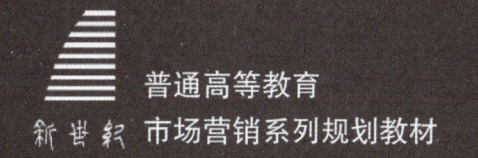

普通高等教育
新世纪 市场营销系列规划教材

市场营销综合教程
（双语版）

Comprehensive Marketing Tutorial

郭国庆 总主编
邓 镝 编 著

大连理工大学出版社

图书在版编目(CIP)数据

市场营销综合教程：双语版 / 邓镝编著. -- 大连：大连理工大学出版社，2024.1(2024.1重印)
普通高等教育市场营销系列规划教材
ISBN 978-7-5685-4343-9

Ⅰ. ①市… Ⅱ. ①邓… Ⅲ. ①市场营销学－双语教学－高等学校－教材 Ⅳ. ①F713.50

中国国家版本馆 CIP 数据核字(2023)第 077156 号

SHICHANG YINGXIAO ZONGHE JIAOCHENG（SHUANGYU BAN）

大连理工大学出版社出版
地址：大连市软件园路 80 号　邮政编码：116023
发行：0411-84708842　邮购：0411-84708943　传真：0411-84701466
E-mail:dutp@dutp.cn　URL:https://www.dutp.cn
辽宁一诺广告印务有限公司印刷　大连理工大学出版社发行

幅面尺寸：185mm×260mm　印张：18.25　字数：444 千字
2024 年 1 月第 1 版　　　　　　2024 年 1 月第 2 次印刷

责任编辑：王晓历　　　　　　　　　　　　责任校对：孙兴乐
封面设计：对岸书影

ISBN 978-7-5685-4343-9　　　　　　　　定　价：59.80 元

本书如有印装质量问题，请与我社发行部联系更换。

普通高等教育市场营销系列规划教材编审委员会

主任委员：
  郭国庆 中国人民大学

副主任委员（按拼音排序）：
  安贺新 中央财经大学
  杜　岩 山东财经大学
  王天春 东北财经大学
  张泉馨 山东大学
  周志民 深圳大学

委员（按拼音排序）：
  常相全 济南大学
  陈转青 河南科技大学
  戴　勇 江苏大学
  邓　镝 渤海大学
  杜海玲 辽宁对外经贸学院
  高　贺 大连交通大学
  关　辉 大连大学
  郝胜宇 大连海事大学
  何　丹 东北财经大学津桥商学院
  姜　岩 大连交通大学
  金依明 辽宁对外经贸学院
  李　丹 大连艺术学院
  李　莉 大连工业大学
  李玉峰 上海海洋大学
  廖佳丽 山东工商学院
  刘国防 武汉工程大学
  刘世雄 深圳大学
  吕洪兵 大连交通大学
  牟莉莉 辽宁对外经贸学院
  乔　辉 武汉工程大学

申文青	广州大学松田学院
史保金	河南科技大学
孙晓红	渤海大学
陶化冶	山东工商学院
王　鹏	山东财经大学
王素梅	长江师范学院
王伟芳	北京石油化工学院
王伟娅	东北财经大学
吴国庆	河南科技学院
姚　飞	天津工业大学
伊　铭	上海商学院
于　宁	东北财经大学
于国庆	大连艺术学院
张德南	大连交通大学
赵瑞琴	河北农业大学
郑　红	北京第二外国语学院
郑锐洪	天津工业大学
朱德明	三峡大学
朱捍华	上海金融学院

前言 Preface

21世纪,中国已真正步入国际化,生存、机遇、挑战和竞争给人们带来了前所未有的危机感。随着世界范围内知识的共享和国际间交流活动的增强,中国对高层次复合型国际英语人才的需求越来越大,也越来越迫切。从事市场营销的人员不仅要熟练掌握营销的基本概念、理论和方法,还要大力提高营销英语水平,以应对目前"国内市场国际化,国际市场国内化"所带来的巨大挑战。与此同时,高校作为人才培养的摇篮,其肩负的历史使命和责任越来越重要。面对新的机遇与挑战,高校必须大刀阔斧地调整自身的教学目的、理念、方法和内容,争取在较短的时间内为国家培养出高素质、外向化、具有国际视野的复合型国际英语人才。

党的二十大报告中指出:"教育、科技、人才是全面建设社会主义现代化国家的基础性、战略性支撑。必须坚持科技是第一生产力、人才是第一资源、创新是第一动力,深入实施科教兴国战略、人才强国战略、创新驱动发展战略,开辟发展新领域新赛道,不断塑造发展新动能新优势。"高质量高等教育体系要发挥高位引领作用,落实立德树人根本任务,培养德智体美劳全面发展的社会主义建设者和接班人,加快建设高质量教育体系,发展素质教育。

教育部《关于加强高等学校本科教学工作提高教学质量的若干意见》明确规定,"本科教育要创造条件使用英语等外语进行公共课和专业课教学"。从目标定位来看,双语教学的初衷是通过第二语言更好地学习专业课程知识。然而,目前许多学校却把双语教学看作英语教学的延伸,将学习重点和精力放在对词汇的掌握,忽视了学科本身的教育和专业知识的获得,存在本末倒置的现象。中国是英语学习的大国,但学习英语并不是目的。如果英语学习与专业学习脱节,就很难培养出具备同国际竞争对手、合作伙伴进行沟通和对抗能力的高层次管理者。按照这样的要求,编写专业类的英语教材,必须突出语言的专业性、实用性和交际性特点,将英语学习渗透到专业知识的学习当中,真正实现语言学习与专业学习的

紧密结合。为此,本教材在编写过程中着力突出以下几个特点:

1. 以能力培养为目标。本教材充分体现市场营销的专业特色,以素质教育和突出应用能力为原则,旨在切实帮助学生解决今后在具体工作中可能会遇到的实际困难,提高他们的岗位适应能力和问题解决能力,并最终将学生塑造成为具有"语言能力＋营销知识＋综合技能"的应用型、复合型人才。

2. 以全面提高为宗旨。学生的语言能力体现在对于听说、阅读、写作各项技能的综合运用。本教材遵循专业类英语学习的科学规律,按照五大模块、十六个专题,以及口语、阅读、写作三个方面对相关英语知识和营销专业知识进行全方位阐述;内容翔实、针对性强,有利于帮助学生全面掌握营销领域的专业热点内容和英语表述。

3. 以任务导向为理念。本教材通篇采用场景模拟,以毕业生于琪2023年加入一个公司后一年的工作经历为主线,让学生在接近现实的任务情境下观察甚至是内化成书中的人物,并和书中其他的人物或事物产生互动,以加深感受,深化认识,提高专业知识水平及实际应用的能力。

4. 以广大学生为主体。建构主义理论认为学生是教学的中心,是认知的主体。"以教师为中心"的教学既不能保证教学的质量与效率,又不利于培养学生的学习兴趣和实践能力。本教材通过不同模拟场景所形成的支架作用,引导学生掌握、建构和内化相关的知识技能,把管理学习的任务逐渐由教师转移给学生自己。

本教材定位于为高等院校市场营销专业提供一本市场营销学双语教材或市场营销专业英语教材,同时也适用于经济类、管理类专业的学生学习使用,还可供企业经营管理人员、商贸人员、营销策划人员,以及广大的英语学习爱好者在实际工作、学习和生活中参考阅读。

笔者由衷地认为,正是菲利普•科特勒、加里•阿姆斯特朗、迈克尔•所罗门、罗杰•贝斯特等一个个闪光的名字和他们的伟大思想提升了本教材的内涵,在此谨向这些先行者们致谢!同时,笔者还要向渤海大学管理学院的领导和师生们致谢!正是他们的鼓励、信任和期待为笔者提供了极大的创作动力。此外,特别的感激还要献给全国人大代表、中国人民大学博士生导师郭国庆教授,他的组织协调、支持帮助和热情指导促成了本套教材的诞生。

本教材由渤海大学邓镝编著。

在编著本教材的过程中,特别是教材的营销理论部分,笔者借鉴了国内外出版物中的相关资料和网络资源,在此表示深深的谢意!相关著作权人看到本教材后,请与出版社联系,出版社将按照相关法律的规定支付稿酬。

限于水平,书中仍有疏漏和不妥之处,敬请专家和读者批评指正,以使教材日臻完善。

编著者
2024年1月

所有意见和建议请发往:dutpbk@163.com
欢迎访问高教数字化服务平台:https://www.dutp.cn/hep/
联系电话:0411-84708445　84708462

目录 Contents

Part 1　Understanding Marketing Target
第一部分　熟悉营销对象

Unit 1　Being a Newcomer	单元1　初入职场	2
Learning Objectives	学习目标	2
Speaking：Meeting New Colleagues	口语：认识新同事	2
Reading：An Overview of Marketing	阅读：营销概述	6
Writing：Signs	写作：标牌	13
Review Questions	复习思考题	16
Unit 2　Why Customers No Longer Like Our Toys	单元2　消费者为何不再喜欢我们的玩具	19
Learning Objectives	学习目标	19
Speaking：Arranging a Business Trip	口语：安排差旅	19
Reading：Understanding Consumers	阅读：了解消费者	23
Writing：Questionnaire	写作：调查问卷	31
Review Questions	复习思考题	34
Unit 3　Here Comes a Large Client	单元3　来了一家大客户	36
Learning Objectives	学习目标	36
Speaking：Meeting Clients at the Airport	口语：在机场迎接客户	36
Reading：Understanding Business Buyers	阅读：了解商业购买者	40
Writing：Memorandum and Note	写作：便笺与便条	48
Review Questions	复习思考题	51

Part 2　Seeking Marketing Opportunity
第二部分　寻找营销机会

Unit 4　Field Investigation	单元4　实地考察	55
Learning Objectives	学习目标	55
Speaking：Visiting the Company	口语：参观公司	55
Reading：Gathering Marketing Information	阅读：收集营销信息	59
Writing：Business Report	写作：商务报告	67
Review Questions	复习思考题	69

Unit 5 Chinese Ice-cream Market	单元 5　中国的冰激凌市场	72
Learning Objectives	学习目标	72
Speaking：Discussing Marketing Environment	口语：讨论营销环境	72
Reading：Thriving in the Marketing Environment	阅读：从营销环境中崛起	76
Writing：Visual Aid	写作：描述图表	83
Review Questions	复习思考题	85
Unit 6 An Olive Branch from the U.K.	单元 6　英国抛来橄榄枝	88
Learning Objectives	学习目标	88
Speaking：Presentation	口语：简报	88
Reading：STP—Building the Right Relationships with the Right Customers	阅读：STP——与正确的顾客建立正确的关系	92
Writing：Intention Agreement on Joint Venture	写作：合资意向书	99
Review Questions	复习思考题	102

Part 3　Formulating Marketing Mix
第三部分　制定营销策略

Unit 7 The Introduction of New Products	单元 7　公司推出新产品	105
Learning Objectives	学习目标	105
Speaking：Discussing New Product	口语：讨论新产品	105
Reading：Formulating Product Strategies	阅读：制定产品策略	109
Writing：Product Description	写作：产品说明书	116
Review Questions	复习思考题	119
Unit 8 At the Negotiating Table	单元 8　谈判桌前	122
Learning Objectives	学习目标	122
Speaking：Negotiation	口语：谈判	122
Reading：Formulating Pricing Strategies	阅读：制定价格策略	126
Writing：Sales Contract or Purchase Contract	写作：买卖合同	133
Review Questions	复习思考题	136
Unit 9 The Children's Day is Coming	单元 9　儿童节快到了	139
Learning Objectives	学习目标	139
Speaking：Festival Promotion	口语：节日促销	139
Reading：Formulating Promotional Strategies	阅读：制定促销策略	143
Writing：Advertisement	写作：广告	150
Review Questions	复习思考题	153

Unit 10　Smoothies Hit the Shelves	单元10　奶昔产品上架了	156
Learning Objectives	学习目标	156
Speaking：Selecting Marketing Channels	口语：渠道选择	156
Reading：Formulating Channel Strategies	阅读：制定渠道策略	160
Writing：Marketing Plan	写作：营销策划书	167
Review Questions	复习思考题	170

Part 4　Enhancing Marketing Management
第四部分　加强营销管理

Unit 11　Increasing Brand's Awareness	单元11　提高品牌的知名度	174
Learning Objectives	学习目标	174
Speaking：Exhibition	口语：会展	174
Reading：Enhancing Brand Management	阅读：加强品牌管理	178
Writing：Business Letter	写作：商务信函	185
Review Questions	复习思考题	188
Unit 12　Getting Support from the Bank	单元12　获得银行的支持	191
Learning Objectives	学习目标	191
Speaking：Borrowing Money from the Bank	口语：银行借款	191
Reading：Enhancing Financial Management	阅读：加强财务管理	195
Writing：Resume or CV	写作：简历	203
Review Questions	复习思考题	206
Unit 13　We Need a Hand	单元13　我们需要人手	208
Learning Objectives	学习目标	208
Speaking：Job Interview	口语：求职面试	208
Reading：Enhancing Human Resources Management	阅读：加强人员管理	212
Writing：Contract of Employment	写作：劳动合同	220
Review Questions	复习思考题	223
Unit 14　Storage and Transportation Problems	单元14　存储和运输问题	225
Learning Objectives	学习目标	225
Speaking：Chairing a Meeting	口语：主持会议	225
Reading：Enhancing Logistics Management	阅读：加强物流管理	229
Writing：Minutes	写作：会议记录	236
Review Questions	复习思考题	239

Part 5　Expanding Marketing Concept
第五部分　拓展营销理念

Unit 15　It's an Insurance Salesperson	单元 15　原来是推销保险的	244
Learning Objectives	学习目标	244
Speaking：Insurance	口语：保险	244
Reading：From Product Marketing to Service Marketing	阅读：从产品营销到服务营销	248
Writing：Notice / Invitation Letter or Card	写作：通知/邀请函（请柬）	255
Review Questions	复习思考题	258
Unit 16　Hearing Some New Words	单元 16　听到一些新名词	261
Learning Objectives	学习目标	261
Speaking：Speech	口语：演讲词	261
Reading：Marketing Innovation in the Twenty-first Century	阅读：21世纪的营销创新	265
Writing：Agency Agreement	写作：代理协议	272
Review Questions	复习思考题	276
References	参考文献	279

书中公司简介

金色童年儿童用品有限公司是一家集儿童用品研发设计、制造及贸易于一体的上海企业,产品主要包括儿童服装和玩具。该公司由研发部、制造部、营销部、财务部、人力资源部以及客服中心等多个部门组成,并拥有自己的生产车间和三家上海本地的旗舰店。公司产品不仅销往中国国内多个大中城市,还出口英、美等国。该公司内部结构如图所示。

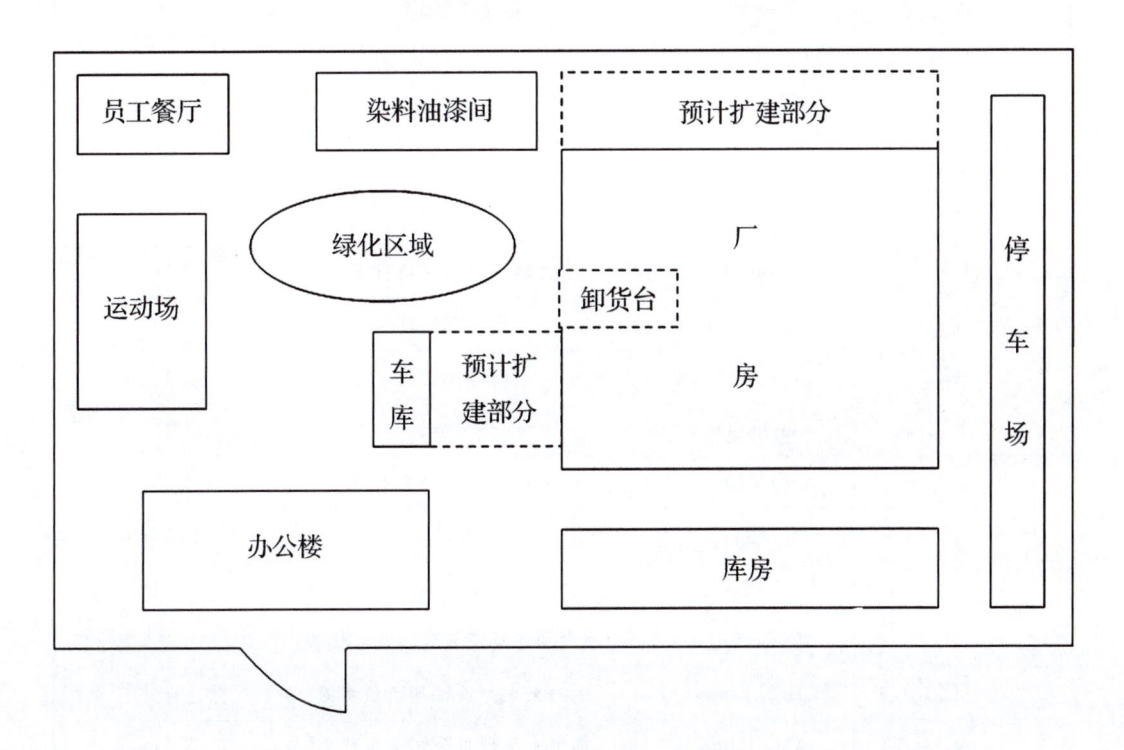

金色童年儿童用品有限公司平面图

书中人物一览表

公司名称（总部）	金色童年儿童用品有限公司（上海）
	Golden Childhood Children's Products Co.，Ltd.（Shanghai）
公司主要产品	儿童服装；儿童玩具
	Children's Wear；Children's Toys

公司员工	姓名	职位	出场章节
A	Robert Liu	总经理兼 CEO	3
B	Michael Douglas	人力资源部经理	1
C	马天跃	销售经理	1
D	于琪	销售经理助理	1
E	Joan Mitchell	儿童服装销售负责人	1
F	Tony Lin	儿童玩具销售负责人	9
G	Peter Phillips	生产部经理	14
H	Leila Peterson	财务部经理	12
I	Sophie Deng	公司会计	12
J	吴晗	公司招聘的财务助理	13

公司客户	姓名	职位	出场章节
K	John Brown	公司在美国纽约的大客户	11
L	David Smith	澳大利亚某童装公司业务代表	3
M	Erick Garcia	上海某大型连锁超市负责人	10
N	Alex Johnson	加拿大某玩具公司业务代表	11

公司合作伙伴	姓名	职位	出场章节
O	Jimmy Wales	英国某冰激凌公司 CEO	5
P	George Stevenson	该冰激凌公司市场部经理	5
Q	Andy Davis	该冰激凌公司董事会主席	5
R	Mark Erwin	中国银行上海分行业务部经理	12
S	Edward White	上海某建筑公司设计师	14
T	Linda Zhang	上海太平洋保险公司业务代表	15

Part 1

Understanding Marketing Target
熟悉营销对象

经典营销名言：

No success is ever-lasting. Many start-up companies vanish at the brink of success. This is incredible but true and the simple reason is that they ignore their customers.

—Jeff Bezos

成功不是永恒的。很多刚刚起步的公司，往往在即将成功的时候却消失了。这似乎难以置信，但确实如此，其实根本原因就在于他们忽略了顾客。

——杰夫·贝索斯

本部分内容导读：

营销的目的在于充分认识和了解顾客（主要包括消费者和商业购买者），以使公司提供的产品或服务能够适合顾客的需要。因此，我们对营销学的研究有必要从了解不同顾客市场的特点以及不同类型顾客的购买行为开始。

内容	口语	阅读	写作
单元1	认识新同事	营销概述	标牌
单元2	安排差旅	了解消费者	调查问卷
单元3	在机场迎接客户	了解商业购买者	便笺与便条

Unit 1 Being a Newcomer

Learning Objectives

◇ 熟悉员工就职报到的常用口语表达；
◇ 理解市场营销的基本含义；
◇ 理解市场营销管理哲学的演变过程和不同营销思想的本质区别；
◇ 理解市场营销的对象；
◇ 掌握公司标牌的书写规则和常用英文标牌的正确写法。

Speaking: Meeting New Colleagues

【场景1】 于琪是一名应届毕业的大学生，刚刚通过面试进入金色童年儿童用品有限公司的营销部。今天是于琪上班的第一天，他怀着紧张、兴奋与期待的心情来到了公司的前台。

【对话1】 A：前台接待 B：于琪

A：Good morning. Welcome to our company. What can I do for you?
早上好。欢迎来到我们公司。能为你做些什么吗？

B：I'm here to report for work at the first day!
我是来这儿报到上班的。

A：Oh, I see. Which position?
哦，知道了。什么岗位呢？

B：Sales Manager Assistant.
销售经理助理。

A：And may I have your name, please?
告诉我你的名字，可以吗？

B：I'm Qi Yu.
我叫于琪。

A：Please go to the HR Department at A402. The manager is just waiting for you.

请去 A402 室的人力资源部。经理正在等你。

B：Excuse me, could you say it again?
劳驾你再说一遍好吗？

A：A402, the second room on the fourth floor. You can take the elevator over there.
A402, 4 楼的第 2 个房间。你可以乘那边的电梯上去。

B：Thanks a lot.
非常感谢。

【场景2】 在公司的人力资源部，经理 Michael Douglas 先生热情地接待了于琪。
【对话2】 A：Michael Douglas 先生　　B：于琪

A：Welcome aboard!
欢迎你来本公司工作！

B：Thank you. I'm delighted to be working here, Mr. Douglas.
谢谢。我很高兴能来这里上班，道格拉斯先生。

A：Call me Doug, will you? Everybody calls me Doug. It's easier.
叫我道格就可以了。大家都叫我道格。这样比较方便。

B：I'd prefer to call you Mr. Douglas. Isn't it rather disrespectful to make a nickname out of one's family name?
我更愿意称呼您道格拉斯先生。用别人的姓作为昵称，不是很不礼貌吗？

A：Well, President Eisenhower was known as Ike. Don't worry about the "disrespectful" business, OK? Of course, everybody in this company is normally called by his or her first name. It's been our tradition ever since the company was small.
嗯，艾森豪威尔总统还被昵称为艾克呢。不要担心不礼貌的事了，好吗？当然，通常情况下在公司里是直呼每个人的名。这是在公司规模很小的时候就已经形成的传统。

B：Got it.
知道了。

A：Good. But when there are outsiders, it might be good to address your higher-ups as Mr., Ms. or whatever is appropriate. To those outside the company, it may be interpreted as a sign of flippancy or lax discipline.
好的。不过，如果有外人在时，最好能称呼你的上司为先生、女士或任何适当的称谓。对外人而言，我们的习惯可能会被解读为轻率和纪律松懈的表现。

B：Yes, sir.
好的，先生。

A：(Laughing) And don't "sir" me either. Now I'll show you the office.
（笑）也不要叫我先生。现在我带你去看看办公室。

【场景3】 人力资源经理Douglas先生带着于琪来到公司的营销部。于琪将接替刚刚调任总经理秘书的玛丽的工作，同事Joan热情地帮助于琪熟悉环境。

【对话3】 A：Michael Douglas先生　B：同事Joan　C：于琪

A：Good morning, Joan. Let me introduce Qi Yu to you. He is new in the Marketing Department.

早上好，琼。让我向你介绍一下于琪。他是营销部的新成员。

B：Hello, Qi. Nice to meet you!

你好，琪。很高兴认识你。

C：Nice to meet you too, Joan.

我也很高兴认识你，琼。

A：Joan, Qi will replace Mary as the Sales Manager Assistant. Would you please help Qi familiarize himself with the working environment?

琼，琪将接替玛丽担任销售经理助理。你能帮他熟悉一下工作环境吗？

B：My pleasure.

非常乐意。

A：(To Qi Yu) I must go back to my work. Have a nice day!

（对于琪）我要回去工作了。祝你过得愉快！

C：Thank you very much, Mr. Douglas. Sorry, Doug. Have a nice day!

非常感谢，道格拉斯先生。对不起，道格。祝你过得愉快！

B：Qi, that is your desk, just near the window.

琪，那是你的办公桌，靠近窗户的那张。

C：It looks fine. Is that my computer?

看上去不错。那是我的电脑吗？

B：Yes. And the duplicating machine is over there. We have a lot of work to do every day. The Sales Manager will let you know your work duties. He is on a business trip and is supposed to be back this morning.

是的。复印机在那边。我们每天要做很多工作。销售经理将会告诉你具体的工作职责。他正在公出，预计今天上午能回来。

C：All right. I'll try my best to get used to my new job.

好的。我将尽快适应我的新工作。

B：I'm sure you can do it well. By the way, the staff lounge is on the left. You can get water, tea or coffee there any time you like. And to its opposite is the washroom. If you have any question, please don't hesitate to ask me.

我相信你肯定能做好。对了，员工休息室在我们的左侧，随时有开水、茶和咖啡供应，它对面就是洗手间。如果你有什么问题，请尽管来问我。

C：Got it. You've really helped me a lot. Thank you!

知道了。你真是帮了我的大忙。谢谢！

【场景4】 上午10点,刚刚出差回来的销售经理马天跃把于琪叫到了经理办公室。寒暄过后,销售经理向于琪介绍了具体的工作职责,以及公司的基本规章制度。

【对话4】 A:销售经理马天跃　B:于琪

A：Nice to meet you. I'm glad you'll be working with us. We're like a big family here. We all work together as a team.
欢迎你的到来,我很高兴你将和我们一起工作。我们这儿就像是一个大家庭,所有人在一起作为一个团队工作。

B：I'm glad to hear that.
很高兴听您这么说。

A：Since today is your first day, I am going to tell you all about your job responsibilities.
今天是你第一天上班,我来跟你说说你的工作职责。

B：Great. I am eager to find out what I will be doing here.
好的。我也很想知道我在这儿要做的事情。

A：The most important job for you will be establishing and maintaining relationships with our overseas partners. Since 2010, we have shifted our focus on trading in the international markets. We export large volumes of children's products every year.
你最主要的任务是与我们的海外客户建立和保持联系。从2010年起,公司的工作重心开始转向国际市场。我们每年都会出口大量的儿童产品。

B：It sounds challenging, but I think I can handle it.
听起来很有挑战性,但是我想我可以应付得了。

A：Good. Let me tell you about some of our policies and practices here.
很好。让我把这里的一些规章制度和你说一下。

B：All right. That will be a big help.
好的。那会对我帮助很大。

A：We require all our employees to punch in before 8 o'clock and punch out after 5 o'clock every work day.
我们要求所有员工每个工作日8点前打卡上岗、5点后打卡下班。

B：I understand. That seems easy to follow. May I ask whether we are allowed to wear casual clothes in the office?
我明白,这很容易做到。方便问一下,我们平时上班可以穿休闲的衣服吗?

A：Sure, company rules are not very strict at this point. But remind you, there are some forbidden activities.
当然可以,在这一点上公司并没有严格的规定。但提醒你一下,公司里还是有些禁令的。

B：What are they? I'll be careful.
有哪些?我会小心遵守的。

Unit 1　Being a Newcomer　5

A：Don't use office phones for personal matters. Also, never come to work drunk.
私人事情不能使用办公电话。另外，绝对不要醉酒上班。

B：Thank you for telling me that.
谢谢您告诉我。

A：We also try to do the best we can for our employees. We feel obligated to provide a safe and cozy working environment, and we make every effort to listen to our employees' concerns.
我们也会尽我们的所能为员工着想。我们觉得有责任为员工提供一个安全且舒适的工作环境，而且我们努力聆听员工的心声。

B：That's great. That's also one of the reasons I wanted to work here.
好极了。这也是我希望到这里工作的原因之一。

Reading: An Overview of Marketing

于琪在大学期间所修的是语言专业，他非常清楚在进入金色童年儿童用品有限公司的营销部后，自己有太多的东西需要学习。在报到的前几天，于琪刚刚从书店购买了一本《市场营销综合教程》。他想利用自己的语言优势系统地了解原汁原味的营销理论。

Chapter 1 The Introduction of Marketing

Section 1 What Is Marketing?

The official definition of marketing the American Marketing Association adopted in late 2007 is as follows: "Marketing is the activity, set of institutions, and processes for creating, communicating, delivering and exchanging offerings that have value for customers, clients, partners, and society at large." The basic idea of this somewhat complicated definition is that marketing is all about delivering value to everyone who is affected by a transaction. Let's take a closer look at some of the different ideas related to this definition.

1.1 Marketing Is about Meeting Needs

One important part of our definition of marketing is that it is about meeting the needs of diverse stakeholders. The term stakeholders here refers to buyers, sellers, or investors in a company, community residents, and even citizens of the nations where goods and services are made or sold—in other words, any person or organization that has a "stake" in the outcome. Thus, marketing is about satisfying everyone involved in the marketing process. One important stakeholder is the consumers. For marketers to be successful, they must develop products that provide one or more benefits that are important to consumers. The challenge is to identify what benefits people look for and then develop a product that delivers those benefits while also convincing consumers that their product is better than a competitor's product—making the choice of which product to buy obvious. As the late management guru Peter Drucker observed, "The aim of marketing is to make selling superfluous."

1.2 Marketing Is about Creating Utility

Marketing activities play a major role in creating utility, which refers to the sum of the benefits we receive when we use a product or service. By working to ensure that people have the type of product they want, where and when they want it, the marketing system makes our lives easier. Utility is what creates value. Marketing processes create several different kinds of utility to provide value for consumers.

Form utility is the benefit marketing provides by transforming raw materials into finished products, as when a dress manufacturer combines silk, thread, and zippers to create a bridesmaid's gown. Creating custom shoes that fit on a particular buyer's feet is another example of form utility. Place utility is the benefit marketing provides by making products available where customers want them. The most sophisticated evening gown sewn in New York's garment district is of little use to a bridesmaid in Kansas City if it isn't shipped to her in time. Time utility is the benefit marketing provides by storing products until they are needed. Time utility occurs when consumers find goods and services available right at the moment they want to purchase them. Overnight courier service DHL emphasizes a combination of time and place utility, as illustrated in its logo "we're #1 international air express and logistics company on the planet. Even to the parts that look like Mars." Possession utility is the benefit marketing provides by allowing the consumer to own, use, and enjoy the product. Some companies allow customers to buy with credit or payment plans, which appeals to consumers or businesses with a desire for immediate possession despite budget constraints.

1.3 Marketing Is about Exchange Relationships

At the heart of every marketing act—big or small—is something we refer to as an "exchange relationship." An exchange occurs when a person gives something and gets something else in return. The buyer receives an object, service, or idea that satisfies a need and the seller receives something he feels is of equivalent value.

For an exchange to occur, at least two people or organizations must be willing to make a trade, and each must have something the other wants. Both parties must agree on the value of the exchange and how it will be carried out. Each party also must be free to accept or reject the other's terms for the exchange. Under these conditions, a gun-wielding robber's offer to "exchange" your money for your life does not constitute a valid exchange. In contrast, although someone may complain that a store's prices are "highway robbery", an exchange occurs if he still forks over the money to buy something there—even if he still grumbles about it weeks later.

小 结

企业营销活动首先是满足利益相关者的需求,特别是消费者的需求。其次,企业营销活动会带来效用,包括形态效用、地点效用、时间效用和占有效用四个方面。形态效用是指市场营销可将原材料制成成品。地点效用指市场营销可将产品送至顾客需要的地点。时间效用是指市场营销可将产品存储至顾客需求之时。占有效用指市场营销使商品从所有者手中过渡到消费者手中,让顾客拥有和享受产品。最后,营销活动反映的是一种交换关系,买卖双方在平等的基础上自由交换。

Section 2 Marketing Management Philosophies

We define marketing management as the art and science of choosing and building profitable relationships with target markets. What philosophy should guide these marketing efforts? What weight should be given to the interests of the organization, customers, and society? Very often these interests conflict. There are five alternative concepts under which organizations conduct their marketing activities.

2.1 The Production Concept

The production concept holds that consumers will favor products that are available and highly affordable. Therefore, management should focus on improving production and distribution efficiency. The production concept is a useful philosophy in two types of situations. The first occurs when the demand for a product exceeds the supply. Here, management should look for ways to increase production. The second situation occurs when the product's cost is too high and improved productivity is needed to bring it down.

However, the production concept can lead to marketing myopia. Companies adopting this orientation run a major risk of focusing too narrowly on their own operations and losing sight of the real objective—satisfying customers' needs.

2.2 The Product Concept

The product concept holds that consumers will favor products that offer the most in quality, performance, and innovative features. Thus, an organization should devote energy to making continuous product improvements. Some manufacturers believe that if they can build a better mousetrap, the world will beat a path to their door. But they are often rudely shocked. Buyers may well be looking for a better solution to a mouse problem but not necessarily for a better mousetrap. The solution might be a chemical spray, an exterminating service, or something that works better than a mousetrap. Further, a better mousetrap will not sell unless the manufacturer designs, packages, and prices it attractively; places it in convenient distribution channels; brings it to the attention of people who need it; and convinces buyers that it is a better product.

Thus, the product concept also can lead to marketing myopia. For instance, Kodak assumed that consumers wanted photographic film rather than a way to capture and share memories and at first overlooked the challenge of digital cameras. Although it now leads the digital camera market in sales, it has yet to make significant profits from this business.

2.3 The Selling Concept

Many companies follow the selling concept, which holds that consumers will not buy enough of the firm's products unless it undertakes a large-scale selling and promotion effort. The concept is typically practiced with unsought goods—those that buyers do not normally think of buying, such as insurance or blood donations. These industries must be good at tracking down prospects and selling them on product benefits.

Most firms practice the selling concept when they face overcapacity. Their aim is to sell what they make rather than make what the market wants. Such marketing carries high risks. It focuses on creating sales transactions rather than on building long-term, profitable customer relationships. It assumes that customers who are coaxed into buying the product will like it. Or, if they don't like it, they will possibly forget their disappointment and buy it again later. These are usually poor assumptions. Most studies show that dissatisfied customers do not buy again. Worse yet, whereas the average satisfied customer tells three others about good experiences, the average dissatisfied customer tells ten others about his or her bad experiences.

2.4 The Marketing Concept

The marketing concept holds that achieving organizational goals depends on knowing the needs and wants of target markets and delivering the desired satisfactions better than competitors do. Under the marketing concept, customer focus and value are the paths to sales and profits. Instead of a product-centered "make and sell" philosophy, the marketing concept is a customer-centered "sense and respond" philosophy. The job is not to find the right customers for your product, but the right products for your customers. Implementing the marketing concept often means more than simply responding to customers' stated desires and obvious needs. Customer-driven companies research current customers deeply to learn about their desires, gather new product and service ideas, and test proposed product improvements. Such customer-driven marketing usually works well when a clear need exists and when customers know what they want.

In many cases, however, customers don't know what they want or even what is possible. For example, 30 years ago, how many consumers would have thought to ask for cell phones, fax machines, home copiers, 24-hour Internet brokerage accounts, DVD players, handheld global satellite positioning systems, or wearable PCs? Such situations call for customer-driving marketing—understanding customer needs even better than customers themselves do and creating products and services that will meet existing and latent needs, now and in the future. As Sony's visionary leader, Akio Morita, puts it: "Our plan is to lead the public with new products rather than ask them what kinds of products they want. The public does not know what is possible, but we do."

2.5 The Societal Marketing Concept

The societal marketing concept holds that the organization should determine the needs, wants, and interests of target markets. It should then deliver superior value to customers to maintain or improve the consumer's and the society's well-being. This philosophy questions whether the pure marketing concept overlooks possible conflicts between consumer short-run wants and consumer long-run welfare. Is a firm that senses, serves, and satisfies individual short-term wants always doing what's best for consumers and society in the long run? Consider the fast-food industry. Most people see today's giant fast-food chains as offering tasty and convenient food at reasonable prices. Yet many consumers and environmental groups have voiced concerns. Critics point out that hamburgers, fried chicken, French fries, and most other foods sold by fast-food restaurants are high in fat and salt. The products are wrapped in convenient packaging, but this leads to waste and pollution. Thus, in satisfying short-term consumer wants, the highly successful fast-food chains may be harming consumers' health and causing environmental problems.

The societal marketing concept calls on marketers to balance three considerations in setting their marketing policies: company profits, consumer wants, and society's interests. Now many companies are beginning to think of society's interests when making their marketing decisions. One such Asian company is Kao, Japan's largest toiletries group. Kao has adapted Buddhist flexibility, transparency, and equality into its corporate culture. Its current president notes that the company "wants to make a larger contribution to society to make life easier for people." Kao invests heavily in R&D and reinvests its profits to realize its long-term vision of cleanliness.

小　结

目前，有五种观念指导企业完成其营销活动。生产观念认为消费者偏爱低价格的产品，因此致力于提高生产效率。产品观念认为消费者喜欢高品质、多功能的产品，因此致力于产品的改进。销售观念的目标是将生产的产品卖出去，而不是生产市场需要的产品。营销观念以消费者需求为中心，并整合各种营销活动影响消费者。社会营销观念强调企业决策时要平衡公司利润、消费者需求和社会利益三个方面的因素。

Section 3　What Can Be Marketed?

Is there any limit to what marketers can market? Marketing applies to more than just canned peas or cola drinks. Some of the best marketers come from the ranks of services companies such as American Express or not-for-profit organizations such as Greenpeace. Politicians, athletes, and performers use marketing to their advantage (just think about that $30 T-shirt you may have bought at a baseball game or rock concert). Ideas such as political systems (democracy, totalitarianism), religion (Christianity, Islam), and art (realism, abstract) also compete for acceptance in a "marketplace."

3.1 Corporate Culture

McDonald's sells not only hamburgers and French fries, but also "Quality, Service, Convenience, and Value (QSCV)." A white-collar professional walks into a Starbucks not just to buy a cup of coffee, but to experience conviviality in a "third place" beyond home and the workplace. Culture marketing is a form of content marketing that showcases a company's culture to help people get to know its brand. Whereas general content marketing may be focused on a specific service, product, industry, or area of expertise, culture marketing focuses on who you are, what you care about, and how you interact with the world. By translating a company's culture into compelling content, the company can introduce people to the humans behind its brand and build a community of people who share the same values. The more a company creates these types of meaningful relationships, the more it'll be able to grow its brand. To give people a behind-the-scenes look at its company culture, Zappos created the Culture Book, an in-depth look at the people, values, and practices that make the company unique. This is a simple piece of content that offers a unique insight into why the brand is so special.

3.2 Consumer Goods and Services

Consumer goods are the tangible products that individual consumers purchase for personal or family use. Services are intangible products that we pay for and use but never own. Service transactions contribute on average more than 60 percent to the gross national product of all industrialized nations. Marketers need to understand the special challenges that arise when marketing an intangible service rather than a tangible product. In both cases, though, keep in mind that the consumer looks to obtain some underlying value, such as convenience, security, or status, from a marketing exchange. That value can come from a variety of competing goods and services, even those that don't resemble one another on the surface. For example, a new CD and a ticket to a local concert may cost about the same, and each may provide the benefit of musical enjoyment, so consumers often have to choose among competing alternatives if they can't afford (or don't want) to buy them all.

3.3 Business-to-Business Goods and Services

Business-to-business marketing is the marketing of goods and services from one organization to another. Although we usually relate marketing to the thousands of consumer goods begging for our dollars every day, the reality is that businesses and other organizations buy a lot more goods than consumers do. They purchase these industrial goods for further processing or to use in their own business operations. For example, automakers buy tons of steel to use in the manufacturing process, and they buy computer systems to track manufacturing costs and other information essential to operations.

3.4 Not for Profit Marketing

Not-for-profit organizations are those with charitable, educational, community, and other public service goals that buy goods and services to support their functions and to attract and serve their members. Many not-for-profit organizations, including museums, zoos, and even churches practice the marketing concept. Local governments are adopting marketing techniques to create more effective taxpayer services and to attract new businesses and industries to their counties and cities. In some not-for-profit organizations, adopting the marketing concept means forming a partnership with a for-profit company to promote the not-for-profit's message or image. The organization Save the Children Federation—which provides food, clothing, and shelter to impoverished children around the world—has 27 licensees, or for-profit companies that use the name of the organization on various products, and donate portions of the proceeds to Save the Children.

3.5 Idea, Place, and People Marketing

Marketing principles also get people to endorse ideas or to change their behaviors in positive ways. Many organizations work hard to convince consumers to use seat belts, not to litter our highways, or to believe that one political system is preferable to another. In addition to ideas, places and people also are marketable. We are all familiar with tourism marketing that promotes exotic resorts like Club Med ("the antidote for civilization"). For many developing countries like Thailand, tourism may be the best opportunity available for economic growth.

You may have heard the expression, "Stars are made, not born." There's a lot of truth to that. Beyonce Knowles may have a killer voice and Ryan Howard may have a red-hot baseball bat, but talent alone doesn't make thousands or even millions of people buy CDs or stadium seats. Entertainment events do not just happen. People plan them. Whether a concert or a baseball game, the application of sound marketing principles helps ensure that patrons will continue to support the activity and buy tickets. Today, sports and the arts are hotbeds of marketing activity. Many of the famous people you pay to see became famous with the help of shrewd marketing: They and their managers developed a "product" that they hoped would appeal to some segment of the population.

小 结

随着营销领域的不断扩展，营销的对象也不再仅仅局限于有形的产品。根据迈克尔·所罗门等学者的观点，企业文化（你是谁，你关心什么，你如何与世界互动）、消费品（或服务）、工业品（或服务）、非营利组织（包括博物馆、动物园、教堂、政府部门和慈善组织等），以及理念、地点和个人等都可以利用营销手段进行宣传和推广，以获得市场的接受和认可。

New Words and Key Terms

01. marketing	营销
02. American Marketing Association	美国营销协会
03. stakeholders	利益相关者
04. form utility	形态效用
05. place utility	地点效用
06. time utility	时间效用
07. possession utility	占有效用
08. marketing management	营销管理
09. production concept	生产观念
10. product concept	产品观念
11. selling concept	销售观念
12. unsought goods	非渴求品
13. marketing concept	营销观念
14. societal marketing concept	社会营销观念
15. culture marketing	文化营销
16. consumer goods	消费品
17. services	服务
18. business-to-business marketing	企业间营销
19. industrial goods	工业品
20. not-for-profit organizations	非营利组织

Writing: Signs

随着墙上的时钟指向两点，午休结束了。这时，办公室的门被推开，销售经理马天跃走了进来。在简单招呼过后，销售经理交给于琪一项任务。为了更好地与国际接轨，公司决定将目前所有的标牌采用中英文对照的形式。这项任务也自然落在了语言专业的于琪身上。

一、标牌写作的基本要求和格式

标牌（Signs）通常是置于公共场所的一块纸板、木板、塑料板或金属板，上面写有文字（有时配有图形），为人们提供指示、管理、宣传等必要的信息。准确、灵活地书写英文标牌,满足外国友人对信息的需求,是做好宣传和服务工作,促进国际交流,提高国际竞争力的重要环节。书写标牌时,应该注意以下几点:

(一)遵循国际惯例(Following International Practices)

标牌的写作强调规范性,要选择那些国际上普遍使用和接受的固定写法,尤其要避免中式翻译。例如,不要将"前台"翻译成"FRONT DESK",应译为"RECEPTION"或"SERVICE DESK";不要将"警务工作站"翻译成"POLICE AFFAIRS STATION",用"POLICE STATION"就可以了。

(二)全部使用大写字母(Using Capitals Only)

为了强调所传递的信息,正规标牌的书写通常只使用大写字母,如 NO SMOKING (禁止吸烟),LOST AND FOUND(失物招领处)等。但在一些不太严格的情况下,也可以只对每个单词的首字母大写。

(三)采用简短、精炼的方式(Putting in a Short and Concise Manner)

标牌的字数要精简到最低限度,在必要的情况下允许进行一定的省略。例如,可以只用一个单词 IN(入口)、OUT(出口)等,甚至可以用一些发音相同的简单的词、字母或数字等,如 4 SALE(出售)。书写标牌时,尽量使用名词、动名词或名词短语,而非句子。如果一定需要使用句子的话,只能用表达命令、请求、劝告、警示、禁止等语气的祈使句。例如,PLEASE BE QUIET 请安静(表示请求);再如,KEEP OFF THE GRASS 请勿践踏草坪(表示禁止)。

(四)禁止使用标点符号(Prohibiting Punctuations)

标牌中不要出现标点符号,但可以使用缩写。例如,"照顾好随身行李"可译为"DON'T LEAVE YOUR LUGGAGE UNATTENDED";"持证进入"可译为"I. D. REQUIRED FOR ENTRANCE"。

(五)体现尊重与礼貌(Showing Respect and Courtesy)

标牌作为一种信息传达的媒体,具有重要的沟通功能,而尊重和礼貌是沟通的基本要素。例如,将"来访者止步"翻译成"NO VISITORS",不仅不符合英语的表达习惯,同时也显得非常生硬,翻译成"STAFF ONLY"即可。再如,"无烟区"的标牌若被译为"SMOKING IS NOT ALLOWED HERE",属于较严厉的限制性警示语,可以换成提示性公示语"SMOKE - FREE AREA"。

二、于琪的解决方案

(一)与企业职位有关的标牌(Signs Associated with Position)

1. CHAIRMAN (CHAIRPERSON) 主席/董事长
2. (VICE) PRESIDENT (副)总裁
3. CHIEF EXECUTIVE OFFICER (CEO) 首席执行官
4. CHIEF OPERATIONS OFFICER (COO) 首席运营官
5. CHIEF FINANCIAL OFFICER (CFO) 首席财务官
6. CHIEF INFORMATION OFFICER (CIO) 首席信息官
7. OPERATIONS DIRECTOR 运营总监

8. MARKETING DIRECTOR 营销总监
9. HUMAN RESOURCES DIRECTOR 人力资源总监
10. FINANCIAL DIRECTOR 财务总监
11. (VICE/DEPUTY) GENERAL MANAGER (副)总经理
12. OPERATIONS MANAGER 运营经理
13. PRODUCTION MANAGER 生产经理
14. PRODUCT MANAGER 产品经理
15. SALES MANAGER 销售经理
16. HUMAN RESOURCES MANAGER 人力资源经理
17. SENIOR CUSTOMER MANAGER 高级客户经理
18. ADMINISTRATIVE ASSISTANT 行政助理
19. MANUFACTURING ENGINEER 制造工程师
20. PACKAGE DESIGNER 包装设计师

(二)与企业场所有关的标牌(Signs Associated with Place)

1. STERILIZATION WORKSHOP 杀菌(或消毒)车间
2. SEMI-FINISHED PRODUCTS WAREHOUSE 半成品仓库
3. WATERING PLACE 饮水处
4. FINISHED PRODUCTS AREA 成品区
5. STAFF DINING ROOM 员工食堂
6. STAFF APARTMENT 员工公寓
7. ADVERTISING DEPARTMENT 广告部
8. PLANNING DEPARTMENT / MARKETING DEPARTMENT 企划部/营销部
9. PURCHASING DEPARTMENT 采购部
10. RESEARCH AND DEVELOPMENT DEPARTMENT 研发部
11. PUBLIC RELATIONS DEPARTMENT 公共关系部
12. HUMAN RESOURCES DEPARTMENT 人力资源部
13. QUALITY CONTROL DEPARTMENT 质检部
14. GENERAL AFFAIRS DEPARTMENT 总务部
15. EXPORT DEPARTMENT / IMPORT DEPARTMENT 出口部/进口部
16. CUSTOMER SERVICE CENTER 客服中心
17. RECEPTION ROOM 会客室(或接待室,传达室)
18. MEETING ROOM / CONFERENCE ROOM 会议室
19. COMPUTER CENTER 电脑室(或计算机中心)
20. VIP CAR PARK 贵宾停车场

(三)与企业活动有关的标牌(Signs Associated with Activity)

1. OPEN FOR BUSINESS / CLOSED FOR STOCK - TAKING 正常营业/停业盘点
2. ROUND-THE-CLOCK BUSINESS 昼夜(或24小时)营业

3. OPEN 7 DAYS A WEEK 每周 7 天开放

4. NO ADMITTANCE EXCEPT ON BUSINESS 非公莫入。其他类似写法还有 MEMBERS ONLY 闲人免进或 VISITORS DECLINED 来宾止步。

5. ASK AT INFORMATION DESK FOR ASSISTANCE 询问请到接待处(或问讯台)

6. OUT OF ORDER / REPAIR IN PROGRESS (机器)故障/正在维修

7. INTERVIEW IN PROGRESS / MEETING IN PROGRESS 正在面试/正在开会

8. OFFICE TO LET 办公室出租

9. ON SALE 大减价

10. FOR SALE / NOT FOR SALE 出售/非卖品

11. CLOSING SALE / FINAL CLEAR OUT 关门大甩卖/清仓大甩卖

12. BUY TWO AND GET ONE FREE 买二赠一

13. 50％ OFF (DISCOUNT) ON SELECTED ITEMS 部分商品半价

14. SPECIAL OFFER 特价

15. TODAY'S SPECIALS (SPECIALITIES) 今日特色菜

16. CHILDREN'S WEAR 童装

17. SPLIT HERE / INSERT HERE 此处撕开/此处插入

18. FRAGILE / HANDLE WITH CARE 易碎/小心轻放

19. DO NOT CRUSH / KEEP TOP SIDE UP 请勿挤压/请勿倒置

20. GUARD (PROTECT) AGAINST DAMP / KEEP DRY 注意防潮/保持干燥

Review Questions

1. Key Terms

Marketing; Stakeholders; Unsought goods; Marketing concept; Consumer goods

2. Multiple Choices (select one)

(1) Central to any definition of marketing is (   ).

    A. demand management   B. transactions

    C. customer relationships   D. making a sale

(2) When backed by buying power, wants become (   ).

    A. social needs   B. demands

    C. physical needs   D. self-esteem needs

(3) (   ) refers to sellers being preoccupied with their own products and losing sight of underlying consumer needs.

    A. Selling myopia   B. Marketing

    C. Selling   D. Marketing myopia

(4) All of the following sentences reflect the marketing concept except (   ).

    A. We don't have a Marketing Department, we have a Customer Department

B. We make it happen for you

C. We stay close to customers

D. Putting profits ahead of customer needs is critical to the health of the firm

(5) The (　　) is a useful philosophy in situations when the product's cost is too high and marketers look for ways to bring it down.

A. selling concept
B. product concept
C. production concept
D. marketing concept

(6) Firms follow the (　　) when they face overcapacity.

A. product concept
B. selling concept
C. production concept
D. marketing concept

(7) Most firms follow the (　　) philosophy, which holds that consumers will not buy enough of the firm's products unless it undertakes a large-scale selling and promotion effort.

A. product-orientation
B. production-orientation
C. marketing-orientation
D. selling-orientation

(8) The (　　) starts with the factory, focusing upon the company's existing products; it calls for heavy selling and promotion to obtain profitable sales.

A. marketing concept
B. production concept
C. product concept
D. selling concept

(9) The (　　) holds that firms must strive to deliver value to customers in a way that maintains or improves both the consumer's and society's well being.

A. marketing concept
B. selling concept
C. product concept
D. societal-marketing concept

(10) (　　) are goods bought by organizations for use in making other goods or in rendering services.

A. Consumer goods
B. Services
C. Industrial goods
D. Tangible goods

3. Questions for Discussion

(1) Briefly explain what marketing is.

(2) What is utility? How does marketing create different forms of utility?

(3) Trace the evolution of marketing concept.

Practical Writing

Scenario: You work in a transportation company. In your daily work, you often come across some traffic signs and business signs in English. Please try to match the following **Signs** on the left with the correct Chinese translation on the right.

Traffic Signs

NO PARKING	步行街
PEDESTRIANS ONLY（或 NO VEHICLES）	禁止停车
NO OVERTAKING	收费站
FOGGY SECTION	服务区
ROAD CLOSED	单行道
ONE WAY	此巷不通
DEAD LANE（或 DEAD END）	限速（重）50
SPEED(LOAD)LIMIT 50	封路
TOLL STATION	多雾路段
SERVICE AREA	禁止超车

Business Signs

INFLAMMABLE COMPRESSED GAS	放射性物品
EXPLOSIVE	易燃压缩气体
PERISHABLE	爆炸物
POISON	易腐物品
RADIOACTIVE SUBSTANCE	有毒物品
NO DROPPING	装于舱内
KEEP IN DARK PLACE	阴凉处存放
STOW IN COOL PLACE	避光保存
KEEP IN HOLD	切勿坠落
KEEP FLAT（或 STOW LEVEL）	保持平放

Unit 2　Why Customers No Longer Like Our Toys

Learning Objectives

◇ 熟悉安排差旅的常用口语表达；
◇ 理解影响消费者购买行为的因素；
◇ 理解消费者购买行为的类型和不同购买类型中消费者的参与程度；
◇ 理解消费者购买决策的整个过程和针对不同购买阶段的营销策略；
◇ 掌握调查问卷的书写规则和常用套语的正确写法。

Speaking：Arranging a Business Trip

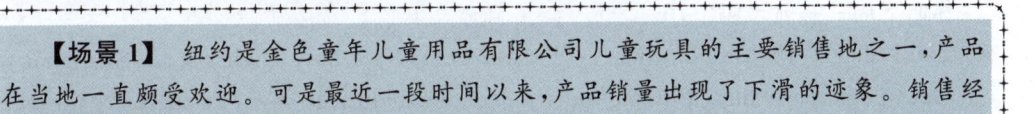

【场景1】　纽约是金色童年儿童用品有限公司儿童玩具的主要销售地之一，产品在当地一直颇受欢迎。可是最近一段时间以来，产品销量出现了下滑的迹象。销售经理马天跃决定亲自去纽约了解情况，并吩咐于琪为其预订机票和当地的旅馆。

【对话1】　A：销售经理马天跃　　B：于琪

A：Good morning, Qi.
　　早上好，小琪。
B：Good morning, Manager Ma. What can I do for you?
　　早上好，马经理。有什么需要我做的吗？
A：Yes, I need you to make some travel arrangements for me.
　　是的，我需要你替我做一下旅行安排。
B：For when?
　　什么时候的？
A：I need to go to New York next Monday and return after six or seven days. Can you see about getting me a flight on March 5th to New York?
　　我下周一要去趟纽约，六七天后回来。你看看能不能帮我订张3月5日去纽约的机票？
B：Do you want window or aisle seating?

您想坐靠窗的还是靠通道的位子？

A：Window, if possible.
如果可能的话，我要靠窗的位子。

B：Do you need me to book a hotel for you?
需要我帮您订酒店吗？

A：Yes. Thank you.
是的，谢谢。

B：OK. I'll get to work on it.
好，我马上去办。

【场景2】 几分钟以后，于琪将电话打到了中国国际航空公司的订票处。
【对话2】 A：售票员 B：于琪

A：This is China Airlines Booking Office. What can I do for you?
这里是国航订票中心，请问能帮您什么？

B：I'd like to book a ticket to New York.
我想订一张去纽约的机票。

A：When would you like to leave?
您想要什么时间的票？

B：Do you have a flight next Monday?
你们下周一有航班吗？

A：I will check. Please hold on... (Pause) Sorry, we have flights from Shanghai to New York every day. But the route is well booked these days, so there are no seats available for next Monday. What about a Tuesday flight? We have a few seats left on Flight CA589 on that day, leaving Shanghai at 11：00 a.m.. Or we can arrange a good connecting flight for you next Monday. You may fly to Los Angeles and then take a connecting flight to New York.
让我查一下，请别挂机……(稍停)对不起，我们每天都有上海去纽约的航班，但是最近座位特别紧张，下周一的票都卖完了。下周二的航班怎么样？周二的CA589次航班还有一些座位，上午11点从上海起飞。或者，我们可以为您安排下周一的联程航班。您可以飞到洛杉矶，然后转机到纽约。

B：Well, I'll take the direct flight next Tuesday.
嗯，我就订下周二的这班直达航班吧。

A：What class will you fly, first class, business class, or economy class?
您要什么舱位的？头等舱，商务舱，还是经济舱？

B：Business class will be fine.
商务舱就可以。

A：Round trip or one way trip?
双程还是单程？

B：Round trip, but please leave the return flight open.
　　我要双程的，不过返程航班先别固定。

A：All right. What name shall I put the reservation under?
　　好的。您的姓名？

B：Qi Yu.
　　于琪。

A：OK. Now Mr. Yu, let me repeat your reservation. I've reserved you one business class seat on Flight CA589 for March 6th, round trip to New York, leaving Shanghai at 11:00 a.m.. Is that correct?
　　好的。于先生，现在让我重复一下您的订票信息。我为您预订的是一张3月6日上午11点，从上海到纽约，国航CA589的往返商务舱的机票。对吗？

B：That's right.
　　没错。

A：Please pick up your ticket either today or tomorrow.
　　请您今天或明天来取票。

B：Could I come the day after tomorrow?
　　我可以后天取票吗？

A：I'm sorry but this is an international flight and you have to pay for the reserved tickets three days in advance. Otherwise, you'll have to try your luck for standby.
　　抱歉，这是国际航班，您需提前三天为所订机票付款。否则您只能碰运气了。

B：All right. I'll go for the ticket tomorrow afternoon.
　　好吧，我明天下午去取票。

A：Thank you very much. Goodbye.
　　多谢，再见。

【场景3】 订完机票后，于琪又继续打电话为销售经理马天跃预定下榻的酒店。他已经从同事那里了解到，秋天宾馆是马天跃经理在纽约公出时经常入住的地方。

【对话3】 A：宾馆前台接待　B：于琪

A：Good morning. Autumn Hotel. May I help you?
　　早上好。这里是秋天宾馆。能为您效劳吗？

B：Yes. I'd like to reserve a room for my manager.
　　是的。我想替我经理预定一间客房。

A：Right, sir. Which date would that be?
　　好的，先生。要定什么时候的？

B：For one week. From March 6th to 12th.
　　从3月6日到12日，总共一个星期。

A：Which kind of room would he prefer?
　　他比较喜欢什么样的房间？

B：A quiet single room away from the street will be OK.
　　一间不临街的安静的单人间就可以了。

A：Could you hold the line, please? I'll check our room availability... Thank you for waiting. We do have some single rooms at ＄500 and ＄800 available. Which do you like?
　　请别挂断,我查查是否有空房间……让您久等了。我们有几间价位 500 美元及 800 美元的单人房间,您要哪种?

B：Do you have anything less expensive?
　　你们是否还有便宜一点的?

A：I'm sorry. So far they are the only single rooms left.
　　对不起。目前就剩这样的单人房间了。

B：OK. I'll take the one at ＄500. Does the price include the breakfast, by the way?
　　好吧。我订 500 美元的单人房。顺便问一下,价格中包括早餐吗?

A：Yes. That includes a continental breakfast and a morning newspaper. Now, could I have the name of your manager?
　　是的。包括欧式早餐和一份早报。现在,能告诉我您经理的姓名吗?

B：Certainly. His name is Tianyue Ma. T-I-A-N-Y-U-E, M-A.
　　当然。他的名字叫马天跃。

A：Thank you. May I know your name and telephone number, please?
　　谢谢。请告诉我您的姓名和电话号码,好吗?

B：Yes, it's 13941677085. My name is Qi Yu.
　　好的,我的电话是 13941677085,我叫于琪。

【场景 4】　快到午休的时间了,销售经理马天跃来到办公室,向于琪询问机票和房间的预定情况。
【对话 4】　A：销售经理马天跃　　B：于琪

A：How's it going with the travel arrangement, Qi?
　　小琪,出差安排得怎么样了?

B：I've managed to book a flight for next Tuesday.
　　我设法预订了一张下周二的机票。

A：OK. And?
　　好的。还有呢?

B：And Mr. Wang will pick you up at your house at 7 o'clock on Tuesday morning and then drive you to the airport.
　　周二早上 7 点钟,王先生会到您家接您并把您送到机场。

A：What about the hotel?
　　那酒店呢?

B：All the three-star rooms in Autumn Hotel are fully booked, so I got you a four-star one.

秋天宾馆的所有三星级房间都已预订一空,所以我给您预订了一间四星级的。

A: I see.

我知道了。

B: When you arrive there, Lucy, the secretary of Mr. Brown will meet you at the airport. Mr. Brown, our largest client in New York, will have dinner with you.

当您到达的时候,布朗先生的秘书露茜会去机场接您。布朗先生,这位我们在纽约最大的客户将与您共进晚餐。

A: Well, he always prefers to talk about business over the table.

嗯,他总是喜欢在饭桌上谈生意。

Reading: Understanding Consumers

产品销量在纽约市场开始下滑让于琪的心情有些郁闷。到底哪些因素会影响消费者的购买行为？消费者购买决策过程又是怎样的？

Chapter 2 Consumer Markets and Consumer Buying Behavior

Section 1 Characteristics Affecting Consumer Behavior

The actions and decisions of individuals who purchase products for their personal use constitute consumer buying behavior. Several factors, some within individuals and some external, affect the buying decisions of consumers. People are influenced by social factors (e. g., family members, peers), psychological factors (motive, attitude), demographic factors (age, personality), and specific conditions that exist at the time of a purchase decision. Table 2.1 explains and gives examples of factors influencing buying behavior.

Table 2.1　　　　　Influences on Consumer Purchase Decisions

Influences	Examples
Social factors	
Family influence: the close, continuing interactions among family members.	A woman buys a whilpool dishwasher her mother recommends.
Roles: as parent, spouse, child, student, employee, club member, etc.	A young man orders flowers to send to his mother on Mother's Day.
Reference groups: people such as friends or co-workers with whom a person identifies and shares attitudes and behaviours.	An accountant chooses the same kind of computer her associates use.

（续表）

Social class: group of people with similar values, lifestyles and behaviours, often classified by income, occupation, education, religion or ethnic background.	Wealthy art lovers from all over the world come to auctions at Sotheby's in New York.
Culture: values, behaviours, and ways of doing things shared by a society and passed down from generation to generation.	An American buys a turkey at Christmas; while a Chinese buys some firecrackers to celebrate the lunar new year.
Psychological factors	
Motivation: reason or internal force that drives a person toward a goal.	A student gets a haircut before a job interview.
Perception: the way people select, organize, and give meaning to the things they see, hear, taste, smell, and touch.	One person sees a Cadillac as a mark of achievement; another sees it as ostentatious.
Attitude: a person's overall feeling about something.	A lady refuses to buy diamonds coming from Sierra Leone — where the stigma of "blood diamonds" prevails.
Learning: changes in an individual's behavior caused by experiences and information.	After a high cholesterol reading, a man cuts down on the amount of meat and fats he eats.
Demographic factors	
Personal characteristics: such as age, sex, marital status, family size, race, income, education and occupation.	Women spend a lot of money on cosmetics, while men on alcohol.
Lifestyle: a pattern of living that determines how people choose to spend their time, money and energy.	Kids happily fork over $80 for skate shoes and T-shirts in addition to the hundreds they may spend on the latest boards.
Personality: traits, experiences, and behaviours that make up a person.	An outgoing young woman with many friends racks up huge long-distance phone bills.
Situational factors	
Conditions that exist when a person is making a purchase decision, such as physical environment, unexpected circumstances, amount of time for the decision, etc.	A man who is laid off from his job puts off buying a new car.

  In order to better understand consumers, businesses have leveraged Internet technologies in developing customer relationship management (CRM). CRM is intended to help integrate information on individual consumers in order to build stronger relationships. The integration of CRM to business applications is best summarized by the researchers of the Trend Convergence Study. They emphasized that "CRM will need to evolve rapidly beyond collecting information on shopping baskets and issuing direct marketing messages to truly listening to and communicating with customers based on their interests, needs and wants."

小 结

消费者的购买行为受到社会、心理、个人,以及偶然因素的影响。社会因素包括家庭、角色和地位、参照群体、社会阶层、文化等;心理因素包括动机、感知、态度、学习四个方面;个人因素包括年龄、性别、婚姻状况、种族、收入、教育、职业、生活方式和个性等;偶然因素指消费者在决策时面临的情况,包括环境因素、未预料的突发状况,以及有限的决策时间等。加强顾客关系管理,可以帮助企业更好地了解消费者。

Section 2 Types of Consumer Buying Decisions and Consumer Involvement

All consumer buying decisions generally fall along a continuum of three broad categories: routine response behavior, limited decision making, and extensive decision making (see Table 2.2). Goods and services in these three categories can best be described in terms of five factors: level of consumer involvement, length of time to make a decision, cost of the product or service, degree of information search, and the number of alternatives considered. The level of consumer involvement is perhaps the most significant determinant in classifying buying decisions. Involvement is the amount of time and effort a buyer invests in the search, evaluation, and decision processes of consumer behavior.

Table 2.2　　　　　　　　Continuum of Consumer Buying Decisions

	Routine	Limited	Extensive
Involvement	Low	Low to moderate	High
Time	Short	Short to moderate	Long
Cost	Low	Low to moderate	High
Information search	Internal only	Mostly internal	Internal and external
Number of alternatives	One	Few	Many

Frequently purchased, low-cost goods and services are generally associated with routine response behavior. These goods and services can also be called low-involvement products, because consumers spend little time on search and decision before making the purchase. Usually, buyers are familiar with several different brands in the product category but stick with one brand. Consumers engaged in routine response behavior normally don't experience need recognition until they are exposed to advertising or see the product displayed on a store shelf. Consumers buy first and evaluate later, whereas the reverse is true for extensive decision making. A parent, for example, will not stand at the cereal shelf in the grocery store for twenty minutes thinking about which brand of cereal to buy for the children. Instead, he or she will walk by the shelf, find the family's usual brand, and put it into the cart.

Limited decision making typically occurs when a consumer has previous product experience but is unfamiliar with the current brands available. Limited decision making is also associated with lower levels of involvement (although higher than routine decisions) because consumers do expend moderate effort in searching for information or in considering various alternatives. Suppose the children's usual brand of cereal, Kellogg's Corn Flakes, is unavailable in the grocery store. Completely out of cereal at home, the parent now must select another brand. Before making a final selection, he or she may pull from the shelf several brands similar to Kellogg's Corn Flakes, such as Corn Chex and Cheerios, to compare their nutritional value and calories and to decide whether the children will like the new cereal.

Consumers practice extensive decision making when buying an unfamiliar, expensive product or an infrequently bought item. This process is the most complex type of consumer buying decision and is associated with high involvement on the part of the consumer. These consumers want to make the right decision, so they want to know as much as they can about the product category and available brands. People usually experience cognitive dissonance only when buying high-involvement products. Buyers use several criteria for evaluating their options and spend much time seeking information. Buying a house or a car, for example, requires extensive decision making.

The type of decision making that consumers use to purchase a product does not necessarily remain constant. For instance, if a routinely purchased product no longer satisfies, consumers may practice limited or extensive decision making to switch to another brand. And people who first use extensive decision making may then use limited or routine decision making for future purchases. For example, a new mother may first extensively evaluate several brands of disposable diapers before selecting one. Subsequent purchases of diapers will then become routine.

小 结

根据查尔斯·兰姆等学者的观点,消费者购买商品分为惯常反应、有限决策和广泛决策三种类型(注:以菲利普·科特勒为代表的学者将消费者购买类型分为复杂购买行为、减少失调购买行为、习惯性购买行为、寻求多样性购买行为四种)。经常被购买的低成本商品或劳务一般与惯常反应行为有关。消费者花在搜寻和评估上的时间短,且常常购买同一个品牌。定期购买的、价格也不十分昂贵的商品或劳务一般与有限决策类型有关。消费者在决策过程中会花一定的时间,并会有不同品牌的比较和选择。当购买不太熟悉且昂贵的商品时,消费者的行为属于广泛决策。这是消费者所表现出的最复杂的购买决策类型,通常需要使用各种不同的标准评估选择,而且花较多的时间搜寻信息。

Section 3 The Consumer Decision-Making Process

Marketers recognize that consumer decision making is an ongoing process—it's much more than what happens at the moment a consumer forks over the cash and in turn receives a product or service. Behind the visible act of making a purchase lies an important decision-making process which involves five stages: problem recognition, information search, alternative evaluation, purchase decision, and postpurchase behavior.

3.1 Problem Recognition

Problem recognition, the initial step in the purchase decision, is perceiving a difference between one's ideal and actual situations big enough to trigger a decision. This can be as simple as finding an empty milk carton in the refrigerator; noting, as a first-year college student, that your high school clothes are not in the style that other students are wearing; or realizing that your stereo system may not be working properly.

In marketing, advertisements or salespeople can activate a consumer's decision process by showing the shortcomings of competing (or currently owned) products. For instance, a company marketing an extremely fuel efficient car might explain that you can use the several thousand dollars a year you will save on gas to pay off credit card debt or fund a family vacation. Table 2.3 provides examples of marketers' responses to consumers' problem recognition and the other steps in the consumer decision-making process.

Table 2.3   Marketers' Responses to Decision-Process Stages

Stage in the Decision Process	Marketing Strategy	Example
Problem recognition	Encourage consumers to see that existing state does not equal desired state	◇ Create TV commercials showing the excitement of owning a new car
Information search	Provide information when and where consumers are likely to search	◇ Target advertising on TV programs with high target-market viewership ◇ Make new-car brochures available in dealer showrooms
Alternative evaluation	Understand the criteria consumers use in comparing brands and communicate own brand superiority	◇ Conduct research to identify most important evaluative criteria ◇ Create advertising that includes reliable data on superiority of a brand (e.g. safety, comfort)
Purchase decision	Focus on building trust (word of mouth) and create right physical surroundings (from store colors to the employees) and circumstances to encourage and facilitate purchase.	◇ Stress long history of the brand to build loyalty ◇ Offer sales promotions and help customers arrange financing or delivery
Postpurchase behavior	Encourage accurate consumer expectations	◇ Provide honest advertising and sales presentations

3.2 Information Search

After recognizing a problem, a consumer begins to search for information, the next stage in the purchase decision process. First, you may scan your memory for previous experiences with products or brands. This action is called internal search. For frequently purchased products such as shampoo, this may be enough. Or a consumer may undertake an external search for information. This is especially needed when past experience or knowledge is insufficient, the risk of making a wrong purchase decision is high, and the cost of gathering information is low.

Suppose you consider buying an expensive or complex product, such as a car. You will probably tap several of these information sources: friends and relatives, car manufacturers' advertisements, and several stores carrying cars (for demonstrations). You might study the comparative evaluation of different car brands that appeared in Consumer Reports, published by a product-testing organization.

3.3 Alternative Evaluation

The information search stage clarifies the problem for the consumer by (1) suggesting criteria to use for the purchase, (2) yielding brand names that might meet the criteria, and (3) developing consumer value perceptions.

For example, you would probably consider certain characteristics of a car, such as power, fuel economy, price, the style of car, and even safety, more important than others when evaluating which one to buy. These criteria establish the brands in your evoked set—the group of brands you would consider acceptable from among all the brands in the product class of which you are aware. You finally narrow down the choices to three models in your evoked set and think about good and bad features of each option (Table 2.4).

Table 2.4   Hypothetical Ratings of Car Brands on Evaluative Criteria Used

Attributes	Importance Weights	Brand A	Brand B	Brand C
Price	0.3	10	6	8
Power	0.2	8	10	4
Fuel economy	0.1	6	8	10
Style	0.3	10	4	8
Safety	0.1	8	8	8
Total score	1	9	6.6	7.4

Marketers attempt to influence the outcome of this stage in three ways. First, they seek to identify the most important evaluative criteria that consumers use when judging brands. With this information, sales and advertising professionals can point out a brand's superiority on the most important criteria. Second, marketers often play a role in educating consumers about which product characteristics they should use as evaluative criteria—usually marketers will emphasize the dimensions in which their product excels. Finally, marketers try to induce a customer to expand the evoked set to include the product being marketed.

3.4 Purchase Decision

Having examined the alternatives in the evoked set, you are almost ready to make a purchase decision. You come to a logical conclusion that even though the Brand B and the Brand C have attractive qualities (power for Brand B and fuel economy for Brand C), the Brand A has the affordability you need and its carefree image is the way you want others to think about you. Generally speaking, a customer's purchase decision will be to buy the most preferred brand (a brand with the highest score). But until the actual purchase, it is still only an "intended" option because any number of events or interactions can happen to dissuade or alter the final purchase decision.

According to Philip Kotler, the final purchase decision may be "disrupted" by two factors. The first factor is attitudes of others. For example, having gone through the previous three stages, a customer chooses to buy a new telescope. However, because his good friend, a keen astronomer, gives him negative feedback, he may change his mind. The second factor is unforeseen situations such as the store atmosphere, salesperson persuasiveness, a sudden job loss or relocation. Or a close competitor may drop its price. Thus, preferences and even purchase intentions do not always result in actual purchase choice.

3.5 Postpurchase Behavior

After buying a product, the consumer compares it with one's own expectations and is either satisfied or dissatisfied. Almost all major purchases result in cognitive dissonance, or discomfort caused by postpurchase conflict. After the purchase, consumers are satisfied with the benefits of the chosen brand and are glad to avoid the drawbacks of the brands not bought. However, every purchase involves compromise. Consumers feel uneasy about acquiring the drawbacks of the chosen brand and about losing the benefits of the brands not purchased. Thus, consumers feel at least some postpurchase dissonance for every purchase.

Sensitivity to a customer's consumption or use experience is extremely important in a consumer's value perception. Studies on automobile purchasing show that satisfaction or dissatisfaction affects consumer communications. Satisfied buyers tell eight other people about their experience. Dissatisfied buyers complain to 22 people. Accordingly, firms like General Electric (GE), Johnson&Johnson, Coca-Cola, and British Airways focus attention on postpurchase behavior to maximize customer satisfaction. These firms, among many others, now provide toll-free telephone numbers, offer liberalized return and refund policies, and engage in staff training to handle complaints, answer questions, and record suggestions. Research has shown that such efforts produce positive postpurchase communications among consumers and contribute to relationship building between sellers and buyers.

小 结

　　消费者购买决策包括5个阶段：认识问题（或需要）—搜集信息—评价方案—购买决策—购后行为。当消费者认识到现实和理想状态存在显著差异时，是其购买过程的开始。随后是搜集信息，主要通过内部、外部两个来源。搜集到的信息是评价购买方案的依据。在方案评价阶段，消费者会使用多个标准并生成备选方案集合。消费者对备选方案进行比较和评价后，形成购买意向，但最终的购买决策依然会受到他人以及不可预见情况的影响。消费者购后的满意程度取决于消费者对产品的预期性能与产品使用中的实际性能之间的对比。购买后的满意程度决定消费者是否会重复购买该产品，并且还会影响到其他消费者。因此，许多公司都积极采取措施避免消费者购买后可能出现的失调感。

New Words and Key Terms

01.	consumer buying behavior	消费者购买行为
02.	social factors	社会因素
03.	psychological factors	心理因素
04.	demographic factors	个人因素
05.	specific conditions	偶然因素
06.	reference groups	参照群体
07.	motivation	动机
08.	perception	感知
09.	attitude	态度
10.	learning	学习
11.	customer relationship management	顾客关系管理
12.	involvement	参与（程度）
13.	routine response behavior	惯常反应行为
14.	limited decision making	有限决策（行为）
15.	extensive decision making	广泛决策（行为）
16.	cognitive dissonance	认知失调
17.	evoked set	参考组，备选方案；诱发集合

Writing: Questionnaire

销售经理马天跃此次的纽约之行,一方面是要向当地的经销商了解本地的市场变化情况,另一方面是要针对当地家长进行一次关于玩具产品消费者喜好的实地调查,获得详细的一手资料。临行之前,他交代于琪为其设计一份详细的调查问卷。

一、调查问卷写作的基本要求和格式

调查问卷(Questionnaire)又称调查表或询问表,是以问题的形式系统地记载调查内容的一种印件。调查问卷可以是表格式、卡片式或簿记式,也可分为自填问卷和访问问卷。一份完整的调查问卷通常包括如下内容:

(一)标题(Title)

问卷标题概括说明调查研究的主题,使被调查者对所要回答什么方面的问题有一个大致的了解。问卷标题应简明扼要,易于引起被调查者的兴趣。例如,Staff Questionnaire on Canteen Service(有关餐厅服务的员工调查问卷)。不要简单采用"Questionnaire"这样的标题,它容易引起被调查者因不必要的怀疑而拒答。

(二)引言(Introduction)

引言放在问卷的开头,通常采用如下书写模式:首先,交代谁在调查(内部调查则不需自我介绍);然后,交代调查内容及目的;接下来,如有必要进行保密承诺。例如,Your survey responses will be strictly confidential and data from this research will be reported only in the aggregate. 如果接受调查有赠品,如酬金、礼物、奖券及产品试用等则还要说明赠品情况;最后,如果有必要,亦应说明问卷填写及交回的方式。当然,填写方式也可出现在问卷主体中并用括号括起来,例如,"(Pick all that apply)",而交回的方式也可出现在结束语中。

(三)问题(Questions)

调查问卷的问题可能是关于被访者的个人情况,可能是关于被访者的行为方式,亦可能是关于被访者的态度或看法。常见的问题类型包括:

1. 封闭式问题(Closed Questions)

封闭式问题指事先设计好备选答案,受访者对问题的回答被限制在备选答案中,即从已有答案中挑选自己认同的选项。例如,Are you going to register for the On-the-Job training this year? Y / N (Please delete)

2. 开放式问题(Open Questions)

开放式问题是指对所提出的问题并不列出可能的答案,而是由被访者自由作答。例如,Please list 3 English training agencies that you think are better than others:

3. 半封闭式问题(Half-closed Questions)

半封闭式问题是上述两种问题的折中,虽然提供了选择,应答者还可以创造自己的答案。例如,What kind of toy do you often buy for your children?
Plush toys □   Electronic toys □   Cartoon toys □   Plastic toys □   Educational

toys☐　　Other (Please be specific)_____

4. 偏好性问题(Rating or Preference Questions)

偏好性问题要求受访者对问题的答案根据重要性进行排序,或给定一个固定的参照系,由调查对象把他认可的分值或喜好程度在参照表中进行分配。

例如,What aspects about our products do you like most? (Please select the options below in sequence. The first one will be the option you concern most.) A：Function　B：Appearance　C：Price　D：Practicability　E：Security　F：After-sales service_____

再如,In thinking about your most recent experience shopping in our store, was the quality of customer service you received... A：Very poor☐　　B：Somewhat unsatisfactory☐　　C：About average☐　　D：Satisfactory☐　　E：Very satisfactory☐

(四)结束语(Concluding Statement)

通常,结束语简单地表示感谢即可。例如,Thank you for taking the time to answer our questions. 谢谢您花费时间回答我们的问题。

二、于琪的解决方案

Questionnaire on Children's Toys

Dear friends,

We are the market researchers of Golden Childhood Children's Products Co., Ltd. In order to better understand the local market and find out how customers perceive our toy products, we make this questionnaire. Please fill in the required information and tick the appropriate boxes below. Your opinion will be greatly valued and of course will be strictly confidential.

1. Your gender?　　☐Male.　　☐Female.
2. Your age?
☐Under 18　　☐18～24　　☐25～34
☐35～44　　　☐45 or above
3. What is your employment status?
☐Employed Full-Time.　☐Employed Part-Time.　☐Student.
☐Unemployed.　　　　☐Retired.　　　　　　☐Prefer not to answer.
If you are employed, what is your occupation?
☐Doctor.　　　　　☐Professor.　　　　　　☐Lawyer.
☐Engineer.　　　　☐Government official.　☐Police officer.　　☐Other.
4. Which of the following is your range of monthly income?
☐Under ＄2,000.　　☐＄2,000～＄2,999.　　☐＄3,000～＄3,999.
☐＄4,000～＄4,999.　☐＄5,000～＄5,999.　　☐＄6,000 or more.
☐Prefer not to answer.
5. What is the highest level of education you received?
☐High school or less　　☐Vocational school or college

☐Bachelor's degree ☐Master's degree
☐Doctorate degree ☐Other

6. How often do you buy a toy for your children?
☐About half a month ☐About a month
☐About three months ☐Half a year or above

7. How much do you usually spend on buying toys for your children each time?
☐$100 or less ☐$100～$300
☐$300～$500 ☐$500 or above

8. Where do you usually buy toys for your children?
☐Convenience store ☐Department store ☐Toy store
☐Supermarket ☐By the Internet ☐Shopping center
☐Other

9. When do you buy toys for your children?
☐Children demand ☐Seeing other children playing with them
☐Children's birthday ☐Important festivals
☐Seeing advertisements ☐Other

10. How do you know about toys?
☐Online ☐Newspapers and magazines
☐Television advertising ☐Friends
☐Stores sales promotion

11. What kind of toy do you often buy for your children?
☐Plush toys ☐Electronic toys ☐Cartoon toys
☐Plastic toys ☐Educational toys
☐Other (Please be specific) _____

12. What factors do you consider when you buy toys? (Pick all that apply)
☐Quality ☐Price ☐Brand ☐Security
☐Creativity ☐The interest of children ☐Following the general trend

13. What brand of toys do you usually buy?
☐Kids II ☐Good Boy ☐Hasbro
☐Little Tikes ☐Carter's ☐Fisher Price
☐Lamaze ☐Other (Please be specific)_____

14. Do you know "Golden Childhood" toys? (If you choose "no", this is the end; if you choose "yes", please go on with it.)
☐yes ☐no

15. What aspects about our products do you like most? (Please select the options below in sequence. The first one will be the option you concern most.)
A: Function B: Appearance C: Price D: Practicability E: Security
F: After-sales service G: Environment friendly _____

16. What suggestions do you have to improve our products/services?

_____

Thank you for spending time helping us with this survey.

Review Questions

1. Key Terms

Reference groups; Perception; Involvement; Cognitive dissonance; Evoked set

2. Multiple Choices (select one)

(1) Many marketers try to identify opinion leaders for their products and direct marketing efforts toward them. What factor do they consider for consumers' behavior? (   )

    A. Social factor   B. Psychological factor

    C. Demographic factor   D. Specific condition or situational factor

(2) (   ) needs are basic to survival and must be satisfied first.

    A. Physiological   B. Safety

    C. Personal   D. Self-actualization

(3) The U.S. Army former advertising theme, "Be all that you can be" relied on which of the psychological influences on behavior? (   )

    A. Motivation   B. Learning

    C. Perception   D. Lifestyle

(4) Consumers will pay more for candy wrapped in expensive-looking foil packages. What factor influences their buying behavior? (   )

    A. Motivation   B. Perception

    C. Attitude   D. Learning

(5) A mother of two toddlers would most likely use an internal search process exclusively when purchasing (   ).

    A. a gift for a best friend   B. a DVD player

    C. disposable diapers   D. perfume

    E. a weekend getaway

(6) Frequently purchased, low-cost goods and services are generally associated with (   ).

    A. routine response behavior   B. limited decision making

    C. extensive decision making   D. common decision making

(7) Consumers practice (   ) when buying an unfamiliar, expensive product or an infrequently bought item.

    A. routine response behavior   B. limited decision making

C. extensive decision making   D. common decision making

(8) After recognizing a problem, a consumer begins to search for information, the ( ) stage in the purchase decision process.

A. first   B. second   C. third   D. fourth

(9) ( ) includes various product-rating organizations such as Consumer Reports, government agencies, and TV "consumer programs".

A. Personal source   B. Public source
C. Marketer-dominated source   D. Internal source

(10) ( ) is the initial step in the consumer purchase decision.

A. Problem recognition   B. Information search
C. Alternative evaluation   D. Purchase decision
E. Postpurchase behaviour

3. Questions for Discussion

(1) Many marketers target opinion leaders with marketing messages. Why are opinion leaders important? How might opinion leaders influence buyer behavior? For which products do opinion leaders appear to be most influential? For which are they least influential?

(2) Assume you are involved in the following consumer decision situations: (a) renting a video to watch with your roommates, (b) choosing a fast-food restaurant to go to with a new friend, (c) buying a popular music compact disc, (d) buying jeans to wear to class. List the factors that would influence your decision in each situation and explain your responses.

(3) Recall an occasion when you experienced cognitive dissonance about a purchase and explain what you did about it.

(4) What are the steps in the consumer decision-making process?

Practical Writing

Scenario: You work at the Personnel and Welfare Department of a large British company in Kuala Lumpur, with 2,000 local employees. It is felt that there has been a decline in using the staff canteen, so you are asked by your boss to draft a *Questionnaire* for employees to complete, showing such things as: how many times a week they use the canteen, how they think of the price, whether they prefer hot or cold meals or snacks and sandwiches, whether they are satisfied with the selection and quality of food available, and also with the service provided. Include any other details you find appropriate.

Unit 3　Here Comes a Large Client

Learning Objectives

◇ 熟悉迎接和安排客户的常用口语表达；
◇ 理解商业组织市场的特点和商业市场需求与消费者市场需求的差异；
◇ 理解商业购买行为的参与者和每个参与者在购买决策中的作用；
◇ 理解商业购买类型和商业购买决策过程；
◇ 掌握便笺与便条的书写规则和常用套语的正确写法。

Speaking：Meeting Clients at the Airport

【场景1】今天，澳大利亚一家儿童服装经销公司的业务代表David Smith先生将拜访公司。他已经于几日前发来传真，告知航班情况。由于销售经理马天跃正在出差，总经理Robert Liu虽然公务繁忙，但仍然在于琪的陪同下一大早便专程来机场迎接。

【对话1】　A：于琪　　B：David Smith先生　　C：总经理Robert Liu

A：If I'm not mistaken, you must be Mr. David Smith from Australia!
如果我没弄错的话，您一定是来自澳大利亚的戴维·史密斯先生吧。

B：Yes, I am, but...
是的，我是。您是……

A：I'm Qi Yu from Golden Childhood Children's Products Co., Ltd. Nice to meet you.
我是来自金色童年儿童用品有限公司的于琪。很高兴见到您。

B：How do you do? Thank you so much for meeting me here.
您好。非常感谢您来接我。

A：My pleasure. May I introduce Mr. Liu to you? Mr. Liu is our general manager.
荣幸之至。我给您介绍刘先生好吗？他是我们的总经理。

C：How do you do, Mr. Smith? I've heard so much about you.
您好，史密斯先生。久仰大名。

B：Thank you. Call me David.
　　谢谢，叫我戴维吧。

C：And call me Robert then. We've been expecting you ever since you faxed us the date of your arrival.
　　那么叫我罗伯特吧。自从收到您的传真后，我们就一直期待着您的光临。

B：Thank you, Robert.
　　谢谢您，罗伯特。

C：Have you had a pleasant journey?
　　旅途还愉快吧？

B：Yes, it was uneventful. I have heard a lot about China in Australia. Now I'm seeing it with my own eyes.
　　是的，一切顺利。我在澳大利亚时已经听说了很多关于中国的事情。现在能够亲眼看见这个国家了。

C：Yes, this is a good chance to know more about China. I hope you'll enjoy your stay here.
　　是啊，这是一个更多了解中国的好机会啊。希望您在这儿过得愉快。

B：Thank you. I'm sure I'll have a wonderful time here.
　　谢谢您。我想我一定会的。

C：(After chatting with the guest for about 5 minutes, Mr. Liu takes a look at his watch.) Well, you must be tired after the long flight. We have reserved you a room at Jinjiang Hotel, one of the best hotels in Shanghai, very close to the embay quarter. I have a meeting at 9 o'clock. Mr. Yu will take you to the hotel and help you settle down.
　　(与客人交谈了5分钟后，刘经理看了看他的手表。)嗯，长途飞行后，您一定累了吧。我们已经在锦江饭店为您预订了一个房间，它是上海最好的宾馆之一，离使馆区很近。我在九点钟还有一个会议。于先生将送您去宾馆，并帮您安顿下来。

B：Thank you again for taking the time to meet me, Robert.
　　再次感谢您抽出时间来接我，罗伯特。

C：My pleasure.
　　我很荣幸。

A：I'll bring the car here, so please wait a moment.
　　请等一下，我把车开过来。

【场景2】 车子一路开到锦江饭店。于琪早就帮Smith先生预订了房间，现在只需在饭店的前台登记入住即可。
【对话2】 A：宾馆前台接待　B：于琪

A：Good morning, sir. May I help you?
　　早上好，先生。需要我为您效劳吗？

Unit 3　Here Comes a Large Client　37

B：Yes. I'd like to check in, please. I made a reservation for my guest a week ago under my name of Qi Yu, for four days from today. And here is my confirmation slip.

是的。请帮我登记住宿。一个礼拜前,我用自己的名字于琪为我的客人预订了一个房间,时间是从今天开始连续四天。这是我的预约确认单。

A：Thank you, Mr. Yu. A second, please... Oh, yes, we've got your reservation. It is a single room with an ocean view. Is it correct?

谢谢,于先生。请稍等片刻……噢,是的,我们有您的预约。是一间带海景的单人间。对吗?

B：Yeah, correct.

是的,没错。

A：Then, please fill out this form, Mr. Yu.

那么,于先生,请把这张表填一下。

B：Sure.（Fill out the registration card.）Is this OK?

没问题。(填好住宿登记表。)这样可以吗?

A：Thank you. Your room number is 666 and here is your room key. Just leave your guest's baggage here and I'll get the porter to carry it up right away.

谢谢。您的房间是666号,这是您房间的钥匙。把您客人的行李留在这儿,我会马上叫行李员把它提上去。

B：Thank you very much.

非常感谢你。

【场景3】 中午12点,已经返回公司的于琪再一次来到锦江饭店。他将就Smith先生来访期间的时间安排进行敲定,并代表总经理邀请Smith先生共进晚餐。

【对话3】 A：于琪　B：David Smith先生

A：Good afternoon, Mr. Smith.

中午好,史密斯先生。

B：Good afternoon, Mr. Yu. Glad to see you again.

中午好,于先生。很高兴再次见到你。

A：Do you enjoy your stay here?

您在这儿住得惯吗?

B：Oh, yes. The room is very nice and the food is delicious.

哦,是的。房间很好,而且饭菜也十分可口。

A：I'm glad you like it. Well, if you don't mind, I'd like to discuss the itinerary with you.

很高兴您喜欢。唔,如果您不介意的话,我想现在和您商讨一下日程安排。

B：Not at all.

当然不介意。

A: Good. Here is a copy of the tentative itinerary we drafted for you. Let's go over it. Please feel free to make changes wherever you feel necessary.

好的。这是一份我们为您草拟的日程表,让我们把它过一遍。只要您觉得需要,可以随时提出修改。

B: OK. Let me see. (Mr. Smith reads the program.)

好的,让我看一下。(史密斯先生读日程表。)

A: As you need a day to get over your jet lag, nothing is fixed up for you this afternoon. You could stay in the hotel for a good rest. You will visit our company tomorrow, starting with the workshop and then the products showroom. You will have lunch at the refectory with general manager Robert Liu and visit our office block at half past two. The day after tomorrow, a car will be at hotel at 8:30 a.m. to drive you to the Oriental Bright Pearl TV Tower and the Huangpu River, which are all features of a complex and diverse Shanghai.

由于您需要一天来克服时差反应,我们今天下午没有给您安排活动。您可以待在宾馆里好好休息。您将在明天参观我们的公司,从生产车间开始,然后是产品展室。中午和总经理在食堂共进午餐,下午两点半参观办公大楼。后天早上八点半有车在宾馆外等您,将带您到东方明珠塔和黄浦江,它们是繁华多样的上海的典型代表。

B: (After having read the program) Well, Mr. Yu, I'm an opera fan myself. Would it be possible for me to go to see traditional Chinese operas, particularly Peking Opera? I've heard so much about Peking Opera. You see, there is no mention of it in your plan.

(看完了日程表)于先生,我是一位戏剧迷。我能去看一看传统的中国戏剧,特别是京剧吗?我对京剧早有耳闻。你看,这在日程表上并没有做安排。

A: Yes, we had it in mind. That's why we have left the last day free. You can either go shopping or see Chinese operas. In China, almost every province has one or more operas with local characteristics. In Shanghai, for example, there is Hu Ju, or Songhu Opera. The most popular opera, of course, is Jing Ju, or Peking Opera.

是的,我们也有此想法,所以才把最后一天留出来。您可以选择去购物,或者去看中国戏剧。在中国,几乎每个省份都有一个或多个地方戏剧。例如在上海,我们有沪剧。当然,最流行的剧种还是京剧。

B: Also I'd like to talk to some of the technicians, if it is possible.

另外,如果可以的话,我想和一些技术人员谈一谈。

A: That can be easily arranged. When you visit the factory, the technicians are happy to answer any questions you may be interested in.

那很容易安排。当您参观工厂的时候,技术员会很乐意回答您感兴趣的任何问题。

B: That's great. Then the plan fits in very nicely with mine.

太好了。那么,这个计划与我的打算完全相符。

A: I'm glad to hear that. Then our plan is made. By the way, our general manager wishes the pleasure of your company at a dinner party this evening.

您这样说我很高兴,我们就这样定了。顺便说一声,我们总经理想请您共进晚餐。

B: How nice of him. I'll be most pleased to go.

他太客气了,我非常乐意前往。

A: Is 6 o'clock convenient for you?

六点钟对您来说方便吗?

B: Yes. In fact, any time will be fine.

方便。实际上,什么时间都行。

A: Very good. I'll pick you up at 6 o'clock this evening. The dinner will start at 6:30.

很好。今晚六点我来接您。晚宴将在六点半开始。

B: That's very kind of you.

太感谢了。

Reading: Understanding Business Buyers

David Smith 先生来自一家大的贸易公司。在商业购买中,不仅单笔的成交额大,而且供需双方往往会通过合作建立长久的关系。商业组织购买行为的特点是什么?商业组织购买类型及决策过程怎样?

Chapter 3 Business Markets and Business Buyer Behavior

Section 1 Characteristics of Business Markets

Like final consumers, a business buyer purchases products to fill needs. A manufacturer buys raw materials to create the company's product, while a wholesaler or retailer buys products to resell. Institutional purchasers such as government agencies and nonprofit organizations buy things to meet the needs of their constituents. These business-to-business markets—also called organizational markets—include manufacturers, wholesalers, retailers, and a variety of other organizations, such as hospitals, universities, and governmental agencies. Although marketing to business customers does have a lot in common with consumer marketing, there are differences that make this basic process more complex.

1.1 Multiple Buyers

In business markets, products often have to do more than satisfy an individual's needs. They must meet the requirements of everyone involved in the company's purchase decision. If you decide to buy a new chair for your room or apartment, you're the only one who has to be satisfied. For your classroom, the furniture must satisfy not only students but also faculty, administrators, campus planners, and the people at your school who actually do the purchasing. If your school is a state or other governmental institution, the furniture may also have to meet certain government-mandated engineering standards.

1.2 Number of Customers

Organizational customers are few and far between compared to end-user consumers. In the United States, there are about 100 million consumer households but less than half a million businesses and other organizations. When most people think of General Electric the first things that come to mind are light bulbs and home appliances. That's because GE spends millions of dollars advertising those products to the consumer marketplace. But GE's tagline isn't "Imagination at Work" for nothing. The "at work" part has a double meaning, including the fact that, by far, GE targets the vast majority of its products and services to the business marketplace. From jet engines to oilfield equipments to healthcare devices, GE's product line for businesses far exceeds the GE-branded items you see at your local Home Depot. Each of these business markets has far fewer customers than the consumer market for their light bulbs and appliances. And their business marketing strategies must be quite different from consumer marketing strategies. For example, a strong sales force is a far better way to promote GE's business products than the extensive advertising the company does when it wants to talk to consumers.

1.3 Size of Purchases

Business-to-business products dwarf consumer purchases both in the quantity of items ordered and how much they cost. A company that rents uniforms to other businesses, for example, buys hundreds of large drums of laundry detergent each year to launder its uniforms. In contrast, even a hard-core soccer mom dealing with piles of dirty socks and shorts only goes through a box of detergent every few weeks. Organizations purchase many products, such as a highly sophisticated piece of manufacturing equipment or computer-based marketing information systems that can cost a million dollars or more. Recognizing such differences in the size of purchases allows marketers to develop effective marketing strategies. Although it makes perfect sense to use mass-media advertising to promote laundry detergent to consumers, selling thousands of dollars' worth of laundry detergent or a million-dollar machine tool is best handled by a strong personal sales force.

1.4 Geographic Concentration

Another difference between business markets and consumer markets is geographic concentration, meaning that many business customers are located in a small geographic area rather than being spread out across the country. Whether they live in the heart of New York City or in a small fishing village in Oregon, consumers buy and use toothpaste and televisions. This is not so for business-to-business customers, who may be almost exclusively located in a single region of the country. For years Silicon Valley, a 50-mile-long corridor along the California coast, has been home to thousands of electronics and software companies because of its high concentration of skilled engineers and scientists. For business-to-business marketers who wish to sell to these markets, this means that they can concentrate their sales efforts and perhaps even locate distribution centers in a single geographic area.

1.5 Buyer-Seller Relationships

As we discussed in Chapter 2, many consumer product companies now focus on building strong relationships with their customers. However, even when a relationship is cultivated with the customer, it is impersonal and exists primarily through electronic communication or direct mail. The opposite is true in business markets. The nature of business markets requires a more personal relationship between buyer and seller. Satisfying one major customer may mean the difference of millions of dollars to a firm. As a result, companies selling in a B2B market invest more resources to foster and maintain personal contact with their customers than in a consumer market. At the same time, technology plays a critical role in connecting buyer and seller. Customers demand not only a personal relationship with their vendors but also an efficient one. Integrating IT systems that enhance sales response times, provide better customer service and increase information flow is now an accepted element in a successful B2B customer relationship.

Besides all these factors that make a difference in business markets, demand in business markets differs from consumer demand. Consumer demand is based on a direct connection between a need and the satisfaction of that need. But business customers don't purchase goods and services to satisfy their own needs. Businesses instead operate on derived demand, because a business's demand for goods and services comes either directly or indirectly from consumers' demand for what it produces. Furthermore, many business markets have inelastic demand; that is, it usually doesn't matter if the price of a business-to-business product goes up or down—business customers still buy the same quantity, because what is being sold is often just one of the many parts or materials that go into producing the consumer product. Business demand also is subject to greater fluctuations than is consumer demand. A product's life expectancy is one reason for fluctuating demand. Business customers may only need to replace some types of large machinery every 10 or 20 years. Thus, demand for such products fluctuates—it may be very high one year when a lot of customers' machinery wears out but low the following year because everyone's old machinery is working fine. Finally, joint demand occurs when two or more goods are necessary to create a product.

小 结

商业市场与消费者市场的差异主要体现在五个方面：第一，在商业市场中，产品往往不仅要满足购买者一个人的需要。它们必须满足参与到公司购买决策的每个人的要求。第二，相比于终端消费者，商业组织购买者的数量较少。第三，企业间产品购买在购买数量和购买花费上比消费者购买要大得多。第四，与消费者市场相比，商业市场地理更加集中。这意味着许多企业的客户分布在一个小的地理区域，而不是散布在全国各地。第五，商业市场的特点要求买卖双方建立更为紧密和有效的个人联系。除了以上这些商业市场与消费者市场的明显差异，商业市场需求与消费者市场需求也有很大的不同。商业市场需求通常是衍生的、非弹性的、波动的以及联合的需求。

Section 2 Participants in the Business Buying Process

Who does the buying of the goods and services needed by business organizations? The decision-making unit of a buying organization is called its buying center: all the individuals and units that participate in the business decision-making process. The buying center includes all members of the organization who play a role in the purchase decision process. This group includes the actual users of the product or service, those who make the buying decision, those who influence the buying decision, those who do the actual buying, and those who control buying information.

Users are members of the organization who will use the product or service. In many cases, users initiate the buying proposal and help define product specifications. Influencers often help define specifications and also provide information for evaluating alternatives. Technical personnel are particularly important influencers. Buyers have formal authority to select the supplier and arrange terms of purchase. Buyers may help shape product specifications, but their major role is in selecting vendors and negotiating. In more complex purchases, buyers might include high-level officers participating in the negotiations. Deciders have formal or informal power to select or approve the final suppliers. In routine buying, the buyers are often the deciders, or at least the approvers. Gatekeepers control the flow of information to others. For example, purchasing agents often have authority to prevent salespeople from seeing users or deciders. Other gatekeepers include technical personnel and even personal secretaries.

The buying center is not a fixed and formally identified unit within the buying organization. It is a set of buying roles assumed by different people for different purchases. Within the organization, the size and makeup of the buying center will vary for different products and for different buying situations. For some routine purchases, one person—say a purchasing agent—may assume all the buying center roles and serve as the only person involved in the buying decision. For more complex purchases, the buying center may include 20 or 30 people from different levels and departments in the organization.

The buying center concept presents a major marketing challenge. The business marketer must learn who participate in the decision, each participant's relative influence, and what evaluation criteria each decision participant uses. Consider a company selling disposable surgical gowns to hospitals. It identifies the hospital personnel involved in this buying decision as the vice president of purchasing, the operating room administrator, and the surgeons. Each participant plays a different role. The vice president of purchasing analyzes whether the hospital should buy disposable gowns or reusable gowns. If analysis favors disposable gowns, then the operating room administrator compares competing products and prices and makes a choice. This administrator considers the gown's absorbency, antiseptic quality, design, and cost, and normally buys the brand that meets requirements at the lowest cost. Finally, surgeons affect the decision later by reporting their satisfaction or dissatisfaction with the brand.

The buying center usually includes some obvious participants who are involved formally in the buying decision. For example, the decision to buy a corporate jet will probably involve the company's CEO, chief pilot, a purchasing agent, some legal staff, a member of top management, and others formally charged with the buying decision. It may also involve less-obvious, informal participants, some of whom may actually make or strongly affect the buying decision. Some buying influences are surprising. Indeed, the most important influence may be the CEO's spouse. Many business buying decisions result from the complex interactions of ever-changing buying center participants.

小 结

一个商业购买组织的决策制定单位称为采购中心。采购中心包括在购买决策过程中所有扮演了以下五个角色中的任何一个的组织成员。其中，使用者是组织中将使用产品或服务的成员。影响者常常协助确定产品规格，并提供评估备选产品的信息。购买者拥有选择供应商和协商购买条件的正式权力。决策者拥有选择或批准最终供应商的正式或非正式的权力。信息流向控制者控制流向他人的信息流。商业市场营销者必须知道谁参与了决策，每个参与者的相对影响力，以及每个决策参与者使用的评估标准。

Section 3 Types and Process of Business Buying Situations

There are three major types of business buying situations. In a straight rebuy, the buyer reorders something without any modifications. Based on past buying satisfaction, the buyer simply chooses from the various suppliers on its list. "In" suppliers try to maintain product and service quality. The "out" suppliers try to offer something new or exploit dissatisfaction so that the buyer will consider them. In a modified rebuy, the buyer wants to modify product specifications, prices, terms, or suppliers. The "in" suppliers may become nervous and feel pressured to put their best foot forward to protect an account. "Out" suppliers may see the modified rebuy situation as an opportunity to gain new business. A company buying a product or service for the first time faces a new-task situation. In such cases, the greater the cost or risk, the larger the number of decision participants and the greater their efforts to collect information will be. The eight-stage model provides a simple view of the business buying process, although some of the stages may be skipped by straight or modified rebuyers.

3.1 Problem Recognition

The buying process begins when someone in the company recognizes a problem or need that can be met by acquiring a specific product or service. Problem recognition can result from internal or external stimuli. Internally, the company may decide to launch a new product that requires new production equipment and materials. Or a machine may break down and need new parts. Perhaps a purchasing manager is unhappy with a current supplier's product quality, service, or prices. Externally, the buyer may get some new ideas at a trade show, see an ad, or receive a call from a salesperson who offers a better product or a lower price. In fact, in their advertising, business marketers often alert customers to potential problems and then show how their products provide solutions.

3.2 General Need Description

Having recognized a need, the buyer next prepares a general need description that describes the characteristics and quantity of the needed item. For standard items, this process presents few problems. For complex items, however, the buyer may have to work with others—engineers, users, consultants—to define the item. The team may want to rank the importance of reliability, durability, price, and other attributes desired in the item. In this phase, the alert business marketer can help the buyers define their needs and provide information about the value of different product characteristics.

3.3 Product Specification

The buying organization next develops the item's technical product specifications, often with the help of a value analysis engineering team. Value analysis is an approach to cost reduction in which components are studied carefully to determine if they can be redesigned, standardized, or made by less costly methods of production. The team decides on the best product characteristics and specifies them accordingly. Sellers, too, can use value analysis as a tool to help secure a new account. By showing buyers a better way to make an object, outside sellers can turn straight rebuy situations into new-task situations that give them a chance to obtain new business.

3.4 Supplier Search

The buyer now conducts a supplier search to find the best vendors. The buyer can compile a small list of qualified suppliers by reviewing trade directories, doing a computer search, or phoning other companies for recommendations. The newer the buying task, and the more complex and costly the item, the greater the amount of time the buyer will spend searching for suppliers. The supplier's task is to get listed in major directories and build a good reputation in the marketplace. Salespeople should watch for companies in the process of searching for suppliers and make certain that their firm is considered.

3.5 Proposal Solicitation

In the proposal solicitation stage of the business buying process, the buyer invites qualified suppliers to submit proposals. In response, some suppliers will send only a catalog or a salesperson. However, when the item is complex or expensive, the buyer will usually require detailed written proposals or formal presentations from each potential supplier. Business marketers must be skilled in researching, writing, and presenting proposals in response to buyer proposal solicitations. Proposals should be marketing documents, not just technical documents. Presentations should inspire confidence and should make the marketer's company stand out from the competition.

3.6 Supplier Selection

The members of the buying center now review the proposals and select a supplier or suppliers. During supplier selection, the buying center often will draw up a list of the desired supplier attributes and their relative importance. These may include quality products and services, on-time delivery, ethical corporate behavior, honest communication, competitive prices, repair and servicing capabilities, technical aid and advice, geographic location, performance history, and reputation. The members of the buying center will rate suppliers against these attributes and identify the best suppliers. Many buyers prefer multiple sources of supplies to avoid being totally dependent on one supplier and to allow comparisons of prices and performance of several suppliers over time.

3.7 Order-Routine Specification

The buyer now prepares an order-routine specification. It includes the final order with the chosen supplier or suppliers and lists items such as technical specifications, quantity needed, expected time of delivery, return policies, and warranties. For maintenance, repair, and operating items, buyers may use blanket contracts rather than periodic purchase orders. A *blanket contract* creates a long-term relationship in which the supplier promises to resupply the buyer as needed at agreed prices for a set time period. It eliminates the expensive process of renegotiating a purchase each time that stock is required. It also allows buyers to write more, but smaller, purchase orders, resulting in lower inventory levels and carrying costs. Blanket contracting leads to more single-source buying and to buying more items from that source. This practice locks the supplier in tighter with the buyer and makes it difficult for other suppliers to break in unless the buyer becomes dissatisfied with prices or service.

3.8 Performance Review

In this stage, the buyer reviews supplier performance. The buyer may contact users and ask them to rate their satisfaction. The performance review may lead the buyer to continue, modify, or drop the arrangement. The seller's job is to monitor the same factors used by the buyer to make sure that the seller is giving the expected satisfaction.

Each organization buys in its own way, and each buying situation has unique requirements. Different buying center participants may be involved at different stages of the process. Although certain buying-process steps usually do occur, buyers do not always follow them in the same order, and they may add other steps. Often, buyers will repeat certain stages of the process. Finally, a customer relationship might involve many different types of purchases ongoing at a given time, all in different stages of the buying process. The seller must manage the total customer relationship, not just individual purchases.

小 结

商业购买有直接重购、修正重购和新任务三种情况。根据菲利普·科特勒等学者的观点,一个完整的商业购买过程包括8个阶段:

1. 问题识别。当公司中有人认识到某个问题或需要应该通过获得一种特定的产品或服务得到满足时,购买过程就开始了。

2. 一般需求描述。说明所需项目的特性和数量。

3. 产品规格说明。购买组织要制定商品的技术产品规格,往往在一个价值分析工程小组的协助下进行。

4. 供应商搜寻。购买者可以通过交易目录、计算机搜索或致电其他公司寻求推荐来编辑一份简单的合格供应商的名单。

5. 方案征集。购买者征求合格的供应商提交供应方案。

6. 供应商选择。采购中心的成员重新审核供应方案并从中选出一个或一组供应商。

7. 常规购买的手续规定。包括购买者与所选择的供应商之间的最后订单和列举的各项条款,例如技术规范、数量需求、期望的交货时间、返还政策和担保。

8. 绩效评价。购买者向产品使用者征询满意度评价。

New Words and Key Terms

01. business-to-business markets	商业市场,组织市场
02. derived demand	衍生需求
03. inelastic demand	非弹性需求
04. fluctuating demand	波动需求
05. joint demand	联合需求
06. buying center	采购中心
07. users	使用者
08. influencers	影响者
09. buyers	购买者
10. deciders	决策者
11. gatekeepers	信息流向控制者
12. straight rebuy	直接重购
13. modified rebuy	修正重购
14. new-task	新任务(购买)
15. value analysis	价值分析
16. blanket contract	一揽子合同

Writing: Memorandum and Note

下午2点,总经理Robert先生将于琪叫到了自己的办公室。公司拟举办一个高级的电脑培训班,为未来的办公自动化以及电脑辅助设计储备人才。当然,公司要事先进行测试,通过者方可参加该培训。总经理Robert先生临时有事需要出门,而自己的秘书Mary小姐又碰巧不在,他让于琪代写一封便笺,通知各部门经理将有培训意向的员工的名单报交人力资源经理,以便测试得以妥善安排。另外,他交代于琪在Mary小姐的桌子上留份便条,让她将原定的与生产经理Peter Phillips先生下午的会面推迟到下周。

一、便笺与便条写作的基本要求和格式

(一)便笺(Memo)

便笺又称便函,通常采用英文单词Memorandum的缩写形式。它经常用于学校、机关、公司、政府部门等组织内部,是联系工作、信息交流、传递指令,以及处理一般公务时使用频率较高的一种简便函件。便函常由主管某项工作的人写给有关人员,其收阅人既可以是个人,也可以是某群体。

一般说来,便函都有固定的格式和特征,这些格式和特征使它们能很容易被识别并存档。许多公司都有专门的便函纸,上面印有信头(Letterhead,公司名称和地址等)和抬头(Memo or Memorandum,便函)以及需要填写的项目栏。这些项目栏通常包括发送(To,收阅人全名和职位或部门)、来源(From,发函人全名和职位或部门)、事由(Subject,用具体精练的语言给出一个短标题)和日期(Date,便函发出日)。各项目栏的位置在不同公司可能会有所不同,发函人只需在对应处填写相应内容即可。在项目栏的下面空两行书写正文。便函的正文部分通常以发函的目的或缘由开头(例如,I was told recently that some of the pens bought from us were leaky.),以号召具体的行动结尾(例如,Please carry out a training program ASAP to make sure this sort of thing will never happen again)。正文要求单倍行距,段落与段落之间最好空一行。写作者应该把每段限制在 5 行之内,并尽量使用正面的语气。例如,不宜采用"Don't be late for the meeting"的写法,建议写成"Please do be on time"。保密性和敏感性的信息不能通过便函传递,而且便函中无须使用称呼和结尾礼词。下面是一些常见的便函类型及正文的写法:

1. 告知便函(Announcement Memo)

告知便函就是让信息接收者了解某件事情,它既不是证实某个观点也不是解决具体问题。例如,Employees are entitled to a 12% discount on books at any of our branches. To obtain a discount, simply present your discount card so that your staff number is keyed in with each purchase. You may collect your employee discount card at my office. 员工在我们任一分店购书可享受八八折优惠。为获得折扣,大家只需在每次购买时出示打折卡以便输入员工号。你们可以到我办公室领取打折卡。

2. 指示便函(Instruction Memo)

指示便函就是做出指示和引导,其目的是让信息接收者按照安排有效地执行指令。例如,Please note that on Monday, 6 June 2000, new car parking arrangements will come into effect. The following are procedures for car parking... 请注意,从 2000 年 6 月 6 日星期一开始,新的停车规定正式生效。停车程序如下……

3. 要求便函(Request Memo)

要求便函是希望信息接收者提供一定的信息或采取一定的行动。例如,Our Annual Staff Dinner is only four weeks away. Please check with all the staff for whom you are responsible and send me a name list of those in your department who intend to come to the dinner. 离我们的年度员工晚宴只剩四个星期了。请与你负责的所有员工核对,并将你部门有意参加晚宴的员工的名单交给我。

4. 移交便函(Transmittal Memo)

移交便函是附着在主要文件之上一起送达接收者的。其目的是介绍随附文件的重要发现和主要结论,也可以邀请收函人的反馈。例如,Here is the report on customer demographics in ABC area. We concentrated on the 20 to 50 age bracket as requested. Our study revealed a growing number of customers in this group responded well to our investment and saving instruments, mortgage financing, and consumer loan programs. 随附的是 ABC 地区消费者人群报告。根据要求,我们重点考察了 20~50 岁年龄段。我们的研究显示在这一人群中越来越多的消费者对我们的投资和储蓄工具、抵押融资,以及贷款方案感兴趣。

(二)便条(Note)

便条通常用于熟悉的同事或朋友之间,其内容可以是预约、告知、致谢、邀请、道歉等。和便函相比,便条在形式上更简单,在语言风格上更接近口语。便条书写格式如下;首先,写上日期或时间(有时如果日期或时间不重要的话,也可省略);然后,写上收条人的姓名(很多时候只写收条人的名而不写他的姓,因为这样显得友好与亲密,而是否用"Dear"也完全取决于两人关系的熟悉程度);这之后,另起一行书写便条的具体内容;最后,署上发条人自己的名字,也通常是只写名不写姓。下面是一些常见的便条类型及正文的写法:

1. 病假条

例如,I very much regret that I won't be able to attend class this morning owing to a bad cold. I am enclosing here with a doctor's certificate and ask you for three days' sick leave. 非常抱歉,我今晨因患重感冒不能前来上课。现附上医生证明,并请假三天。

2. 告知条

例如,Lynn just rang up. Please call her at 534689. She will be there all day. 林恩刚刚打来电话,请给她回个电话,号码为534689。她整天都在。

3. 邀请条

例如,We are going on a two-day trip to Shenzhen next weekend. Are you keen on joining us? Please give me a call or send me an E-mail. 下周末我们准备去深圳游玩两天,不知你是否有兴趣参加? 请给我挂个电话或发个电子邮件。

4. 借(收)条

例如,Borrowed from Michael Johnson US＄3,000 only, payable within one year from this date with annual interest rate at four percent. 兹从迈克尔·约翰逊处借到3,000美元整,从即日起1年还清,利率4%。(借条常用写法为:Borrowed from... 或 I.O.U. 意思是兹借到…… 相应的收条常用套语为:Received from... 意思是兹收到……)

需要说明的是,虽然便条写作的语言风格总体上比较随意,但根据写条人和收条人的不同关系,在语言使用上仍然会存在细微的差异。体会下面四句同样表示邀请的便条正文的不同写法。当然,正式的邀请宜采用邀请函或请柬的形式。

◇ 熟悉、亲密的关系:Let's go to the movie.

◇ 稍有距离的关系:Shall we meet at the office to talk about the thesis topic?

◇ 表示尊重、礼貌:Is it possible for us to meet at the office to discuss the new teaching plan?

◇ 表示特别尊重、礼貌:If it doesn't trouble you much, shall we meet at the Zhongshan bus station at 7 this evening?

二、于琪的解决方案

(一)便笺

MEMORANDUM

To:Department Managers

From:Robert Liu,General Manager

Subject:An advanced computer course

Date:12th March,2023

An advanced part-time computer course is starting on 2nd April, from 7:00 p.m. to 8:30 p.m. every weekday's evening (Friday is included), and finishing on 20th April. Textbooks are free but only those who can pass the test held on 28th March are eligible to attend the course.

Please collect the names of the staff in your department who want to take the course and send the list to Mr. Michael Douglas, the HR manager, by 4 p.m. Friday (March 16) as the test can be arranged properly.

(二) 便条

2:30 p.m.

Mary,

I've got an urgent meeting today. Please contact Mr. Peter Phillips to postpone the appointment for this afternoon till next week.

Robert

Review Questions

1. **Key Terms**

Derived demand; Gatekeeper; Modified rebuy; Value analysis; Blanket contract

2. **Multiple Choices (select one)**

(1) (　　) refers to the buying behavior of the organizations that buy goods and services for use in the production of other products and services that are sold, rented, or supplied to others.

 A. Consumer buying behavior   B. Business buying behavior
 C. Buying situation   D. Buying center

(2) All of the following are accurate descriptions of the business market, except which one? (　　)

 A. Business markets are geographically concentrated.
 B. Business demand is derived demand.
 C. Business marketers deal with far more and smaller buyers than consumer marketers do.
 D. Business buying usually involves a team-based decision and a more complex buying situation than consumer buying decisions.

(3) A (　　) is a fairly routine buying decision.

 A. straight rebuy   B. modified rebuy
 C. new buy   D. buying center

(4) In a new-task situation, the buyer must decide on (　　).

 A. product specifications   B. suppliers
 C. price limits   D. all of the above

(5) The decision-making unit of a buying organization is called its (   ).

  A. buying center   B. user

  C. gatekeeper   D. CEO

(6) In order-routine specification, a (   ) creates a long-term relationship in which the supplier promises to resupply the buyer as needed at agreed prices for a set time period.

  A. supplier search   B. proposal

  C. blanket contract   D. buying center

(7) All of the following activities are examples of business buying behavior, except which one? (   )

  A. General Mills, maker of Cheerios and Betty Crocker cake mixes, sells its products to wholesalers and retailers.

  B. P&G, maker of Ivory soap, Head and Shoulders shampoo and Folgers coffee, sells directly to wholesalers.

  C. A nurse brings home a sample of a prescription drug to treat her son.

  D. Intel sells the Pentium 4 microprocessor to Dell computers.

(8) Which of the following statements is not an accurate description of the business market? (   )

  A. Goodyear Tire deals globally with various suppliers of steel to make tires.

  B. Wal-Mart has a contractual relationship with P&G to serve its customers efficiently.

  C. Costco is a wholesale establishment that deals with various manufacturers.

  D. Lavanya Pradeep, a retail buyer for Lord & Taylor, does all the shopping for her family at the same store.

(9) Having recognized a need, the buyer next prepares a (   ) that describes the characteristics and quantity of the needed item.

  A. problem recognition   B. general need description

  C. value analysis   D. proposal solicitation

(10) (   ) is the final step in the business purchase decision.

  A. Problem recognition   B. Order-routine specification

  C. Performance review   D. Proposal solicitation

3. Questions for Discussion

(1) How do business-to-business markets differ from consumer markets? How do these differences affect marketing strategies?

(2) What is a buying center? What are the roles of the various people in a buying center?

(3) Describe new-task buys, modified rebuys, and straight rebuys. What are the different marketing strategies each calls for?

(4) What are the steps in the business buying decision process? What happens in each step?

Practical Writing

Scenario: You work as HR Manager in a large American company in London. You have just received an application from Alain Nikro, a staff in Records Section, asking for a paid education leave. Since the subject he is going to study (Chinese history) is not directly related to his present position, you are going to draft a **Memo**, telling him such a paid leave can not be granted. Include any details you find appropriate. Also, you want to go shopping with one of your colleagues, John Thomson, during weekend. So you decide to leave a **Note** on his table to tell him that you will meet him at 10 a.m., Sunday at McDonald's.

Part 2

Seeking Marketing Opportunity
寻找营销机会

经典营销名言：

Obviously, every investor will make mistakes. But by confining himself to a relatively few, easy-to-understand cases, a reasonably intelligent, informed and diligent person can judge investment risks with a useful degree of accuracy.

—Warren Buffett

当然，每个投资人都会犯错。但只要将自己集中在相对较少、容易了解的投资个案上，一个理性、知性与勤勉兼具的投资人可以将投资风险限定在可接受的范围之内。

——沃伦·巴菲特

本部分内容导读：

从管理决策的角度来说，营销活动首先要找到市场机会所在。这样一来，如何在科学的方法和手段帮助下收集、发现、鉴别、评价市场机会就成为企业营销活动的首要任务。而根据机会分析做出的 STP 战略决策，对企业成败有着至关重要的影响。

内容	口语	阅读	写作
单元4	参观公司	收集营销信息	商务报告
单元5	讨论营销环境	从营销环境中崛起	描述图表
单元6	简报	STP——与正确的顾客建立正确的关系	合资意向书

Unit 4 Field Investigation

Learning Objectives

◇ 熟悉参观公司的常用口语表达；
◇ 理解营销调研的含义和类型；
◇ 理解营销调研的过程；
◇ 理解销售预测的基本方法和每种预测方法的适用性；
◇ 掌握调查报告的书写规则和常用套语的正确写法。

Speaking：Visiting the Company

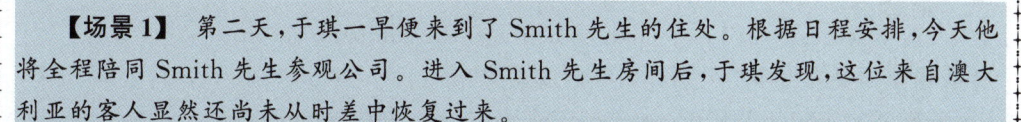

【场景1】 第二天，于琪一早便来到了Smith先生的住处。根据日程安排，今天他将全程陪同Smith先生参观公司。进入Smith先生房间后，于琪发现，这位来自澳大利亚的客人显然还尚未从时差中恢复过来。

【对话1】 A：于琪 B：David Smith先生

A：Good morning, Mr. Smith. Did you have a good rest?
早上好，史密斯先生。昨晚睡得好吗？

B：Not really. There is a two-hour time difference between China and Australia, you know.
不太好。你知道，中国和澳大利亚在时间上差了两个小时。

A：I'm sorry to hear that. I hope you can recover from the time lag soon.
真遗憾听您这么说。我希望您能很快从时差中恢复过来。

B：Don't worry. I'm used to traveling around the world.
别担心。我已经习惯了在世界各地到处走。

A：Well... According to the time schedule, we are going to visit our company today. I bet you will know our products better after this visit.
嗯……根据日程安排，今天我们将要去参观公司。我相信，这次参观后您一定会更深入地了解我们的产品。

B：Great.

　　好的。

A：It's 8:30 now. Shall we go? I have a car outside.

　　现在是 8 点 30 分,我们可以走了吗? 我的车就在外边。

B：Wait a minute, please. I'll make some preparations.

　　请稍等一会儿,我准备一下。

A：All right. Take your time.

　　没关系。您不用着急。

> 【场景2】 在去公司的路上,Smith 先生向于琪进一步了解公司的一些基本情况。
> 【对话2】 A：于琪　B：David Smith 先生

A：(On the way to the company) If you are interested in children's wear, you have come to the right place.

　　(去公司的路上)如果您对童装感兴趣,您可找对地方了。

B：Good. How big is your company?

　　很好。贵公司的规模有多大?

A：It covers an area of 5 hectares. We have 2,000 employees, and about 1,400 in the workshop, 150 in the office, the rest in our own flagship shops.

　　整个公司占地 5 公顷。我们有 2,000 名员工,大约有 1,400 人在车间,150 人在办公室,剩下的人在我们自己的旗舰店工作。

B：It's much larger than I expected. When was the company set up?

　　比我想象的要大得多。公司什么时候成立的?

A：In the early 1980s. We'll soon be celebrating the 40th anniversary.

　　20 世纪 80 年代早期。我们很快就要庆祝成立 40 周年了。

B：Congratulations! How is your company's profit and trade?

　　祝贺你们。你们公司的利润和贸易情况如何?

A：It's the third in trading volume and the top in profit in China in this line. And we have 30% market share in China. Here are some brochures. They will give you a brief account of our company.

　　在中国同行业中贸易总额第三,利润则高居第一位。在中国我们拥有 30%的市场占有率。这里有几本小册子,这些小册子会让您对我们公司有个大概的认识。

B：Oh, they are well printed.

　　哦,这些小册子印刷得很精美啊。

> 【场景3】 进入公司大门后,于琪引领 Smith 先生首先来到服装生产车间。
> 【对话3】 A：于琪　B：David Smith 先生

A：(Entering the gate of the company) This way please. Let's start with the workshop.

And would you please put on these work clothes?
(进入公司大门)这边请。让我们从生产车间开始吧。请您穿上工作服可以吗？

B：Certainly. You are thoughtful. What's that building opposite us?
当然。你想得很周到。对面那座楼是什么场所？

A：That's our office block. We have all the administrative departments there: Sales, Accounts, Personnel, and Product Research and so on.
那是我们的办公楼。行政管理部门都在那座楼里：销售部、财务部、人事部和产品研发部等。

B：What's the long building over there?
那边的长条形建筑是什么？

A：That's the warehouse. We try and keep a stock of the faster-moving items so that urgent orders can be met quickly from stock.
那是库房。我们对那些周转快速的物品留有库存，以便应对紧急订货的需要。

B：If I placed an order today, how long would it be before I got delivery in Sydney?
如果我今天下了订单，在悉尼收货将需要多长的时间呢？

A：I think perhaps you'd better speak to our Production Manager. (Entering the workshop) This is our workshop. You can see our factory is very advanced. Look at the drawings on the wall. These drawings are process sheets. They describe how each process goes on to the next.
我想您最好还是和我们的生产经理谈谈。(进入生产车间)这就是我们的生产车间了。可以看到我们的工厂是非常先进的。看到墙上的图表了吗？这些图表是工艺流程表，表述着每道工序间的衔接情况。

B：Yeah... I see. Is the production line fully automatic?
嗯，我明白了。生产线都是全自动化的吗？

A：Not completely. We use robots on the production line for routine jobs like cutting, pressing, etc. What a worker does is simply to push buttons. So the efficiency is greatly raised and the intensity of labor is decreased. Some of the work, however, still needs to be done manually.
不完全是。我们使用机器人在生产线上从事裁剪、熨压等常规工作。操作工人需要做的只是简单地按下电钮。因此，工作效率极大提高，而劳动强度却降低了。但是，有些工作还是需要手工完成。

B：(Looking around for a while) It's wonderful. Even in Europe your equipments are very advanced, and your layout is scientific and logical. What kind of quality control do you have?
(看了一会儿)真是太好了。你们的设备即使在欧洲都是非常先进的，并且你们的布局非常科学合理。你们是如何进行质量控制的呢？

A：All products have to pass strict inspection before they go out. We believe that the quality is the soul of an enterprise. Therefore we always put quality as the first consideration.

所有产品出厂前必须要经过严格检查。我们认为质量是一个企业的灵魂。因而我们总是把质量放在第一位来考虑。

B：Yes, quality is even more important than quantity. Would you like to show me around your exhibition room?

没错，质量比数量更为重要。你愿意带我到你们的产品陈列室看看吗？

A：Certainly. Please step this way.

当然可以。请这边走。

> 【场景4】 从生产车间出来，Smith先生又兴致勃勃地参观了公司的产品陈列室。
> 【对话4】 A：于琪 B：David Smith先生

A：（A moment later）These are our company's new products which are about to come into the children's wear market.

（片刻之后）这就是我们公司即将投放童装市场的新产品。

B：This one looks so adorable, doesn't it?

这件衣服看起来真可爱，是不是？

A：I'm glad you said that. This extravagant dress designed especially for a birthday girl features an appliquéd cupcake with embroidery and tiered tulle skirt with grosgrain ribbon and bow detail at the waist. Buttons and elasticized waist in back for easy dressing.

很高兴您这样说。这种特别针对生日女孩设计的奢华服饰，以生日蛋糕的贴花刺绣图案和腰部为罗缎丝带和蝴蝶结的分层薄纱裙为设计特点。纽扣和收腰置于后部方便穿着。

B：When is it going to be on the market?

它什么时候上市？

A：It will be out next month.

下个月即可推出。

B：And what about this? Who's this one designed for?

那这个呢？这是为谁设计的？

A：This is a boy outerwear. Super soft fleece-lined hoodie features contrast raglan sleeves plus a bright big wheel in appliqués and embroidery. Kangaroo pockets complete the casual look.

这是一件男孩外套。超软羊毛内衬帽衫，以对比套袖配以贴花和刺绣的明亮大轮为设计特点。袋鼠形的口袋尽显休闲。

B：You really have some interesting products. Are all products designed on your own?

你们的确有一些令人感兴趣的产品。所有产品都是你们自己设计吗？

A：Yes. We have many well-known, hard working and fashionable designers. We often send our designers abroad to participate in big international competitions to keep up with the modern fashion trend.

是的。我们有许多知名、尽心尽力并且时尚的设计师。我们经常将设计师派往国外参加一些大型的国际赛事以便紧随现代时装的潮流。

B：How about the after-sales service?

售后服务如何？

A：If there are any quality problems, we would accept refund and replacement. Oh... I think that's everything. Is there anything else you'd like to see?

对于任何质量问题，我们接受退款和调换。嗯……我想就这些了。您还想看些什么？

B：No. That's enough.

不，已经足够了。

A：You must be tired, having seen so many places of our company. Would you like to have a break with a cup of tea?

看了我们公司这么多地方，您一定累了吧。要不要休息一下，来杯茶？

B：I'm glad to. Thank you. Oh, may I ask any questions about technique in detail?

非常愿意。谢谢。对了，我可以详细询问一些技术方面的问题吗？

A：I'm not familiar about that part. Let me call Mr. Bush who has it at his fingers.

我对那部分不太熟悉。让我把布什先生叫来，他对技术问题很精通。

Reading: Gathering Marketing Information

销售经理马天跃已经走了几天了，于琪知道这次实地考察对公司的决策十分重要。虽然帮助设计了问卷，但对于调研的过程和方法，于琪并不十分清楚。

Chapter 4 Marketing Research and Forecasting

Section 1 What Is Marketing Research?

Marketing Research is the process of systematically gathering, analyzing and interpreting data pertaining to the company's market, customers and competitors, with the goal of improving marketing decisions. Years ago, the attitudes of many business people toward marketing research could be summarized as "If it's not broken, don't fix it." Firms conducted research in response to problems, such as decreasing profits, failure to reach sales quotas, or losses of customers. But today many firms realize that research should be ongoing. Successful firms, regardless of size, continually talk to customers and study the market. As Table 4.1 shows, marketing research can be proactive to prevent "breakdowns" or reactive to respond to a problem and try to fix it. Unfortunately marketing research conducted after serious problems emerge may be too late. Forward-looking companies take a proactive stand to help keep ahead of the competition.

Table 4.1　　　　　　　　Proactive and Reactive Research Questions

Proactive	Reactive
Are we attracting new customers	Why are we losing customers
How do we maintain and increase sales	Who has surpassed us in our sales
Are we satisfying our current customers	How do we get lost customers back
What new products does our target market need	Can we develop a new product to keep up with our major competitor

In general, there are two kinds of marketing research. A research study which is conducted and funded by a market research firm but not for any specific client is called a syndicated research. The result of such research is often provided in the form of reports, presentations, raw data etc. and is made available in open market for anyone to purchase. INC/The QScores Company, for instance, reports on consumers' perceptions of over 1,700 celebrity performers for companies that want to feature a performer in their advertising. The company also rates consumer appeal of cartoon characters, sports stars, and even deceased celebrities. As valuable as it may be, syndicated research doesn't provide all the answers to marketing questions because the information it collects typically is broad but shallow; it gives good insights about general trends such as who is watching what television shows or what brand of perfume is hot this year. In contrast, custom research is the research a single firm conducts to provide answers to specific questions. This kind of research is especially helpful for firms when they need to know more about why certain trends have surfaced.

Some firms maintain an in-house research department that conducts studies on its behalf. Many firms, however, hire outside research companies, like Plan-it Marketing, that specialize in designing and conducting projects based on the needs of the client. Marketers may use marketing research to identify opportunities for new products, to promote existing ones, or to provide data about the quality of their products, who uses them, and how.

小　结

营销调研是系统地收集、分析和解释有关公司的市场、客户和竞争对手数据,以改进营销决策的过程。如今的企业更多的是以一种主动的态度开展调研活动。一般来说,营销调研可分为两种类型。辛迪加调研(联合调研)一般指研究公司定期开展调研,然后出售给其他公司。联合调研不提供特定营销问题的答案,因为它收集的信息通常是宽泛而浅显的。相反,定制调研是对企业某个特定问题进行的研究。这种研究对于公司深入了解为什么某些趋势会出现特别有帮助。

Section 2 The Marketing Research Process

The marketing research process consists of six steps: forming the research question, research design, sample design, data collection, data analysis, and choosing the best solution.

2.1 Forming the Research Question

Marketing researchers must first define what they want to find out—the research question. For example, suppose a luxury car manufacturer wants to find out why its sales have fallen off dramatically over the past years. The researcher knows that the real problem is not the company's declining sales; falling sales are the result, a symptom, of the real issue. The research objective could revolve around the following possible questions: Is the firm's advertising failing to send right message to the right consumers? Do the firm's cars have a particular feature (or lack of one) that's turning customers away? Is there a problem with the firm's reputation for providing quality service? Do consumers believe the price is right for the value they get? A research study should address a specific topic or problem rather than several different issues at once. Researchers need to clearly state their purpose and their plan for using the information they gather.

2.2 Research Design

After defining the research question, marketers formulate a plan for collecting information essential to the study. If little is known about the question being investigated, marketers engage in exploratory research. They may look at company records and government or industry publications or talk to knowledgeable people inside or outside their organization. Focus group interviews, in which a researcher informally discusses an idea or issue with a small group of employees, consumers, or others, can provide helpful insights. Sometimes organizations conduct causal research, which is useful to explore the cause and effect relationship between two or more variables. Like descriptive research mentioned later, it uses quantitative methods, but it doesn't merely report findings; it uses experiments to predict and test theories or hypotheses about a product or market. For example, researchers may change product packaging design or material, and measure what happens to sales as a result. Marketers often want to know the age, sex, education, income, lifestyle, buying habits, or buying intentions of consumers. To obtain such information, they conduct descriptive research.

2.3 Sample Design

Because reaching all consumers in the target market (e.g., all television viewers) is often impossible or impractical, researchers collect data from a sample. A sample is a portion of a larger group and accurately represents the characteristics of the larger group. There are two main types of samples: probability and nonprobability samples. In a probability sample, each member of the population has some known chance of being included.

The most basic type of probability sample is a *simple random sample* in which every member of a population has a known and equal chance of being included in the study. For example, if we simply take the names of all 40 students in your class and put them in a hat and draw one out, each member of your class has a one in 40 chance of being included in the sample. In most studies, the population from which the sample will be drawn is too large for a hat, so marketers use a computer program to generate a random sample from a list of members.

Sometimes researchers may choose a *nonprobability sample*, which entails the use of personal judgment in selecting respondents—in some cases they just ask whomever they can find. With a nonprobability sample, some members of the population have no chance at all of being included. Thus, there is no way to ensure that the sample is representative of the population. Results from nonprobability studies can be generally suggestive of what is going on in the real world but are not necessarily definitive. A *convenience sample* is a nonprobability sample composed of individuals who just happen to be available when and where the data are being collected. For example, if you simply stand in front of the student union and ask students who walk by to complete your questionnaire, the "guinea pigs" you get to agree to do it would be a convenience sample.

2.4 Data Collection

After settling on a research design and deciding from whom to obtain the needed information, marketers accumulate the information that will answer the research question. Researchers sometimes rely on *secondary data*—published information already available inside the organization or from government, industry, or other sources. Secondary data offers tremendous advantages, being obtainable quickly and at relatively little cost, which may be especially important to small firms and non-profit organizations. Marketers generally start all research projects by looking for secondary data. Often secondary data is unavailable, or inadequate. In such cases, marketers obtain *primary data*—information collected for the first time and specific to the study. Researchers use experiments, observation, or surveys to collect primary data.

Researchers conduct *experiments* either in a controlled, isolated setting (laboratory experiments) or in actual marketplace settings such as a store (field experiments). *Observation* involves watching a situation and recording relevant facts. A marketer may observe supermarket shoppers and record the purchases made. Through *surveys*, researchers question respondents to obtain needed information. Mail, telephone, and in-person surveys are becoming more and more common.

2.5 Data Analysis

To determine what all the information means, and to help find useful alternatives to specific marketing challenges, researchers analyse the data they collect. Usually they enter the data into a computer and run special programs to find the frequency of responses and how different items of information are related. To understand the important role of data analysis, let's take a look at a hypothetical research example. In our example, a company that markets frozen foods wishes to better understand consumers' preferences for varying levels of fat content in their diets. They conducted a descriptive research study where they collected primary data via telephone interviews from a sample that includes 175 males and 175 females.

Typically, marketers first tabulate the data as Table 4.2 shows—that is, they arrange the data in a table or other summary forms so they can get a broad picture of the overall responses. The data in Table 4.2 show that 43 percent of the sample prefers a low-fat meal. In addition, there may be a desire to cross-classify or cross-tabulate the answers to questions by other variables. Cross-tabulation means that we examine the data by breaking down into subgroups, in this case males and females separately, to see how results vary between categories. The cross-tabulation in Table 4.2 shows that 59 percent of females versus only 27 percent of males prefer a meal with a low fat content. Other statistical analysis techniques will not be discussed here.

Table 4.2 Examples of Data Tabulation and Cross-Tabulation

Fat Content Preference (number and percentage of response)		
Questionnaire Response	Number of Response	Percentage of Response
Do you prefer a meal with high fat content, medium fat content, or low fat content?		
High fat	21	6
Medium fat	179	51
Low fat	150	43
Total	350	100

Fat Content Preference by Gender (number and percentage of response)						
Questionnaire Response	Number of Females	Percentage of Females	Number of Males	Percentage of Males	Total Number	Total Percentage
High fat	4	2	17	10	21	6
Medium fat	68	39	111	63	179	51
Low fat	103	59	47	27	150	43
Total	175	100	175	100	350	100

2.6 Choosing the Best Solution

After collecting and analysing data, market researchers determine alternative strategies and make recommendations as to which strategy may be the best and why. For example, the study results in Table 4.2 may lead to the conclusion that females are more likely than males to be concerned about a low-fat diet. Based on these data, the researcher might then recommend that the firm should target females when it introduces a new line of low-fat foods. It should be pointed out, however, in today's customer-driven market, conscientious marketers face many moral dilemmas. Companies and managers should apply high standards of ethics and morality when making corporate decisions and do what's right as well as what's profitable.

小 结

营销调研活动首先以营销人员界定需要研究的问题开始。然后，营销人员需要制订一个收集信息的基本方案。由于获得目标市场所有消费者的数据往往是不可能或不切实际的，研究人员还必须确定收集数据的样本。明确了研究问题和决定从谁那里得到所需要的信息后，营销人员着手收集回答研究问题的数据信息。接下来，为明确所有信息的含义并帮助找到具体的应对营销挑战的方法，研究人员要对收集的数据进行分析。最后，在收集和分析数据的基础上，市场研究人员确定可行的策略和建议。

Section 3 Marketing Forecasting

Forecasting is the act of estimating future demand by anticipating what buyers are likely to do under a given set of future conditions. Since most markets do not have stable total demand, good forecasting becomes a key factor in company success. Qualitative forecasting techniques rely on subjective data that report opinions rather than exact historical data. Quantitative forecasting methods, by contrast, use statistical computations such as trend extensions based on past data, computer simulations, and econometric models.

3.1 Qualitative Forecasting Techniques

The first technique called the jury of executive opinion combines and averages the outlooks of top executives from such areas as finance, production, marketing, and purchasing. Top managers bring the following capabilities to the process: experience and knowledge about situations that influence sales, open-minded attitudes toward the future, and awareness of the bases for their judgments. This quick and inexpensive method generates good forecasts for sales and new-product development. It works best for short-run forecasting.

Like the jury of executive opinion, the Delphi technique solicits opinions from several people, but it also gathers input from experts outside the firm, such as university researchers and scientists, rather than relying completely on company executives. It is most appropriately used to predict long-run issues, such as technological breakthroughs, that could affect future sales and the market potential for new products. The Delphi technique works as follows: A firm selects a panel of experts and sends each a questionnaire relating to a future event. After combining and averaging the answers, the firm develops another questionnaire based on these results and sends it back to the same people. The process continues until it identifies a consensus of opinion. Although the experts never need to be brought together physically, and indeed could reside anywhere in the world, the method is both expensive and time-consuming.

The sales force composite technique develops forecasts based on the belief that organization members closest to the marketplace—those with specialized product, customer, and competitor knowledge—offer the best insights concerning short-term future sales. It typically works from the bottom up. Management consolidates salespeople's estimates first at the district level, then at the regional level, and finally nationwide to obtain an aggregate forecast of sales that reflects all three levels. The sales force composite approach has some weaknesses, however. Since salespeople recognize the role of their sales forecasts in determining sales quotas for their territories, they are likely to make conservative estimates. Moreover, their narrow perspectives from within their limited geographic territories may prevent them from considering the impact on sales of trends developing in other territories, forthcoming technological innovations, or the major changes in marketing strategies. Consequently, the sales force composite gives the best forecasts in combination with other techniques.

Finally, a survey of buyers' intentions forecast involves asking prospective customers whether they are likely to buy the product during some future time period. For industrial products with few prospective buyers who are able and willing to predict their future-buying behavior, this can be effective. The survey of buyers' intentions method is ideally suited for short and medium-term sales forecasts for marketing organizations. The results can be fairly accurate and realistic.

3.2 Quantitative Forecasting Techniques

One quantitative technique, the market test, frequently helps planners in assessing consumer responses to new-product offerings. The procedure typically begins by establishing a small number of test markets to gauge consumer responses to a new product under actual marketplace conditions. Market tests also permit experimenters to evaluate the effects of different prices, alternative promotional strategies, and other marketing mix variations by comparing results among different test markets. The primary advantage of market tests is the realism that they provide for the marketer. On the other hand, these expensive and time-consuming experiments may also communicate marketing plans to competitors before a firm introduces a product to the total market.

Besides market tests, sales forecasts can be developed on the basis of past sales. Time-series analysis consists of breaking down past time series into four components (trend, cycle, seasonal, and erratic) and projecting these components into the future. Exponential smoothing consists of projecting the next period's sales by combining an average of past sales and the most recent sales, giving more weight to the latter. Statistical demand analysis consists of measuring the impact level of each of a set of causal factors (e.g., income, marketing expenditures and price) on the sales level. Finally, econometric analysis consists of building sets of equations that describe a system and proceeding to fit the parameters statistically.

小 结

一般来说,营销预测中常用的定性预测方法有四种:高级经理意见法是依据高级经理的经验与直觉进行营销预测的方法。德尔菲法是以不记名方式根据多轮专家意见做出营销预测的方法。销售人员意见法是利用销售人员对未来销售进行预测。预测结果以街区、地区、全国展开并逐级汇总,最后得出企业的销售预测结果。购买者意图法是根据现有或潜在顾客未来购买意向进行未来销售预测的方法。用来进行营销预测的定量方法可分为两大类:产品试销法主要用于对新产品的销售预测,而时间序列分析、指数平滑分析、统计需求分析和计量分析四种方法则是通过对过去销售状况的分析来预测未来。

New Words and Key Terms

01. marketing research	营销调研
02. syndicated research	联合调研
03. custom research	定制调研
04. exploratory research	探测性调研
05. causal research	因果性调研
06. descriptive research	描述性调研
07. sample	样本
08. probability sample	概率样本
09. simple random sample	简单随机样本
10. nonprobability sample	非概率样本
11. convenience sample	便利样本
12. secondary data	第二手资料,二手数据
13. primary data	第一手资料,一手数据
14. experiments	实验法
15. observation	观察法
16. surveys	调查法
17. forecasting	预测
18. qualitative forecasting techniques	定性预测方法
19. quantitative forecasting methods	定量预测方法
20. jury of executive opinion	高级经理意见法
21. Delphi technique	德尔菲法
22. sales force composite technique	销售人员意见综合法
23. survey of buyers' intentions	购买者意图调查法
24. market test	产品试销法
25. time-series analysis	时间序列分析法
26. exponential smoothing	指数平滑分析法
27. statistical demand analysis	统计需求分析法
28. econometric analysis	计量分析法

Writing: Business Report

下午，销售经理马天跃终于从美国回来了。这次美国之行收获很大。他不仅与当地经销商进行了会谈，并且组织开展了一次大规模的消费者问卷调查，获得了丰富的一手资料。马经理交代于琪对回收的问卷进行整理，并根据整理的数据编写一份调查报告，以便向总经理 Robert 进行汇报。

一、报告写作的基本要求和格式

商务报告（Business Report）通常是根据上司的要求，由下级向上级呈报。在通常情况下，商务报告的目的是发现问题、分析问题和解决问题，为公司或组织制定正确决策提供可靠的信息和切实可行的建议。一份正式的商务报告通常需要一个题目（题目下面紧接着的是作者的名字、职位及提交日期。作者名字通常是由"Submitted by..."短语引出，有时也可以直接写出作者名字）和如下子标题：

（一）导言（Terms of Reference）

导言是报告的引入部分，应该清楚地阐述报告为谁而写、报告关于什么事情、报告的目的和意图是什么。例如，The purpose of the report is to find out reasons for the Music Society's declining attendance figures and make recommendations for improvement, as requested by Mr. Andrew Wong, the Chairman, on 1 June 2000.（这篇报告是根据音协主席 Andrew Wong 先生 2000 年 6 月 1 日的要求而写，目的是寻找欣赏音乐协会演出的观众人数不断下滑的原因，并提出改进的建议。）如果需要，导言还可以对报告主体中各章节的内容，以及它们之间的联系作简单的介绍。

（二）调研方式（Proceedings）

这部分主要说明报告的具体调查程序，即如何获取所需的资料。搜集资料是写好任何一份报告的前提，只有拥有详细、充分的资料，才能进行科学的研究、分析和判断，进而为管理部门制定方针、做出决策等提供客观依据。资料来源是多渠道的，主要包括档案（Files）、个人的观察（Personal Observation）、采访及书信（Interviews and Letters）、调查表（Questionnaires），以及图书馆（Library）等。例如，Questionnaires were issued to 50 people who attended concert on Sunday 6 June, asking for opinions. Personal calls were also made to 50 private houses during the week commencing 2 June to speak to householders personally.（调查表被分发给 50 位参加 6 月 6 日星期天音乐会的观众询问意见。从 6 月 2 日起一周时间，电话也打给了 50 位私人家庭与他们进行了个人交流。）如果有必要，在这一部分也可以描述数据分析方案，并证实所采用的数据分析方法和技术是合理的。尽量使用简单、非技术性的语言对数据分析方案进行描述。

（三）具体发现（Findings）

报告这一部分应当包含通过调研所发现的所有信息。写作者需要使用事实和数据，如果必要还可以使用表格、图形等来帮助描述和阐释所有的相关信息。例如，The results of the investigation can be summarized as follows: (a) Music performed has so far been mainly classical and 70% of people commented that a greater variety of tastes should be catered for. Popular and contemporary music was suggested; (b) Many comments were received that advertising was poor, as people had never seen any of the Society's concerts advertised. 30 people interviewed were not even aware of the existence of the Society.(调查结果概述如下:表演的音乐目前主要是经典音乐,70%的受访者认为应该照顾到更广泛的口味。流行和当代音乐应该被考虑;另外,许多受访者认为广告宣传不够,人们根本没见过协会音乐会的任何广告。受访者中有30人根本不知道音协的存在。)如果发现的内容较多,可以根据不同的内容,将报告的这部分划分为若干章节,每个章节中都有讨论的中心问题、用于说明该问题的数据、对该问题的解释,以及对问题进行分析的结果。

(四)结论(Conclusions)

这部分阐述写作者如何看待所获得的信息,以及这些信息的重要性。例如,From the figures presented in the findings it can be concluded that:(a) If a wider variety of music was performed, more people would attend concerts; (b) Publicity and selling of tickets is unsatisfactory.(根据调查中发现的数字,可以做出以下结论:首先,如果更多的音乐种类被表演的话,更多的人会来欣赏音乐会;另外,门票的宣传和销售工作不到位)。结论不是对具体发现的简单重复,而是经过综合分析、逻辑推理,将各种数据材料连贯起来,形成总体论点。结论也可以指出目前研究中存在的不足之处,以及所受到的限制。

(五)建议(Recommendations)

这部分提出如何解决问题(或将来进一步研究的行动方案)。建议必须基于报告中的发现。例如,In view of the research, it was proposed that a series of changes should be made. For instance, (a) popular and contemporary music should be incorporated into future concerts; (b) thought should be given to methods of improving advertising and publicity of the Society's concerts, as well as new ways of selling tickets.(根据本次研究,建议可以做以下一系列改变。首先,流行和当代音乐应该被结合到未来的音乐会中;另外,考虑改善协会音乐会的广告和宣传,以及各种新的售票方式。)报告中可以提出短期或长期的建议,也应该清楚表述该如何落实这些建议。

商务报告的题目和子标题,便于读者对相关内容一目了然,因此必不可少。同时,和其他所有文体的写作一样,报告要求结构严谨、条理分明、简明扼要。

二、于琪的解决方案

Report on the Sales of Children's Toys

Submitted by Qi Yu

March 15, 2023

Terms of Reference

Since the middle of last year, among the 11 categories of exported toys of our company, 8 categories experienced declines, of which, the export value of plastic toys was down 24.2%. This report is for Mr. Robert Liu, the General Manager of Golden Childhood Children's Products Co., Ltd. The underlining aim is to find out the possible reasons for declined sales and determine the company's development direction in the children's toys market.

Proceedings

In view of the declined sales of our children's toys in the international market, Mr.

Ma, the Sales Manager, conducted on-the-spot investigation in New York from March 6 to March 12, 2023. A survey was conducted by means of questionnaire given to 1,000 families with at least one child aged between 3 and 10 to complete.

Findings

The results of the investigation can be summarized as follows:

1. About 80 percent of the parents indicated that their children liked electric toy cars.

2. More than 50 percent of the parents mentioned that their children liked toys that they can dismantle and reassemble, such as transformers.

3. The biggest concern of all the parents was the safety of the toys, especially the raw material used and the size.

4. About 70 percent of parents would choose toys which were helpful for children's intelligence development, so that their children can learn while playing.

5. Almost all the parents questioned were quite satisfied with our price, but unhappy about the function, security and service.

Conclusions

From the figures presented in the findings it can be concluded that developed countries have diverted their demands of toys to top-grade types such as high-tech electric toys, intellectual & educational toys from traditional medium and low-grade products like plastic toys and stuffed toys.

Recommendations

In view of the research, it was proposed that a series of changes should be made.

1. Since outdoor games could give positive impact for children's development both in body and in mind, the company should design a kind of electric toy cars with off road wheels and strong power to let kids experience the riding fun.

2. The company should produce toys with natural raw material such as organic and naturally-dyed cotton, bamboo, wool, and unpainted wood to meet parents' health concern.

3. The company should control toys' size, including parts that can break off from the toy, to avoid the danger of choking.

4. The company should produce various puzzle or block toys to help children practice problem-solving ability and fine motor skills.

5. Training program should be introduced to our staff to enhance after-sales service standard.

Review Questions

1. Key Terms

Syndicated research; Observation; Convenience sample; Delphi technique; Market test

2. Multiple Choices (select one or more)

(1) Marketing research is the (　　) of data relevant to marketing decision-making and the communication of the results of this analysis to management.

 A. planning   B. screening   C. analysis   D. collection

(2) The function of marketing research is (　　).

 A. identifying and evaluating opportunities

 B. analyzing segments and selecting target markets

 C. planning and implementing marketing mix

 D. analyzing marketing performance

(3) There are three types of marketing research, including (　　).

 A. formal research   B. descriptive research

 C. causal research   D. exploratory research

(4) Marketers often want to know the age, sex, education, income, lifestyle, buying habits, or buying intentions of consumers. To obtain such information, they conduct (　　).

 A. formal research   B. descriptive research

 C. experimental research   D. exploratory research

(5) In a (　　), each member of the population has some known chance of being included.

 A. probability sample   B. simple random sample

 C. nonprobability sample   D. convenience sample

(6) There are several ways of administering a survey, including (　　).

 A. interview   B. mail

 C. exploratory research   D. telephone

(7) Primary data can be collected by the following ways: (　　).

 A. causal research   B. focus-group

 C. exploratory research   D. observation

(8) The most famous methods of marketing forecasting are (　　).

 A. past-sales analysis   B. market-test method

 C. expert opinion   D. Delphi method

(9) (　　) frequently helps planners in assessing consumer responses to new-product offerings.

 A. Past-sales analysis   B. Market-test method

 C. Expert opinion   D. Delphi method

(10) In focus-group research, the moderator needs to be (　　).

 A. objective   B. knowledgeable

 C. skilled   D. dynamic

3. Questions for Discussion

(1) What are the differences between proactive and reactive research questions?

(2) What are the steps in the marketing research process? Why is defining the problem to be researched so important to ultimate success with the research project?

(3) What are the main advantages and disadvantages of Delphi Method for forecasting future demand?

Practical Writing

Scenario: You work in the General Office of Country Joy Co. Ltd., a reputable tourist agency in London. The General Manager gives you the following information and asks you to write a **Report** for him outlining the main points about last year's performance, and give some recommendations for future trade.

Responses of Customer Questionnaire			
2,000 issued			1,607 returned
Levels of satisfaction with holiday			
Very satisfied 56%	Satisfied 31%	Disappointed 12%	Very disappointed 1%
Letters of praise were received from several customers: efficiency, politeness, value for money, superb hotels.			Of those customers who were "very disappointed" 15 were on a coach tour of European cities which was delayed for 24 hours by a dock-strike; all passengers received compensation.

Causes for complain				
Unfurnished hotels (10% of those who went to Greece)	Food (5% of those in Spain)	Delays at dock or airport (2% of intercontinental flights)	Rudeness (one complaint from Italy)	Cost (a few from up-market hotels on South Coast)

Destination of Holidays						
Spain	UK	France	Italy	Greece	US	Elsewhere
11%	46%	12%	6%	8%	8%	9%

Unit 5　Chinese Ice-cream Market

Learning Objectives

◇ 熟悉讨论营销环境的常用口语表达；
◇ 理解分析公司宏观环境的 PEST 工具；
◇ 理解分析公司所处行业环境的五种力量模型；
◇ 理解 SWOT 分析方法和对应的四种战略选择；
◇ 掌握描述图表的书写规则和比较类图表的基本写法。

Speaking：Discussing Marketing Environment

【场景 1】　Sunshine Food Company 是英国一家知名的冰激凌生产企业，产品主要针对欧洲、美国等高端市场。公司首席执行官 Jimmy Wales、市场部经理 George Stevenson 和董事会主席 Andy Davis 正在为如何开发中国市场进行着磋商。

【对话 1】　A：Jimmy Wales 先生　　B：George Stevenson 先生　　C：Andy Davis 先生

A：This year we are going to focus on the development of Chinese market. We are going to set up an ice-cream plant in China. The reason why we place such heavy investment in China is that we can sense the great potential in Chinese ice-cream market. George, could you tell us something about Chinese ice-cream market?

今年我们将把精力集中在中国市场的发展上。我们将在中国建一个冰激凌厂。我们之所以在中国投入大量资金，是因为我们可以觉察到中国冰激凌市场的巨大潜力。乔治，你能跟我们谈谈中国的冰激凌市场吗？

B：Of course, yes. Before we go through Chinese ice-cream market，I'd like to talk something about the world ice-cream market. As you know, the biggest consumer market in the world is the U. S. , where the consumption of ice-cream is 23kg each person. Following are：Australia 17kg, Sweden 16kg, Japan 11kg and Netherlands 10kg, but China only 1.7kg after almost 10-year's development. So there is much room for us to launch our products in China.

好的。在我们了解中国冰激凌市场之前,我想说一说全世界冰激凌的销售情况。正如你们所知道的,世界上最大的冰激凌市场在美国,人均消耗冰激凌23公斤,其后依次是澳大利亚17公斤,瑞典16公斤,日本11公斤,荷兰10公斤,而中国人均消费量经过将近十年的发展仅达到1.7公斤。所以,我们可以在中国投放产品,大展拳脚。

C: Yeah, what you are saying sounds attractive, but perhaps you are over-evaluating China's buying ability. Our products are mainly oriented at the top range of the market and Chinese market is still a preliminary market, in which low range of the products are the mainstream. I don't think we can achieve many sales in Chinese market. We should focus on our existing markets.

是的,你所说的很吸引人,但也许你高估了中国人的购买力。我们的产品主要面向高端市场,中国市场还是一个初级市场,低端产品占主流地位。我认为我们在中国市场上不一定能卖得多好。我们应该集中于我们现有的市场。

B: You are a little bit conservative, Andy. In the past ten years, China's economy is experiencing a skyrocketing rise. There must be an increasing demand for top-range products. Besides, the living standards in some super metropolises in China, like Beijing, Shanghai, Guangzhou, are at the same level of middle cities in the U.S. We can certainly expect our products being popular in these big markets.

安迪,你有一点保守呀。在过去的十年中,中国的经济有着飞跃的发展。这就一定会拉动对高端产品的需求。而且,一些如北京、上海、广州等超大城市的生活水平与美国中等城市的生活水平差不多。可以预见,我们的产品一定会在这些巨大的市场上受到欢迎的。

A: It is estimated by the UTO institute in Stanford that the scale of China ice-cream market will expand to 3.2 million tons in 2025, which is 17 times the U.S. market. If we stand off this delicious cake at present, we will miss a good timing to expand our market share and gain higher profit.

据斯坦福的UTO研究所预测:到2025年中国冰激凌市场规模将达到320万吨,是美国市场的17倍。如果我们面对这块蛋糕而无动于衷的话,我们会错过一个扩大我们市场份额和获取更高利润的好时机。

C: OK, for the benefit of shareholders, I agree with your proposal. But I think we should take cautious steps into investing in a new market which we have never entered. Could you please profile the existing competitors in Chinese market, George?

好吧,从股东的利益来看我同意你们的建议。但我认为我们应当在投资新市场时采取谨慎的态度,毕竟这是一个我们从未接触过的市场。乔治,你能给我们大致讲讲中国市场现有竞争者的情况吗?

B: Fine. There are two main local manufacturers, Yili and Mengniu, and one major foreign manufacturer, Nestle, in Chinese ice-cream market. The local manufacturers are targeted at the lower range of the market. As study shows, 70% to 80% of the sales in this market are from the products at the price from 1 to 1.5 yuan. Accordingly, these

two local manufacturers are covering around 35% of the market share. Since our products are oriented at the top range of the market, Nestle could be our major competitor.
好的。目前在中国冰激凌市场上有两家主要的本土制造商——伊利和蒙牛，一家主要的外资制造商——雀巢。本土制造商目标定位于低端市场上。经研究表明，在中国冰激凌市场有 70%～80% 的销量来自 1～1.5 元之间的产品。因此，这两家本土制造商占有大约 35% 的市场份额。因为我们的产品定位于高端市场，所以雀巢可能是我们主要的竞争对手。

A：What's the strength and weakness of Nestle?
雀巢的优势和弱势是什么呢？

B：Nestle has established a much more impressive dealer network and its promotion is a lot more sophisticated than ours. It has a much stronger presence in the market both in terms of sales and profile, because it is famous for its coffee products. But this is also its weakness. People don't consider it a professional ice-cream manufacturer. In this point, we've got the more-known reputation for ice-cream manufacturing and better range of the products.
雀巢已经建立起一套很有效的销售网络，而且他的促销手段比我们先进得多。无论是产品销售还是企业形象方面，他比我们都要深入人心，因为他的咖啡非常有名。但这也正是他的弱点。人们会觉得他不是一个专业的冰激凌生产商。在这一点上，我们的冰激凌品牌比他更响亮些，产品更好一些。

C：As far as I know, Nestle has occupied 48% of the market share in the top range market. How can we compete with this big crocodile?
据我所知，雀巢已经占有高端市场 48% 的市场份额，我们怎么来应对这只大鳄呢？

B：Actually the kinds of its products are very limited and the flavor is rather unchanging. We could be achieving higher sales than Nestle—I estimate fifty to sixty percent more with our wide range of ice-cream. What's more, Nestle didn't gain much popularity among white-collars, which has always been our focus. I'm quite convinced that we can grasp a bigger market share if we stand this opportunity.
实际上，他的产品品种非常有限，口味也单一。我们可以比雀巢卖得更好，我估计通过我们多样化的产品，我们的销售能比他高 50% 到 60%。而且，雀巢在白领人士间并没有受到普遍欢迎，这正是我们的主打。我相信如果我们能抓住这个机会，我们就能获得更大的市场份额。

A：I think we should keep an eye on the local manufacturers as well. By some reliable sources, they are going to launch two brands targeted at top-range products this year, which shows they have adapted their strategy under the pressure of production cost.
我认为我们还应当注意本土制造商。根据可靠信息来源，他们今年准备推出两款高端产品。这表明他们在生产成本的压力下也开始调整战略了。

C：Why don't we develop some low-range products to cater to the taste of Chinese consumers and share the cake of low-range market?

为什么我们不开发一些低端产品来迎合中国消费者的口味呢？还能分享低端市场的份额。

B: I'm afraid I can't stand by your side, Andy. I think we should first maintain our reputation for high-quality products. You see, with the trends of growing price of sugar and chocolate, only top-range products can be profitable in the market. Our ultimate goal is to make profit rather than expand our market share without benefits or even at the price of getting a loss.

安迪，恐怕我不能同意你的看法。我认为我们首先应当维持我们高质量产品的声誉。你看，随着糖和巧克力价格的上涨，只有高端产品才是有利可图的。我们的终极目标是为了赚钱，而不是盲目扩大市场份额，甚至是以亏损为代价。

【场景2】 在激烈的讨论过后，公司首席执行官 Jimmy Wales 终于将他这段时间以来一直在思考的想法提了出来。

【对话2】 A: Jimmy Wales 先生　B: George Stevenson 先生　C: Andy Davis 先生

A: To ensure our success there, the first thing we need to know is what our potential customers need, I think. Surely we can't sell the same products to them as we do to the Americans.

为确保我们的成功，我认为我们首先需要了解的是潜在顾客的需求。我们卖给他们的产品肯定不能和卖给美国人的一样。

B: I agree with you.

我同意你的看法。

A: To find out what people need, we should not only take their purchasing power into account, but also pay more attention to their preferences, cultural background, etc. You know what, I've been thinking the possibility to set up a joint venture in China to reduce our risk.

为了解人们的需求，我们不仅要考虑他们的购买力，还要注意他们的偏好、文化背景等。你们知道吗？我一直在思考能否在中国建立一家合资企业来降低我们的经营风险。

C: But, as both partners have investment, they both must have a say in the management of the venture. And both partners will have representatives on the board of directors and the management.

但是，既然双方都有投资，那么他们必定都有权管理企业。双方在董事会和管理人员中都将会有代表。

B: Then I'd imagine that it would be much more complicated to run a joint venture than a company of our own.

那样的话,我猜想管理一个合资企业比管理一个我们自己的公司要复杂得多吧。

A: My answer is both yes and no. Because the board directors and managers come with different backgrounds, some misunderstandings and even conflicts are unavoidable, especially at the beginning. But if both sides keep their mutual interests in mind and try their best to adjust to the new relationship, the venture may eventually benefit rather than suffer from such mixed management. Because the venture operates in China, the mixed management can understand this special environment better and therefore function better than an all-foreigner management.

我的回答是既肯定又否定。由于董事们和经理们的背景不同,有些误解,甚至冲突是不可避免的,尤其是在开始阶段。但是,如果双方都把共同的利益放在心上,尽力去适应这种新型的关系,混合式的管理最终会使合资企业受益,而不是受损。因为企业是在中国运营,混合式的管理要比清一色的外国人管理更能清楚地了解这一特殊环境,从而更好地进行运营。

Reading: Thriving in the Marketing Environment

企业从事任何商业活动,事先都需要对其所处的营销环境有所了解。怎样认识外部环境?有哪些具体的分析工具?如何在环境分析和自我了解的基础上进行战略选择?

Chapter 5 The Marketing Environment

Section 1 The Company's Macroenvironment

Marketing does not occur in a vacuum. As Table 5.1 shows, the company and all of the other actors operate in a larger macroenvironment of forces that shape opportunities and pose threats to the company. The political and legal environment is composed of laws, government agencies, and pressure groups that influence and limit various organizations and individuals. The economic environment consists of factors that affect consumer purchasing power and spending patterns. Demography is the study of human populations in terms of size, density, location, age, gender, race, occupation, and other statistics. The demographic environment is of major interest to marketers because it involves people, and people make up markets. The social and cultural environment is made up of institutions and other forces that affect a society's basic values, perceptions, preferences, and behaviors. People grow up in a particular society that shapes their basic beliefs and values. The natural environment involves the natural resources that are needed as inputs by marketers or that are affected by marketing activities. Finally, the technological environment is perhaps the most dramatic force now shaping our destiny. Technology has released such wonders as antibiotics, organ transplants, notebook computers, and the Internet. New technologies create new markets and opportunities. However, every new technology replaces an older technology. Transistors hurt the vacuum tube industry, the auto hurt the railroads, and compact discs hurt phonograph records. Companies that do not keep up with technological change soon will find their products outdated.

Table 5.1   Major Forces in the Company's Macroenvironment

Political/Legal factors	Economic factors
◇ Form of government ◇ Monopolies legislation ◇ Environmental protection laws ◇ Taxation policy ◇ Foreign trade regulations ◇ Employment law ◇ Government stability ◇ Foreign policies ◇ Protectionist sentiment ◇ Terrorist	◇ GDP/GNP ◇ Economic growth rate ◇ Interest rate ◇ Inflation ◇ Currency convertibility ◇ Unemployment ◇ Per capita income ◇ PDI ◇ Membership in regional economic association
Demographic, Sociocultural, Natural factors	Technological factors
◇ Population demographics ◇ Social mobility ◇ Lifestyle changes ◇ Attitudes to work and leisure ◇ Religious beliefs ◇ Consumerism ◇ Levels of education ◇ Life expectancies ◇ Natural resources ◇ Ecological environment	◇ Government spending on research ◇ Government and industry focus on technological effort ◇ New discoveries/development ◇ Speed of technology transfer ◇ Rates of obsolescence ◇ Transportation network ◇ Infrastructure ◇ Skill level of work force ◇ Patent/Trademark protection

Marketing management cannot always control macroenvironmental forces. For example, a company would have little success trying to influence geographic population shifts, the economic environment, or major cultural values. But whenever possible, smart marketing managers will take a proactive rather than reactive approach to the marketing environment. Such companies hire lobbyists to influence legislation affecting their industries and stage media events to gain favorable press coverage. They run advertorials (ads expressing editorial points of view) to shape public opinion. They press lawsuits and file complaints with regulators to keep competitors in line, and they form contractual agreements to better control their distribution channels.

小 结

企业营销活动所面临的宏观环境包括以下几个方面：政治法律环境由法律、政府机构和影响、限制各种组织及个体的压力集团组成；经济环境由那些影响消费者购买力和消费方式的因素构成；人口环境指人口数量、密度、地点、年龄、性别、种族、职业等；文化社会环境包括影响社会基本价值观、感知、偏好和行为的各种制度和其他力量；自然环境涉及营销者需要用作投入要素或受营销活动影响的自然资源；而没有跟上技术环境变化的企业很快会发现他们的产品过时，并将错过新的产品和市场机会。企业虽然无法控制宏观环境，但精明的营销人员可以采取主动的行动来影响环境。

Section 2 The Company's Industry Environment

Porter's five forces analysis is a framework for industry analysis and business strategy development formed by Michael E. Porter of Harvard Business School in 1979. It draws upon industrial organization (IO) economics to derive five forces that determine the competitive intensity and therefore attractiveness (i.e., overall industry profitability) of a market.

2.1 Threat of New Competition

Profitable markets that yield high returns will attract new firms. This results in many new entrants, which eventually will decrease profitability for all firms in the industry. Unless the entry of new firms can be blocked by incumbents, the abnormal profit rate will tend towards zero (perfect competition). Barriers to entry are obstacles that make it difficult to enter a given market or industry—such as government regulation, capital requirements, switching costs or sunk costs, customer loyalty to established brands, or a large, established firm taking advantage of economies of scale. The most attractive industry is one in which entry barriers are high and exit barriers are low. Few new firms can enter and non-performing firms can exit easily.

2.2 Threat of Substitute Products or Services

The existence of products outside of the realm of the common product boundaries increases the propensity of customers to switch to alternatives. The more substitute products available to customers, the easier it is for them to switch. Ease of switching intensifies competition and lowers profit potential and industry attractiveness. Note that this should not be confused with competitors' similar products but entirely different ones instead. For example, tap water might be considered a substitute for Coke, whereas Pepsi is a competitor's similar product. Increased marketing for drinking tap water might "shrink the pie" for both Coke and Pepsi, whereas increased Pepsi advertising would likely "grow the pie" (increase consumption of all soft drinks), albeit while giving Pepsi a larger slice at Coke's expense. Here are some typical factors to measure the threat of substitute products or services: buyer propensity to substitute; relative price performance of substitute; buyer switching costs; perceived level of product differentiation; number of substitute products available in the market; ease of substitution; substandard product; quality depreciation.

2.3 Bargaining Power of Customers (buyers)

The bargaining power of customers is also described as the market of outputs: the ability of customers to put the firm under pressure, which also affects the customer's sensitivity to price changes. When relatively few customers buy in large quantities and can easily switch suppliers, the customers' strong buying power diminishes market attractiveness. Here are some typical factors to measure the bargaining power of customers (buyers); buyer concentration to firm concentration ratio; degree of dependency upon existing channels of distribution; bargaining leverage, particularly in industries with high fixed costs; buyer switching costs relative to firm switching costs; buyer information availability; availability of existing substitute products; buyer price sensitivity; differential advantage (uniqueness) of industry products.

2.4 Bargaining Power of Suppliers

The bargaining power of suppliers is also described as the market of inputs. Suppliers of raw materials, components, labor, and services (such as expertise) to the firm can be a source of power over the firm, when there are few substitutes. Suppliers may refuse to work with the firm, or, e. g., charge excessively high prices for unique resources. Here are some typical factors to measure the bargaining power of suppliers: supplier switching costs relative to firm switching costs; degree of differentiation of inputs; impact of inputs on cost or differentiation; presence of substitute inputs; strength of distribution channel; supplier concentration to firm concentration ratio; employee solidarity (e. g., labor unions); supplier competition.

2.5 Intensity of Competitive Rivalry

For most industries, the intensity of competitive rivalry is the major determinant of the competitiveness of the industry. Here are some typical factors to measure the intensity of competitive rivalry: sustainable competitive advantage through innovation; competition between online and offline companies; level of advertising expense; powerful competitive strategy; flexibility through customization, volume and variety. Intense competitive rivalry invariably leads to lower prices and margins, as well as higher marketing expenses, in the battle to attract and retain customers. The net effect is an unattractive industry, one in which the profit potential is relatively low.

小 结

根据波特的五种力量分析模型,一个行业的竞争程度是五种力量共同作用的结果。第一,新进入者的威胁。有利可图的市场所产生的高回报将吸引新公司,最终将降低行业中所有公司的盈利能力。第二,替代品的威胁。替代产品的存在增加了顾客切换到替代品的可能性。第三,客户的议价能力。当相对较少的客户大量购买,并可以很容易地更换供应商时,客户强大的购买力将减少市场的吸引力。第四,供应商讨价还价的能力。原材料、零部件、劳动和服务(如知识)的供应商也可能对公司构成压力,尤其当有较少替代品时。最后,行业现有企业间的竞争是产业竞争强度的主要决定因素。

Section 3 Assessing Organizational Resources and External Environment

Before specific marketing activities can be defined, marketers must understand the organization's internal and external environment. This process is called situation analysis. SWOT analysis (alternately SLOT analysis) is a strategic planning method used to specify the objective of the business venture or project and identify all the factors that are favorable and unfavorable to achieve that objective. It is applicable to either the corporate level or the business unit level.

3.1 Generating a SWOT Profile

SWOT is an acronym for Strengths, Weaknesses, Opportunities and Threats. By definition, strengths (S) and weaknesses (W) are considered to be internal factors over which a firm has some measure of control. Opportunities (O) and threats (T) are considered to be external factors over which a firm has essentially no control.

◇ Strengths are resources and capabilities that can be used as a basis for a firm to develop a competitive advantage. Michael Porter identified two basic types of competitive advantage: cost advantage and differentiation advantage. A competitive advantage exists when the firm is able to deliver the same benefits as competitors but at a lower cost (cost advantage), or deliver benefits that exceed those of competing products (differentiation advantage). Thus, a competitive advantage enables the firm to create superior value for its customers and superior profits for itself.

◇ Weaknesses are the qualities that prevent a firm from accomplishing its mission and achieving its full potential. For example, each of the following may be considered weaknesses: lack of patent protection, a weak brand name, poor reputation among customers, high cost structure, lack of access to the best natural resources, and lack of access to key distribution channels. In some cases, a weakness may be the flip side of a strength. Take the case in which a firm has a large amount of manufacturing capacity. While this capacity may be considered a strength that competitors do not share, it also may be considered a weakness if the large investment in manufacturing capacity prevents the firm from reacting quickly to changes in the strategic environment.

◇ Opportunities are external chances to improve performance (e.g., make greater profits) in the environment. Some examples of such opportunities include: an unfulfilled customer need, arrival of new technologies, loosening of regulations, and removal of international trade barriers. Organization should be careful and recognize the opportunities and grasp them whenever they arise.

◇ Threats are external elements in the environment that could cause trouble for the business or project. Some examples of such threats include: shifts in consumer tastes away from the firm's products, emergence of substitute products, new regulations, and increased trade barriers. Threats compound the vulnerability when they relate to the weaknesses. They are uncontrollable. When a threat comes, the stability and survival can be at stake.

A consistent study of the environment in which the firm operates helps in forecasting or predicting the changing trends and also helps in including them in the decision-making process of the organization. When the analysis has been completed, a SWOT profile can be generated and used as the basis of goal setting, strategy formulation, and implementation.

3.2 Identifying Strategic Options

A firm should not necessarily pursue the more lucrative opportunities. Rather, it may have a better chance at developing a competitive advantage by identifying a fit between the firm's strengths and upcoming opportunities. In some cases, the firm can overcome a weakness in order to prepare itself to pursue a compelling opportunity. To develop strategies that take into account the SWOT profile, a matrix of these factors can be constructed. The SWOT matrix is shown below (Table 5.2).

Table 5.2 SWOT Matrix

Internal factors / External factors	Strengths 1. ..., ... 2. ..., ... 3. ..., ...	Weaknesses 1. ..., ... 2. ..., ... 3. ..., ...
Opportunities 1. ..., ... 2. ..., ... 3. ..., ...	S-O Strategies Offensive make the most of these	W-O Strategies Defensive watch competition closely
Threats 1. ..., ... 2. ..., ... 3. ..., ...	S-T Strategies Adjust restore strengths	W-T Strategies Survive turn around

◇ S-O Strategies pursue opportunities that match the company's strengths. These are the best strategies to employ, but many firms are not in a position to do so. Companies will generally pursue one or several of the other three strategies first to be able to apply S-O strategies.

◇ S-T Strategies identify ways that the company can use its strengths to reduce its vulnerability to external threats. The aim is to maximize the former while minimizing the latter. Thus a company may use its technological, financial, managerial or marketing strengths to cope with the threats of new products introduced by the competitors.

◇ W-O Strategies overcome weaknesses to pursue opportunities. Thus a firm with certain weaknesses in some areas may either develop those areas within the enterprise or acquire the needed competencies such as technology or people with needed skills from the outside, making it possible to take advantage of opportunities in the external environment.

◇ W-T Strategies establish a survival plan to prevent the organization's weaknesses from making it highly susceptible to external threats. This kind of strategies aims to minimize both weaknesses and threats. They may require that the company, for example, form a joint venture, retrench or even liquidate.

The biggest advantages of SWOT analysis are that it is simple and only costs time to do. It can help generate new ideas as to how a company can use a particular strength to defend against threats in the market. If a company is aware of the potential threats then it can have responses and plans ready to counteract them when they happen. It should be pointed out, however, SWOT analysis is just one method of categorization and has its own weaknesses. For example, it may tend to persuade its users to compile lists rather than to think about what is actually important in achieving objectives. It also presents the resulting lists uncritically and without clear prioritization so that, for example, a long list of weaknesses may appear to be "cancelled out" by a longer list of strengths, regardless of how significant those weaknesses are.

小 结

　　SWOT分析是用来明确企业或项目的目标,并识别对实现这一目标有利和不利的内部和外部因素的战略规划方法。一个企业的优势指可产生竞争优势的资源和能力。而限制企业实现目标的因素可以被看作劣势。机会是指提高企业性能(例如,更大的利润)的外部环境机遇。而外部环境也可能为企业或项目带来麻烦和威胁。在明确了以上要素后,企业可以有四种战略选择。S-O战略追求符合公司优势的机会。S-T战略识别公司可以利用的优势,从而减少其对外部威胁的脆弱性。W-O战略克服弱点来追求机会。W-T战略建立生存计划防止组织的弱点对外部威胁的高度敏感。

New Words and Key Terms

01. political and legal environment	政治和法律环境
02. economic environment	经济环境
03. demographic environment	人口环境
04. social and cultural environment	社会文化环境
05. natural environment	自然环境
06. technological environment	技术环境
07. Porter's five forces analysis	波特五种力量分析模型
08. threat of new competition	新进入者的威胁
09. barrier to entry	进入障碍
10. threat of substitute products or services	替代品或服务的威胁
11. bargaining power of customers	购买者的议价能力
12. bargaining power of suppliers	供应商的议价能力
13. intensity of competitive rivalry	同业竞争者的竞争程度
14. situation analysis	情境分析
15. SWOT analysis	SWOT分析
16. strengths	优势,强项
17. competitive advantage	竞争优势

(续表)

18. weaknesses	劣势,弱点
19. opportunities	机会
20. threats	威胁
21. SWOT matrix	SWOT 矩阵
22. S-O Strategies	优势—机会战略
23. S-T Strategies	优势—威胁战略
24. W-O Strategies	劣势—机会战略
25. W-T Strategies	劣势—威胁战略

Writing：Visual Aid

这天下午,总经理 Robert 将销售经理马天跃叫到了自己的办公室。他刚刚收到英国阳光食品公司发来的传真,对方有意与金色童年儿童用品有限公司成立一家合资企业专门从事冰激凌产品的生产。总经理 Robert 希望了解一下近些年来冰激凌产品在国内的销售情况。从总经理室出来,马天跃交代于琪收集相关数据,并将结果向他汇报。很快,于琪查到了所需数据,但如何将图表数据转变为文字向经理们汇报呢?

一、图表写作的基本要求和格式

议案、报告、文章以及各种考试中会经常出现一些直观图表(Visual Aids),包括馅饼图(Pie Charts)、柱状图(Bar Graphs)、线性图(Line Charts)、流程图(Flow Charts)、表格(Tables)等。总体说来,上述直观图表主要可分为两种类型:比较图(表)和流程图。比较图(表)展示同一描述对象随着时间变化而不断发展变化的趋势,或对于不同描述对象的数据在同一时点进行对比;而流程图展示一系列的活动、变化、功能、阶段、程序共同作用,从而导致某一结果的发生。于琪面临的任务属于比较图(表)的写作。对于这类图表的写作,通常情况下应采用一般过去时,因为图表中出现的数据往往都是以前的统计数据。具体的描述步骤如下:

(一)引言(Introduction)

引言部分一般用一到两句话,简明扼要地告诉读者该图表显示的是什么,即图表类型、研究的时间段、研究的对象、数据形式(数字还是百分比)等。例如,The two pie charts show the proportion of males and females in employment in 6 broad categories, divided into manual and non-manual occupations in 2000. (两幅饼状图表明了 2000 年体力劳动与非体力劳动 6 个基本工种中男性与女性的受雇比例。)如果可能,写作者还应在引言部分对该图表所反映的主要特征或总体趋势进行概括。例如,In general, a greater percentage of women work in non-manual occupations than work in manual occupations, and the reverse is true for men. (总的来说,以非体力劳动为职业的女性所占比例高于以体力劳动为职业的女性,而男性情况恰好相反。)

(二)主体(Body)

在主体段落,写作者需要详细地介绍图表,即通过使用文字信息、数字信息和比较来具体描述发生了怎样的变化或到底存在哪些不同。例如，In detail, the amount of money spent on A decreased gradually, from 65% of total income in 1996 to 35% in 1998. In contrast, there has been a rapid increase in the amount of money spent on B and C, from… to…（具体说来，人们在 A 商品上的消费支出从 1996 年的占总收入的 65% 逐渐减少到 1998 年的占总收入的 35%。相反，人们在 B 和 C 商品上的消费支出迅速增长，从……上升到……）。多数情况下，需要描述的比较图（表）中会包含许多信息。写作者要选择出那些最重要、最有代表性、最核心的信息，不必面面俱到。例如，In detail, between 1990 and 1992, the output of rice increased significantly by almost 90 percent from 500 thousand tons in 1990 to 930 thousand tons in 1992.（具体说来，1990 年到 1992 年间，粮食产量显著增加了将近 90%，从 1990 年的 50 万吨到 1992 年的 93 万吨）。写作者在文中略去了 1991 年的数值，避免了行文拉杂。

需要特别指出的是，比较图（表）写作往往需要使用一些固定句型和表达法，写作者事先应对此融会贯通，切忌简单地罗列图表所给出的信息。同时，应尽量保证写出的句子美观、简洁。试比较下面的两组表达。

◇ The average US family had 4.5 people in 1915, 3.3 in 1967 and 2.6 in 2006.

◇ Average family size in the US has been shrinking, from 3.3 people in 1967 to 2.6 people in 2006, compared to 4.5 people in 1915.

点评：在这组句子中，第一句话虽然清楚地交代了数据，但整个句子行文呆板。而经过改进后的第二句话，不仅交代了图表所给出的信息，而且通过对信息的组织，增强了行文的艺术性。

◇ Notebooks represented the fastest-growing segment of the worldwide PC market, and they accounted for 40% of all PC units sold in 2004. It was up from 18% in 2003.

◇ Notebooks represented the fastest-growing segment of the worldwide PC market, accounting for 40% of all PC units sold in 2004, compared with 18% in 2003.

点评：对于这组句子，第一种表述中的 they 与 notebooks 重复，it 与 40% 重复，而且是分开的两句话。而经过改进后的第二句话，通过现在分词 accounting for 和过去分词 compared with 的使用，不仅交代了同样的信息，而且整个句子显得流畅简练。

（三）结论（Conclusion）

如果需要的话，图表写作可以在最后做出结论。结论是写作者对主要发现进行的归纳，应该尽量简单扼要。例如，In summary, we can see that area devoted to grain production was affected by both government policy and market forces.（总之，我们可以看出粮食种植面积受到政府政策和市场规律两个方面的影响。）

二、于琪的解决方案

The first pie chart shows the percentage of ice-cream consumption among different brands in Chinese market. As can be seen from the chart, Yili was the most popular brand, which accounted for 18% of total ice-cream expenditure. The next two significant ice-cream brands were Mengniu and Nestle, which were 15% and 10% respectively. If we take into account Wall's, which made up 8%, the four major brands in China's ice-cream market accounted for up to 51% of the total market share in 2022.

The second line graph shows the changes in the consumption of ice-cream from 2018 to 2022 in China. Overall, the amount rose considerably with a slight drop in 2020 during that period. In detail, between 2018 and 2019, the consumption of ice-cream increased significantly by almost 30 percent from 23 billion yuan in 2018 to 29 billion yuan in 2019. A sharp increase was followed by a slight fall in 2020, when the total consumption was 28 billion yuan. Since then, the amount began to recover and reached 34 billion yuan in the year 2021. The consumption of ice-cream in China remained almost the same in the year 2022.

In conclusion, although China's ice-cream consumption increased dramatically during the past five years, the market still has great potential. And the concentration in the industry is not high thanks to the fierce competition. On the other hand, Yili and Mengniu, the two local brands in the industry occupy the leading position in China, and foreign ice-cream products face enormous opportunities and challenges as well.

2022中国冰激凌市场份额分布

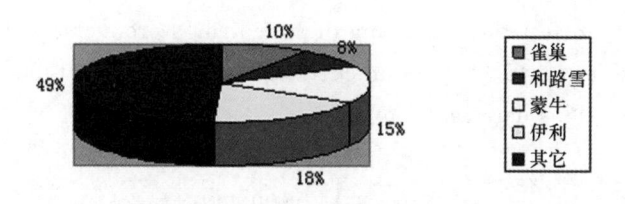

中国冰激凌市场销售额变化

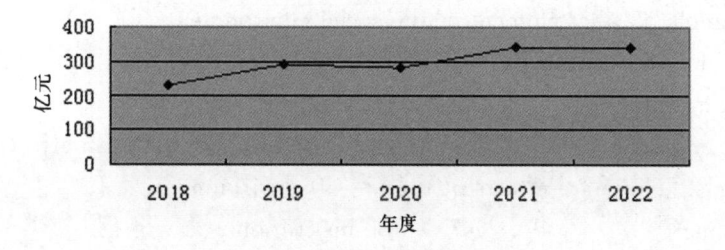

Review Questions

1. **Key Terms**

Social and cultural environment; Barrier to entry; Competitive advantage; S-O Strategies

2. **Multiple Choices (select one)**

(1) All factors external to an organization that can affect the organization's marketing

activities and that are mostly uncontrollable are termed as (   ).

  A. marketing mix   B. target market

  C. marketing environment   D. marketing transaction

(2) The marketing environment includes all of the following except (   ).

  A. competitive environment   B. political/legal environment

  C. production environment   D. social environment

(3) Through the review of (   ), Ford Motor Company discovers that those customers aged 18 to 29 like brighter colors, the exciting elements of a car, like spoilers, and a loud music system.

  A. demographic environment   B. economic environment

  C. competitive environment   D. social environment

(4) Which of the cultural trends could the emphasis on all natural, caffeine-free and preservative-free drinks relate to? (   )

  A. Desire for convenience.   B. Consumerism.

  C. Changing roles.   D. Emphasis on health and fitness.

(5) In performing research for your organization, you have come across the following information that will affect the marketing of your firm's products: the largest percentage of growth occurred in the 45~64 age brackets and the number of typical family household units have declined. This data refers to the (   ) environment.

  A. social   B. demographic

  C. political/legal   D. economic

(6) No longer are household chores, child care, or grocery shopping solely the responsibility of women, more men spend time on these household and shopping chores. This is an example of what element of the social environment? (   )

  A. Desire for convenience.   B. Popular culture.

  C. Changing roles.   D. Consumerism.

(7) High unemployment, high interest rates, and high debt can affect the marketing of your products. These are effects of the (   ) environment.

  A. economic   B. institution

  C. technology   D. demographic

(8) Hans Muller operates a small retail bakery in Germany. Until recently he was forced to close at 6:30 p.m. on weekdays and 2 p.m. on Saturdays, and was not allowed to operate on Sundays. These restrictions were due to (   ).

  A. economic environment.   B. social environment.

  C. political/legal environment.   D. None of the above.

(9) The (   ) is also described as the market of outputs: the ability of customers to put the firm under pressure, which also affects the customer's sensitivity to price changes.

  A. bargaining power of customers   B. barrier to entry

C. bargaining power of suppliers   D. intensity of competitive rivalry

(10) (   ) establish a survival plan to prevent the organization's weaknesses from making it highly susceptible to external threats.

A. S-O Strategies   B. S-T Strategies
C. W-O Strategies   D. W-T Strategies

3. **Questions for Discussion**

(1) The single most important demographic trend may be the changing age structure of the population. Characterize the differences among baby boomers, Generation X, Generation Y. How might a marketer selling computers target a person in each of these groups? Let's call the next generation Generation D (the digital generation). What preferences and buying patterns might emerge for this group?

(2) How could the industry forces for a regional phone company be different from the industry forces for a regional bank?

(3) Explain the meaning of S-O Strategies and S-T Strategies, using examples to illustrate your answer.

Practical Writing

Scenario: The **Table** below gives information on consumer spending on different items in five different countries in 2002. Summarise the information by selecting and reporting the main features, and make comparison where relevant.

Percentage of National Consumer Expenditure by Category—2002

Country	Food/Drinks/Tobacco	Clothing/Footwear	Leisure/Education
Ireland	28.91%	6.43%	2.21%
Italy	16.36%	9.00%	3.20%
Spain	18.80%	6.51%	1.98%
Sweden	15.77%	5.40%	3.22%
Turkey	32.14%	6.63%	4.35%

Unit 6　An Olive Branch from the U.K.

Learning Objectives

◇ 熟悉简报的常用口语表达；
◇ 理解市场细分的含义和基本的细分方法；
◇ 理解目标市场选择的基本策略；
◇ 理解市场定位的含义和基本的定位方法；
◇ 掌握合资意向书的书写规则和常用套语的正确写法。

Speaking: Presentation

【第一部分】这天早晨，阳光食品公司的 George Stevenson 先生出现在金色童年儿童用品有限公司的会议室。他要凭借自己雄辩的口才和精准的分析，展现成立合资企业共同开发中国冰激凌市场的美好前景。在方案说明会上，待来自金色童年公司的经理们坐定之后，史蒂文森先生带着从容和悦的神情，起身上台开始了这场简报。

Good morning, ladies and gentlemen. It is an honor to have the opportunity to address such a distinguished audience. My name is George Stevenson, the Marketing Manager of Sunshine Food Co. I'm here today to present our company's investment plan, which is designed to introduce our ice-cream products to the huge Chinese market. In fact, we have been selling our products to Asian countries including Japan and Singapore for some years and realized the Chinese market was expanding rapidly in the past decade. To better serve the Asian customers and to increase our profit margin, maybe it is time for us to set up a joint venture to carve up the booming Chinese ice-cream market.

女士们，先生们，早上好，很荣幸有此机会向各位尊敬的来宾做简报。我是乔治·史蒂文森，阳光食品公司营销经理。今天在这里向各位说明本公司的投资方案，这是针对将我们的冰激凌产品打入巨大的中国市场所拟定的。实际上，我们向日本和新加坡等亚洲国家销售我们的产品已经有些年头了，并且认识到近十年中国市场增长很快。为了更好地服务亚洲消费者并提高我们的利润率，也许现在是我们成立合资企业共享蓬勃发展的中国冰激凌市场的合适时机。

I'll start with a few facts and figures about the current ice-cream products market in China. Next, I'll go over the top four players in China. Finally, I'll introduce some products especially designed for Chinese customers and targeted different market segments. A booklet of the investment plan will be handed out after the presentation, which will give you all the details.

我首先将报告一些有关中国目前冰激凌产品市场的实际情况与数据。然后,深入探讨中国目前冰激凌产品的四个主要生产商。最后,我会介绍一些我们专门为中国顾客设计的针对不同细分市场的冰激凌产品。简报之后,我将发给各位一本关于这份投资计划的报告书,里面写得非常详细。

【第二部分】 一般来说,统计数字可以增加简报的可信度。George 早就准备好了一连串的统计数字来向他的听众传递最直接的证据。

Because we all have tight schedules, I'd like to introduce the first point, the current state of China's ice-cream products market...

由于我们大家都很忙,我想马上就开始介绍今天的第一项主题:中国冰激凌产品市场现况……

Currently, the Chinese ice-cream market scale is a mere 34 billion yuan, but it has kept an annual growth rate of 10%. Besides, the Chinese only consume 1.7 kg of ice-cream per capita every year, about 1/7 of the figure in the U.K., 1/13 of the U.S. On the other hand, growing purchasing power of Chinese people, resulting from the booming economic development, offers good business opportunities for the ice-cream market in the country. It can be inferred from all the above information that the Chinese ice-cream market still has great potential.

目前,中国冰激凌产品市场规模只有 340 亿元,但却保持了每年 10% 的增长率。而且,中国人目前人均每年消费冰激凌 1.7 公斤,这个数字仅相当于英国的 1/7,美国的 1/13。另外,经济发展所带来的中国人不断增长的购买力,也为冰激凌市场提供了良好的商业机会。从上述信息可以看出,中国冰激凌市场依然蕴涵巨大的潜力。

【第三部分】 在分析了中国冰激凌产品市场巨大潜力后,接下来要做的是对竞争对手有所了解。George 知道,成功的演说者不仅仅要提供数字,更应该充分利用图表。图表就像是"数字地图",可以让看的人一目了然。

Now, let's move on to the next topic—the top four players in China's ice-cream products market. I've prepared a few diagrams showing which companies dominate the market, and the market share each of them has gotten.

现在,让我们进入下一个话题——中国目前冰激凌产品市场的前四位生产商。我已经准备了一些图表来说明目前是哪几家公司主宰着这个市场,以及这些公司各自所获得的市场份额情况。

This bar chart shows the top four companies and their market shares: Inner Mongolia Yili Industrial Group Co., Ltd. is the leading player in the Chinese ice-cream market, generating an 18% share of the market's value, followed by another domestic firm, Mengniu, at 15%. The Swiss Nestle is next with 10%, and Unilever's Wall's, is last with 8%. The four major brands in China's ice-cream market, that is, Yili, Mengniu, Nestle and Wall's, account for up to 51% of the total market share.

从这个条形图可以看出四家主要的生产公司以及他们的市场占有率。内蒙古的伊利公司以18%的市场份额领先群雄；其次是本土的另一家公司蒙牛，拥有15%的市场占有率；接下来是瑞士的雀巢公司，拥有10%；联合利华的和路雪居末，占据8%的市场份额。这四个中国目前冰激凌产品的主要品牌，即伊利、蒙牛、雀巢和和路雪占了整个市场份额的51%。

【第四部分】 在提供给在场听众所需要的背景数据后，George便进入了简报的核心部分。他非常清楚，自己必须以专业者的眼光指出将本公司的冰激凌产品打入中国市场的可行方案。

To succeed in this market, we must not only manufacture quality products that taste good, but also keep up with local taste and lifestyle trends and be able to turn product concepts into real products quickly. That's why we are thinking of your company. You have a very good distribution network, have a good understanding of the local culture, and are also familiar with the investment environment, the procedures for getting things done, and so on.

为了能在这块市场上获得成功，我们不仅要生产出口感好的产品，还要符合本地的口味和生活方式，并且能够快速将产品构想转变成实际的产品。这就是为什么我们会考虑与贵公司进行合作。你们有很好的分销网络，了解地方文化，并且熟悉投资环境、办事程序等。

For Chinese market, we are going to bring out products that are especially designed for meeting local consumers' preferences, such as Golden Snow targeted white-collars (a rice pastry filled with vanilla ice-cream that resembles dim-sum) and Golden Health for fashion-oriented women segment who are concerned about their weight and health (an ice milk product with natural flavors like red bean and green tea). There is also other product segmentation by age involved; for example, we are going to introduce Golden Kitty strawberry-flavored ice-cream especially targeted children under eight. The innovative ice-cream needs to be peeled off before eating, similar to eating bananas. I must emphasize that all these products are positioned as better quality, and thus we will charge a higher price for our products.

对于中国市场，我们将推出专门为满足地方消费者偏好而设计的产品，例如针对白领阶层推出的金色雪花(一种充满香草冰激凌的类似点心的大米糕点)和针对喜欢时尚关注体重和健康的女性细分市场推出的金色健康(一种具有红豆和绿茶等天然口味的冰奶产品)。我们也会有其他根据年龄细分而推出的产品，例如，我们将专门针对8岁以下儿童推出草莓口味的金色小猫。这种具有创新性的产品吃前需要剥皮,就像吃香蕉一样。我必须强调,我们的这些产品都定位在高品质,因此我们也将为它们制定一个较高的价格。

> 【第五部分】 George 即将结束这一场简报了。总结对他而言是件轻松愉快的事情,因为只需遵循三个步骤:(1)重述主要的论点与建议;(2)告知与会者简报就要结束;(3)再次感谢在座听众的参与并接受提问。

To sum up then, we feel that the Chinese market is ready for Sunshine's unique line of products. Given the fact that the Chinese ice-cream market is highly fragmented and the fierce competition coming from top four players, we think it is high time to combine our two companies' strength together. With the products that are especially designed for Chinese market, we are confident that the joint venture will provide both of us with high and stable cash flow. That's all I have to say for now. Thank you for your time and attention. Are there any questions?

总的来说,我们认为阳光公司独特的产品线进军中国市场的时机已经来临了。鉴于中国冰激凌产品市场高度分散的事实,以及来自四个主要厂商的激烈竞争,我们觉得应该将我们两家公司的优势联合起来。依靠专门针对中国市场开发的产品,我们相信合资企业一定会为双方提供高额和稳定的现金流。这就是现在我想要说的。非常感谢各位抽空参加!有没有任何问题?

I see that Mr. Liu, the general manager, has a question…

我看到总经理刘先生有疑问……

That's a good question. Mr. Liu asked how we are going to make our contributions. We think the size of the company should be $15 million in terms of the total investment. We hope our Chinese partner contributes 40% by the land you have, the channels you possess, and a portion of the funds for the infrastructure. We will cover the other 60% with capital funds, machinery, and advanced technology. Of course, we can discuss all these issues in detail in the afternoon.

这是个很好的问题,刘先生问道,我们将如何出资。我想公司的总投资应该达到1500万美元。我们希望中方以土地、销售渠道、基础设施建设资金的方式出资40%,我方以资金、设备、先进技术的方式出资60%。当然,我们可以在下午的时候继续讨论这些细节。

Do I see another question? Yes, Mr. Ma.

还有问题吗?是的,马先生。

Mr. Ma asked for some figures on what children spend yearly on ice-cream products. I'm afraid I don't have those figures on hand at the moment. If you don't mind waiting until Monday, I'll be able to fax you those figures when I'm back in the U. K.

马先生想知道儿童每年花费在冰激凌产品上的统计数字。很抱歉,此刻我手边没有这些数据。如果您不介意等到周一,我一回到英国就传真给您。

I hate to call time here, but I have exactly half an hour before I'm due at another meeting. I'll be happy to meet all of you in the afternoon and talk it over then. Thank you once again.

我实在很不愿意说时间已经到了,但我距离另一个会只有半个小时了。我很乐意在下午的时候再与大家会面协商此事。再次感谢各位!

Reading: STP—Building the Right Relationships with the Right Customers

在上午的简报中,于琪听到了一些新鲜的词汇,如 Segmentation、Target 等。于琪想知道,这些新名词到底是什么意思呢?

Chapter 6 Market Segmentation, Targeting and Positioning

Section 1 Market Segmentation

Market segmentation is a marketing strategy that involves dividing a broad market into subsets of consumers who have common needs and applications for the relevant goods and services. Depending on the specific characteristics of the product, these subsets may be divided by criteria such as age and gender, or other distinctions, like location or income. Marketing campaigns can then be designed and implemented to target these specific market segments.

1.1 Segmenting Consumer Markets

There is no single way to segment a market. A marketer has to try different segmentation variables, alone and in combination, to find the best way to view the market structure. The four common bases for segmenting consumer markets are geographic segmentation, demographic segmentation, psychographic segmentation, and behavioral segmentation.

Table 6.1　　　　Major Segmentation Variables for Consumer Markets

	Geographic
World region or country	North America, Western Europe, Middle East, Pacific Rim, China, India, Canada, Mexico
Country region	North, South, East, West, Central
City or metro size	Under 100,000; 100,000~250,000; 250,000~500,000; 500,000~1,000,000; 1,000,000~4,000,000; 4,000,000 or over
Density	Urban, suburban, rural
Climate	Northern, southern
	Demographic
Age	Under 6, 6~11, 12~19, 20~34, 35~49, 50~64, 65+
Gender	Male, female
Family size	1~2, 3~4, 5+
Family life-cycle	Young, single; young, married, no children; young, married with children; older, married with children; older, married, no children under 18; older, single; other

（续表）

Income	Under $10,000; $10,000～$20,000; $20,000～$30,000; $30,000～$50,000; $50,000～$100,000; $100,000 and over
Occupation	Professional and technical; managers, officials, proprietors; clerical; sales; craftspeople; supervisors; operatives; farmers; retired; students; homemakers; unemployed
Education	Grade school or less; some high school; high school graduate; some college; college graduate
Religion	Buddhist, Catholic, Protestant, Muslim, Hindu, other
Race	Chinese, Indian, Malay, other
Generation	Baby boomer, Generation X, Generation Y
Nationality	Chinese, Japanese, Korean, Thai
Psychographic	
Social class	Lower lowers, upper lowers, working class, middle class, upper middles, lower uppers, upper uppers
Lifestyle	Achievers, strivers, strugglers
Personality	Filial, gregarious, authoritarian, ambitious
Behavioral	
Occasions	Regular occasion; special occasion
Benefits	Quality, service, economy, convenience, speed
User status	Nonuser, ex-user, potential user, first-time user, regular user
User rates	Light user, medium user, heavy user
Loyalty status	None, medium, strong, absolute
Readiness stage	Unaware, aware, informed, interested, desirous, intending to buy
Attitude toward product	Enthusiastic, positive, indifferent, negative, hostile

1.2 Segmenting Business Markets

Like consumer markets, business-to-business markets include wide varieties of customers. Though the specific variables used for segmenting business customers may differ, the underlying logic of classifying the larger market into manageable pieces that share relevant characteristics is the same whether the product being sold is clothing or machinery.

Table 6.2　　Major Segmentation Variables for Business Markets

Demographics	
Industry	Which industries that buy this product should we focus on?
Company size	What size companies should we focus on?
Location	What geographical areas should we focus on?
Operating Variables	
Technology	What customer technologies should we focus on?
User-nonuser status	Should we focus on heavy, medium, or light users or nonusers?

(续表)

Customer capabilities	Should we focus on customers needing many services or few services?
Purchasing Approaches	
Purchasing-function organization	Should we focus on companies with highly centralized or decentralized purchasing?
Power structure	Should we focus on companies that are engineering dominated, financially dominated, or marketing dominated?
Nature of existing relationships	Should we focus on companies with which we already have strong relationships or simply go after the most desirable companies?
General purchase policies	Should we focus on companies that prefer leasing? Service contracts? Systems purchases? Sealed bidding?
Purchasing criteria	Should we focus on companies that are seeking quality? Service? Price?
Situational Factors	
Urgency	Should we focus on companies that need quick delivery or service?
Specific application	Should we focus on certain applications of our product rather than all applications?
Size of order	Should we focus on large or small orders?
Personal Characteristics	
Buyer-seller similarity	Should we focus on companies whose people and values are similar to ours?
Attitudes toward risk	Should we focus on risk-taking or risk-avoiding customers?
Loyalty	Should we focus on companies that show high loyalty to their suppliers?

小 结

市场细分是一种营销策略，它将一个广阔的市场细分为那些对相关商品和服务具有共同需求和应用的购买群体。根据菲利普·科特勒等学者的观点，消费者市场细分的四种常见方法是地理细分、人口统计细分、心理细分和行为因素细分。与消费者市场一样，商业市场也包括广泛的客户群体。虽然细分商业市场所使用的具体变量可能不同，但细分的逻辑基础是一样的。商业市场细分的变量主要包括人口统计因素、经营因素、采购方式、情境因素，以及个性特征等。

Section 2 Selecting Target Market

After the market has been separated into smaller groups that share certain characteristics, the marketers evaluate the attractiveness of each potential segment and decide in which of these groups they will invest resources to try to turn them into customers. The customer group or groups they select are the firm's target market. The strategies to be adopted are usually characterized as undifferentiated, differentiated, or concentrated. The names are fairly self-explanatory.

An undifferentiated strategy means making a single offering to the whole market; the offering is directed towards what most people want, what is common to the majority. Henry Ford's first mass-produced car, the Model T, is a famous example; Coca-Cola and Guinness, for much of their histories, are others. Many major companies adopt such a strategy at certain stages of a market's development, since that is the way to achieve high sales and brand share. The strategy usually demands high investment in manufacturing and marketing support, so may not be an option for smaller competitors.

A differentiated strategy means that the company offers different things to different segments. The Ford Motor Company today has a model for almost every segment in the market. Most Japanese car manufacturers have moved from an undifferentiated strategy at the beginning to compete in more and more segments. Such an approach can produce higher total sales than an undifferentiated strategy, but there are risks of "cannibalization" (eating away at your own sales) and of reducing profitability.

Concentrated marketing obviously focuses on only a part of the total market. Dunhill operates only at the high-priced, luxury end of its markets; Volvo until recently aimed only at a certain segment of the car market, those who wanted a large, safe, solid family/executive car. Ideally, marketers should be able to define segments so precisely that they can offer products that exactly meet the unique needs of each target market. This level of concentration does occur in the case of personal or professional services we get from doctors, lawyers, and hairstylists, as well as in industrial contexts where a manufacturer works with one or a few large clients and develops products that only these clients will use.

In 1980, Derek F. Abell suggested a slightly more complex classification, based on a matrix of product/market segments: Single segment concentration is concentrating on only one market segment. Through concentrated marketing, these firms gain a thorough understanding of the chosen segment's needs and achieve a strong market presence. However, companies adopting such strategy have increased risk if the segment collapses or if a stronger competitor enters the market.

Selective specialization is choosing a few segments unrelated to each other. Because the segments can stand alone, the risk of failure is minimized by the diversification—the assumption is that at least one, or more, of chosen segments will be successful at any one time.

Product specialization is marketing a particular type of product or service that all segments want. By expanding market through product specialization the company can build a very strong brand for its product and business. The risk is on the product desirability itself—does the product have a long product life cycle or a short one?

Market specialization is focusing on a segment, and offering all the products/services it requires. For example, a company might be supplying all types of sporting goods to sporting goods stores (e. g., soccer, tennis, snowboards, etc). This strategy is very dependent on the health of the industry and a specific customer group.

Full market coverage is offering a product in every segment. This strategy by definition means the company must be large with strong distribution channels, abundant resources, and many products to be capable of providing this type of coverage into the market. Small businesses should not attempt total market coverage.

Which strategy a company chooses will depend partly on its strengths and weaknesses. Smaller competitors are more likely to be able to implement a concentrated strategy. Companies which are flexible and innovative may be better able to cover many segments with a differentiated strategy than more monolithic, rigid competitors. The nature of the market, too, will affect what is feasible—what stage of the product life cycle has been reached, for example, and the degree of differentiation which is actually possible in the products.

Of major importance, of course, will be what competitors are doing or may do in the future, and your freedom of action relative to those competitors. A small newcomer to the toilet soap market could not afford to tackle the dominating majors head-on, but could adopt a concentrated strategy and focus on one segment; Simple Soap did just that, concentrating on people who wanted a product with no additives. This example also suggests that the decision as to which segments to choose is affected by similar considerations, in particular who you are and what your objectives are, compared with other competitors. The large, established company will want to be in the big segments, and will have the resources to cover a number of segments. A small company with limited resources will opt for segments more suited to its size and capabilities, and preferably undefended by the majors.

小 结

当市场已被分成较小的共享某些特征的子市场后，营销人员评估每个细分市场的吸引力并决定将在哪些细分市场上投入资源，把他们变成自己的客户。企业采取的策略通常可分为无差异性策略、差异性策略，以及集中性策略。无差异性策略意味着向整体市场提供同样的产品和一套营销方案。差异性策略是指公司向不同市场提供不同产品。集中性策略则只关注整个市场的一部分。1980年Abell先生提出了更为复杂的分类建议：单一市场策略只专注于一个细分市场；选择性专业化选择几个彼此无关的细分市场；产品专业化是向所有的细分市场销售特定类型的产品或服务；市场专业化的重点是向一个细分市场提供所有需要的产品或服务。完全市场覆盖是向每个细分市场提供产品。

Section 3 Choosing a Position

The aim of choosing a position is to match the company's skills and resources with the needs of the consumers in the target segment. Position is the place a product, brand, or group of products occupies in consumers' minds relative to competing offerings. Effective positioning requires assessing the positions occupied by competing products, determining the important dimensions underlying these positions, and choosing a position in the market where the organization's marketing efforts will have the greatest impact. For example, Ford Motor Company is styling the new Taurus models with conventional lines and installing new high-tech protection features. They will position the Taurus as a safe, family sedan, based on marketing research that revealed consumers view safety as a top priority in automobiles. Firms use a variety of bases for positioning. It is not unusual, however, for a marketer to use more than one of these bases.

◇ Attribute: A product is associated with an attribute, product feature, or customer benefit. Communicating the unique benefits of a product or service that no competitor can claim and that are valuable to the consumer has long been a popular positioning strategy. Consider the well-known and ever-bored Maytag repairman: Maytag built its brand on the benefits of owning a machine that almost never requires repair. Similarly, Colgate toothpaste uses a benefit strategy with an effective message: Brush with Colgate and prevent cavities and gingivitis, a benefit promise that appeals to consumers.

◇ Price and quality: This positioning base may stress high price as a signal of quality or emphasize low price as an indication of value. Neiman Marcus uses the high-priced strategy; Kmart has successfully followed the low price and value strategy. The mass merchandiser Target has developed an interesting position based on price and quality. It is an "upscale discounter", sticking to low prices but offering higher quality and design than most discount chains.

◇ Use or application: AT&T telephone service advertising emphasized communicating with loved ones using the "Reach Out and Touch Someone" campaign. Stressing uses or applications can be an effective means of positioning a product with buyers. Kahlua liqueur uses advertising to point out 228 ways to consume the product.

◇ Product user: This positioning base focuses on a personality or type of user. Zale Corporation has several jewelry store concepts, each positioned to a different user. The Zale stores cater to middle-of-the-road consumers with traditional styles. Their Gordon's stores appeal to a slightly older clientele with a contemporary look. Guild is positioned for the more affluent fifty-plus consumers.

◇ Product class: The objective here is to position the product as being associated with a particular category of products; for example, positioning a margarine brand with butter. Several brands have changed their positioning only by changing the product class they were in. For example—Horlicks, which was initially into the medical sector, changed itself to the consumer health drink segment.

◇ Competitor: Positioning against competitors is part of any positioning strategy. The Avis rental car positioning as number two exemplifies positioning against specific competitors.

As the products in many markets are now so similar, and deliver an expected level of quality—as in the car market—the positioning takes on greater importance. It may also become more challenging, as consumers are sophisticated in understanding marketing programmes, and will not be fooled by mere empty claims. A winning position must always centre around a product or service that delivers what the target segment wants. BMW has done this superbly for its relatively expensive cars, but so has McDonald's for its inexpensive fast-food restaurants, which deliver the speed, convenience, quality and entertainment that its consumers prefer.

Once a position has been chosen, the company must take strong steps to deliver and communicate the desired position to target consumers. All the company's marketing mix efforts must support the positioning strategy. Positioning a product or brand calls for concrete action, not just talk. If the company decides to build a position on better quality and service, it must first deliver that position. Designing the marketing mix—product, price, place, and promotion—involves working out the tactical details of the positioning strategy. Thus, a firm that seizes on a more-for-more position knows that it must produce high-quality products, charge a high price, distribute through high-quality dealers, and advertise in high-quality media. It must hire and train more service people, find retailers who have a good reputation for service, and develop sales and advertising messages that broadcast its superior service. This is the only way to build a consistent and believable more-for-more position.

小 结

定位的目的是使公司的能力和资源与目标市场消费者的需求相匹配。定位是让自己的产品、品牌，或一组产品在消费者心中相对于竞争产品占据某种位置。公司可以使用各种方法进行定位，包括产品特征、产品的价格和质量、产品用途或使用场合、产品使用者、产品类别，以及竞争对手等。一旦明确了定位，公司必须采取强有力的措施来将定位情况沟通和传递给目标消费者。相应的营销组合（产品、价格、促销、渠道）设计必须能对企业的定位策略提供良好支持。

New Words and Key Terms

01.	market segmentation	市场细分
02.	target market	目标市场
03.	undifferentiated strategy	无差异性营销策略
04.	differentiated strategy	差异性营销策略
05.	concentrated marketing	集中性营销策略
06.	single segment concentration	单一市场策略
07.	selective specialization	选择性专业化
08.	product specialization	产品专业化
09.	market specialization	市场专业化
10.	full market coverage	完全市场覆盖
11.	position	定位
12.	marketing mix	营销组合

Writing: Intention Agreement on Joint Venture

整个下午,经过进一步的磋商,金色童年儿童用品有限公司终于与英国的阳光食品公司初步达成了合作的意向。会谈结束后,总经理 Robert 交代于琪起草一份合资意向书。

一、意向书写作的基本要求和格式

意向书(Intention Agreement)是国家、单位、企业以及经济实体或个人之间,对某项事务在正式签订条约、达成协议之前,表明各方基本态度或初步设想的一种具有协商性的草约文书。意向书的主要作用是传达"意向",不具备法律效力。但作为各方真诚合作的重要凭证,可以在一定程度上约束彼此的行动,保证业务朝着健康有利的方向发展,并为最终正式签订协议或合同打下基础。由于意向书以及随后将介绍的合同、协议等文体通常具有预见性,各方就未来发生、可能发生,以及应避免发生的事宜进行约定,因此在时态上多选择一般将来时和一般现在时,在句式上多采用 if, in the event of, provided, in case, should, subject to 等引导的条件句。尤其需要注意的是,一些通常在现代英语中不再使用的老式表达,如 hereinafter(在下文), hereinbefore(在上文), hereof(在文中), hereto(至此), hereby(由此), whereby(据此), in witness whereof(特此证明)等,在意向书以及合同、协议等文体中经常出现。意向书(以及合同、协议等文体)的书写基本采用条款式。对于合资经营意向书,通常包括如下内容:

(一)约首(Head)

包括意向书名称、编号、各方当事人的单位全称和地址,以及序言等。序言明确意向书的指导思想和政策依据,以及最终目标,并帮助转入正文。例如,In accordance with the relevant laws and regulations of the People's Republic of China and the Republic of India, China Guangzhou Tiantian Co., Ltd. (hereinafter referred to as Party A) and Evans Co. (hereinafter referred to as Party B), adhering to the principle of equality and mutual benefit, through visiting each other and friendly consultations, agree to jointly invest to set up a joint venture enterprise, INDIA-CHINA TEXTILE MILL CO., LTD. of 100,000-spindle. The Intention Agreement is being worked out. 根据中华人民共和国和印度共和国的有关法规,中国广州天添有限公司(以下简称甲方)和伊万斯公司(以下简称乙方),本着平等互利的原则,通过互访和友好协商,同意联合投资建立十万纱锭的印中棉纺厂有限公司,特定立本意向书。

(二)正文(Body)

1. 投资总额和各方出资比例

例如,The approximate total amount of investment is US $20,000,000, of which Party A shall invest 61% and Party B shall invest 39%. 投资总额为 2,000 万美元,其中甲方出资 61%,乙方出资 39%。

2. 各方出资方式

例如,The investment to be contributed by Party A is the machinery and equipment, technology and a portion of working capital. The investment to be contributed by Party B is the land, the factory and office building, installation of power, gas, electricity and waters, and a portion of working capital. The value of machineries and equipment, technology, land, factory and office building and other utilities will be determined and decided at a meeting by the two parties. 甲方以机械设备、技术和一定比例的流动资金作为投资。乙方以土地、厂房、办公楼、动力、燃气、水电设备和一定比例的流动资金作为投资。机械设备、技术、土地、厂房、办公楼和其他设施计价将以双方会谈认定为准。

3. 各方的责任和义务

例如，Party A shall be responsible for handling application for approval, registration, business license and other matters concerning the establishment of the joint venture company from relevant departments in India. Party B shall be responsible for providing needed technical personnel for installing, testing and trial production of the equipment, as well as the technical personnel for production and inspection. 甲方负责建立合资公司所需的向印度相关部门申请批准、登记注册、领取营业执照等事宜。乙方负责提供设备安装、调试以及试生产所需要的技术人员和生产、检验技术人员。

4. 经营管理机构

例如，The Board of Directors will be composed of 13（thirteen）directors, of which Party A will nominate 7（seven）directors and Party B 6（six）directors. The Chairman, Managing Director and Deputy Managing Director shall be appointed by the Board of Directors. The Managing Director will be nominated by Party A who will be the chief executive of the proposed Textile Mill, who will discharge his responsibilities in consultation with the Deputy Managing Director. The Chairman will have the right to advise and to be informed of all managerial and financial matters. The joint venture company shall establish a management office to be in charge of day-to-day work. The management office shall have a General Manager appointed by Party A and a Deputy General Manager by Party B, in both cases the Chairman will be consulted. 董事会由13名董事组成，其中甲方委任7名，乙方6名。主席、董事长、副董事长均由董事会委任，董事长由甲方提名，他将兼任该棉纺厂的首席执行官，和副董事长一起协商共同负责；主席有权提出建议，过问一切管理和财务问题。合资公司将建立经理部，处理日常工作，经理部设总经理一人，由甲方委任，副总经理一人，由乙方委任，且均要和主席磋商。

5. 合资企业预计建成投产日

例如，The joint venture company will be set up and put into operation by the end of 2002. 合资公司将于2002年年底建成投产。

6. 正式合同签署日期及未尽事宜处理

意向书主体的最后通常要写明"未尽事宜，在签订正式合同或协议书时再予以补充"一语，以便留有余地。例如，All parties agree to sign a formal contract by September 30th, 2001. Any problem undecided in the Intention Agreement shall be settled in the formal contract. 各方同意在2001年9月30日之前签订正式合同。本意向书中的未尽事宜将在正式合同中解决。

（三）约尾（End）

完整的约尾应包括意向书使用的文字及效力、正本的份数、定约时间和地点及生效时间

（定约时间和地点也可置于约首）、各方当事人单位的名称、代表人签名，并加盖印章。例如，The Intention Agreement is signed in Guangzhou, P. R. China, by the authorized representatives of two parties on June 24th, 2001 in the witness whereof. 本意向书于2001年6月24日由甲、乙双方的授权代表在中国广州签字，特此证明。

二、于琪的解决方案

INTENTION AGREEMENT
BETWEEN
Sunshine Food Corporation
and
Golden Childhood Children's Products Corporation

In the interest of forming a collaborative relationship of mutual benefit, and for the purpose of establishing jointly an ice-cream manufacturing plant in China, the Intention Agreement between Sunshine Food Co., Ltd. and Golden Childhood Children's Products Co., Ltd. is being worked out.

1. The above named two companies shall promote a joint venture company to manufacture ice-cream products in China.

2. The equity will be jointly subscribed in the ratio of [60/40] by the above two companies.

3. Golden Childhood will source out all the required documentation and formalities to register a joint venture company in China with the above equity participation.

4. Golden Childhood shall arrange for a fresh feasibility study report along with market research, and submit the proposed project to the concerned government authorities for approval.

5. Sunshine Corporation will assist Golden Childhood in meeting equity participation by way of equipment, technology, capital funds, etc.

6. Sunshine Corporation and Golden Childhood shall maintain secrecy at all times.

7. The Board of Directors will be composed of 13 (thirteen) directors, of which Sunshine Corporation will nominate 7 (seven) directors and Golden Childhood 6 (six) directors.

8. This Intention Agreement shall be in effect for a period of eight months, ending December 31st, 2023, at which time the Intention Agreement may be renewed by the two parties to the formal agreement.

The agreement is signed on April 30th, 2023 by the authorized representatives of both parties in Shanghai.

[George Stevenson (signed), 　　　　[Robert Liu (signed),
　Marketing Manager]　　　　　　　　　General Manager]
　(Sunshine Corporation)　　　　　　(Golden Childhood Corporation)

Review Questions

1. Key Terms

Market segmentation; Target market; Market specialization; Position; Marketing mix

2. Multiple Choices (select one)

(1) (　　) is the process of dividing a market into smaller groups of buyers with distinct needs, characteristics, or behaviors who might require separate products of marketing mixes.

 A. Target marketing   B. Market segmentation
 C. Positioning   D. None of the above

(2) Requirements for effective market segmentation include that the segment be (　　).

 A. measurable   B. accessible and actionable
 C. substantial and differential   D. all of the above

(3) (　　) divides the market into groups based on variables such as age, gender, family size, family life cycle, income, occupation, education, religion, race, generation, and nationality.

 A. Geographic segmentation   B. Demographic segmentation
 C. Behavioral segmentation   C. Psychographic segmentation

(4) (　　) divides buyers into groups based on their knowledge, attitudes, uses, or responses to a product.

 A. Geographic segmentation   B. Demographic segmentation
 C. Market segmentation   D. Behavioral segmentation

(5) In evaluating different market segments, firms look at factor(s), namely (　　).

 A. segment size and growth   B. segment structural attractiveness
 C. company objectives and resources   D. all of the above

(6) A(n) (　　) is especially appealing when a company's resources are limited.

 A. undifferentiated marketing strategy   B. mass marketing strategy
 C. concentrated marketing   D. differentiated marketing strategy

(7) (　　) is focusing on a segment, and offering all the products/services it requires.

 A. Single segment concentration   B. Selective specialization
 C. Product specialization   D. Market specialization

(8) A product's (　　) is the place the product occupies in consumers' minds relative to competing products.

 A. distribution   B. position
 C. life-cycle stage   D. location

(9) Mercedes Benz offers superior quality, craftsmanship, durability, performance and charges a high price that is difficult to match. Mercedes Benz uses (　　) positioning strategy.

  A. "more for more"　　　　　　　B. "more for the same"
  C. "the same for less"　　　　　　D. "less for much less"

(10) Through (　　), companies divide large, heterogeneous markets into smaller segments that can be reached more efficiently and effectively with products and services that match their unique needs.

  A. target marketing　　　　　　　B. market segmentation
  C. market positioning　　　　　　D. intuition

3. Questions for Discussion

(1) List and explain the major demographic characteristics frequently used in segmenting consumer markets.

(2) What are some of the ways marketers segment industrial markets?

(3) Discuss alternative strategies for selecting target markets.

(4) What is product positioning? How do marketers use perceptual maps to help them develop effective positioning strategies?

Practical Writing

Scenario: You work in Yin Long Business Management Consulting Co., Ltd. After a mutual negotiation, your company (Party A) has agreed to lease the premises in shopping centers it manages to Mr. Lewis Hershey (Party B). You are going to draft an **Intention Agreement** with regard to the lease of the premises between your company and Mr. Hershey. The intention agreement should include at least the following items: the location of the leased premises, the permitted use, lease term, rent, security deposit, the date of signing the formal lease contract, etc.

Part 3

Formulating Marketing Mix
制定营销策略

经典营销名言：

There is only one winning strategy. It is to carefully define the target market and direct a superior offering to that target market... Sell the right product at right price and right place in right way to right person.

—Philip Kotler

只有一种取胜战略。那就是，精心确定目标市场并提供一种卓越的价值……把正确的产品以正确的价格在正确的地点用正确的方法出售给正确的人。

——菲利普·科特勒

本部分内容导读：

为实施特定的STP营销战略，必须设计与之匹配的战术方案。企业营销活动就是利用内部可控因素适应外部环境的过程，即通过对产品、价格、渠道、促销的周密计划，对外部不可控因素做出积极动态的反应，以促成商品交易，实现企业目标。

内容	口语	阅读	写作
单元7	讨论新产品	制定产品策略	产品说明书
单元8	谈判	制定价格策略	买卖合同
单元9	节日促销	制定促销策略	广告
单元10	渠道选择	制定渠道策略	营销策划书

Unit 7　The Introduction of New Products

Learning Objectives

◇ 熟悉产品开发和送别客户的常用口语表达；
◇ 理解产品层次、分类，以及产品组合的含义；
◇ 理解新产品开发的基本程序；
◇ 理解产品生命周期不同阶段的特点和相应的营销策略；
◇ 掌握产品说明书的书写规则和常用套语的正确写法。

Speaking：Discussing New Product

【场景1】从美国回来，销售经理马天跃便意识到新产品开发已经迫在眉睫。针对儿童喜好户外运动的特点，公司正在加紧研制一种电动玩具车，主要针对欧、美男童市场。这天一早，总经理 Robert Liu 和销售经理马天跃将为马上回国的 David Smith 先生送行。在去宾馆接 Smith 先生的路上，Robert 向马天跃询问起产品开发的进展情况。

【对话1】A：总经理 Robert Liu　　B：销售经理马天跃

A：How is our new product going?
　　我们的新产品进展得如何？
B：It's going very well. We have almost finished making it and we're testing the product.
　　进展非常顺利。我们几乎已经完成制造，正在测试产品。
A：Are we going to be able to apply for a patent soon?
　　我们不久就能够申请专利了吗？
B：I hope so. I'm having drawings prepared now.
　　希望如此。我已经交代准备图纸了。
A：What about the market research, by the way?
　　市场调研情况如何，顺便问一下？
B：Well. We made lots of enquires to potential users and asked for their opinions. More

than 85% of the children think our new car is cute and fashionable. About 70% of the young parents interviewed are interested in buying one if the car is available.

嗯。我们对潜在消费者进行了大量调查,并询问他们的意见。超过85%的孩子认为我们的新车可爱时尚。大约70%被访问的年轻父母表示如果该车上市愿意购买。

A: It sounds that we stand a very good chance of success.

听起来我们成功的概率很大。

B: It looks as if there's a good market for the product at the moment, but it'll take at least a few months for it to really catch on.

目前看该产品具有较好的市场前景,但是要流行至少需要几个月的时间。

A: That's understandable. We'll have to run a good advertising campaign.

可以理解。我们必须开展大量的广告宣传活动。

B: That's for sure.

那是一定的。

A: What special features does this product have?

该产品具有哪些特点呢?

B: One of the major advantages of this product is that it is designed to conserve energy. Compared with other products, the driving time of our product is much longer. Several new design features such as remote control, automatic brake and water proof also make it more attractive than many similar, more expensive products made by our competitors.

该产品的主要优点之一是节能。和其他产品相比,我们产品的驾驶时间要长得多。一些新的设计特点,例如遥控、自动制动和防水保护也使得它比我们竞争对手的同类、价格更高的产品更有吸引力。

A: For manufacturing, we must ensure that the products confirm to specifications.

对于生产,我们必须确保产品完全符合设计标准。

B: Please rest assured. I have discussed it with the manufacturing department. They are thinking about personnel training.

请放心,我已经就这个问题和生产部门进行了讨论。他们正在考虑进行人员培训。

A: Good. Has the pricing been worked out yet?

很好。如何定价已经决定了吗?

B: Not completely. The pricing should be appropriate for communicating a high-quality product image to our consumers.

还没有定下来。定价应该适宜向我们的消费者传递高品质的产品形象。

A: We must move carefully. Pricing is a key factor to the success of a new product. Well, another thing I'd like to remind you of is that good service such as maintenance must be offered to our customers.

我们必须小心行事。定价是新产品成功的关键因素。对了,另外我还要提醒你的是,良好的服务例如维修必须向我们的顾客提供。

B: Yes. I'll discuss it with Customer Service Center next week.

是的。我将在下周和客服中心讨论这件事。

> 【场景2】 从宾馆接到 Smith 先生后,一行三人乘车驶向机场。得知 Smith 先生昨天晚上在销售经理马天跃的陪同下刚刚看了一场京剧,总经理 Robert 饶有兴趣地向他询问对中国京剧的印象。
>
> 【对话2】 A:总经理 Robert Liu   B:David Smith 先生

A: I'm an opera fan myself, too. Is Peking Opera similar to the operas you go to in the West?

我本人也是歌剧迷。京剧像不像你们在西方看的歌剧?

B: My answer is both yes and no. Peking Opera is similar to Western operas in that both have arias and dialogues, tragedies and comedies, etc. But they are very different too. While Western operas are generally realistic, Peking Opera is highly symbolic and extremely free to express the changes in time and space. Performers use gesture and body language to represent actions such as opening or closing the door, going up or down a building or a mountain. A decorated whip represents a horse, and a general with four soldiers represent an army.

我的回答是既像又不像。京剧同西方歌剧的相似之处是都有唱段和道白,悲剧和喜剧,等等。但它们又很不一样。西方歌剧(的表现手法)一般比较现实主义,而京剧则大量采用象征手法,对时空变化的表现非常灵活。表演者用手势或身体语言表示开门或关门、上下楼或上下山。一个装饰的鞭子代表一匹马,一个将军和四个士兵代表一支军队。

A: Yes. Peking Opera is highly stylized. There are four basic acting skills and four main types of performers. Another feature of Peking Opera...

没错。京剧是高度程式化的。它包括四项基本功和四类主要的表演人物。京剧的另一特点是……

B: Sorry, but could you explain what the four acting skills and four main types of performers are?

对不起,你能否解释一下什么是四项基本功和四类主要的表演人物?

A: Sure. Peking Opera combines stylized acting with singing, dialogue, pantomiming, and acrobatics and features four main types of performers namely the Sheng, the Dan, the Jing and the Chou. The Sheng is the main male role in Peking Opera. The Dan refers to all the female roles in Peking Opera. The Jing is a name for the male role that has some special characteristic or appearance. The Chou is easily understood from the role's name as a clown with an ugly appearance. His function in a performance is to provide light relief and comedy.

当然。京剧将程式化的表演与唱、念、做、打相结合,并且包括"生""旦""净""丑"四种主要人物。"生"一般指剧中扮演主要男子的演员。京剧中把女性统称为"旦"。"净"一般扮演品貌或者性格有特点的男子。"丑"根据名字就可以知道是外貌难看的小丑。他在剧中的作用是带来幽默和滑稽。

B: I see.

我明白了。

A：Another feature of Peking Opera is the so-called masks. Many foreigners find them fascinating.

京剧的另一特色是所谓的脸谱。它们使很多外国人着了迷。

B：Yes. I have read about them. They are symbolic of natures of the characters, am I right?

是啊。我看过这方面的书。它们象征着人物的性格,我说得对吗?

A：Yes. Different colors denote different characteristics. Black, for example, stands for uprightness. White means treachery. And red often signifies loyalty. Got it?

是的。不同的颜色表示不同的性格。举例来讲,黑色代表刚直,白色代表背叛和狡诈,红色则通常表示忠诚。明白了吗?

B：Yes. It's truly fascinating.

听懂了。真让人着迷。

【场景3】 车到机场了。此次上海之行历时一个多月,Smith 先生考察了包括"金色童年"在内的多家公司,并对"金色童年"留下了深刻印象。分手之际,双方都表达了进一步合作的愿望。

【对话3】 A:总经理 Robert Liu　B:David Smith 先生　C:销售经理马天跃

A：Now, it's 9:30. We arrive just on time.

现在是九点半。我们正好按时到达。

B：OK. I think I should check in first.

噢,我想我需要首先办理登机手续。

C：Let me do it for you.

我为您办吧。

B：Thank you very much. (To Robert) It's very nice of you to come and see me off, but you really shouldn't have bothered.

非常感谢。(对罗伯特)非常高兴您亲自为我送行,其实您不必如此麻烦的。

A：My pleasure. But I'm sorry you're leaving us so soon.

为您送行是我的荣幸。只是您这么快就离开我感到有些遗憾。

B：Time goes quickly and all good things must come to an end. I wish I could stay a little longer, but I've lots to do back home. For a businessman, business always comes first, you know.

时间过得真快,天下没有不散的宴席。真希望能再多待几天,但国内还有很多工作要做。您知道,对于商人来说,工作总是第一位的。

A：Yup. I hope you have lived through a good time here.

是啊。我希望您在这儿度过了一段美好的时光。

B：Certainly. Thanks for all the trouble you have taken. I have had a wonderful time in Shanghai.

当然是的。连日来给你们添了很多麻烦,太谢谢你们了。我在上海过得很愉快。

A：I am delighted to hear that. I'm looking forward to seeing you again and having a discussion over the possibility of further cooperation.

听您这么说我很高兴。盼望能再次见到您,并和您一起探讨进一步合作的可能。

B：So am I. I must go. Let's get together again in the near future.

我也是。我得走了。让我们在不远的将来再见吧。

A：Have a pleasant journey and good luck. Please keep in touch.

祝您旅途愉快、平安。请保持联系。

B：Sure. I will. Goodbye!

当然,我会的。再见!

Reading：Formulating Product Strategies

开发新产品、改进老产品,是企业不断发展壮大的根本途径,也是企业提高经济效益和竞争能力的重要手段。企业应如何对待现有产品,新产品开发工作该怎样进行,于琪发现自己有太多的知识需要了解。

Chapter 7 Product Strategies

Section 1 Product and Product Mix

A product is anything that can be offered to a market to satisfy a want or need. Products that are marketed include physical goods, services, experiences, events, people, places, properties, organizations, information, and ideas.

1.1 Levels of Product

In planning its market offering, the marketer needs to think through five levels of the product. Each level adds more customer value, and the five constitute a customer value hierarchy. The most fundamental level is the *core benefit*—the fundamental service or benefit that the customer is really buying. A hotel guest is buying "rest and sleep". The purchaser of a drill is buying "holes". Marketers must see themselves as benefit providers.

At the second level, the marketer has to turn the core benefit into a *basic product*. Thus a hotel room includes a bed, bathroom, towels, desk, dresser, and closet.

At the third level, the marketer prepares an *expected product*, a set of attributes and conditions buyers normally expect when they purchase this product. Hotel guests expect a clean bed, fresh towels, working lamps, and a relative degree of quiet. Because most hotels can meet this minimum expectation, the traveler normally will settle for whichever hotel is most convenient or least expensive.

At the fourth level, the marketer prepares an *augmented product* that exceeds customer expectations. A hotel can include a morning newspaper, fresh flowers, rapid check-in, and fine dining and room service. Today's competition essentially takes place at the product-augmentation level. According to Levitt: "The new competition is not between what companies produce in their factories, but between what they add to their factory output in the form of packaging, services, advertising, customer advice, financing, delivery arrangement, warehousing, and other things that people value."

At the fifth level stands the potential product, which encompasses all the possible augmentations and transformations the product might undergo in the future. Here is where companies search for new ways to satisfy customers and distinguish their offer. All-suite hotels where the guest occupies a set of rooms represent an innovative transformation of the traditional hotel product.

1.2 Product Classifications

The two broad general categories of products are consumer goods and industrial goods. Consumer goods are goods and services that are bought and used by the ultimate buyer. They can be classified as convenience goods, shopping goods, specialty goods, and unsought goods depending on how much effort consumers are willing to exert to get them. Convenience goods are goods that the customer usually purchases frequently, immediately, and with a minimum of effort. Examples include tobacco products, soaps, and newspaper. Shopping goods are goods that the customer, in the process of selection and purchase, characteristically compares on such bases as suitability, quality, price, and style. Examples include furniture, clothing, used cars, and major appliances. Specialty goods are goods with unique characteristics or brand identification for which a sufficient number of buyers are willing to make a special purchasing effort. Examples include cars, stereo components, photographic equipment, and men's suits. Specialty goods do not involve making comparisons; buyers invest time only to reach dealers carrying the wanted products. Unsought goods are goods the consumer does not know about or does not normally think of buying. The classic examples of known but unsought goods are life insurance, cemetery plots, gravestones, and encyclopedias. Unsought goods require advertising and personal-selling support.

Industrial goods can be classified in terms of how they enter the production process and their relative costliness. We can distinguish four groups of industrial goods: materials and parts, capital items, supplies and business services. Materials and parts are goods that enter the manufacturer's product completely. They fall into two classes: raw materials (farm products and natural products) and manufactured materials and parts. Capital items are long-lasting goods that facilitate developing or managing the finished product. They include two groups: installations and equipment. Supplies are the equivalent of convenience goods; they are usually purchased with minimum effort on a straight basis. Price and service are important considerations, because supplies are standardized and brand preference is not high. Business services include maintenance and repair service (window cleaning, typewriter repair, etc.) and business advisory services (legal, management consulting, etc).

1.3 Product Mix Decisions

A product mix (also called product assortment) is the set of all products and items that a particular seller offers for sale. NEC's (Japan) product mix consists of communication products and computer products. Michelin has three product lines: tires, maps, and restaurant-rating services. A company's product mix has a certain width, length, depth, and consistency. The width of a product mix refers to how many different product lines the company carries. The length of a product mix refers to the total number of items in the mix. We can also talk about the average length of a line. This is obtained by dividing the total length by the number of lines. The depth of a product mix refers to how many variants are offered of each product in the line. If Crest comes in three sizes and two formulations (regular and mint), Crest has a depth of six. The average depth of P&G's product mix can be calculated by averaging the number of variants within the brand groups. The consistency of the product mix refers to how closely the various product lines are related in end use, production requirements, distribution channels, or some other way.

Businesses need to regularly look for new products and markets for future growth. There are four main ways in which growth can be achieved through a product strategy: market penetration is increasing sales of an existing product in an existing market. The best way to achieve this is by gaining competitors' customers (part of their market share). Other ways include attracting non-users of your product or convincing current clients to use more of your product/service (by advertising, etc). Product development is improving present products and/or developing new products for the current market. McDonald's is always within the fast-food industry, but frequently markets new burgers. Market development is selling existing products into new markets. Lucozade was first marketed for sick children and then rebranded to target athletes. And finally diversification seeks to increase profitability through greater sales volume obtained from new products and new markets.

小 结

第一,产品具有五个层次:核心利益是顾客真正购买的基本服务或利益;基础产品是核心利益所形成的外在产品;期望产品是顾客通常希望产品应具备的属性和条件;附加产品指超过顾客期望的产品利益;潜在产品涵盖所有可能在将来发生的产品扩增和转换。第二,产品通常分为消费品和工业品两种类型。消费品包括便利品、选购品、特殊品、非渴求品。工业品则包括材料和部件、资本品,以及供应品和商业服务(维修和维护,业务咨询等)。第三,产品组合由销售者提供或出售的所有产品线和产品项目组成。产品组合的宽度指该公司具有多少条不同的产品线。长度指公司在每条产品线内的所有产品项目的数目。深度指产品线中每种产品有多少种类型。产品组合的相关性指不同产品线相互关联的程度。第四,公司产品策略通常包括市场渗透(追求当前市场上更多的销售)、产品开发(现有市场推出全新或改进产品)、市场开发(以现有产品开拓新市场),以及多元化经营(新市场上推出新产品)四种类型。

Section 2 New-Product Development Strategy

Product development doesn't simply mean creating totally new stuff. Of course a lot of companies do that, but for many other firms product development is a continuous process of looking for ways to make an existing product better.

2.1 Idea Generation

In the initial idea generation phase of product development, marketers use a variety of sources to come up with great new product ideas that provide customer benefits and that are compatible with the company mission. Sometimes ideas come from customers. Ideas also come from salespeople, service providers, and others who have direct customer contact.

2.2 Product Concept Development and Screening

The second phase in developing new products is product concept development and screening. Although ideas for products initially come from a variety of sources, it is up to marketers to expand these ideas into more-complete product concepts. Product concepts describe what features the product should have and the benefits those features will provide for consumers.

2.3 Marketing Strategy Development

The third phase in new-product development is to develop a marketing strategy to introduce the product to the marketplace. This means that marketers must identify the target market, estimate its size, and determine how they can effectively position the product to address the target market's needs. And, of course, marketing strategy development includes planning for pricing, distribution, and promotion both for the introduction of the new product and for the long run.

2.4 Business Analysis

Even though marketers have evidence that there is a market for the product, they still must find out if the product can make a profitable contribution to the organization. The business analysis for a new product begins with assessing how the new product will fit into the firm's total product mix. Will the new product increase sales, or will it simply cannibalize sales of existing products? Are there possible synergies between the new product and the company's existing offerings that may improve visibility and the image of both? And what are the marketing costs likely to be?

2.5 Technical Development

If it survives the scrutiny of a business analysis, a new product concept then undergoes technical development, in which a firm's engineers work with marketers to refine the design and production process. The better a firm understands how customers will react to a new product, the better its chances of commercial success. For this reason typically, a company's research-and-development (R&D) department usually develops one or more physical versions or prototypes of the product. Prospective customers may evaluate these mockups in focus groups or in field trials at home.

2.6 Test Marketing

The next phase of new-product development is test marketing. This means the firm tries out the complete marketing plan—the distribution, advertising, and sales promotion—in small geographic area that is similar to the larger market it hopes to enter. There are both pluses and minuses to test marketing. On the negative side, test marketing is extremely expensive. It also gives the competition a free look at the new product, its introductory price, and the intended promotional strategy—and an opportunity to get to the market first with a competing product. On the positive side, by offering a new product in a limited area of the market, marketers can evaluate and improve the marketing program. Sometimes test marketing uncovers a need to improve the product itself. At other times, test marketing indicates product failure; this advanced warning allows the firm to save millions of dollars by "pulling the plug."

2.7 Commercialization

The last phase in new-product development is commercialization. This means the launching of a new product, and it requires full-scale production, distribution, advertising, and sales promotion. For this reason, commercialization of a new product cannot happen overnight. A launch requires planning and careful preparation. Marketers must implement trade promotion plans that offer special incentives to encourage dealers, retailers, or other members of the channel to stock the new product so that customers will find it on store shelves the very first time they look. They must also develop consumer sales promotions such as coupons. Marketers may arrange to have point-of-purchase displays designed, built, and delivered to retail outlets. If the new product is especially complex, customer service employees must receive extensive training and preparation.

小 结

产品开发的第一步是创意产生阶段,营销人员利用各种资源想出好的新产品构想。接下来,营销人员扩展这些想法变成更完整的产品概念。新产品开发的第三个阶段是制定将产品打入市场的营销策略。随后,市场营销人员还需要进行商业分析。经过商业分析的严格审查,一个新的产品概念进入技术开发阶段,公司的工程师与营销人员改进设计和生产工艺。通常情况下,开发的新产品会在与目标市场相似的较小地理区域进行试销。最后,产品开发进入商业化阶段,这意味着一个新产品的推出。

Section 3 Product Life Cycle Strategies

After a product reaches the marketplace, it enters the product life cycle—a series of stages in sales and profits over a period of time. The cycle typically has four stages: introduction, growth, maturity, and decline (and death).

3.1 Introduction Phase

The introduction phase starts when a firm first launches a brand-new product or service into the market. When the product is introduced, sales will be low until customers become aware of the product and its benefits. Some firms may announce their product before it is introduced, but such announcements also alert competitors and remove the element of surprise. Advertising costs are typically high during this stage in order to rapidly increase customer awareness of the product and to target the early adopters. During the introduction stage the firm is likely to incur additional costs associated with the initial distribution of the product such as inducing channel members to carry the product. These higher costs coupled with a low sales volume usually make the introduction stage a period of negative profits. During the introduction phase, the primary goal is to establish a market and build primary demand for the product class rather than a specific brand.

3.2 Growth Phase

If a product category survives the introductory stage, it advances to the growth phase of the life cycle. In this stage, sales typically grow at an increasing rate, many competitors enter the market, and large companies may start to acquire small pioneering firms. Educating the market remains a goal, but now the company must also meet the competition. Emphasis switches from primary demand promotion (for example, promoting personal digital assistants [pdas]) to aggressive brand advertising and communication of the differences between brands (for example, promoting Casio versus Palm and Visor). Distribution becomes a major key to success during the growth stage, as well as later stages. Manufacturers scramble to sign up dealers and distributors and to build long-term relationships. Without adequate distribution, it is impossible to establish a strong market position.

3.3 Maturity Phase

A period during which sales increase at a decreasing rate signals the beginning of the maturity phase of the life cycle. Brand awareness is strong; consequently advertising expenditures will be reduced. However competition may result in decreased market share and/or prices. Sales promotions may be offered to encourage retailers to give the product more shelf space over competing products. During the maturity phase, the primary goal is to maintain market share and try to extend the maturity stage. For instance, during the summer months, Butterball—traditionally known for its Thanksgiving turkeys—advertises "turkey on the grill" (Increasing frequency of use). In recent years, the Walt Disney Company has spent time and money on advertising its theme parks to attract adults, in addition to young families (Increasing the number of users). Still another strategy for extending a product's life cycle is to identify new uses for it. New applications for mature products include oatmeal as a cholesterol-reducer, mouthwash as an aid in treating and preventing plaque and gum disease. The company might also try modifying the product—changing characteristics such as quality, features, or style to attract new users and to inspire more usage.

3.4 Decline Phase

During the decline phase, the firm generally has three options. Firstly, management may decide to maintain the product in hopes that competitors will exit or reformulate the brand to move it back into the growth stage. In fact, a firm may continue to carry an unprofitable item in order to provide a complete line for its customers. For example, while most grocery stores lose money on bulky, low-unit-value items such as salt, they continue to carry these items to meet shopper demand. Secondly, harvest it, reducing marketing support and coasting along until no more profit can be made. Thirdly, discontinue the product when no more profit can be made or there is a successor product.

The term "life cycle" implies a well-defined curve as observed in living organisms, but products do not have such a predictable life and the specific life cycle curves followed by different products vary substantially. Consequently, the life cycle concept is not well-suited for the forecasting of product sales. Furthermore, critics have argued that the product life cycle may become self-fulfilling. For example, if sales peak and then decline, managers may conclude that the product is in the decline phase and therefore cut the advertising budget, thus precipitating a further decline.

小 结

在产品生命周期引入期阶段,公司主要目标是建立对产品类的市场需求而不是特定的品牌。成长期的重点从基本需求推动变为对不同品牌间的攻击性广告与品牌传播。在成熟阶段,主要目的是维持市场份额,延长产品的生命周期。常采用的手段有增加使用频率,增加用户数量,增加产品新用途,以及改进产品等。衰退期可以采取维持或重塑、收割,以及停止该产品三种策略选择。但是,企业营销人员必须充分认识到,产品生命周期理论本身也存在缺陷。

New Words and Key Terms

01.	core benefit	核心利益,实质产品
02.	basic product	基础产品,形式产品
03.	expected product	期望产品
04.	augmented product	附加产品,延伸产品
05.	potential product	潜在产品
06.	convenience goods	便利品
07.	shopping goods	选购品
08.	specialty goods	特殊品
09.	unsought goods	非渴求品
10.	materials and parts	材料和部件
11.	capital items	资本品
12.	supplies	供应品
13.	business services	商业服务
14.	product mix	产品组合
15.	product lines	产品线
16.	width of a product mix	产品组合宽度
17.	length of a product mix	产品组合长度
18.	depth of a product mix	产品组合深度
19.	consistency of the product mix	产品组合相关性
20.	market penetration	市场渗透
21.	product development	产品开发
22.	market development	市场开发
23.	diversification	多元化
24.	product life cycle	产品生命周期
25.	introduction phase	引入期
26.	growth phase	成长期
27.	maturity phase	成熟期
28.	decline phase	衰退期

Writing：Product Description

在电动玩具车开发工作紧张进行的同时,与阳光公司的合作也让金色童年儿童用品有限公司意识到食品市场的巨大潜力。公司刚刚购买了一份奶昔产品的配方并申请了生产许可。在产品上市前,编写说明书的任务落在了于琪的身上。

一、产品说明书写作的基本要求和格式

产品说明书(Description,Instruction 或 Direction)又称为产品使用手册(Operating Manual),是厂商在销售其产品时所附的对产品构造、性能、规格、用途、使用方法、维修保养等方面进行文字说明的活页或小册子,用来告诫买者如何正确使用所购物品,以免因使用不

当或保管不当而造成不良后果。产品说明书一般由标题(包括副标题)和正文两大部分组成,有的说明书在最后还附注厂商的名称。说明书的书写可采用概述式(通篇浑然一体,类似一篇短文)、条文式(分条列款,逐项说明)或复合式,多使用动词的现在时态,并经常通过各种省略手段进行简化和避免重复。

(一)非耐用品类产品说明书(Directions for Nondurable Goods)

非耐用品(Nondurable Goods)指使用时间较短,甚至一次性消费的商品,如手纸、糖果、牙膏等。这类产品通常单位价值较低,消耗快,消费者往往经常、反复购买,大量使用。非耐用品类说明书的内容通常包括:

1. 产品概况

例如,Wahaha, a children's nourishing oral liquid, is co-developed by Wahaha Nutritious Food Product Factory and the Department of Medical Nutrition of Zhejiang Medical University. The liquid contains rich amino acids, vitamins and particularly supplies children with Ca and trace elements such as Fe and Zn essential to healthy growth. It occupies the leading position in the development of nourishing products and has passed the nation-level evaluation of newly-developed products. 娃哈哈儿童营养液是由娃哈哈集团和浙江医科大学医学营养系共同开发的。产品富含氨基酸、维生素,以及儿童生长发育所需的钙、铁、锌等微量元素。本品已经通过国家级新产品鉴定,在国内同类产品中处于领先地位。

2. 性质、性能、特点

例如,The Pond's Block Cream contains Vitamin E and unique protective ingredients which form a breathing protective screen on your skin's surface, protecting the skin from damage caused by UV rays. 旁氏隔离霜富含维生素E和特效防护成分,在皮肤表面形成一层透气的保护膜,保护皮肤免受紫外线的伤害。

3. 使(食)用方法及注意事项

例如,Dosage and Administration: The usual dose is two pills once, three times a day. The dose can be increased by one or two pills if the stomachache grows worse. Contraindication: Due to the presence of sorbitol, this medicine is contra-indicated in patients who are intolerant to fructose. 用法用量:一般用量为每天三次,一次两粒,胃不舒服时可以加服1到2粒。禁忌:由于本品含有山梨糖醇,对果糖不耐受的患者慎用。

4. 包装、贮存方法,以及保质期

例如,Package: Paper / Aluminium / PE complex sachet; each box contains 10 sachets. Storage: To be kept in a cool place. Quality guarantee for one year and storage period one and a half years. 包装:纸铝塑复合膜袋,每盒10袋。贮藏:阴凉地方存放,保质期一年,存储期一年半。

5. 其他(如执行标准、批准文号等)

例如,Sanction No.: Zhejiang Food Hygiene Permit (89) 0004-35. Standard Code: Q/WJB0201-8. 批准文号:浙卫食准字(89)第0004-35号。标准代号:Q/WJB0201-8。

(二)耐用品类产品说明书(Directions for Durable Goods)

所谓耐用品(Durable Goods)是指三、四年或更长使用时间的产品,既包括生产资料(如机器设备等)又包括消费品(如汽车、冰箱、电视机、家具等)。在实际生活中,耐用品的说明书一般比较长,很多情况下需要在首页以目录的形式先将各条目列出,并标示页码。该类产品说明书的内容通常包括:

1. 产品概况。例如,The Lifecare PROVIDER 5500 System is a portable infusion pump, specially designed to deliver analgesic drugs, antibiotics, and chemotherapeutic agent. 产品"生命关爱者5500"是一种便携式输液泵,特别适合传送镇痛药、抗生素,以及化疗剂。

2. 性质、性能、特点。例如,In clinical trials the product was shown to be highly effective in improving and normalizing the alternated cerebral circulation and those disorders related to insufficient arterial flow in the limbs. 临床试验证实,本品疗效高,可改善已病变的脑循环,使之恢复正常,并治疗与四肢动脉血流不畅有关的疾病。

3. 安装调试。例如,Before installing the machine rub off the original rust-protective grease and daub the surface with a thin film of light oil. Make sure the two protrusions on the large gear fit firmly into the slots in the end of the spool. 安装本设备前,应除去原始防锈油,并在表面涂上薄层的轻质油。务必将大齿轮上的两个突起部分与卷轴端子的凹槽牢固配合。

4. 使用方法及注意事项。例如,Easy Print:(1)In playback mode, display the picture you want to print out on the monitor. (2)Turn the printer on and plug the USB cable provided with the camera into the multi-connector of the camera and the printer's USB port. (3)Press "△", printing starts. Troubles and Troubleshooting: If the unit makes no response when power button is pressed, please check if ① the power supply is already turned on ② the main unit is set at the "mute" mode. 简单打印操作:(1)选择播放模式,在显示屏上显示想要打印的图像。(2)开启打印机电源并将照相机附带的 USB 电缆插入照相机的多功能接口和打印机的 USB 接口。(3)按"△"键,打印开始。常见故障及排除:如果按动开关却没有反应,请检查是否①电源已接通②主机处于静音状态。

5. 保养与维修。例如,Do not store the device in hot areas. High temperatures can shorten the life of electronic devices, damage batteries, and warp or melt certain plastics. To claim under warranty the customer must take the product and this Warranty Certificate before the end of the one year warranty period to the dealer where the product was purchased or any authorized service station listed in the instructions and request the necessary repairs. 请勿将本品存放在热源附近。高温可能会缩短电子装置的寿命、损坏电池,并使某些塑料部件变形或熔化。如需保修服务,顾客应携带该产品和保修卡,在一年保修期之内,在产品经销商处或任何在说明书中指明的授权服务点进行必要的维修。

6. 其他(产品成套明细、附属备件及工具、标准等)。例如,Package Content: fingerprint security access system; mounting adapter ring; CD with demo software; operating instructions. 包装内容:指纹安全门禁系统;安装转接环;带演示软件的CD;操作说明。

二、于琪的解决方案

Golden Childhood Smoothie

Golden Childhood Smoothie is a fruit-and-yogurt-based beverage that contains only natural ingredients (no additives) and is high in essential nutrients. It is made from high-quality fresh fruit, milk and other materials by advanced technology and latest formula. The nutriments of these materials are kept well during processing. It is really an ideal delicious convenience food for both the old and the young at home or in tour.

Ingredients:

Fresh fruit, Low-fat milk, Mint, Olive kernel, Honey

Nutrition: (Per 340g)

Fat	<0.5g	Carbohydrates	10g
Cholesterol	6mg	Dietary fiber	5g
Sodium	70mg	Iron	2mg
Potassium	100mg	Protein	25g

Direction: Open the screw-off cap and serve. Or add suitable amount of fresh fruit juice or vegetable, blend and keep in an ice-box to make a pleasing ice-cream or salad.

Execution Standard: Q/HWL 009

Net Weight: 340g

Date of Production: see the seal

Shelf Period: 365 days

Storage: Keep in a cool, dry place

Manufacturer: Golden Childhood Co. Ltd.

Address: 299 Chengxin Road, Pudong District, Shanghai, P. R. China

Post Code: 200010

Tel: (021) 5322673 5329888-816888

Fax: (021) 5323896 5322443

Under the supervision of the Nutrition and Food Hygiene Institute of Shanghai Hygiene and Epidemic Prevention Station.

Review Questions

1. **Key Terms**

Augmented product; Shopping goods; Width of a product mix; Product development; Market development

2. **Multiple Choices (select one)**

(1) A(n) (　　) is anything that can be offered to a market for attention, acquisition, use, or consumption that might satisfy a want or need.

　A. product　　　B. icon　　　C. tangible good　　　D. price

(2) Product planners think about products and services on five levels. The most basic level is the (　　), which addresses the question, "What is the buyer really buying?"

A. basic benefit　　　　　　　　B. actual product

C. augmented product　　　　　D. core benefit

(3) When Sony and its dealers give buyers a warranty on parts and workmanship, instruction on how to use the camcorder, quick repair services when needed, and a toll-free number to call if they have problems or questions, Sony is building a(n) (　　) by offering additional consumer services and benefits.

A. core benefit　　　　　　　　B. actual product

C. image　　　　　　　　　　　D. augmented product

(4) (　　) are usually low priced, and marketers place them in many locations to make them readily available when customers need them.

A. Core products　　　　　　　B. Actual products

C. Shopping products　　　　　D. Convenience products

(5) Most major innovations are (　　) products and services until the consumer becomes aware of them through advertising.

A. shopping　　B. convenience　　C. specialty　　D. unsought

(6) If a consumer buys a lawn mower for personal use in the home, the lawn mower is a (　　). If the same consumer buys the lawn mower for use in a landscaping business, the lawn mower is an (　　).

A. unsought good; industrial product

B. sought good; consumer product

C. consumer product; industrial product

D. industrial product; consumer product

(7) A (　　) is a group of products that are closely related because they function in a similar manner, are sold to the same customer groups, are marketed through the same type of outlets, or fall within given price ranges.

A. product mix　　B. product line　　C. brand　　D. brand equity

(8) Procter and Gamble's product lines are (　　) insofar as they are consumer products that go through the same distribution channels.

A. inconsistent　　B. wide　　C. deep　　D. consistent

(9) (　　) refers to increase sales of an existing product in an existing market.

A. Market penetration　　　　　B. Product development

C. Market development　　　　D. Diversification

(10) In (　　), sales typically grow at an increasing rate, many competitors enter the market, and large companies may start to acquire small pioneering firms.

A. introduction phase　　　　　B. growth phase

C. maturity phase　　　　　　　D. decline phase

3. Questions for Discussion

(1) What is the difference between the core product, the actual product, and the augmented product?

(2) What are the main differences among convenience, shopping, and specialty products?

(3) List and explain the steps marketers undergo to develop new products.

(4) Place the personal computer on the product life cycle curve, and give reasons for placing it where you did.

Practical Writing

Scenario: You just bought some pianos for the university you work in and come across the following **Manual**. Translate it into Chinese to make sure you understand all the instruction.

Instruction Manual for Piano

1. Care must be taken during transportation and unpacking.

2. Keep the piano at a proper place with the back around 10cm against the wall. The four rollers should rest squarely on the floor.

3. A stable temperature 20℃~25℃ and relative humidity 40%~70% should be maintained. In wet season, put a drier or install an electric drying tube into the instrument. In dry season, put a jug of water in it.

4. Put bagged insect-killers inside the piano to prevent the felt parts from being eaten by insects, and renew them regularly.

5. Use soft velvet for wiping the piano cabinet so as to avoid scratching the shiny surface.

6. Use an alcohol cotton pad to clean up the keyboard, do not use benzine or lacquer thinner.

7. The piano needs tuning twice a year or more, depending on the frequency of use. The action and pedals also need regulating at the same time.

8. Clothe the piano after use so as to protect it.

Unit 8　At the Negotiating Table

Learning Objectives

◇ 熟悉商务谈判的常用口语表达；
◇ 理解影响产品价格的诸多因素；
◇ 理解产品定价的基本策略；
◇ 理解产品调价的原因、可能出现的问题，以及处理方法；
◇ 掌握商务合同的书写规则和常规条款的正确写法。

Speaking：Negotiation

【场景1】　这天早上9点，在金色童年公司的会议室，销售经理马天跃与David Smith先生又见面了。刚刚离开的Smith先生此次风尘仆仆地从澳大利亚回来，是打算购买一批儿童服装。谈判刚刚开始，马经理便感到这位澳大利亚人粗犷的外表下藏有狡兔的心思。

【对话1】　A：销售经理马天跃　　B：David Smith先生

A：Good morning, Mr. Smith. How good to see you again! How's everything going?
　　早上好, 史密斯先生。再次见到你真高兴！一切都好吗？
B：Fine, thanks. How's everything with you?
　　很好, 谢谢。你一切都好吗？
A：Very well, thank you.
　　非常好, 谢谢。
B：Now, shall we get down to business?
　　现在, 我们来谈谈正事吧。
A：Sure. I'd be happy to answer any questions you may have.
　　好的。我非常愿意回答你的任何问题。
B：Your products are very good. But I'm a little worried about the prices you're asking.
　　你们的产品非常不错, 但是对于要价我却有些担忧。

A：You think we should be asking for more? (Laughs)
你觉得我们应该要价更高？（笑）

B：(Chuckles) That's not exactly what I had in mind. I know your products are of high quality, but what I'd like is a reasonable discount.
（咯咯笑）那并不是我的意思。我知道你们的产品具有良好的质量,但我希望能得到一个合理的折扣。

A：I'm certainly happy to talk about the discount. But can you indicate to me the quantity you'd like to order?
我很愿意和你谈论折扣问题。但你能不能告诉我你大概要订多少货呢？

B：Fair enough. What discount would you offer on an order of say 2,000 suits?
嗯,应该的。比方我要订2,000套的话,你能给我什么样的折扣？

A：For an order of that size, Mr. Smith, I can give you a discount of ten percent.
如果是这么多的话,史密斯先生,我可以给你百分之十的折扣。

B：Ten percent!
百分之十！

A：Just let me finish. Yes, ten percent, but with a guarantee of delivery within one month.
让我说完。是的,百分之十,但可以保证一个月内交货。

B：Delivery must be within one month, or I'm not interested. I want the goods to arrive well before the Children's Day. Let's be clear about one thing. I hope you realize I must have a larger discount than what you've offered.
当然要一个月内交货呀,否则我可不会买你们的产品。我希望这批货能在儿童节之前到埠。你要清楚的是,我希望你能给个比刚才更大的折扣。

A：You know the fabric used in the production undergoes a special process that prevents shrinkage and increases durability. This price, actually, leaves us with a very small profit margin.
你知道,我们使用的布料经过特殊的工艺处理,能有效防止缩水并增加牢固度。事实上,这个价格对我们来说已经没有什么利润可言了。

B：Although we are anxious to open up business with you, we find your price is out of line with the current market level.
尽管我们渴望与贵方开展业务,但我们认为你方的报价与现行市场价格脱节。

A：Well, if you commit to buy 3,000 suits, then I could consider a larger discount.
那么,如果你承诺购买3,000套的话,我可以考虑给你更大的折扣。

B：How much larger?
有多大？

A：If you order 3,000 suits I can offer you a twenty percent discount.
如果你定3,000套的话,我给你百分之二十的折扣。

B：Ten percent, twenty percent. I'm getting tired of this. You are playing games. I'm looking for a much larger discount. I'm ordering in large quantities and I operate on small margins, you see?

百分之十,百分之二十,我受够了,你老是在兜圈子。我想要更大的折扣。我订了这么多,但却赚不了什么钱,你看是不是?

A: If you want a big discount, then you must make the order a large one.
如果你想要更大的折扣,那你就必须要订更多的货。

B: We're going in circles. Isn't an order of 2,000 suits large enough? Unless you make a concession, we're getting nowhere.
又回到老路上了。难道2,000套不是一笔很大的订单吗?除非你有所让步,否则我们就做不成生意了。

A: I don't think I can change it right now. Why don't we talk again in an hour?
我觉得我现在不能改变什么。我们一个小时后接着谈怎么样?

B: Sure. I must talk to my office anyway. I hope we can find some common ground on this.
好的。我也必须向总部汇报。我希望我们能对此找到共同立场。

【场景2】 在谈判间隙,销售经理马天跃向Robert汇报了Smith先生的提案。Robert很满意对方的采购计划,但在折扣方面则希望马天跃能继续维持强硬的态度,尽量探出对方的底线。一个小时后,双方又坐到了谈判桌前。

【对话2】 A:销售经理马天跃 B:David Smith先生

A: Have you made up your mind, Mr. Smith?
史密斯先生,下定决心了吗?

B: Mr. Ma, I've been instructed to reject the numbers you proposed; but we can try to come up with something else.
马先生,总部指示我拒绝你们提出的数字,但是我们可以努力达成其他的一些协议。

A: I hope so, Mr. Smith. My instructions are to negotiate hard on this deal—but I'll try very hard to reach some middle ground.
希望如此,史密斯先生。我获得的指示也是在这个问题上采取强硬的立场——但我会尽最大的努力来找到我们彼此的利益均衡点。

B: I understand. We propose an order of 2,000 suits with a discount of 25%.
我明白。我们的提议是购买2,000套,产品七五折。

A: Mr. Smith, I can't bring those numbers back to my boss—he'll turn it down flat.
史密斯先生,我不能将这些数字上报回老板,他会打回票的。

B: Then you'll have to think of something better, Mr. Ma.
那么你就来想出一个更好的主意吧,马先生。

A: How about 25%, with a minimum order of 3,000 suits?
产品七五折,最低订购3,000套如何?

B: That's a lot to order, with very low profit margins.
那需要订购很多的产品,毛利率却很低。

A: It's about the best we can do, Mr. Smith. (Pause) We need to hammer something out today. If I go back empty-handed, I may be coming back to you soon to ask for a job.
这几乎是我们所能做到的最好的了,史密斯先生。(停顿)今天我们需要敲定一些事情,如果两手空空地回去,我可能不久就要向你讨工作了。

B: (Smiles) All right. Mr. Ma, don't let us get stuck over the question of price. We can meet each other half way: we increase our order to 2,500 suits and you increase the discount to 25%. Is that agreeable?
(笑)好吧。马先生,我们不要老在价格这个问题上兜圈子了。让我们各让一步吧:我方加订到2,500套,你方给我们七五折,你说呢?

A: That's a deal.
成交。

> 【场景3】 经过激烈的讨价还价,双方终于在价格上达成一致。销售经理马天跃清楚,自己必须趁热打铁,尽快敲定其他细节。
>
> 【对话3】 A:销售经理马天跃 B:David Smith先生

A: Oh, thank God, we have finally settled the price. Shall we discuss the mode of payment next?
哦,感谢上帝,我们终于在价格上达成了一致。我们接下来探讨一下付款方式好吗?

B: OK.
好的。

A: Our terms of payment are 100% irrevocable letter of credit payable against shipping document.
我们接受的付款方式是100%不可撤销的信用证,见装运单据付款。

B: Would you agree to accept D/A or D/P payment? You see, our order is large.
你们是否能接受承兑交单或付款交单? 你看,我们的订货量是很大的。

A: Since the total amount is so big and the world monetary market is rather unstable at the moment. We can't accept any other modes of payment than a L/C.
由于订货量很大,目前的世界货币市场又不太稳定,我们不能接受除信用证以外的其他付款方式。

B: In order to conclude the business, I hope you'll meet me halfway. What about 50% by L/C and the balance by D/P?
为了达成交易,我希望我们能彼此让步。50%通过信用证支付,剩余部分通过付款交单支付如何?

A: We regret we can't make an exception. L/C is the normal mode of payment universally adopted in international business. We must adhere to this customary practice.
很遗憾我们不能破例。信用证支付是国际贸易的惯例,我们必须坚持。

B: Hmm... OK, an irrevocable sight L/C.
嗯……好吧。一个不可撤销的即期信用证。

A: Great! The L/C must reach us 25 days before the month of shipment and remain valid for negotiation in Shanghai until the 15th day from the date of shipment.
很好！信用证必须在装运月份前25天送达，有效至装运后15天在上海议付。

B: I can agree to that.
我同意。

A: Well, let's iron out the remaining details...
嗯，让我们来解决剩下的细节问题吧……

Reading：Formulating Pricing Strategies

显而易见，价格是贸易中最核心的问题。于琪觉得，自己有必要深入了解一下到底哪些因素会影响商品的价格，以及产品定价和调价的一些基本技巧。

Chapter 8 Pricing Strategies

Section 1 Factors Affecting Pricing Decisions

Before any pricing decisions can be undertaken, it is important that the factors influencing price are understood. These factors can be categorized as follows.

1.1 Customer Demand

Much of pricing theory is derived from economics. The basic idea, according to such theories, is that demand will be different at each possible price. Demand is normally assumed to fall as price increases. Similarly supply is expected to increase as price increases (the reverse of demand). A downward sloping demand curve and an upward sloping supply curve can determine the equilibrium price. Equilibrium means a state of equality between demand and supply. Without a shift in demand and/or supply there will be no change in market price. Changes in the conditions of demand or supply will shift the demand or supply curves. This will cause changes in the equilibrium price and quantity in the market. Marketers also need to know price elasticity—how responsive demand will be to a change in price. If demand is elastic rather than inelastic, sellers will consider lowering their price to gain more total revenue.

1.2 Product Life Cycle

At the introduction stage price may be set high to capitalize on its uniqueness or recover its development cost (skimming), as the first video recorders were priced. This high price may be carried through to maturity or later, taking skimming to its logical conclusion—as a niche player, such as Mercedes-Benz in the automobile industry might do. At the growth stage, competition will grow as other companies develop competitive products. Although the market leader or first company in the industry to create the product usually maintains its starting price to keep its premium image, some competitors may try to lower prices to gain market share. It is only at the end of maturity, when the market moves into saturation that, according to this theory, price competition increases and inefficient, high-cost firms are eliminated. Manufacturers that remain in the market typically offer similar prices. The decline stage may see further price decreases as the few remaining competitors try to salvage the last vestiges of demand.

1.3 Competition and Environment

Competition and environment in the market may also have an important impact and may often be the ultimate determinant of prices. If the business is a monopolist, then it has price-setting power. At the other extreme, if a firm operates under conditions of perfect competition, it has no choice and must accept the market price. The reality is usually somewhere in between. In such cases the chosen price needs to be considered relative to those of close competitors and with one eye to the likely reaction of rival firms when a business changes its pricing strategy. In addition, economic factors such as boom or recession, inflation, and interest rates may affect pricing decisions because they affect both the costs of producing a product and consumer perceptions of the product's price and value. There are also various aspects of legislation that impact a firm's pricing practices. The Sherman Act, for example, forbids price fixing, which could result in overall higher prices for consumers since various competitors are all pricing the same to maximize their profits.

1.4 Business Objectives and Strategies

Pricing policy should be consistent with the overall objectives of the firm. Many companies use current profit maximization as their pricing goal. They estimate what demand and costs will be at different prices and choose the price that will produce the maximum current profit, cash flow, or return on investment. Other companies want to obtain market share leadership. To become the market share leader, these firms set prices as low as possible. A company might also use price to attain other more specific objectives. It can set prices low to prevent competition from entering the market or set prices at competitors' levels to stabilize the market. One product may be priced to help the sales of other products in the company's line. Furthermore, price decisions must be coordinated with product design, distribution, and promotion decisions to form a consistent and effective marketing program. For example, producers using many resellers who are expected to support and promote their products may have to build larger reseller margins into their prices.

1.5 Cost

Before pricing a new product or service, business owners must have a thorough understanding of the total cost of production and distribution. Total cost includes expenses for research and development, manufacturing, distribution, capital, labor and overhead. All expenses involved with initially creating the product or service fall under research and development costs. Costs directly associated with raw materials used in production of the product are manufacturing costs. Distribution costs include everything related to direct distribution and marketing, specifically sales commissions, advertising, packaging, promotional materials, trade shows, business travel, etc. All long-term fixed assets are capital expenses. Labor costs are those costs associated with the time spent making the product. A business owner must include his or her time as part of the labor costs. Overhead expenses that are not directly related to production also need to be included. Examples of these costs are rent, utilities, telephone, insurance, supplies, etc. In order to make a profit, a business should ensure that its products are priced above their average cost.

小 结

多种因素会影响企业产品的价格。首先，需求（或供给）的改变会造成需求（或供给）曲线的移动，从而导致价格的变化。其次，根据产品生命周期理论，通常在引入期时可以制定高价以充分利用其独特性，而在成长阶段，虽然市场领导者或行业内第一家生产该产品的公司通常会保持起始价格以维护其优质形象，一些竞争对手可能会降低价格以获得市场份额。成熟阶段的后期，价格开始趋于平稳，而在衰退期将会出现价格的进一步下降。另外，竞争和环境因素也会对价格产生影响。垄断企业拥有制定高价的能力，自由竞争企业只能接受市场价，而经济和法律等因素对价格的影响同样非常重要。再有，价格决策应该与企业目标和战略相吻合。以利润最大化为目标的企业将制定高价，以市场份额最大化为目标的企业将尽量制定低价。最后，产品成本在企业价格决策时也要充分考虑。

Section 2 Price-Setting Strategies

2.1 New-Product Pricing Strategies

Many companies that invent new products initially set high prices to "skim" revenues layer by layer from the market. Sony frequently uses this strategy, called market-skimming pricing. When Sony introduced the world's first high-definition television (HDTV) to the Japanese market in 1990, the high-tech sets cost $43,000. These televisions were purchased only by customers who could afford to pay a high price for the new technology. Sony rapidly reduced the price over the next several years to attract new buyers. By 1993, a 28-inch HDTV cost a Japanese buyer just over $6,000. In 2001, a Japanese consumer could buy a 40-inch HDTV for about $2,000, a price that many more customers could afford. In this way, Sony skimmed the maximum amount of revenue from the various segments of the market. Market skimming makes sense only under certain conditions. First, the product's quality and image must support its higher price, and enough buyers must want the product at that price. Second, the costs of producing a smaller volume cannot be so high that they cancel the advantage of charging more. Finally, competitors should not be able to enter the market.

Rather than setting a high initial price to skim off small but profitable market segments, some companies use market-penetration pricing. They set a low initial price to penetrate the market quickly and deeply—to attract a large number of buyers quickly and win a large market share. Several conditions must be met for this low-price strategy to work. First, the market must be highly price sensitive so that a low price produces more market growth. Second, production and distribution costs must fall as sales volume increases. Finally, the low price must help keep out the competition, and the penetration pricer must maintain its low-price position—otherwise, the price advantage may be only temporary.

2.2 Product Mix Pricing Strategies

Companies usually develop product lines rather than single products. In product line pricing, management must decide on the price steps to set between the various products in a line. The price steps should take into account cost differences between the products in the line, customer evaluations of their different features, and competitors' prices. In many industries, sellers use well-established price points for the products in their line. Thus, men's clothing stores might carry men's suits at three price levels: $185, $325, and $495. The customer will probably associate low-, average-, and high-quality suits with the three price points. The seller's task is to establish perceived quality differences that support the price differences.

Many companies use optional-product pricing—offering to sell optional or accessory products along with their main product. For example, a car buyer may choose to order power windows, cruise control, and an extended warranty. Pricing these options is a sticky problem as companies must decide which items to include in the base price and which to offer as options. GM's pricing strategy was to advertise a stripped-down model at a base price to pull people into showrooms and then to devote most of the showroom space to showing option-loaded cars at higher prices.

Companies that make products that must be used along with a main product are using captive-product pricing. Examples of captive products are razor blades, camera film, video games, and printer cartridges. Producers of the main products (razors, cameras, video game consoles, and printers) often price them low and set high markups on the supplies. For example, Nintendo sells its game consoles at low prices and makes money on video game titles. In the case of services, this strategy is called two-part pricing. The price of the service is broken into a fixed fee plus a variable usage rate. The fixed amount should be low enough to induce usage of the service; profit can be made on the variable fees.

In producing processed meats, petroleum products, chemicals, and other products, there are often by-products. If the by-products have no value and if getting rid of them is costly, this will affect the pricing of the main product. Using by-product pricing, the manufacturer will seek a market for these by-products and should accept any price that covers more than the cost of storing and delivering them. By-products can even turn out to be profitable. For example, Malaysia's Golden Hope Plantations used to burn old rubber trees after their productive life. Now, it cuts them down and uses the wood to supply the fast-growing markets for rubber wood furniture, parquet flooring, and particle and medium-density fiber boards.

Using product bundle pricing, sellers often combine several of their products and offer the bundle at a reduced price. Thus, theaters and sports teams sell season tickets at less than the cost of single tickets; computer makers include attractive software packages with their personal computers; and Internet service providers sell packages that include Web access, Web hosting, e-mail, and an Internet search program. Price bundling can promote the sales of products consumers might not otherwise buy, but the combined price must be low enough to get them to buy the bundle.

2.3 Segmented Pricing

Segmented pricing takes several forms. Under customer-segment pricing, different customers pay different prices for the same product or service. Bus companies may charge a lower admission for students and senior citizens. Under product-form pricing, different versions of the product are priced differently but not according to differences in their costs. For instance, Black&Decker prices its most expensive iron at $54.98, which is $12 more than the price of its next most expensive iron. The top model has a self-cleaning feature, yet this extra feature costs only a few more dollars to make. Using location pricing, a company charges different prices for different locations, even though the cost of offering each location is the same. For instance, theaters vary their seat prices because of audience preferences for certain locations, and state universities charge higher tuition for out-of-state students. Finally, using time pricing, a firm varies its price by the season, the month, the day, and even the hour. Telephone companies offer lower off-peak charges, and resorts give seasonal discounts.

2.4 Psychological Pricing

In using psychological pricing, sellers consider the psychology of prices and not simply the economics. For example, consumers may perceive higher-priced products as having higher quality. Another aspect of psychological pricing is reference prices—prices that buyers carry in their minds and refer to when looking at a given product. For example, a company could display its product next to more expensive ones to imply that it belongs in the same class. In addition, even small differences in price can suggest product differences. Consider a stereo priced at $300 compared to one priced at $299.95. The actual price difference is only 5 cents, but the psychological difference can be much greater.

2.5 Distribution-based Pricing

Often a company states a price as FOB factory or FOB delivered. FOB factory or FOB origin pricing means that the cost of transporting the product from the factory to the customer's location is the responsibility of the customer. FOB delivered pricing means that the cost of transporting to the customer is included in the selling price. Delivery terms for pricing of products sold in international markets are especially important. CIF, for example, is the term used for ocean shipments and means the seller quotes a price covering cost of goods, insurance, and all transportation fees to the point of debarkation.

Other distribution-based pricing tactics should also be understood. Basing-point pricing means marketers choose one or more locations to serve as basing points. Customers pay shipping charges from these basing points to their delivery destinations. For example, a customer in Los Angeles may order a product from a company in San Diego. The product ships to Los Angeles from the San Diego warehouse. However, if the designated basing point is Dallas, the customer pays shipping charges from Dallas to Los Angeles, charges that the seller never incurred. When a firm uses uniform delivered pricing, it adds an average shipping cost to the price, no matter what the distance from the manufacturer's plant is. Internet sales, catalog sales, home television shopping, and other types of nonstore retail sales usually use uniform delivered pricing. Freight absorption pricing means the seller takes on part or all of the cost of shipping. Marketers are most likely to use freight absorption pricing in highly competitive markets or when such pricing allows them to enter new markets.

小 结

就企业定价策略而言，首先，新产品定价策略主要有撇脂定价（首先制定很高的价格，以便从市场中逐层赚取利润）和渗透定价（首先制定较低价格，以便赢得市场份额）。其次，产品组合定价策略包括产品线定价（确定产品线中不同产品的价差空间）、可选品定价（提供可选择的配件价格）、附属品定价（一般将主产品制定一个低价，利润在附属产品上实现）、副产品定价（制造商为生产过程中的副产品寻找市场）和捆绑定价（将几种产品组合在一起，售价低于分别购买的总价格）。差别定价指以不同价格销售产品或服务。心理定价考虑价格的心理影响而不仅仅是简单的经济影响。最后，基于分销的定价策略指在出厂价基础上再考虑运输费用，主要包括FOB原产地定价（价格是出厂价）、FOB目的地定价（价格中含实际运费）、基点定价（厂家根据顾客所在地到基点距离收取运输费用）、统一运输定价（厂家向所有顾客收取同样的运输费用）、免运费定价等。

Section 3　Initiating Price Changes

After developing their pricing structures and strategies, companies often face situations in which they must initiate price changes.

3.1　Initiating Price Cuts

Several situations may lead a firm to consider cutting its price. One such circumstance is excess capacity. In this case, the firm needs more business and cannot get it through increased sales effort, product improvement, or other measures. It may drop its "follow-the-leader pricing"—charging about the same price as its leading competitor—and aggressively cut prices to boost sales. But as the airline, fast-food, and other industries have learned in recent years, cutting prices in an industry with excess capacity may lead to price wars as competitors try to retain market share. Another situation leading to price cuts is falling market share in the face of strong price competition. Several American industries—automobiles, consumer electronics, cameras, watches, and steel, for example—lost market share to Japanese competitors whose high-quality products carried lower prices than their American counterparts did. In response, American companies resorted to more-aggressive pricing action. A company may also cut prices in a drive to dominate the market through lower costs. Either the company starts with lower costs than its competitors, or it cuts prices hoping to gain market share that will further cut costs through larger volume. This is the approach employed by many Asian businesses venturing overseas.

3.2 Initiating Price Increases

A successful price increase can greatly increase profits. For example, if the company's profit margin is three percent of sales, a one percent price increase will increase profits by 33 percent if sales volume is unaffected. A major factor in price increases is cost inflation. Rising costs squeeze profit margins and lead companies to pass cost increases along to customers. Another factor leading to price increases is overdemand: When a company cannot supply all its customers' needs, it can raise its prices, ration products to customers, or both. In passing price increases on to customers to keep up with rising costs, the company must avoid being perceived as a price gouger. Customer memories are long, and they will eventually turn away from companies or even whole industries that they perceive as charging excessive prices.

There are some techniques for avoiding this problem. One is to maintain a sense of fairness surrounding any price increase. Price increases should be supported with a company communication program telling customers why prices are being increased. Making low-visibility price moves first is also a good technique: Eliminating discounts, increasing minimum order sizes, and curtailing production of low-margin products or adding higher-priced units to the line are some examples. Finally, the company should consider ways to meet higher costs or demand without raising prices. For example, it can consider more cost-effective ways to produce or distribute its products. It can shrink the product instead of raising the price, as candy bar manufacturers often do. It can substitute less expensive ingredients or remove certain product features, packaging, or services.

小 结

在几种情况下,公司会考虑降价。一是存在过剩的生产能力,或者是面对强有力的价格竞争,市场份额正在下滑。此外,一个公司降价还可能是为了利用低成本而成为市场领导者。导致提价的主要因素是成本膨胀或过度需求。但是,公司向顾客收取高价应该保持一种公平的感觉。在提高价格的同时向顾客做出解释,为什么要涨价。执行不引人注意的价格变动技术也不失为一种很好的策略。当然,只要有可能,公司应该考虑那些能弥补成本膨胀和需求过度而不必提高价格的措施。

New Words and Key Terms

01. equilibrium price	均衡价格
02. price elasticity	价格弹性
03. price fixing	固定价格
04. research and development costs	研发成本
05. manufacturing costs	生产成本
06. distribution costs	分销成本
07. capital expenses	资本费用
08. labor costs	人工成本
09. overhead expenses	间接费用，管理费用
10. market-skimming pricing	撇脂定价
11. market-penetration pricing	渗透定价
12. product line pricing	产品线定价
13. optional-product pricing	可选品定价
14. captive-product pricing	附属品定价
15. two-part pricing	两部制定价
16. by-product pricing	副产品定价
17. product bundle pricing	捆绑定价
18. segmented pricing	分层定价；差别定价
19. psychological pricing	心理定价
20. reference prices	参考价格
21. FOB origin pricing	FOB原产地定价
22. FOB delivered pricing	FOB目的地定价
23. CIF	成本＋保险费＋运费定价
24. basing-point pricing	基点定价
25. uniform delivered pricing	统一运输定价
26. freight absorption pricing	免运费定价

Writing: Sales Contract or Purchase Contract

经过一整天激烈的谈判，双方终于在各项内容上达成一致，敲定了第一笔交易。谈判结束后，销售经理马天跃让于琪着手准备合同，以备签署。

一、合同写作的基本要求和格式

合同（Contract）也称契约，是缔约方依据所在国的法律或国际惯例就各自的责任、权利和义务达成的协议，是定约双方必须遵循的法律文件。商品买卖合同包括如下内容：

（一）约首（Head）

所包括内容与意向书类似。其中，序言写法通常如下：This contract is made by and between the Buyer and the Seller, whereby the Buyer agrees to buy and the Seller agrees to sell the under-mentioned commodity according to the terms and conditions stated below：本合同由买卖双方共同签订，根据如下合同条款，买方同意购买，卖方同意出售所述商品。

（二）正文(Body)

1. 商品的品名(Name of Commodity)、品质(Quality of Goods)条款

例如,Sample S22, Teddy Bear, Size 26″, as per the samples dispatched by the Seller on 20th October, 2004. 样品号 S22,玩具熊,尺码 26 英寸,根据卖方于 2004 年 10 月 20 日寄送的样品。

2. 数量条款(Quantity)

包括数量、计量单位,以及合理的机动幅度。例如,Northeast Soybean 60,000 M/T, Gross for Net, 5% more or less at Seller's option at contract price. 东北大豆 60,000 公吨,以毛作净,5%溢短装,由卖方决定,增减部分按合同价计。

3. 包装条款(Packing)

包括材料、方式、费用负担和运输标志。例如,In poly bags, 25 pounds in a bag, 4 bags in a sealed wooden case which is lined with metal. The cost of packing is for Seller's account. Each case shall be marked... 涤纶袋包装,25 磅一袋,4 袋装一箱。箱子用以金属作衬里的木箱。包装费用由卖方负担。每个木箱上刷制如下唛头……

4. 装运条款(Shipment)

例如,Shipment during May from London to Shanghai. The Seller shall advise the Buyer 45 days before the month of shipment of the time the goods will be ready for shipment. Partial shipments and transshipment allowed. 5 月份装运,由伦敦至上海。卖方应在装运月份前 45 天将备妥货物的时间通知买方。允许分批装运和转船。

5. 保险条款(Insurance)

包括投保人、险别、金额、保险依据等。例如,To be covered by the Seller for...% of total invoice value against..., as per Institute Cargo Clauses... dated.... 卖方按发票金额×%投保×险,按伦敦保险业协会×日货物×险条款负责。

6. 价格条款(Price)

包括计价数量单位、价格金额、计价货币和贸易术语四部分。例如,Unit Price: at USD 0.70 Per box FOB Tianjin 单价:每箱 0.70 美元 FOB 天津。

7. 支付条款(Payment)

以国际贸易广泛采用的信用证结算为例,The Buyer shall open through a bank acceptable to the Seller an Irrevocable Sight Letter of Credit to reach the Seller 45 days before the month of shipment, valid for negotiation in China until the 15th days after the month of shipment. 买方应通过为卖方所接受的银行于装运月份前 45 天开立并送达卖方不可撤销即期信用证,有效至装运月份后第 15 天在中国议付。

8. 商品检验检疫条款(Commodity Inspection)

例如,It is mutually agreed that the Certificate of Quality and Weight (Quantity) issued by the China Exit and Entry Inspection and Quarantine Bureau at the port of shipment shall be part of the documents to be presented for negotiation under the relevant L/C. 双方同意货物在装运港装运前由中国出入境检验总局进行检验,签发的质量和重量(数量)检验证书作为 L/C 项下议付单据的一部分。

9. 索赔与罚金条款(Claim and Penalty)

例如,Should the Buyer fail to open the L/C on time stipulated in the contract, the

Buyer shall pay a penalty to the Seller. The penalty shall be charged at the rate of 1% of the amount of the L/C for every ten days. 买方不能按合同规定的时间开立信用证,应向卖方支付罚金。罚金按迟开证每10天收取信用证金额的1%。

10. 不可抗力条款(Force Majeure)

包括不可抗力范围、发生后的通知义务,以及证明等。例如,If the shipment of the contracted goods is prevented or delayed in whole or in part by reason of war, earthquake, flood, storm, heavy snow or other causes of Force Majeure, the Seller shall not be liable... 如由于战争、地震、水灾、暴风雨、雪灾或其他不可抗力的原因,致使卖方不能全部或部分装运或延迟装运合同货物,卖方对此不承担责任……

11. 仲裁条款(Arbitration)

包括仲裁地点、机构、规则、效力,以及费用负担。例如,The arbitration shall be conducted by the Foreign Trade Arbitration Commission of Council for the Promotion of International Trade N.Y. according to its rules of arbitration... 仲裁由纽约国际贸易促进委员会对外贸易仲裁委员会根据其仲裁规则进行仲裁……

(三)约尾(End)

所包括内容与意向书类似。例如,This contract is made out in Chinese and Russian languages, both texts being equally binding. One copy each is kept by either party. 本合同书有中、俄两种文本,两种文本具有同等的效力。双方各持一份。

二、于琪的解决方案

Sales Confirmation

Commercial Contract No.:　　　　　　　　　　　　　　　　　　**Date**:

The Seller: Golden Childhood Children's Products Co., Ltd. China

The Buyer: Happy Kids Co., Ltd. Australia

This contract is made by and between the Buyer and the Seller according to the terms and conditions stated below:

1. Commodity & Specification	2. Quantity (Suits)	3. Unit Price (USD)	4. Amount (USD)
MC-01 Boys Wear FC-01 Girls Wear	1,500 (Suits) 1,000 (Suits)	FOB Shanghai USD40.00 USD45.00	USD60,000.00 USD45,000.00
TOTAL VALUE: SAY US DOLLARS ONE HUNDRED FIVE THOUSAND ONLY			USD105,000.00

5. Packing: To be packed in strong wooden cases or cartons, suitable for long distance ocean, and with good resistance to moisture and shocks. The cost of packing is for Seller's account.

6. Shipping Mark: The Seller shall mark on each package with fadeless paint the package number, gross weight, measurement and such warnings as "KEEP AWAY FROM HEAT".

7. Time of Shipment: Within 30 days after receipt of L/C allowing transshipment.

8. Port of Shipment: Shanghai

9. Port of Destination: Sydney

10. Insurance: To be borne by the Buyer after shipment.

11. Payment: The Buyer, on receipt from the Seller of the delivery advice, shall open an irrevocable letter of credit, in favor of the Seller for the total value of shipment 25 days prior to the date of delivery. The credit shall be available against Seller's draft drawn at sight on the opening bank for 100% invoice value accompanied by the shipping documents. The letter of credit shall be valid until the 15th day after the shipment is effected.

12. Inspection: It is mutually agreed that the Inspection Certificate of Quality and Quantity (Weight) issued by the China Import and Export Commodity Inspection Bureau at the port of shipment shall be part of the documents to be presented for negotiation under the relevant L/C. The Buyer shall have the right to re-inspect the Quality and Quantity (Weight) of the cargo. The re-inspection fee shall be borne by the Buyer. Should the Quality and/or Quantity (Weight) be found not in conformity with that of the contract, the Buyer shall be entitled to lodge with the Seller a claim which should be supported by survey reports issued by a recognized surveyor approved by the Seller within 20 days after the arrival of the goods.

13. Force Majeure: The Seller shall not be held responsible for delay in shipment or non-delivery of the goods due to Force Majeure, which might occur during the process of manufacturing or in the course of loading. The Seller shall advise the Buyer of the occurrence mentioned above within 15 days and send by airmail a certificate of the incident issued by the local government to the Buyer.

14. Arbitration: All disputes in connection with this contract or the execution thereof shall be settled through friendly consultations. Should no settlement be reached, the case may then be submitted for arbitration to the Foreign Economic and Trade Arbitration Commission of the CCPIT in accordance with the rules and procedures of the said Arbitration Commission. The decision of the Arbitration Commission shall be final and binding on both parties. The arbitration fee shall be borne by the losing party.

In witness whereof, this contract is signed by both parties in two original copies; each party shall keep one copy.

THE SELLERS(SIGNED)   THE BUYERS(SIGNED)

Review Questions

1. Key Terms

Overhead expenses; Market-skimming pricing; Reference prices; Segmented pricing; Basing-point pricing

2. Multiple Choices (select one)

(1) Which of the following is NOT an external influence on price? (   )

A. Demand   B. Market structure
C. Product Life Cycle   D. Experience
(2) Internal influences on price include (   ).
A. cost   B. business objectives
C. economies of scale   D. all of the above
(3) A firm's pricing objectives could be (   ).
A. to maximize profits   B. to achieve a target sales level
C. to maintain or enhance market share   D. all of the above
(4) A successful penetration pricing may lead to (   ).
A. image of quality   B. large sales
C. maximizing profit   D. all of the above
(5) Which of the following is NOT an advantage of price skimming? (   )
A. The practice of price-skimming allows for some return on the set-up costs.
B. A company can build a high-quality image for its product.
C. It may also promote complimentary and captive products.
D. Skimming can be an effective strategy in segmenting the market.
(6) Setting a low initial price to attract a large number of buyers is called (   ).
A. market-skimming pricing   B. market-penetration pricing
C. product line pricing   D. optional-product pricing
(7) Theaters and sports' teams sell season tickets at less than the cost of single tickets. This pricing strategy is called (   ).
A. product-bundle pricing   B. discount pricing
C. captive-product pricing   D. optional-product pricing
(8) All of the following are the examples of price discrimination except for (   ).
A. variations in prices for the same candy in package and in bulk
B. prices of fruit at the road-side sellers
C. variations in price for different sizes of bottles of shampoo
D. charges for business and residential telephone service
(9) (   ) means that the goods are placed free on board a carrier; the customer pays the freight from the factory to the destination.
A. Uniform-delivered pricing   B. Zone pricing
C. FOB-origin pricing   D. Basing-point pricing
(10) Several situations may lead a firm to consider cutting its price except (   ).
A. excess capacity   B. falling market share
C. lower costs   D. rising costs

3. Questions for Discussion

(1) Explain how the demand curves for normal products and for prestige products differ. What are demand shifts and why are they important to marketers?

(2) For new products, when is skimming pricing more appropriate, and when is pen-

etration pricing the best strategy?

(3) Give situations that force companies to initiate price changes, and possible problems they may face.

Practical Writing

Scenario: The company you work in (Hunan Native Products Import and Export Corporation) has just made a deal with Rotterdam Foodstuffs Import and Export Company to sell Hunan Lotus Seeds. The **Contract** is supposed to be made out in Chinese and English languages. Translate the following Chinese version into English.

合同号:2010-120

卖方:湖南土特产品进出口公司

买方:荷兰鹿特丹食品进出口公司

本合同经买卖双方同意,按如下条款建立:

货物名称:湖南湘莲

规格:2010年产大路货

数量:80公吨

单价:每公吨25,000元人民币,CIF鹿特丹

总值:2,000,000元人民币

包装条款:双层麻袋装

保险条款:卖方按发票金额110%投保一切险和战争险

装运期:2010年11月期间

装运港:中国湖南岳阳

目的港:荷兰鹿特丹

运输标志:由卖方自定

支付条款:不可撤销的即期信用证

签订于中国湖南岳阳,2010年9月18日。

买方签字: 卖方签字:

Unit 9　The Children's Day is Coming

Learning Objectives

◇ 熟悉促销活动的常用口语表达；
◇ 理解不同促销工具的含义和作用；
◇ 理解促销组合策略的基本类型；
◇ 理解整合营销传播方案开发和评估的具体运作过程及方法；
◇ 掌握广告的书写规则和常用套语的正确写法。

Speaking：Festival Promotion

【场景1】 儿童节快到了，公司决定在上海的三家旗舰店内搞一次促销活动。销售经理马天跃与儿童服装销售负责人 Joan Mitchell 及儿童玩具销售负责人 Tony Lin 就如何利用节日开展促销活动进行着仔细的讨论。
【对话1】 A：销售经理马天跃　　B：Joan Mitchell 女士　　C：Tony Lin 先生

A：The Children's Day is round the corner. It is high time for us to decide how to make the most of this occasion. First，let's decide what's going to be our special offers this year. Joan，what do you have in mind about this?
儿童节马上就要到来了。现在是我们决定如何充分利用这一节日的关键时刻。首先，我们要决定今年将要推出的特别优惠。琼，你对这事有什么想法？

B：As far as our sector is concerned，I'd like to suggest a joint promotion with McDonald's apart from a 20％ discount as usual.
就我们部门而言，除了与往常一样的20％的价格折扣，我建议与麦当劳搞一次联合促销活动。

A：How would it work?
具体如何开展？

B：Well，most parents would buy new clothing for their children around the Children's Day and they are also more likely to offer their children a treat to the kids' tastes. And every kid likes McDonald's, you know. So we can cooperate with McDonald's and let our customers meet two needs within one purchase. For example, every purchase beyond 300 yuan entitles the buyer a coupon for a set meal at McDonald's.

嗯，大多数父母会在儿童节期间为他们的孩子购买新衣服，父母也通常会给予特别奖赏满足孩子的口福。你知道，每个孩子都喜欢麦当劳。因此我们可以和麦当劳合作，让我们的顾客一次购买就能满足两项需求。比如说，购物超过300元的顾客可以得到一张麦当劳套餐的优惠券。

A：Sounds pretty good. What's your opinion, Tony?

听起来很不错。你有什么想法，托尼？

C：That's a great idea. But I'm afraid it doesn't apply to our sector, for we usually don't have so many big deals as the clothing sector. So I'm thinking of giving different freebies such as popular cartoon cards, picture books and batteries for electrical toys, based on the money paid of course. That worked well last year. And if there is any purchase beyond 300 we can also offer a McDonald's coupon.

主意不错。但是恐怕不太适合我们部门，因为我们通常不会像服装部门那样有很多大额购买。因此，我想采用免费赠品的方式，如流行的卡通卡、图画书，以及电动玩具电池等，当然是基于他们的购买额。这一招去年就很有效。如果购物超过300元，我们也可以提供一张麦当劳套餐的优惠券。

A：What else can we do to attract more customers?

我们还能做什么来吸引更多的顾客呢？

B：We can also carry out a buy-one-get-one policy. For example, those who buy an expensive dress can get a pair of sandals or a beautiful sunbonnet to go with the dress. And those who buy shoes can get a tube of shoeshine.

我们也可以实行买一赠一策略。比如说，那些购买昂贵服装的顾客可以得到与之匹配的一双凉鞋或一顶漂亮的太阳帽。另外，那些购买鞋子的顾客也可以得到一管鞋油。

C：And those who buy remote-controlled toy cars can get a set of building blocks.

那些购买遥控玩具车的顾客可以得到一套积木。

A：OK. That's almost settled. Now what about the festive decoration of the store as a whole?

好的。问题基本解决了。那么整体店面该如何进行节日装饰呢？

C：I think we need to repaint the front of the store with cartoon patterns to make it look new and attractive. We can also dress the salespeople as if they were characters in fairy tales. At the center of the store we can build a wonderland full of beautiful and interesting things from which every kid can choose two items for themselves if their parents pay a certain amount of money.

我想我们需要用卡通图案将商店的前部重新粉刷，使它看起来是全新的而且是吸引人的。我们还可以把售货员打扮成童话中的人物。在店的中央我们可以建一个仙境，里面充满漂亮有趣的东西。如果父母支付了一定金额，孩子就可以从中任选两个。

B: That'll be something really new and exciting for all kids. I'm sure a great many kids will beg their parents for a chance. Besides, we can't forget to hang two big cartoon balloons with the words "Come in and get me" on them in front of the entrance. And each counter can also be decorated with colorful balloons. As you know, balloons are indispensable in creating a festive atmosphere on such occasions.

对于所有孩子来说那真是既新奇又激动。我确信许多孩子会求他们的父母给他们这样的机会。此外,我们不要忘了在入口处悬挂两个写有"进来带走我"的大卡通气球。每个柜台也可以装饰彩色气球。你知道,气球对于烘托这种场合下的节日气氛是必不可少的。

C: I agree with you on that.
我同意你的建议。

A: Well, that's all for the time being. Thank you for your good ideas.
嗯,现在就这样吧。谢谢你们的好主意。

【场景2】 结束了节日促销方案讨论会,销售经理马天跃径直来到总经理办公室。总经理 Robert Liu 听完马天跃的汇报后,向他询问起即将上市的系列奶昔产品的促销计划。对于马天跃提出的赞助活动,Robert 似乎有些犹豫。

【对话2】 A:总经理 Robert Liu　　B:销售经理马天跃

A: What kind of promotional events are scheduled for the new product line?
对新的产品系列安排了什么样的促销活动呢?

B: We are going to set up with product launches in five major cities, as well as some sponsoring events throughout the year. All together, there will be 15 events.
我们将在五大城市举行产品发布会,并且在全年内开展一些赞助活动。总共加在一起有15场活动。

A: What kind of sponsoring are we talking about? I don't know how effective sponsorship really is...
什么样的赞助活动?我不知道赞助的真正效果……

B: It's not what you're thinking. These events will give us a wider exposure than most. Take the tri-city marathon for starters. This is a highly publicized event. The television exposure alone will nearly double our customer awareness.
不是你想的那样。这些活动将给我们提供更多抛头露面的机会。我们一开始要赞助3个城市举办的马拉松比赛,这是个大家普遍关注的活动。光电视一项的曝光率就会使我们的顾客认知度几乎翻倍。

A: Other than the marathon, what else is on the list?
除了马拉松比赛,还准备搞什么活动?

B: We've got a spot in Olympic Stadium sponsoring one of a team's equipment, then a rally for cancer research, and a connection to the inner-city education program.
我们在奥林匹克体育馆得到赞助其中一个参赛队伍装备的机会,还有就是癌症康复研究，以及与城市内部教育项目的联系。

A：Sports, medicine, education... seems kind of random, don't you think?
体育、医药、教育……好像有点儿杂乱，你不这么看吗？

B：It might seem that way, but these events were all carefully chosen based on marketing research. These are the events that our customers and potential customers care about.
似乎是有点儿乱，但是这些活动都是在市场调查的基础上认真做出的选择。这些都是我们顾客和潜在顾客关心的活动。

> 【场景3】 广告一直是金色童年主要运用的常规促销方式，公司以前一直选择费用较高的电视媒体做广告。目前，一本季刊杂志在国内颇为流行。从总经理室出来，销售经理马天跃让于琪了解一下在该杂志刊登广告的相关事宜。
> 【对话3】 A：某杂志广告部工作人员 B：于琪

A：Market classifieds, how may I help you?
市场分类广告部，需要我帮什么忙吗？

B：Yes, I would like to find out about placing an advertisement in your magazine. Can you tell me a little about your rates for advertisements?
是的，我想了解一下在你们杂志上登广告的事情。你能给我介绍一下你们的广告收费情况吗？

A：Certainly. Our advertising rates are divided according to size, substrate, and location. If you are a corporate partner with our publication, we can offer you a slight discount. Also, our rates are different according to which publication you wish to advertise in. Our fall edition is pricier than the spring edition. When are you looking to advertise?
当然可以。我们的广告收费按照大小、印纸和所登的位置分成几档。如果是我们的刊物合作单位，我们可以稍微打点儿折扣。另外，广告费用也会根据你想登在哪一期而有所不同。我们秋季版就比春季版的收费高。你想什么时候登广告？

B：We would like to get in with the summer publication, if possible...
如果可能的话，我们想在夏季版上登……

A：We can do that... Timing might be a little tight because our press date is July 15th, but it can be done. Do you have a predetermined design? You can use either your own designers, or if it is more convenient for you, we have a team of in-house graphic designers that can put something together for you...
我们可以安排……由于我们的出版日期是7月15日，所以时间上可能有点儿紧张，但是可以完成。你有提前定好的设计方案吗？你可以用自己的设计师，或者对你们来说更方便的话，我们有室内美术设计小组也能帮你们设计……

B：That won't be necessary, we already have the image. If we run a full page ad in your summer edition on a normal gloss paper, tri-color, what do you think that will cost me?
那倒没有必要，我们已经有了设计图。如果我们在你们夏季版上登一整页的广告，用一般的光纸、三色印刷,你看得需要多少钱?

A: It depends on the location in the magazine. Are you interested in a front or back page ad? Those are more prime spots. We also have six tab page positions available.
那要看所登的广告在刊物中的位置。你喜欢封面广告或封底广告吗?这些都是比较好的位置。我们还有六个插页广告的位置。

B: I think a tab spot would be nice...
我想插页广告就很好……

A: For a customer supplied design, full page tab page ad, you're looking at about $785.
顾客自己提供设计的话,整页的插页广告费用大约要785美元。

B: Thanks a lot.
非常感谢。

Reading: Formulating Promotional Strategies

于琪早就听说一个好的促销策略往往能起到多方面作用,如引导采购、激发购买欲望、建立产品形象、巩固市场地位等。那么促销活动到底应该如何开展?有多少工具手段可以运用?针对消费者和商家的促销有哪些不同?所有这些,他都急于深入了解。

Chapter 9 Promotional Strategies

Section 1 Promotion Tools

Promotion is the set of activities concerned with communicating information to potential buyers. Promotional activities are traditionally grouped in four areas: personal selling, advertising, publicity, and sales promotion. While coordinated under the concept of promotion, each of these areas may be considered an area of specialization in marketing. Taken together, these activities are called the "tools" of the promotional mix.

1.1 Personal Selling

Personal selling is a communication method that involves paid, personal contact in the form of a seller's representative who meets with customers, usually in a face-to-face situation. Personal selling is a unique form of communication in that it involves personal, interactive contact between the buyer and the seller. This is important for many kinds of selling situation because the seller's representative, in the form of a salesperson, can respond to direct feedback provided by the buyer. For many products, and especially for products sold in the business-to-business marketplace, personal selling is a critical part of the overall promotion effort. While personal selling may be used with other tools of the promotion in any given context, it is of over-riding importance for some classes of products. In general, if the cost of a product is high, the product is complex, the risk (to the buyer) of making a poor choice is great, or the uses and benefits of the product are difficult to understand, then personal selling activities may be the most important part of the promotion effort coordinated by the seller.

1.2 Advertising

Advertising can be defined as any paid, impersonal communication by the seller to the buyer or prospective buyer. By paid, we mean that advertisements are created, controlled, and paid for by the selling organization. Advertising is usually conducted through a channel of mass communication such as television, radio, newspapers, magazines, or billboards. It is considered impersonal because it does not involve face-to-face interaction between the buyer and the seller. In this respect, advertising differs from personal selling in that the seller cannot gauge the reaction of the buyer to the advertising message. This is true even if the advertisement itself uses a person or more people to project the message the seller wishes to convey. For example, a television advertisement, or ad, for insurance services may feature an insurance salesperson telling the viewers to call an 800 number for a free quote on insurance rates. Even though the salesperson may be an employee of the seller sponsoring the ad, the transmission of the communication via the television means that the seller and the buyer do not actually interact and so the contact is considered impersonal.

1.3 Publicity

Publicity is any unpaid, impersonal form of communication about a company or its products. It is unpaid in that the seller does not pay for the communication itself. Publicity is a distinct part of the promotion mix in that the source of the communication is not the company itself. For example, a story about a new type of microprocessor manufactured by Intel that appears in the Wall Street Journal is a form of publicity. Intel may provide the Wall Street Journal with substantial information in the hope that the new product is reported in a favorable context. But Intel cannot ultimately control what the article will say about the new product. Because the source of publicity is not under the control of the seller, publicity is thought to have a high degree of credibility with potential buyers.

1.4 Sales Promotions

Sales promotions are paid, impersonal programs that consist of short-term incentives to encourage buyers to try a product and/or purchase it. Sales promotions usually support promotional activity conducted by personal selling or advertising or both. For example, a print advertisement in a newspaper may explain the benefits of a new hair shampoo. If the ad includes a coupon for a free sample of the shampoo, then the coupon is a sales promotion. There are two kinds of sales promotions. Trade promotions are sales promotions used by manufacturers to provide incentives to firms in the channel of distribution to increase the activity of those firms in moving the product toward retail outlets. Customer promotions are sales promotions targeting end-users of the product. Typical tools for customer promotions include price deals and rebates, samples, coupons, premiums, point-of-purchase promotions, contests, sweepstakes, continuity/loyalty programs, and conventions and trade shows.

Price deals and rebates offer a price reduction for purchase of a specific product during a specific time period. The price deal may be printed on the package itself, or it may be a price-off flag or banner on the store shelf. Alternatively, rebates allow the consumer to send a "proof of purchase" to the manufacturer, who then refunds part of the purchase price by mail. Samples are small amount of a product offered to consumers for trial. Sampling is the most effective—but most expensive—way to introduce a new product. Coupons are certificates that give buyers a saving when they purchase specified products. Coupons can stimulate sales of a mature brand or promote early trial of a new brand. Premiums are goods offered either free or at low cost as an incentive to buy a product, ranging from toys included with kids' products to phone cards and CDs. Point-of-purchase (POP) promotions include displays and demonstrations that take place at the point of purchase or sale. A contest calls for consumers to submit an entry—a jingle, guess, suggestion—to be judged by a panel that will select the best entries. A sweepstakes calls for consumers to submit their names for a drawing. A contest is a test of skill, while a sweepstakes is based on chance. Continuity/loyalty programs reward consumers for repeat purchases through points that lead to reduced price or free merchandise. Finally, conventions and trade shows give manufacturers the chance to display their products to a large audience of potential buyers (mainly industrial customers) at relatively low cost.

小 结

促销是向潜在买家交流信息的一系列活动。包括人员销售、广告、公共宣传和销售促进四种促销工具。人员销售是一种有偿的以卖方代表会见客户为形式的面对面的沟通方式。广告可以被定义为任何需要付费的、由卖方向买方或潜在买家进行的非人员的沟通。宣传是任何不需要支付费用的、对一个公司或其产品进行的非人员的传播。而销售促进是有偿的、非人员的活动,它包括鼓励买家尝试和/或购买产品的短期奖励办法。销售促进的对象可以是最终使用者和渠道成员。其中,对最终使用者的销售促进主要采用价格折扣和返款、样品、优惠券、赠品、售点陈列、竞赛、抽奖、积分奖励计划,以及会议和商业展览等形式。

Section 2 Promotion Mix Strategies

Marketers can choose from two basic promotion mix strategies—push promotion or pull promotion. Figure 9.1 contrasts the two strategies. The relative emphasis on the specific promotion tools differs for push and pull strategies. A push strategy involves "pushing" the product through distribution channels to final consumers. The producer directs its marketing activities (primarily personal selling and trade promotion) toward channel members to induce them to carry the product and to promote it to final consumers. Using a pull strategy, the producer directs its marketing activities (primarily advertising and consumer promotion) toward final consumers to induce them to buy the product. If the pull strategy is effective, consumers will then demand the product from channel members, who will in turn demand it from producers. Thus, under a pull strategy, consumer demand "pulls" the product through the channels.

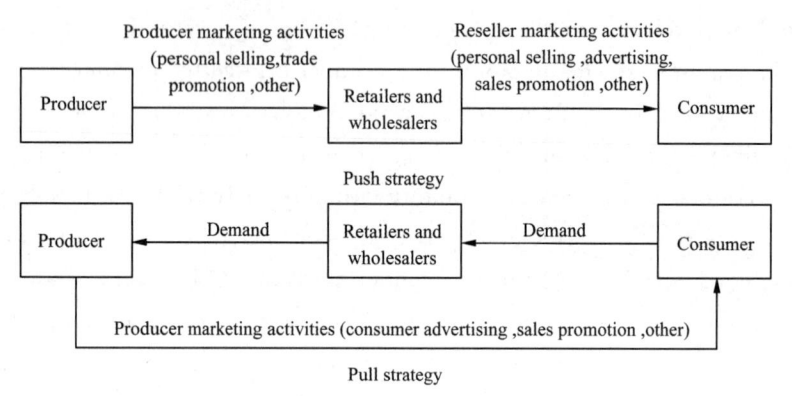

Figure 9.1　Push versus Pull Promotion Strategy

Some industrial goods companies only use push strategies; some direct-marketing companies only use pull. However, most large companies use some combination of both. For example, P&G's uses mass-media advertising and consumer promotions to pull its SKII skin products and a large sales force and trade promotions to push SKII products through the channels. In recent years, consumer goods companies have been decreasing the pull portions of their mixes in favor of more push. This has caused concern that they may be driving short-run sales at the expense of long-term brand equity.

Companies consider many factors when designing their promotion mix strategies, including the type of product/market and the product life-cycle stage. For example, the importance of different promotion tools varies between consumer and business markets. B2C companies usually "pull" more, putting more of their funds into advertising, followed by sales promotion, personal selling, and then public relations. In contrast, B2B marketers tend to "push" more, putting more of their funds into personal selling, followed by sales promotion, advertising, and public relations. In general, personal selling is used more heavily with expensive and risky goods and in markets with fewer and larger buyers.

The effects of different promotion tools also vary with stages of the product life cycle. In the introduction stage, advertising and public relations are good for producing high awareness, and sales promotion is useful in promoting early trial. Personal selling must be used to get the trade to carry the product. In the growth stage, advertising and public relations continue to be powerful influences, whereas sales promotion can be reduced because fewer incentives are needed. In the mature stage, sales promotion again becomes important relative to advertising. Buyers know the brands, and advertising is needed only to remind them of the product. In the decline stage, advertising is kept at a reminder level, public relations are dropped, and sales people give the product only a little attention. Sales promotion, however, might continue strong.

小 结

营销者可以从两类基本的促销组合策略中做出选择,即推动促销或者拉动促销。推动策略是指将产品顺着分销渠道推向最终顾客。生产商将其营销活动(主要是人员销售和商业促销)指向中间渠道成员,来促使他们接受产品并向最终顾客促销。采用拉动策略,生产商会将它的营销活动(主要是广告和消费者促销)直接指向最终顾客并促使他们购买产品。如果拉动策略有效的话,消费者会向渠道成员提出要求购买该产品,而渠道成员则会转向生产商处购买。公司在设计它们的促销组合策略时需要考虑许多因素,包括产品或市场的类型,以及产品生命周期等。

Section 3 Developing the Integrated Marketing Communication Plan

Integrated Marketing Communication (IMC) plan is one that delivers just the right message to a number of different target audiences when and where they want it in the most effective and cost-efficient way. Just as any other strategic decision-making process, the development of this plan includes several steps.

3.1 Identifying the Target Audiences

An important part of overall marketing planning is to identify the target audience(s). Although IMC marketers recognize that a company must communicate with a variety of stakeholders to satisfy everyone involved in the marketing process, the target audience, of course, is the most important stakeholder and the one that the company should focus on. With a well-designed database, marketers can know who their target audience is as well as the buying behavior of different segments within the total market. This means they can develop targeted messages for each customer.

3.2 Understanding the Communication Objectives

The whole point of communicating with customers and prospective customers is to let them know that the organization has a product to meet their needs in a timely and affordable way. Although the final response companies seek is customer purchase, the marketing communicator needs to know where the target audience now stands and what task communication should perform. Communication can perform one or more of three tasks. Informative communication may seek to convert an existing need into a want or to stimulate interest in a new product. It is generally more prevalent during the early stages of the product life cycle. People typically will not buy a product, service or support a nonprofit organization until they know its purpose and its benefits to them. Persuasive communication is designed to stimulate a purchase or an action. Persuasion normally becomes the main communication objective when the product enters the growth stage of its life cycle. By this time, the target market should have general product awareness and some knowledge of how the product can fulfill their wants. Therefore, the communication task switches from informing consumers about the product category to persuading them to buy the company's brand rather than the competitor's. Reminder communication is used to keep the product and brand name in the public's mind. This type of communication prevails during the maturity stage of the life cycle. It assumes that the target market has already been persuaded of the goods' or service's merits. Its purpose is simply to trigger a memory.

3.3 Determining and Allocating the Marketing Communication Budget

Most firms rely on two budgeting techniques to determine the total promotion budget: top-down and bottom-up. Top-down budgeting techniques require top management to establish the overall amount that the organization allocates for promotion activities. The most common top-down technique is the percentage-of-sales method in which the promotion budget is based on last year's sales or on estimates for the present year's sales. The percentage may be an industry average provided by trade associations that collect objective information on behalf of member companies. The advantage of this method is that it ties spending on promotion to sales and profits. Unfortunately, this method can imply that sales cause promotional outlays rather than viewing sales as the outcome of promotional efforts. Bottom-up budgeting techniques, on the other hand, attempt to identify promotion goals and allocate enough money to accomplish them. This bottom-up logic is at the heart of the objective-task method, which is gaining in popularity. Using this approach, the firm first defines the specific communication goals it hopes to achieve, such as increasing by 20 percent the number of consumers who are aware of the brand. It then tries to figure out what kind of promotional efforts it will take to meet that goal. Although this is the most rational approach, it is hard to implement because it obliges managers to specify their objectives and attach dollar amounts to them.

Once the organization decides how much to spend on promotion, it must divide its budget among the elements in the promotion mix. Several factors influence how companies divide up the promotional pie. For example, the characteristics of the organization itself may influence budget allocation; managers may simply have a preference for advertising versus sales promotion or other elements of the promotion mix. Also, consumers vary widely in the likelihood that they will respond to various communication elements. Some thrifty consumers like to clip coupons or stock up with two-for-one offers while others throw away those Sunday newspaper coupons without a glance. College students are notorious for not reading newspapers (except perhaps for campus papers they browse during lectures), but they do spend a huge amount of time on-line. The size and makeup of a geographic market also influence promotion decisions. In larger markets, the cost of buying media, such as local TV, can be quite high. If only a small percentage of the total market includes potential customers, then mass media advertising can be a very inefficient use of a promotion budget.

3.4 Designing the Promotion Mix

Designing the promotion mix is the most complicated step in marketing communication planning. It includes determining the promotion strategy (push strategy versus pull strategy, or both), the specific promotion tools to use, what message to communicate, and the communication channel(s) on which to send the message. Planners must ask how they can use advertising, sales promotion, personal selling, and public relations most effectively to communicate with different target audiences. Each element of the promotion mix has benefits and shortcomings, so often a combination of a few techniques works the best. A company should create compatible themes, tones, and quality across all communications tools and media to spread its unique selling points. This consistency achieves greater impact and prevents the unnecessary duplication of work across functions.

3.5 Evaluating the Effectiveness of the Communication Program

The final step in managing marketing communication is to decide whether the plan is working. It would be nice if a marketing manager could simply report, "The $3 million campaign for our revolutionary glow-in-the-dark surfboards brought in $15 million in new sales!" It's not so easy. There are many random factors in the marketing environment: a rival's manufacturing problem, a coincidental photograph of a movie star toting one of the boards, or perhaps a surge of renewed interest in surfing sparked by a cult movie hit like Blue Crush.

As a rule, various types of sales promotion are the easiest to evaluate because they occur over a fixed, usually short period, making it easier to link to sales volume. Advertising researchers measure brand awareness, recall of product benefits communicated through advertising, and even the image of the brand before and after an advertising campaign. The firm can analyze and compare the performance of salespeople in different territories, although again it is difficult to rule out other factors that make one salesperson more effective than another. Public relations activities are more difficult to assess because their objectives relate more often to image building than sales volume.

小　结

如今，越来越多的公司采用整合营销传播的理念，其具体步骤如下：首先，识别目标顾客。其次，明确沟通目标。告知式沟通寻求将一个现有的需要变为需求或诱发对新产品的兴趣。说服式沟通的目的是刺激购买或行动。提醒式沟通用来保持产品和品牌在公众心目中的地位。再其次，决定和分配营销预算。可以采用自上而下和自下而上两种预算技术；接下来,设计促销组合,包括确定促销策略(推动策略还是拉动策略)、特定的促销工具、什么样的促销信息,以及具体的沟通渠道。最后,评估营销传播的效果。

New Words and Key Terms

01. promotion	促销
02. personal selling	人员推销
03. advertising	广告
04. publicity	公共宣传
05. sales promotions	销售促进;营业推广
06. price deals and rebates	价格折扣和返款
07. samples	样品
08. coupons	优惠券
09. premiums	赠品
10. point-of-purchase (POP) promotions	卖场促销
11. contests	竞赛
12. sweepstakes	抽奖
13. continuity/loyalty programs	积分奖励计划
14. conventions and trade shows	会议和商业展览
15. push strategy	推动策略
16. pull strategy	拉动策略
17. Integrated Marketing Communication	整合营销传播
18. informative communication	告知式沟通
19. persuasive communication	说服式沟通
20. reminder communication	提醒式沟通
21. top-down budgeting techniques	自上而下预算技术
22. percentage-of-sales method	销售比例法
23. bottom-up budgeting techniques	自下而上预算技术
24. objective-task method	目标任务法

Writing:Advertisement

专门针对欧美男童而开发的电动玩具车——大男孩(BIG BOY)终于研制成功并即将登陆美国市场。为了保证该产品的销售效果,公司决定采取密集广告策略,并打算自己设计广告文案。于琪主动提出愿意为此做一些尝试。

一、广告写作的基本要求和格式

广告(Advertisement)是其发起者以公开支付费用的做法,以非人员的任何形式对产品、劳务或某项行动的意见和想法的介绍。按篇幅大小,广告可分为小广告(又称分类广告,

Classified Advertisement)和大广告(又称排印广告,Displayed Advertisement)。分类广告一般是指版面位置相对固定、篇幅较小的非工商广告。多数情况下"扎堆"出现,并按主题进行科学分类,以便于浏览者根据自身需要主动查找。排印广告一般是指来自工商企业的市场供求性商业广告,或为公众利益服务,旨在以倡导或警示等方式传播某种公益观念的非商业性广告。广告写作的目的是说服或提醒人们采取行动来满足某种需要和欲望。为了建立人们对广告产品或服务的认知,写作者首先要吸引人们的注意(Attention,简写为A),例如通过使用醒目的视觉效果和煽动性的语言。随后,广告写作者要努力使潜在消费者产生对该产品或服务的兴趣(Interest,简写为I)。接下来,通过提供充分的证据和原因使产生兴趣的潜在买家相信(Conviction,简写为C)企业对该产品或服务的宣传。进而,广告写作者使用激发想象的语言让消费者产生购买欲望(Desire,简写为D),并最终引领他们实施购买行动(Action,简写为A)。如果遵循以上的规则(亦称为AICDA),那么一个标准的由五部分构成的广告文案的结构如下(*号为可选项,口号的位置有时也出现在随文后)(表9-1)。

表9-1　　　　　　　　　　　　广告文案结构表

序号	结构内容	阶段效果	
1	标题	引起注意	A
2	副标题*	产生兴趣	I
3	正文	建立信心	C
4	口号*	挑动欲望	D
5	随文	促使行动	A

(一)标题(Headline)

标题是放在广告文案最前面的,起引导和提示作用的简短语句。标题作为广告的眼睛,要明确醒目,新颖生动,具有吸引力。下表列出了一些常用的标准广告标题(表9-2)。

表9-2　　　　　　　　　　　　常用标准广告标题

出租广告	FOR RENT	承租广告	WANTED TO RENT
求职广告	POSITIONS WANTED	招聘广告	HELP WANTED
售物广告	FOR SALE	宣传广告	常以要宣传的产品或公司名称作标题

在广告写作中,既可以采用这些标准标题,亦可独创。例如,同样是出租校园内房屋的广告,"BEST ON CAMPUS"就比"FOR RENT"更有冲击力。再如,某钻石饰品的广告标题,"How big is your love for her?"(你对她的爱有多深?)采用疑问句式吸引消费者的注意和兴趣。又如,摩尔香烟的广告标题,"I am More satisfied."(我更加满意)。比较级 more 的运用既强调了吸摩尔香烟的舒适,同时又与香烟品牌一语双关。标题通常不会太长,但也有例外的情况。例如,某戒烟公益广告标题,"If people keep telling you to quit smoking, don't listen... They're probably trying to trick you into living longer."(如果有人劝你戒烟,千万别听……他们可能想诱使你活得更长)。正话反说的方式,发笑之余让人深思。

（二）正文（Body）

国外学者曾经概括出这样一个广告文案创作公式,即 KISS 公式（Keep It Simple and Sweet),意为"令其简洁并甜美"。和其他文体相比,广告对语言的简洁性提出了更加严格的要求。广告文案要求摒弃任何无关的、无用的信息。即使是有用的信息也要分清主次,抓住要点。同时,句子的写作要尽量简单明了,可以不使用完整的句子。对于分类广告,甚至连单词也要尽可能地采取简写形式。表 9-3 列出了一些分类广告中常用单词的简写形式。

表 9-3　　　　　　　　　　　常用单词简写表

简写形式	完整拼写	中文含义	简写形式	完整拼写	中文含义
apt	apartment	公寓	Xmas	Christmas	圣诞节
Jan	January	一月	mon	month	月份
sgle	single	单人	even	evening	晚上
dble	double	双人	Sts	Streets	街道
bdrm	bedroom	卧室	expwy	express way	高速公路
furn	furniture	家具	P/T	part time	非全日
gar	garage	车库	F/T	full time	全日
ht	heating	供暖	EXP	experienced	有经验的
incl	including	包含	btwn	between	在……之间
A/C	alternating current	交流的	M/F	Monday through Friday	星期一至星期五

除了文字精练,保证广告甜美的要领则是要打动人心。当然,打动人心有许多方法和途径。有切中消费者需求和欲望的,可称之为利益打动（Rational Advertising）。还可以通过煽起消费者强烈的情感体验,可称之为情感打动（Emotional Advertising）。同时,为了强化广告的视觉效果并增加冲击力,对于分类广告通常要把正文部分前几个重点词大写并加黑。对于排印广告,还可采用图片和色彩等艺术处理手段。例如,某承租分类广告的正文,"2-BDRM PLACE wanted. Hopefully under 180/mon. Thanks. 800-1234."（拟租有两间卧室的住所,月租希望在 180 美元以下,谢谢。电话 800-1234。）

（三）口号（Slogan）

广告口号又称广告语,是为表达企业理念或产品特征而长期使用的宣传短句。虽然在个别情况下可以用口号作为标题,但标题和口号仍然存在着较大的区别。首先,广告标题的基本功能是诱导和吸引受众阅读正文;而广告语则是对企业个性或产品特征进行人性化的概括,侧重于如何用最精练的语言沟通物性与人性,它强调信息的穿透力（打动人心的力量）。其次,标题对音律的要求不严格,个别情况下为传达一个准确的信息也不得不长一点;而广告语更讲究顺口、流畅、言简意赅,易读易记,更讲究句子的锤炼、词语的推敲和音韵的和谐。再有,广告标题的效用比较短暂,一般只用于一个广告作品中;而广告语是企业长期使用的宣传口号,因而"富有持久的鼓动性和号召力",在同一产品不同的广告作品中被反复使用,甚至是同一企业不同产品的广告也使用统一的企业形象广告语。例如,麦斯威尔咖啡的经典广告口号,"Good to the last drop"（滴滴香浓,意犹未尽）。又如,摩托罗拉手机的经典广告口号,"Communication unlimited"（沟通无极限）。口号是广告中最体现创意的地方,某鸡蛋销售商的广告口号——"We know eggsactly how to sell eggs"(我们完全懂得如何销售鸡蛋)甚至使用了自造词。利用 eggsactly 和 exactly 之间的谐音,既突出了产品,又宣传了销售理念。

(四)随文(Supplementary Items)

在广告文案中,最后的这一部分称为随文,以方便消费者与企业的直接沟通和联系。随文中应注明通信地址、电传、电话、邮箱等联系方式,也可包含一些附加信息。例如 Ramada Hotel 宣传广告随文,To honor your presence, we are offering a 20% reduction of all room rates until the end of May, 2005. Booking is easy, please call our Sales and Reservations Office at (850)27330398. 为欢迎您的光临,我们对所有房间费用实行 20%的优惠,截止日期为 2005 年 5 月末。预订非常方便,拨打我们的预约电话(850)27330398 即可。

二、于琪的解决方案(随文略)

How Big Is Your Love for Him?

YOUR KIDS ARE AMAZING—especially compared with everybody else's (who seem to cry all the time). How do you show your love for your kids this holiday season? With toys that are smooth and colorful, interactive and exciting. And with ones that have educational value—because you are the boss.

BIG BOY is an electric toy car designed for kids to experience the riding fun and boost his hand-eye coordination at the same time. The multifunctional steering wheel can play music. With over-current protection, this kiddie car makes a great toy for your little one.

BIG BOY Electric Toy Car,
The envy of your kid's friends!

Review Questions

1. **Key Terms**

Samples; Coupons; Push strategy; Pull strategy; Percentage-of-sales method

2. **Multiple Choices (select one)**

(1) Any form of paid communications in which a sponsor or company is identified is the definition of (   ).

    A. advertising   B. the promotional mix

    C. sales promotion   D. publicity

(2) Through which element of the promotional mix does the communication sender receive the greatest amount of feedback? (   )

    A. Advertising.   B. Personal selling.

    C. Public relations.   D. Sales promotion.

(3) Influencing customers to buy a product now is accomplished by (   ) promotion.

A. informative   B. advocacy
C. persuasive   D. reminder

(4) Which of the elements of the promotional mix is most effective in stimulating action in the target market? ( )

A. Advertising.   B. Personal selling.
C. Sales promotion.   D. Public relations.

(5) Products with high value are usually best suited to use ( ) as the primary element of the promotional mix.

A. advertising   B. personal selling
C. sales promotion   D. public relations

(6) ( ) usually focuses on the name and prestige of an organization or industry.

A. Product advertising   B. Institutional advertising
C. Publicity   D. Media planning

(7) Which one is NOT the advantage of using personal selling as a means of promotion? ( )

A. Personal selling is a face-to-face activity.

B. The face-to-face sales meeting gives the sales force chance to demonstrate himself or herself.

C. The two-way nature of the sales process allows the sales team to respond directly and promptly to customer questions and concerns.

D. Personal selling is a good way of getting across large amounts of technical or other complex product information.

(8) Which of the following is NOT a buying signal? ( )

A. "Yes, it sounds really good to me, but..."

B. "I'd like to think about this for a while..."

C. "I hope you can close a sale next time..."

D. "I was thinking about getting these but with the new budget being approved..."

(9) Using a ( ), the producer directs its marketing activities toward channel members to induce them to carry the product and to promote it to final consumers.

A. push strategy   B. pull strategy
C. public relations   D. personal selling

(10) In terms of the effectiveness of different promotional tools, various types of ( ) are the easiest to evaluate because they occur over a fixed, usually short period, making it easier to link to sales volume.

A. advertising   B. personal selling
C. sales promotion   D. public relations

3. Questions for Discussion

(1) List the elements of the promotion mix and describe how they are used to deliver personal and mass appeals.

(2) Explain the difference between a "push" and "pull" promotional strategy. Under what conditions should each strategy be used?

(3) What is IMC? How is IMC different from traditional promotion strategies? How do marketers evaluate the effectiveness of their communication programs?

Practical Writing

Scenario: There is a kindergarten in your hometown and you are asked to write a *Displayed Advertisement* for it. In the advertisement, you have to provide such information as the special features of the kindergarten (the location, the commuting, the facility, the faculties, service, etc.), the fees it charges, and the contacting way. Meanwhile, the kindergarten needs a part-time worker to do some cleaning half day per week, and asks you to write a *Classified Advertisement* as well. Please make up all the necessary information.

Unit 10　Smoothies Hit the Shelves

Learning Objectives

◇ 熟悉渠道选择的常用口语表达；
◇ 理解营销渠道的含义和消费品与工业品营销渠道的基本类型；
◇ 理解影响渠道设计的因素、渠道成员之间的关系类型，以及不同的渠道选择策略；
◇ 理解渠道冲突的含义、类型，以及渠道成员激励、评价的基本方法；
◇ 掌握营销策划书的书写规则和常用套语的正确写法。

Speaking: Selecting Marketing Channels

【场景1】金色童年推出的奶昔已经开始投入生产了，这是公司首次经营食品类产品。在分销渠道的选择上，营销部里产生了分歧。
【对话1】　A：销售经理马天跃　　B：Joan Mitchell 女士　　C：Tony Lin 先生

A: Normally we find wholesalers to distribute our products and leave a mark-up for them, typically around 30% of the cost. The wholesaler deals with the logistics of the products and reports the sales figure to us on a regular basis.
通常我们会让批发商来分销我们的产品，给他们留出一部分价格加成，一般来说是价格的30%左右。批发商会处理商品的物流运输，并每隔一段时间向我们报告销售情况。

B: Well, I think it's a big deduction from our margins. Why don't we try going straight to the retailers? It saves us a lot of distributing costs.
嗯，我认为这是从我们的利润中分走了一大笔钱呀。为什么我们不尝试直接面向零售商呢？这可省去不少分销的费用呀。

A: Yes, that's what I want to discuss with you. Direct distribution to retailers is really an economical way but we should devote a great deal of time and energy to determining our retailers. You know, if we sold the products to someone with bad reputation or poor after-sales service, we would ruin our own reputation.
是的，这正是我想跟你们讨论的。直接分销给零售商是一个很省钱的方法，但我们要花很多时间和下大力气去决定零售商的人选。你要知道,如果我们把产品分销给一个信誉差或售后服务不佳的零售商,就等于是自毁声誉呀。

C: I happened to have some reliable retailers in hand. We can get in touch with them about the new proposal of distribution. But one thing I want to mention here is that they are also engaged in distribution work for many other manufacturers.

我手头正好有一些可靠的零售商。我们可以跟他们联系一下新的分销方案。但有一件事我想要说,他们也在分销很多其他厂商的商品。

A: Yeah, it poses a problem to us. If the distributors are not committed themselves in our products, the turnover may be not satisfying at the end of the year.

是的,这对我们来说确实是个问题。如果分销商不能完全投入到我们产品的销售中来,那么到年底,销售额可能不会让人满意。

B: Sorry to interrupt. I don't see this problem in this way. Our products are targeted at high-end of the market and have distinguished features from other brands. When they are put together with other brands, customers would realize how excellent our products are. Obviously, it will reinforce the competitiveness of our products.

抱歉打断一下,我不这么看这个问题。我们的产品定位于高端市场,与其他品牌有着很明显的区别。当它们与其他品牌放在一起时,顾客会意识到我们的产品有多么好。很明显,这个有利于增强我们产品的竞争力。

A: Well, this is a good point.

嗯,你说得不错。

B: May I suggest something? I think we could adopt some favorable policies to encourage the retailers to sell our products.

我能建议一下吗?我觉得我们应该采取一些优惠政策来鼓励零售商销售我们的产品。

A: Could you give us an example?

你能举个例子吗?

B: Yeah, we can offer trade allowance to give retailers free goods, such as one free case for every ten ordered, or deduct specified amounts from their invoice, say 5%, if they order certain quantities. We can also give retail salespeople push money for every unit of our product they sell, which increases the likelihood that the salesperson will try to convince a consumer to buy our product rather than a competing brand.

好的,我们可以以商业折让的形式向零售商提供免费商品,比如每订购十箱就有一箱免费,或者如果他们订购一定数量的商品,我们可以从他们的发票中扣除规定的金额,比如说5%。我们还可以为零售店销售人员每销售一件商品提供销售提成,这将增加销售人员试图说服顾客购买我们的产品而不是竞争品牌的可能性。

A: Sounds great. But I don't think we have to go for one at one time. Why don't we plan the sales channel through both of the two ways? Partly we send the products to our long-standing wholesalers, which can assure us of the basis sales volume. And partly we go through our reliable retailers at hand so that we can save the time and energy to find suitable retailers and save some costs.

听起来不错。但我觉得我们不一定二者必居其一。为什么我们不通过两种途径同时销售呢？我们将部分商品通过长期合作的批发商来出货，这就可以保证我们基本的销量。另一部分商品从我们手头可靠的零售商那儿出货，这样我们就可以节省找合适的零售商所花的时间和精力了，还能节省成本。

C：Excuse me for interrupting. But I don't think the wholesalers would be for this strategy. If the retailers get a relatively low price directly from us, how can the wholesalers make a profit from distribution? I don't think they are willing to give in at this point.

抱歉打断一下。但我觉得批发商可能不会赞成这种策略。如果零售商从我们这儿以一个较低的价格拿货，那批发商如何从分销工作中赚到钱呢？我认为他们是不会在这一点上妥协的。

A：That's true. However, I think we can figure out a way to compromise the interest of both parties, can't we?

是的。但是，我觉得我们可以找一种方法来中和双方的利益，不是吗？

【场景2】 对于奶昔产品，公司最终决定采取批发和零售两种途径同时销售。于琪已经和 Tony Lin 先生手头掌握的一家信誉好的零售商——某大型连锁超市的负责人 Erick Garcia 通过了电话。这天一早，他如约来到 Erick 的办公室。

【对话2】 A：于琪　B：某超市负责人 Erick Garcia 先生

A：Hello, Erick.

你好，埃里克。

B：Hello, Qi. Nice to see you here again.

你好，琪。很高兴在这里又见到你。

A：Glad to see you, too. As I told you on the phone, today I am here to introduce you one of our new products, the Golden Childhood Smoothie. I've brought some samples. Would you like to have a taste?

我也很高兴见到你。就像我在电话里谈到的，今天我到这儿来是向你推荐一款我们的新产品——金色童年奶昔。我带来了一些样品，你愿意品尝一下吗？

B：Yes, of course. (Drinking a bottle of smoothie)

是的，当然。（品尝一罐奶昔）

A：How do you like it?

你觉得它怎么样？

B：It's cool, I should say. What is it made from?

非常好，我不得不承认。它是由什么做的？

A：The main ingredients are fresh fruit, low-fat milk, and mint. That's why it gives out such a nice and refreshing fragrance. It is also full of vitamin C and other kinds of nutrition. What's more, it's sugar free and helps to keep people fit. I'm sure you'll make a great profit soon if you put it on your shelves.

该产品的主要原料是新鲜水果、低脂牛奶和薄荷。那就是为什么它能释放出如此美好和清新的芳香的原因。它也富含维生素 C 和其他营养成分。此外，本产品不含糖，能保证人体健康。我确信，一旦你将本品上架，一定会获得丰厚的利润。

B: But the problem is our customers are not familiar with it. Do you know how many strong competitors you've already got at our market?

但问题是我们的顾客对该产品并不熟悉。你知道在市场上已经出现了多少强有力的竞争对手吗？

A: Well, just as what you've tasted, our product is really unique in its flavor and you know our company also enjoys a good reputation for the quality of its products. You can put it together with other items from our company and feature it.

嗯，就像你所品尝到的，我们的产品具有非常独特的口感，并且你也清楚我们公司的产品质量享有很好的口碑。你可以将本品和我们公司的其他产品摆放在一起，做成特色。

B: Still we have to make strenuous efforts to promote a new item. So I think it's reasonable for us to claim a slotting fee of 50,000 yuan. Do you agree?

我们仍然需要花费很大的努力去推销一款新产品。因此，我认为收取 5 万元的进场费是比较合理的。你觉得呢？

A: Well, Erick, you are really driving a hard bargain today. We have never heard a slotting fee like that before. I think 30,000 yuan is more acceptable.

嗯，埃里克，你今天的条件实在是太苛刻了。我们以前从未听过像你提出的进场费。我觉得 3 万元是一个更容易接受的价格。

B: To tell you the truth, we now claim a slotting fee no less than 38,000 yuan.

老实说，我们现在收取进场费不会低于 3.8 万元。

A: OK, I agree to that. How much shelf space can you offer us, then?

好吧，我同意这个数额。那么，你能提供给我们多少货架空间呢？

B: Half of a shelf on the main aisle.

主要通道上的半个货架。

A: That's not bad.

不错。

B: What about the price?

产品价格是多少？

A: The list price is 180 yuan per box. Each box contains a dozen. However, with a view to supporting your sales, you can have it at the price of 150 yuan per box.

产品标价是每箱 180 元。内含 12 罐。但为了支持你们的销售，你们可以每箱以 150 元拿货。

B：What kind of sales rebate can you offer us, then?

那么,你能给我们什么样的销售折扣呢?

A：It depends on the sales volume. If you can reach a turnover beyond 200,000 yuan, you will get a 5% of rebate.

这取决于销售量。如果你们能超过 20 万元的成交量,将会得到 5% 的销售折扣。

B：Sounds attractive. How should we arrange for the payment?

听起来很吸引人。我们如何付款呢?

A：Just as usual business practice, we expect you to pay us 30 days after delivery at latest.

像通常的商业惯例一样,发送货物后最迟 30 天付款。

B：Good. It's settled, then.

好的。那么就这么定吧。

Reading: Formulating Channel Strategies

营销渠道到底是企业的伙伴还是分割企业利润的一分子?如何合理地对营销渠道进行设计和管理?这些问题让于琪困惑迷惘。

Chapter 10 Channel Strategies

Section 1 Types of Distribution Channels

A channel of distribution or marketing channel is a sequence of marketing organizations that directs a product from the producer to the ultimate user. Every marketing channel begins with the producer and ends with either the consumer or industrial user. Marketing organizations that link producer and user within a marketing channel are called middlemen or marketing intermediaries. A merchant middleman (or, more simply, a merchant) is a middleman that actually takes title to products by buying them. A functional middleman, on the other hand, helps in the transfer of ownership of products but does not take title to the products.

1.1 Consumer Channels

The channels used for consumer products include: the direct channel from producer to consumer; the channel from producer to retailer to consumer; the channel from producer to wholesaler to retailer to consumer and that from producer to agent to wholesaler to retailer to consumer. The producer-wholesaler-retailer-consumer channel is a common distribution channel in consumer marketing. Take ice cream for example. A single ice-cream factory supplies, say, four or five regional wholesalers. These wholesalers then sell to 400 or more retailers such as grocery stores. The retailers, in turn, each sell the ice cream to thousands of customers. Because the regional wholesalers combine many manufacturers' products to supply grocery stores and the grocery stores do business with many wholesalers, this arrangement results in a broad selection of products.

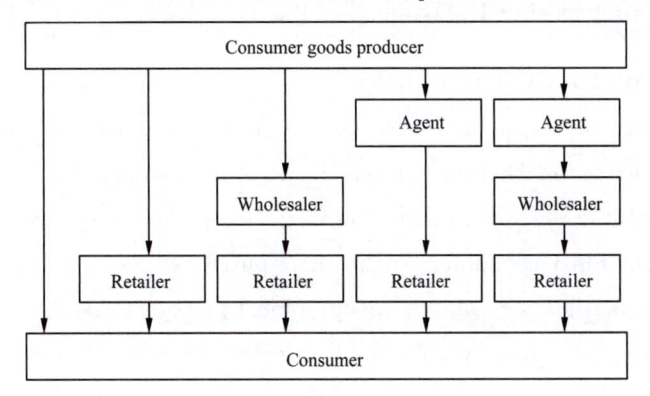

Figure 10.1　Marketing Channels for Consumer Products

1.2 Business-to-Business Channels

The major channels for industrial products are producer to user, producer to industrial distributor to user, and producer to agent to user. Direct channels are more common to business-to-business markets than to consumer markets. This is because business-to-business marketing often means a firm sells high-dollar, high-profit items (a single piece of industrial equipment may cost hundreds of thousands of dollars) to a market made up of only a few customers. In such markets, it makes sense financially for a company to develop its own sales force and sell directly to customers—in this case the investment in in-house sales force pays off.

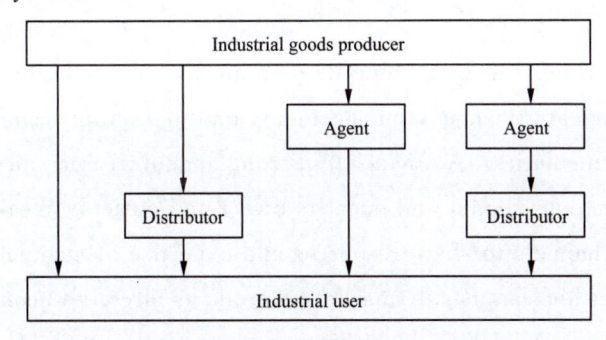

Figure 10.2　Marketing Channels for Industrial Products

小 结

分销渠道或营销渠道是指一系列的将产品从生产者转移到最终消费者的营销组织。在营销渠道范围内,联系生产者和用户的市场组织叫作中间商或市场中间人。商业中间商(或简称商人)是指实际通过购买产品而取得产品所有权的商人。职能性中间商协助产品所有权的转移,但却不取得产品所有权。用于消费品的销售渠道包括:由生产商到消费者的直接渠道、由生产商经批发商和零售商再到消费者的渠道，以及由生产商经代理商、批发商和零售商再到消费者的渠道。而用于工业产品的销售渠道主要是从生产商到用户的直接渠道，由生产商经经销商再到用户的渠道，以及由生产商经代理商和经销商再到用户的渠道。

Section 2 Channel Design Decisions

2.1 Factors Affecting Channel Choice

A variety of factors impact the selection of a marketing channel. Some channel decisions are dictated by the marketplace in which the company operates. Business purchasers usually prefer to deal directly with manufacturers (except for routine supplies or small accessory items), but most consumers make their purchases from retailers. Other market factors include the market's needs, its geographical location, and its average order size. To serve a concentrated market with a small number of buyers, a direct channel offers a feasible alternative. To serve a geographically dispersed potential market in which customers purchase small amounts in individual transactions—the conditions in the consumer goods market—distribution through marketing intermediaries makes sense.

Product characteristics also guide the choice of an optimal marketing channel strategy. Perishable goods, such as fresh fruit and vegetables, seasonal goods like swimsuits and fashion products with short life cycles, typically move through short channels, since getting the product to the final user quickly is a priority. Longer channels with more intensive distribution are generally best for inexpensive, standardized consumer goods that need to be distributed broadly and that require little technical expertise. Complex products, such as custom-made installations and computer equipment, are often sold directly to ultimate buyers.

The organization must also examine its own ability to handle distribution functions. Companies with adequate financial, management, and marketing resources feel little need for help from intermediaries. A financially strong manufacturer can hire its own sales force, warehouse its own goods, and open its own retail outlets. Weaker companies have to opt for indirect channels to share resources and expertise of channel members. A firm with a broad product line can usually market its products directly to consumers or business users since high sales volume spreads selling costs over a large number of items. Single-product firms often view direct selling as unaffordable. The manufacturer's desire for control over marketing of its product also influences channel selection. If a company desires to have direct and close control over production and selling activities, direct channels are preferred and vice-versa.

2.2 Deciding about Channel Relationships

Participants in any distribution channel form an interrelated system. In general, these marketing systems take one of three forms: conventional, vertical, or horizontal. A conventional marketing system is a multilevel distribution channel in which members work independently of one another. Their relationships are limited to simply buying and selling from one another. Each firm seeks to benefit, with little concern for other channel members. Even though channel members work independently, most conventional channels are highly successful. For one thing, all members of the channel work toward the same goals—to build demand, reduce costs, and improve customer satisfaction. And each channel member knows that it's in everyone's best interest to treat other channel members fairly.

A vertical marketing system (VMS) is a channel in which there is formal cooperation among channel members at two or more different levels: manufacturing, wholesaling, and retailing. Firms develop vertical marketing systems as a way to meet customer needs better by reducing costs incurred in channel activities. Often, a vertical marketing system can provide a level of cooperation and efficiency not possible with a conventional channel, maximizing the effectiveness of the channel while also maximizing efficiency and keeping costs low. Members share information and provide services for other members; they recognize that such coordination makes everyone more successful when they want to reach a desired target market. In turn there are three types of vertical marketing systems: administered, corporate, and contractual.

In an administered VMS, channel members remain independent but voluntarily work together because of the power of a single channel member. Strong brands are able to manage an administered VMS because resellers are eager to work with the manufacturer so they will be allowed to carry the product. In a corporate VMS, a single firm owns manufacturing, wholesaling, and retailing operations. Thus, the firm has complete control over all channel operations. Retail giant Sears, for example, owns a nationwide network of distribution centers and retail stores. In a contractual VMS, cooperation is enforced by contracts (legal agreements) that spell out each member's rights and responsibilities and how they will cooperate. This arrangement means that the channel members can have more impact as a group than they could alone.

In a horizontal marketing system, two or more firms at the same channel level agree to work together to get their product to the customer. Sometimes unrelated businesses forge these agreements. For example, many 7-Eleven locations feature a Citibank Vcom electronic banking kiosk complete with ATM services, check cashing, bill paying, and Western Union money transfers. 7-Eleven leases the space to Citibank, and customers like it because they can do their shopping and their banking in one stop.

2.3 Choosing Distribution Intensity

How many wholesalers and retailers should carry the product within a given market? If the product goes to too many outlets, there may be inefficiency and duplication of efforts. For example, if there are too many Honda dealerships in town, there will be a lot of unsold Hondas sitting on dealer lots and no single dealer will be successful. But if there are not enough wholesalers or retailers to carry a product, this will fail to maximize total sales of the manufacturer's products (and its profits). If customers have to drive hundreds of miles to find a Honda dealer, they may instead opt for a Toyota, Mazda, or Nissan. Thus, a distribution objective may be to either increase or decrease the level of distribution in the market. The three basic choices are intensive, exclusive, and selective distribution.

Intensive distribution aims to maximize market coverage by selling a product through all wholesalers or retailers that will stock and sell the product. Marketers use intensive distribution for products such as chewing gum, soft drinks, milk, and bread that consumers quickly consume and must replace frequently. Intensive distribution is necessary for these products because availability is more important than any other consideration in customers' purchase decisions.

In contrast to intensive distribution, exclusive distribution means to limit distribution to a single outlet in a particular region. Marketers often sell pianos, cars, executive training programs, television programs, and many other products with high price tags through exclusive distribution arrangements. They typically use these strategies with products that are high-priced and have considerable service requirements, and when a limited number of buyers exist in any single geographic area. Exclusive distribution enables wholesalers and retailers to better recoup the costs associated with long-selling processes for each customer and, in some cases, extensive after-sales service.

Finally, we call market coverage that is less than intensive distribution but more than exclusive distribution selective distribution. This model fits when demand is so large that exclusive distribution is inadequate, but selling costs, service requirements, or other factors make intensive distribution a poor fit. Selective distribution strategies are suitable for so-called shopping products, such as household appliances and electronic equipment for which consumers are willing to spend time visiting different retail outlets to compare alternatives. For producers, selective distribution means freedom to choose only those wholesalers and retailers that have a good credit rating, provide good market coverage, serve customers well, and cooperate effectively. Wholesalers and retailers like selective distribution because it results in higher profits than are possible with intensive distribution, in which sellers often have to compete on price.

小 结

各种因素会影响营销渠道的选择。首先,渠道决策要受企业所处市场的影响,包括购买者类型、市场的需求、地理位置、平均订单大小等因素。其次,产品特点也会影响渠道的选择。易腐品、季节产品,以及生命周期短的时尚产品通常选择短通道,密集分销的长渠道更适合廉价、标准化的消费品,而复杂的产品往往是直接销售给最终买家。企业还必须检查自己的能力来优化营销渠道决策。同时,渠道成员构成了一个营销系统,他们之间的关系可能有三种情况。传统的营销系统是一个由彼此独立工作的成员构成的多级分销渠道。垂直营销系统中渠道成员之间在两个或两个以上不同层次上正式合作。而在水平营销系统中,两个或两个以上同一渠道层次的公司同意一起工作将他们的产品送达客户。最后,对于渠道策略的选择,密集分销的目的是最大限度地提高市场覆盖率;独家分销是将分销限制在一个特定区域的单一经销商;而当需求很大,独家分销不够,但销售成本、服务要求或其他因素使密集分销不适合时通常采用选择分销的方式。

Section 3 Channel Management Decisions

3.1 Channel Conflict

Ideally, because the success of individual channel members depends on overall channel success, all channel firms should work together smoothly. They should understand and accept their roles, coordinate their activities, and cooperate to attain overall channel goals. However, individual channel members rarely take such a broad cooperative view. Cooperating to achieve overall channel goals sometimes means giving up individual company goals. Although channel members depend on one another, they often act alone in their own short-run best interests. They often disagree on who should do what and for what rewards. Such disagreements over goals, roles, and rewards generate channel conflict.

Horizontal conflict occurs among firms at the same level of the channel. This often happens to economies in which regional distributors have different cost structures (due to varying provincial or regional government levies, fees) in selling the same products. Accordingly, the lower cost distributors willingly price their products lower and sell outside of their assigned territories. Horizontal conflict may also happen in franchise chains. Holiday Inn franchisees might complain about other Holiday Inn operators overcharging guests or giving poor service, hurting the overall Holiday Inn image.

Vertical conflict, conflict between different levels of the same channel, is even more common. For example, McDonald's may create conflict with some of its dealers if it placed new stores in areas that took business from existing locations. A few years ago, United Airlines tried to stimulate its sales by selling directly to consumers in China Hong

Kong—it gave significant mileage bonuses and price discounts directly to them without proper coordination with Hong Kong travel agents. In return, the travel agents protested by refusing to sell United Airlines tickets. Seeing the dramatic decline in sales, United Airlines reverted to the old agent distribution system.

Some conflict in the channel takes the form of healthy competition. Such competition can be good for the channel—without it, the channel could become passive and non-innovative. But severe or prolonged conflict can disrupt channel effectiveness and cause lasting harm to channel relationships. Companies should manage channel conflict to keep it from getting out of hand. This is especially salient in Asian markets where multiple channels are usually the norm.

3.2 Motivating and Evaluating Channel Members

Once selected, channel members must be continuously managed and motivated to do their best. The company must sell not only through the intermediaries but to and with them. Most companies see their intermediaries as first-line customers and partners. They practice strong partner relationship management (PRM) to forge long-term partnerships with channel members. High intermediary profit margins, training programs, cooperative advertising, and expert marketing advice are invisible to end customers but are motivating factors in the eyes of wholesalers and retailers. Haggar Apparel, for example, finds ways to help its retail channel partners—especially the smaller ones—become more successful. By improving the speed and accuracy of reorders, retailers are able to maintain inventory levels necessary to satisfy customers while avoiding ordering errors.

Meanwhile, the producer must regularly check channel member performance against standards such as sales quotas, average inventory levels, customer delivery time, treatment of damaged and lost goods, cooperation in company promotion and training programs, and services to the customer. The company should recognize and reward intermediaries who are performing well and adding good value for consumers. Those who are performing poorly should be assisted or, as a last resort, replaced. A company may periodically "requalify" its intermediaries and prune the weaker ones. Finally, manufacturers need to be sensitive to their dealers. Those who treat their dealers poorly risk not only losing dealer support but also causing some legal problems.

小 结

渠道成员对目标、角色和回报的不一致产生了渠道冲突。水平渠道冲突发生在渠道内同一层级的公司之间。垂直渠道冲突是渠道中不同层级之间的冲突。渠道内的有些冲突是有好处的——没有竞争,渠道会变得过于消极和缺乏创造力。但是严重的或者过久的冲突就会破坏渠道的有效性,并对渠道关系产生持久的损害。因此,选定渠道成员以后,公司应该对他们进行持续的管理与激励,以保证他们处于最佳的工作状态。公司应将中间商看作自己的第一线顾客和伙伴。通过实施强有力的合作伙伴关系管理同渠道成员打造长期的合作伙伴关系。同时,制造商还要定期对渠道成员的销售定额、平均存货水平、客户交付速度、损毁及丢失产品的处理、对公司促销和培训项目的配合以及售后服务等方面进行检查,以确定他们在这些方面是否符合标准。

New Words and Key Terms

01.	channel of distribution	分销渠道
02.	merchant middleman	商业中间商
03.	functional middleman	功能中间商
04.	retailer	零售商
05.	wholesaler	批发商
06.	conventional marketing system	传统营销系统
07.	vertical marketing system	垂直营销系统
08.	administered VMS	管理式垂直营销系统
09.	corporate VMS	公司式垂直营销系统
10.	contractual VMS	合同式垂直营销系统
11.	horizontal marketing system	水平营销系统
12.	intensive distribution	密集分销
13.	exclusive distribution	独家分销
14.	selective distribution	选择分销
15.	channel conflict	渠道冲突
16.	horizontal conflict	水平冲突
17.	vertical conflict	垂直冲突
18.	partner relationship management	伙伴关系管理

Writing: Marketing Plan

　　金色童年推出的奶昔虽然口感好,但毕竟公司以前从未经营过食品类的产品。为确保上市后能够获得成功,总经理交代营销部提供策划方案并编制营销策划书。

一、营销策划书写作的基本要求和格式

　　营销策划书(Marketing Plan)是对企业在一定时期内的营销活动方针、目标、战略以及实施方案进行的设计和计划。营销策划书正文通常包括如下内容:

　　(一)概要(Executive Summary)

　　概要是对企业主要营销目标和措施进行的简短概括,目的是使管理部门迅速了解计划的主要内容,抓住计划的要点。概要有时也可省略。

(二)使命陈述(Mission Statement)

使命陈述用于回答"我们公司从事何种业务"这一问题。例如,Our company is in the business of providing advanced communications technology and communications convenience to mobile users. 我们公司致力于向手机用户提供先进的通信技术和通信便利。

(三)当前营销状况或风险机会分析(Situation or SWOT Analysis)

通过分析企业目前营销状况的背景资料,包括市场、产品、竞争、分销以及宏观环境状况等因素,归纳出企业所面临的外部机会和威胁,以及自身存在的优势和劣势。

1. 优势(Strength)

例如,Highly skilled workforce with low turnover, excellent relationships with suppliers. 低跳槽率的高级技能劳动力,与供应商的良好的关系。

2. 劣势(Weakness)

例如,No long-term contracts with distributors, inexperience in the wireless communications market. 与经销商没有长期合同,无线通信市场上缺乏经验。

3. 机会(Opportunity)

例如,Explosive growth of wireless phone users, newly available digital networks. 无线电话用户的爆炸式增长,新的数字网络的出现。

4. 威胁(Threat)

例如,Heavy competition, potential governmental regulation. 激烈的竞争,潜在的政府法规。

(四)目标(Objective)

目标是指通过营销活动所要达到的效果,可设立总目标、阶段目标、长期目标和短期目标。目标要可衡量并有时限性,例如,To achieve 20 percent, in dollar volume, of the wireless telephone market by year-end. 到年末,销售额达到无线电话市场的20%。

(五)营销战略(Marketing Strategy)

1. 目标市场的选择和定位战略(Target Market Strategy)

即企业准备服务于哪个或哪几个细分市场,如何进行市场定位,确定何种市场形象。例如,Young, mobile executives in North America and Europe, with incomes over $200,000 per year. 年薪20万美元以上的年轻的北美和欧洲的移动高管。

2. 营销组合战略(Marketing Mix Strategy)

即企业在其目标市场上拟采取的具体营销战略,包括产品、渠道、定价和促销等方面。以促销战略为例,Fifty manufacturer's representatives for selling force, with 25 percent commissions; advertising in print media, cable television, and outdoor billboards; sales promotion in the form of product rebates, technology trade shows; public relations efforts to news media and sponsorship of world-championship sporting events. 50个厂商代表组成销售队伍,享受25%的佣金;在印刷媒体、有线电视、户外广告牌上做广告;以产品折扣和科技展览会的形式进行销售促进;对新闻媒体开展公关以及对世界锦标赛进行赞助。

(六)行动方案(Implementation or Action Plan)

阐述每项营销活动何时开始、何时完成、由谁来做、如何来做等,使整个营销战略落实于行动,循序渐进地贯彻执行。例如,First quarter: Complete marketing research on price, design promotional campaign, sign contracts with manufacturers reps (Responsible Party: ××). Second quarter: Public relations campaign, product introduction at trade shows, rollout of advertising... 第一季度:完成关于价格的市场调研,设计促销方案,与生产商代表签订合同(负责人:××)。第二季度:开展公关,展销会产品介绍,首次播放广告……

(七)营销预算(Budget)

预算是采购、生产、人事安排、营销运营的基础。以广告费用预算为例:

Media	Estimated Quantity	Estimated Cost per Unit	Estimated Subtotal
Brochures	5000	USD 0.15	USD 750.00
Television	2	USD 600.00	USD 1,200.00
Newspapers	6	USD 220.00	USD 1,320.00
Magazines	2	USD 300.00	USD 600.00
Total			USD 3,870.00

(八)营销控制(Control)

审查企业各部门的业务实绩,找出未达到预期目标的部门及原因,并提出改进措施,以争取实现既定目标。例如,To keep implementation results in files and compare with the plan quarterly. 记录执行结果并将执行结果与策划书按季度进行对照。

二、于琪的解决方案

Marketing Plan of Golden Childhood Co., Ltd.

Business Mission	Golden Childhood seeks to meet the needs of discriminating, health-conscious consumers for high-quality, superior-tasting smoothie beverages and other similar products.
Situation Analysis	
Strengths	◇ A high-quality product recipe that provides exceptional flavor with high levels of nutrition; ◇ A strong network of distributors.
Weaknesses	◇ Limited financial resources for advertising and other marketing communications; ◇ Less experience in producing and marketing food products.
Opportunities	◇ A strong and growing interest in healthy living, among both young, upscale consumers and older consumers; ◇ Continuing consumer interest in low-carb alternatives that offers opportunities for additional product lines.
Threats	◇ A major economic downturn that might affect potential sales; ◇ Increase in market for energy drinks like Rockstar, Red Bull etc.
Marketing Objectives	To increase the awareness of Golden Childhood Smoothie products among the target market and achieve 20% market share and an average of 5 million yuan in annual sales over the next three years.

(续表)

Marketing Strategies	
Target Market	◇ Demographics: male and female teens and young adults (Gender); 15-39 (Ages); $50,000 and above (Household income); college degree or above (Education of head of household). ◇ Psychographics: Health-conscious, interested in living a healthy lifestyle; Enjoy holidays that include physical activities.
Positioning Strategy	Golden Childhood will position its products as the first-choice smoothie for the serious health-conscious consumer, including those who are seeking to lower their carbohydrate intake.
Product Strategy	Golden Childhood will introduce two new product lines, each identifiable through unique packaging and labeling: Smoothie Gold, a product in six unique flavors; Low-Carb Smoothie, a product with 50 percent fewer grams of carbohydrates.
Pricing Strategy	Golden Childhood will charge high prices to communicate a high-quality product image.
Promotion Strategy	Golden Childhood will augment personal selling efforts with television and magazine advertising, with sponsorships of marathons in major cities, and with a sampling program.
Distribution Strategy	Golden Childhood will expand its existing wholesaler distribution network to include supermarkets, hotels and resorts, golf and tennis clubs, and college campuses.
Implementation	To be developed by marketing department soon.
Budget	10% of annual sales.
Control	Golden Childhood needs to keep implementation results in files and compare with the plan quarterly, which will allow Golden Childhood to take corrective action when necessary.

Review Questions

1. **Key Terms**

Functional middleman; Conventional marketing system; Corporate VMS; Intensive distribution; Vertical conflict

2. **Multiple Choices (select one)**

(1) Which of the following is NOT another name for a channel member? (   )

A. Intermediary.　　　　　　　　B. Reseller.

C. Middleman.　　　　　　　　　D. None of the above.

(2) Marketing channels overcome (   ) by maintaining inventories in anticipation of future demand for products.

A. discrepancies of quantity　　　B. discrepancies of assortment

C. temporal discrepancies　　　　D. spatial discrepancies

(3) Channels can help simplify distribution by reducing the number of transactions re-

quired to get products from manufacturers to consumers. This function is (   ).

A. providing specialization of labor　　B. providing division of labor

C. overcoming discrepancies　　D. providing contact efficiency

(4) Which of the following types of channels would most likely be used when there are many manufacturers and many retailers who often lack the resources to find each other? (   )

A. Direct channel.　　B. Agent/broker channel.

C. Retailer channel.　　D. Wholesaler channel.

(5) How about the marketing channel structure for candy bars? (   )

A. Producer-retailer-consumer.　　B. Producer-agent-retailer-consumer.

C. Producer-consumer.　　D. Producer-wholesaler-retailer-consumer.

(6) A producer's decisions on the number of intermediaries to use at each channel level determine the channel's (   ).

A. width　　B. length　　C. depth　　D. both A and B

(7) In a (   ), two or more firms at the same channel level agree to work together to get their product to the customer.

A. administered VMS　　B. corporate VMS

C. contractual VMS　　D. horizontal marketing system

(8) (   ) is distribution that is aimed to maximize marketplace coverage.

A. Intensive distribution　　B. Selective distribution

C. Strategic distribution　　D. Exclusive distribution

(9) Cause(s) of the channel conflict is/are (   ).

A. role incongruities　　B. resource scarcities

C. perceptual differences　　D. all of the above

(10) (   ) often happens to economies in which regional distributors have different cost structures in selling the same products.

A. Channel conflict　　B. Horizontal conflict

C. Vertical conflict　　D. Mixed conflict

3. Questions for Discussion

(1) Describe the types of distribution channels.

(2) What factors are important in determining whether a manufacturer should choose a direct or indirect channel? Why do some firms use hybrid marketing systems?

(3) Explain intensive, exclusive, and selective forms of distribution.

(4) Explain how companies motivate and evaluate channel members?

Practical Writing

Scenario: Marketing plan elements can apply to marketing an organization or an individual. Put yourself in the situation of looking for a new job, and write down a **Marketing Plan** to assist your job-hunting.

First, what is your mission? Are you looking only for part-time or temporary experience to enhance your resume, or a career stepping stone, or a full-time, long-term career choice? Next, what are your objectives? Are there specific job activities you would like to perform?

It's now time for your SWOT analysis. Do you have a competitive advantage? What about opportunities and threats in the marketplace? Who is your competition? Are there aspects in the external environment that provide strategic windows for your employment?

What is your target market? Are you only looking for jobs with big, established organizations or small entrepreneurial firms? Companies in a particular industry? Do you have any geographic preferences?

You are the product. How can you best present yourself? Think of your own packaging with regard to dress, appearance, mannerisms, and speech. What about place? How will you travel to the employer? Is telecommuting an option? How will you promote yourself? Careful construction of a cover letter, resume, business card, and personal website are all methods that help communicate your skills to a potential employer. Think carefully about pricing issues, including salary, commission, bonuses, overtime, flexible time, insurance, and other benefits. What is a fair price for you?

Finally, have you set up an implementation plan for applying to companies? Contacting them for potential interviews? Working on your wardrobe and interviewing skills? When job offers come in, how will you evaluate them? If job offers don't come in, can you find out why and control for those aspects?

Part 4

Enhancing Marketing Management
加强营销管理

经典营销名言：

A decision will not become effective unless the action commitments have been built into the decision from the start... To be effective, is the job of the executive.

—Peter Drucker

我们应该将行动纳入决策当中，否则就是纸上谈兵……管理者的工作，必须要卓有成效。

——彼得·德鲁克

本部分内容导读：

思想和战略固然重要，但实施这些思想和战略才是真正的挑战。因此，在战略、战术方案规划完成后，企业要在具体行动过程中对品牌、财务、人员和物流等方面进行积极、有效的管理和控制，以避免执行结果偏离规划目标。

内容	口语	阅读	写作
单元11	会展	加强品牌管理	商务信函
单元12	银行借款	加强财务管理	简历
单元13	求职面试	加强人员管理	劳动合同
单元14	主持会议	加强物流管理	会议记录

Unit 11　Increasing Brand's Awareness

Learning Objectives

◇ 熟悉参加展会的常用口语表达；
◇ 理解品牌的含义和作用；
◇ 理解品牌的各种使用策略；
◇ 理解品牌开发和维护的基本策略；
◇ 掌握商务信函的书写规则和常用套语的正确写法。

Speaking：Exhibition

【场景1】 为了提高公司产品的知名度，金色童年决定参加一个在广州举办的国际儿童用品展销会。在预订了展位后，于琪提前一天到达会场。

【对话1】　A：于琪　B：展会前台接待　C：展会器材室工作人员

A：Excuse me, sir. I'm Qi Yu from Golden Childhood Co., Ltd. Do you know where I can find my booth?
对不起，先生。我是金色童年公司的于琪，请问我的摊位在哪里？

B：Hmm. Let me see. You're in booth number 286-E. Here's a map of the exhibition hall, and here we are at the service desk.
嗯，我看一下。您的摊位是286-E。这是展厅的布置图，我们服务台的位置在这儿。

A：(Looking at the map) Okay, and where exactly is our booth? Oh! There it is. Thanks for your help. (After a while, return to service desk again.) Pardon me, sir. Our goods were sent from Shanghai more than ten days ago, and they're not in our booth!
（看布置图）好，那我们的摊位具体在哪儿呢？喔，找到了。谢谢。（一会儿，又回到服务台。）对不起，先生。我们的展品十多天前就从上海寄出，可还没摆到摊位上！

B：Ah... hold on, let me check our records. Oh yes, your goods arrived late yesterday evening, so we haven't had the time to bring your goods to your booth.
喔……您等会儿，我查一下记录。有了，你们的货昨天晚上很晚才到，所以我们还来不及把它们搬到您的摊位上。

A：When can I expect them? I really need to set up before the exhibition!
什么时候能搬来呀？我一定得在展会开始前布置好！

B：You don't have to worry; I promise you'll have your goods before 1:00p. m. .
别着急,我保证您的货会在下午一点前送到。

A：Good, that makes me feel a lot better. (After a while, in the equipment office) Is this the equipment office? I'm afraid there's a problem with the power socket in my booth.
好,这样我就放心多了。(一会儿,出现在器材室)这里是不是器材室？我想我摊位上的电源插座似乎有点问题。

C：All of our technicians are busy at the moment. What booth are you in?
现在我们的技术员都在忙。请问您是几号摊位？

A：286-E. I'm very concerned about this problem, for tomorrow is the opening day!
286-E。我很担心这个问题,展览会明天就开始了！

C：One of our technicians will help you in about ten minutes. Please take a seat.
大约十分钟,就会有技术人员来帮您。请先坐一下。

【场景2】 产品展销会如期开幕了。在展销会的第一天,一位来自加拿大的客户对公司的玩具产品表现出了极大的兴趣。

【对话2】 A：于琪 B：加拿大客户 Alex Johnson 先生

A：Good morning. Anything particular you are interested in? We have wide varieties for you to choose from. They are all our best selling lines.
早上好。您有什么特别感兴趣的商品吗？我们的产品种类齐全,都是我们的畅销商品。

B：Yes, I'm interested in your range of toys for children. Could you tell me something about them?
是的,我对你们的儿童玩具系列产品比较感兴趣。能为我介绍一下吗？

A：Right. The toys on the right are machine toys, electronic toys, electric toys and intellectual toys, suitable for children from the age of five upwards. The toys on the left are bamboo & wooden toys, plastic toys and plush toys, suitable for children under five. They are all available from stock. Well, we've also got some new models there. If you come this way, I will show them to you.
好的。右手边的是器械玩具、电子玩具、电动玩具和益智玩具,适合五岁以上儿童。左手边的是竹木玩具、塑料玩具和毛绒玩具,适合五岁以下儿童。它们目前都有现货。嗯,在那边我们还有一些新型玩具。这边请,我为您介绍一下。

B：OK.
好的。

A：This is our new designed electric toy car. One of the major advantages of this product is that it is designed to conserve energy. Compared with other products, the driving time of our product is much longer. Several new design features such as remote control, automatic brake and water proof also make it more attractive than many similar, more expensive products made by our competitors. Let me show you how it works now...

这是我们新设计的一款电动玩具车。该产品的主要优点之一是节能。和其他产品相比，我们产品的驾驶时间更长。一些新的设计特点例如遥控、自动制动和防水也使得它比我们竞争对手所生产的同类、价格更高的产品更有吸引力。现在让我为您做一下展示吧……

B：Quite interesting. What's that?

真有趣。那是什么？

A：This is a battery-powered teddy panda with nursery rhyme in it. Just press this button. Listen..."Teddy panda, teddy panda, turn around. Teddy panda, teddy panda, touch the ground..."

这是一个由电池供电的带童谣的玩具熊猫。只需按下这个按钮。听……"玩具熊猫，玩具熊猫，转个圈。玩具熊猫，玩具熊猫，摸摸地……"

B：All your products look very attractive. How about the prices?

你们所有的产品看起来都非常吸引人。它们的价格如何？

A：The recommended retail prices can be found on the price list. Here is the price list, sir.

建议零售价可以在报价单中找到。这是报价单，先生。

B：Thank you. I'd also like to get some information about the discount. Can you give me a good discount on a large order?

谢谢。我还想了解一下折扣的情况。大量订货可以获得大的折扣吗？

A：It's hard to say. It depends on what you choose and how large the quantity you want.

难说。这取决于你选哪种产品，量有多大。

B：Mr. Yu, your products and presentation really impressed me. And I'm willing to give your products a try, but your delivery must be up to the sample.

于先生，你们的产品及介绍给我留下了深刻印象。我愿意试销你们的产品，不过交付的货品必须和这里展示的样品相符。

A：Certainly. It's our principle in business to "Honor the contract and keep our promise."

当然。我们做生意的原则就是"履行合同，从不食言"。

【场景3】 今天是产品展销会的最后一天了。一大早，销售经理马天跃竟然在展位上见到了老熟人John Brown先生。

【对话3】 A：销售经理马天跃 B：John Brown先生

A：Hello, Mr. Brown. I am so glad to meet you here at the fair.

你好，布朗先生，真高兴在交易会上见到你。

B：Likewise. It seems your business is prosperous. There are many customers here.
我也很高兴。看起来你们的生意很兴旺,这么多客户光临。

A：Yes, it's not too bad. Our sales are going up year after year. And we still have a large potential production capacity.
是的,还不错。我们的销量年年递增,我们的生产潜力还很大。

B：Mr. Ma, we have done business with each other for nearly ten years, if I'm not mistaken.
马先生,如果我没有记错的话,我们之间的业务往来有近十年了吧。

A：Yes, and I have to say that we get along with each other quite satisfactorily.
对,我得说我们之间的业务往来是相当令人满意的。

B：Did it ever occur to you that we might take a new step forward? Have you ever considered appointing us as your sole agent in North America?
你考虑过我们可以再向前迈出新的一步吗?是否考虑过委托我们作为你们在北美的独家代理?

A：It all depends on what you can do.
这全看你方能做些什么了。

B：I'm coming to that. As your agent, we shall spare no effort to promote the sale of your toys on North American market.
我就要谈到这一点了。作为你方的代理,我们将不遗余力地在北美市场上推销你们的玩具。

A：I would like to know the definite quantities of your annual turnover.
我想知道你们年销售量的确切数字。

B：Well, how about US$ 4 million annually for a start?
哦,开始阶段每年销售400万美元如何?

A：That sounds good.
听起来不错。

B：Then, what's your usual commission rate for your agents?
那么,你们通常给代理商的佣金率是多少?

A：Usually, we give a commission of 4% to our agents.
通常我们给代理商4%的佣金。

B：It is too low, I think. You see, we have a lot of work to do in sales promotion such as advertising on radio or TV, printing booklets, leaflets, catalogues and so on. It all costs money.
我认为太低了。你知道,为了推销你方的产品,我们要做很多工作。比如,在电台或电视上做广告,印刷小册子、传单和商品目录等。这一切都需要花销。

A：Don't worry. We'll allow you a higher commission rate if your sales score a substantial increase.
别担心,如果你们的销量大幅度增长,我们会给予更高的佣金。

B：You mean...

你的意思是……

A：Now, if you sell US＄4 million worth of children's toys annually, we can only allow 4％ commission. If the annual turnover exceeds US＄6 million, you can get 6％ commission. What do you think of that?

如果你方儿童玩具的年销量为400万美元,我们只能给4％的佣金。如果年销量超过600万美元,你就可得到6％的佣金,你看怎么样?

B：It sounds OK. Then how do you pay the commission?

这还差不多。那么,佣金如何支付呢?

A：We may deduct the commission from the invoice value directly or remit it to you after payment.

我们可以直接从发票金额中扣除佣金,或在(买方)付款后再汇给你方。

B：All right. If it's Okay, I would like to sign an agency agreement with you as soon as possible.

那好。如果可以,我希望与你们尽快签订代理协议。

Reading：Enhancing Brand Management

在营销中,品牌是唤起消费者或客户重复购买的最原始的动力,是企业的生命力和灵魂。如何合理地对品牌进行开发、推广、维护,通过成功的品牌管理保障企业持续的成长和未来的辉煌,于琪陷入了深深的思索中。

Chapter 11 Brand Management

Section 1 The Benefits of Branding

Brands represent consumers' perceptions and feelings about a product and its performance—everything that the product or service means to consumers. As one branding expert suggests, "Ultimately, brands reside in the minds of consumers." The essence of any brand is that it is more than an undifferentiated, commodity product. In the perception of buyers, it has a unique identity. It has a unique name, and it may have its own logo, design and packaging, although these are not essential; it is probably supported by advertising, though even that is not necessary in special cases such as Marks&Spencer (though even M&S has now adopted advertising to support its weakened brand). A brand should wherever possible be legally protected, that is the brand name and identity should be registered as a trade mark and the design elements copyrighted.

Branding has three main purposes: product identification, repeat sales, and new-product sales. The most important purpose is product identification. Branding allows marketers to distinguish their products from all others. Many brand names are familiar to consumers and indicate the quality. The term brand equity refers to the value of company and brand names. A brand that has high awareness, perceived quality, and brand loyalty among customers has high brand equity. A brand with strong brand equity is a valuable asset. The term master brand has been used to refer to a brand so dominant in consumers' minds that they think of it immediately when a product category, use, attribute, or customer benefit is mentioned.

The best generator of repeat sales is satisfied customers. Branding helps consumers identify products they wish to buy again and avoid those they do not. Brand loyalty, a consistent preference for one brand over all others, is quite high in some product categories. Over half the users in product categories such as cigarettes, mayonnaise, toothpaste, coffee, headache remedies, photographic film, bath soap, and catsup are loyal to one brand. Brand identity is essential to developing brand loyalty.

The third main purpose of branding is to facilitate new-product sales. For example, premium ice-cream maker Haagen-Dazs decided to get into the growing low-fat ice-cream market. Its choices were to create a new brand or modify the existing one. The result was Haagen-Dazs Light, which it proclaimed to have "all the taste and texture of original Haagen-Dazs with only half the fat." The Haagen-Dazs Light was an immediate success, and the company now offers 14 flavors under the Light banner, many of which are available only in a Light version.

小 结

品牌代表消费者对某种产品及其性能的认知与感觉。品牌化最重要的目的是识别产品。品牌使营销人员将自己的产品与其他产品区分开来。其中,霸主品牌是指在消费者心目中有十分重要地位的品牌,一提到该产品的类别、使用环境、特性或消费者获得的利益,人们就会立刻想起的品牌。其次,重复销售最有力的推动者是感到满意的消费者。品牌有助于消费者识别他们想要再次购买的商品而避开不想要的商品,从而培养品牌忠诚。品牌化的第三个主要目的是促进新产品销售。许多公司通过对现有品牌的利用成功地推出新的产品。

Section 2 Brand Sponsorship Strategy

2.1 Individual Brands versus Family Brands

Part of developing a branding strategy is to decide whether to use a separate, unique brand for each product item—an individual brand strategy—or to market multiple items under the same brand name—a family brand or umbrella brand strategy. Individual brands may do a better job of communicating clearly and concisely what the consumer can expect from the product, while a well-known company like Apple may find that its high brand equity in other categories (like computers) can sometimes "rub off" on a new brand (like the iPod). The decision often depends on characteristics of the product and whether the company's overall product strategy calls for introduction of a single, unique product or for the development of a group of similar products. For example, Microsoft serves as a strong umbrella brand for a host of diverse individually branded products like Office, Internet Explorer, Xbox 360, and Microsoft Live or Live Search, while Procter&Gamble prefers to brand each of its household products separately.

But there's a potential dark side to having too many brands, particularly when they become undifferentiated in the eyes of the consumer due to poor positioning. Recently, venerable General Motors suffered from muddy differentiation among the eight brands in its portfolio—namely, Chevrolet, GMC, Pontiac, Saturn, Cadillac, Buick, Hummer and Saab. The brands often compete with each other—both for customers and a slice of GM's marketing budget. For example, GM has four mainstream midsize sedans. It backs its top selling Chevy Malibu with an aggressive ad campaign, while the Buick LaCrosse, Pontiac G6, and Saturn Aura struggle to build the awareness and recognition these lines need to compete. To put things into perspective, Toyota has but one midsize sedan—the Camry—and in 2007, it alone outsold GM's four models 473,308 to 386,024!

2.2 National and Store Brands

Retailers today often are in the driver's seat when it comes to deciding what brands to stock and push. In addition to choosing from producers' brands, called national manufacturer brands, retailers decide whether to offer their own versions. Private-label brands, also called store brands, are the retail store's or chain's exclusive trade name. Wal-Mart, for example, sells store brand Sam's cola and Sam's cookies along with national brands such as Coke and Oreos. Store brands are gaining in popularity for many value-conscious shoppers. Retailers continue to develop new ones, and some add services to the mix: Target and others now offer walk-in medical care in select locations, staffed by a nurse practitioner or physician's assistant. And Wal-Mart has set the pharmacy business on end by offering some types of generic prescriptions, such as basic antibiotics, for $4.00.

Retailers may prefer a private-label branding strategy because they generally make more profit on these than on national brands. Even midrange retailers such as JCPenney now offer private-label clothing to lure millions of customers away from more upscale department stores as well as lower-end discounters. Penney's Stafford and St. John's Bay brands for men have become a significant competitive force against national brands like Dockers, Haggar, and Levi's. In addition, it recently added a new American Living line that the company bills as "a new tradition in American style for your family and home."

In addition, if you stock a unique brand that consumers can't find in other stores, it's much harder for shoppers to compare "apples to apples" across stores and simply buy the brand where they find it sold for the lowest price. Loblaws, Canada's largest supermarket chain, sells over 4,000 food items under the "premium quality" President's Choice label, from cookies to beef, olive oil, curtains, and kitchen utensils. Sales of President Choice items run from 30 to 40 percent of total store volumes. Under the private label, Loblaws can introduce new products at high quality but for lower prices than brand names. It can also keep entire categories profitable by its mix of pricing options. Competitors that sell only national brands can cut prices on those brands, but that hurts their overall profitability. Loblaws can bring prices down on national brands but still make money on its private-label products.

2.3 Generic Brands

An alternative to either national or store branding is generic branding, which is basically no branding at all. Generic branded products are typically packaged in white with black lettering that names only the product itself (for example, "Green Beans"). Generic branding is one strategy to meet customers' demand for the lowest prices on standard products such as dog food or paper towels. Generic brands first became popular during the inflationary period of the 1980s when consumers became especially price conscious because of rising prices. However, today generic brands account for very little of consumer spending.

2.4 Licensing

Some firms choose to use a licensing strategy to brand their products. This means that one firm sells another firm the right to use a legally protected brand name for a specific purpose and for a specific period of time. Licensing can provide instant recognition and consumer interest in a new product, and this strategy can quickly position a product for a certain target market as it trades on the high recognition of the licensed brand among consumers in that segment. For example, distiller Brown-Forman licensed its famous Jack Daniel's bourbon name to T.G.I. Friday's to use on all sorts of menu items from shrimp to steak to chicken. In addition to this "Jack Daniel's Grill," Friday's features menu items inspired by the popular Food Network reality show Ultimate Recipe Showdown.

A familiar form of licensing occurs when movie producers license their properties to manufacturers of a seemingly infinite number of products. Each time a blockbuster Harry Potter movie hits the screens, a plethora of Potter products packs the stores. In addition to toys and games, you can buy Harry Potter candy, clothing, all manner of back-to-school items, home items, and even wands and cauldrons.

2.5 Cobranding

Frito-Lay sells K.C. Masterpiece-flavored potato chips, and Post sells Oreo O's cereal. Strange marriages? No, these are examples of cobranding, as are the Jack Daniel's and Food Network combinations with T.G.I. Friday's that we already mentioned. This branding strategy benefits both partners when combining the two brands provides more recognition power than either enjoys alone. For example, Panasonic markets a line of digital cameras that use Leica lenses, which are legendary for their superb image quality. Panasonic is known for its consumer electronics. Combining the best in traditional camera optics with a household name in consumer electronics helps both brands.

A new and fast-growing variation on cobranding is ingredient branding, in which branded materials become "component parts" of other branded products. This was the strategy behind the classic "Intel inside" campaign that convinced millions of consumers to ask by name for a highly technical computer part (a processor) that they wouldn't otherwise recognize if they fell over it. Today, consumers can buy Breyer's Ice-cream with Reese's Peanut Butter Cups or M&M's candies, Twix cookies or Snickers bars. Van De-Camp's Fish&Dips come with Heinz ketchup dipping cups. The ultimate cobranding deal may be an Oscar Meyer Lunchables Mega Pack, which includes up to five brands in a single package. Its Pizza Stix pack, for example, comes with Tombstone pizza sauce, Kraft cheese, a Capri Sun Splash Cooler, and a 3 Musketeers bar. Brand heaven!

The practice of ingredient branding has two main benefits. First, it attracts customers to the host brand because the ingredient brand is familiar and has a strong brand reputation for quality. Second, the ingredient brand's firm can sell more of its product, not to mention the additional revenues it gets from the licensing arrangement.

小 结

制造商在如何使用品牌上有五种策略可以选择。第一，使用单独品牌或家族品牌。单独品牌指为每个产品设立独立的品牌，家族品牌指在同一品牌下营销不同的产品。第二，使用制造商品牌或自有品牌。除了选择生产商的品牌，如今许多零售商也开始提供他们自己的品牌产品。第三，无品牌策略。该策略用来满足客户对低价格、标准产品的需求。第四，许可品牌策略。这意味着一家公司出于某一目的卖给另一家公司在特定一段时间内使用该公司受法律保护的品牌名称的权利。最后，合作品牌策略。这种品牌策略结合两个品牌后将提供比任何单一品牌更多的识别力，从而使合作双方受益。

Section 3 Brand Development and Maintenance Strategy

3.1 Brand Development

A company has four choices when it comes to developing brands. Line extensions occur when a company introduces additional items in a given product category under the same brand name, such as new flavors, forms, colors, ingredients, or package sizes. Thus, Tiger Balm introduced several line extensions, including medicated plaster, muscle rub, oil, and liniment. The vast majority of all new-product activity consists of line extensions. A company might introduce line extensions as a low-cost, low-risk way to introduce new products. Or it might want to meet consumer desires for variety, to utilize excess capacity, or simply to command more shelf space from resellers. However, line extensions involve some risks. An overextended brand name might lose its specific meaning, or heavily extended brands can cause consumer confusion or frustration. Another risk is that sales of an extension may come at the expense of other items in the line. A line extension works best when it takes sales away from competing brands, not when it "cannibalizes" the company's other items.

A brand extension involves the use of a successful brand name to launch new or modified products in a new category. For example, Honda uses its company name to cover different products such as its automobiles, motorcycles, snowblowers, lawn mowers, marine engines, and snowmobiles. This allows Honda to advertise that it can fit "six Hondas in a two-car garage." A brand extension gives a new product instant recognition and faster acceptance. It also saves the high advertising costs usually required to build a new brand name. At the same time, a brand extension strategy involves some risk. Brand extensions such as Virgin Cola, Virgin Mobile, Virgin Vodka, and Virgin Cosmetics have not been successful. The extension may confuse the image of the main brand. And if a brand extension fails, it may harm consumer attitudes toward the other products carrying the same brand name. Further, a brand name may not be appropriate to a particular new product, even if it is well made and satisfying—would you consider buying Nissan milk or a Lee Kum Kee watch? A brand name may lose its special positioning in the consumer's mind through overuse. Companies that are tempted to transfer a brand name must research how well the brand's associations fit the new product.

Companies often introduce additional brands in the same category. Thus, P&G markets many different brands in each of its product categories. Multibranding offers a way to establish different features and appeal to different buying motives. It also allows a company to lock up more reseller shelf space. Or the company may want to protect its major brand by setting up flanker or fighter brands. Seiko uses different brand names for its higher-priced watches (Seiko Lasalle) and lower-priced watches (Pulsar) to protect the flanks of its mainstream Seiko brand. A major drawback of multibranding is that each brand might obtain only a small market share, and none may be very profitable. The company may end up spreading its resources over many brands instead of building a few brands to a highly profitable level. These companies should reduce the number of brands they sell in a given category and set up tighter screening procedures for new brands.

A company may create a new brand name when it enters a new product category for which none of the company's current brand names is appropriate. For example, Toyota created the Lexus brand to differentiate its luxury car from the established Toyota line. Japan's Matsushita uses separate names for its different families of products: Technics, Panasonic, and Quasar. Or, a company might believe that the power of its existing brand name is waning and a new brand name is needed. As with multibranding, offering too many new brands can result in a company spreading its resources too thin. And in some industries, such as consumer packaged goods, consumers and retailers have become concerned that there are already too many brands, with too few differences between them. Thus, Procter&Gamble and other large consumer-product marketers are now pursuing megabrand strategies—weeding out weaker brands and focusing their marketing dollars only on brands that can achieve leading market share positions in their categories.

3.2 Brand Maintenance

Companies must carefully manage their brands. First, the brand's positioning must be continuously communicated to consumers. Major brand marketers often spend huge amounts on advertising to create brand awareness and to build preference and loyalty. For example, McDonald's spends more than $660 million annually on advertising. Such advertising campaigns can help to create name recognition, brand knowledge, and maybe even some brand preference. However, the fact is that brands are not maintained by advertising but by the brand experience. Today, customers come to know a brand through a wide range of contacts and touch points. These include advertising, but also personal experience with the brand, word of mouth, personal interactions with company people, telephone interactions, company Web pages, and many others. Any of these experiences can have a positive or negative impact on brand perceptions and feelings. The company must put as much care into managing these touch points as it does into producing its ads.

The brand's positioning will not take hold fully unless everyone in the company loves the brand. Therefore, the company needs to train its people to be customer-centered. Even better, the company should build pride in its employees regarding their products and services so that their enthusiasm will spill over to customers. Companies such as Giordano, Lexus, and Singapore Airlines have succeeded in turning their employees into enthusiastic brand builders. Companies can carry on internal brand building to help employees to understand, desire, and deliver on the brand promise. Many companies go even further by training and encouraging their distributors and dealers to serve their customers well.

Finally, companies need to periodically audit their brands' strengths and weaknesses. They should ask: Does our brand excel at delivering benefits that consumers truly value? Is the brand properly positioned? Do all of our consumer touch points support the brand's positioning? Do the brand's managers understand what the brand means to consumers? Does the brand receive proper, sustained support?

小 结

当公司准备开发品牌时,有四种方法可以选择。可以进行产品线延伸(利用现有产品类别中已存在的品牌名称延伸出新的形式、规格和口味)、品牌延伸(将已有的品牌名称延伸到新的产品类别)、多品牌(将新品牌名称引入到已有的产品类别)或新品牌(在新产品类别中使用新的品牌名称)。同时,公司必须小心地管理他们的品牌。首先,为使品牌定位持续地传达给消费者,公司必须对顾客了解品牌的各种途径(接触点)加强管理。其次,公司可以实施内部品牌建设来帮助员工理解、渴望和传递品牌承诺。许多公司做得更好,它们培训和鼓励分销商和经销商为顾客提供高质量的服务。最后,公司需要定期审查它们品牌的优势和劣势。

New Words and Key Terms

01.	brands	品牌
02.	brand equity	品牌权益
03.	master brands	霸主品牌
04.	brand loyalty	品牌忠诚
05.	individual brands	单独品牌
06.	family brands	家族品牌
07.	national manufacturer brands	制造商品牌
08.	private-label brands	私有品牌,自有品牌
09.	generic branding	无品牌
10.	licensing	许可品牌
11.	cobranding	合作品牌,联合品牌
12.	ingredient branding	成分品牌,要素品牌
13.	line extensions	产品线延伸
14.	brand extensions	品牌延伸
15.	multibranding	多品牌
16.	new brands	新品牌
17.	megabrand strategies	大品牌战略

Writing：Business Letter

这天下午,刚刚结束产品展销会回来的销售经理马天跃收到已经成为公司老主顾的 Smith 先生发来的一封信函,谈到他近期接收的一批童装出现破损。公司对此高度重视,专门开会并责成营销部进行调查。调查结果显示,服装破损是由于船到澳大利亚后,当地的装卸公司违规使用了吊钩。查明原因后,马天跃让于琪代他起草回信。

一、商务信函写作的基本要求和格式

商务信函(Business Letter)是商务活动的重要组成部分,是通过邮寄或其他电信手段进行的文字形式的商务对话。商务信函的特点是简洁明了,故多数信函只写一页。

(一)信头(Letterhead)

信头主要包括发信人公司的名称、地址、邮编、电话、电传以及电子邮箱,通常印在信纸的正上方或右上角。信头的目的是保证收信人能够识别发信人并且知道如何联系。日期应写在信头下面隔一行处,或写在信头内作为信头的一部分。日期的书写要求是:年份写全且放在最后,并与日、月之间用逗号隔开;月份要写英文名称,但可以使用缩写;日期使用基数词和序数词均可;月份放在日期的前后均可。有些信头上发信人还会注明编号或查询号(Reference Number),希望对方回信时引用,以方便接收方查阅原件。

(二)封内地址(Inside Address)

封内地址包括收信人姓名和地址。封内地址应出现在信纸页面的左侧,并且通常同信头间隔二至四行。与信封上的地址一样,封内地址包括详细的公寓或公司名称、大街号、地区、城市、省或州、邮政编码,以及国家名称。对于写信人来说,封内地址准确地指明了收信人,从而保证信体被放入正确的信封。看下面一些封内地址的典型写法。

1. 基本式写法

一般三行或四行,不要超过五行。若加收信人的头衔,写在第一或第二行为佳。同时,还要注意整体的美观和平衡。例如,

Dr. John Dixon, Claims Supervisor
State Insurance Corporation
286 Hightower Boulevard
Prince Town, 100258, US

2. 转交式写法

在个人或公司名称的前面加 c/o(care of 的缩写),意思是此信将由该公司或该人转交给收信人。例如,

Mr. David Peters
c/o London Export Corporation
16 Clifford Street
London, SW7 2DY, England

3. 经办式写法

在收信人所在公司地址下面加上 Attention 或 Attention of 字样(Attention 可简写为 ATT),然后标明收信人姓名(和/或职位)或经办部门名称。例如,

The Universal Trading Company
151 Gower Street
London, SC7 6DY, England
Attention: Mr. R. Jameson, Export Manager.

(三)称呼(Salutation)

封内地址下面隔一行从页面的左侧写称呼。对个人规范的称呼通常是 Dear Mr. Smith(先生),Dear Miss Smith(小姐),Dear Mrs. Smith(已婚女士),or Dear Ms. Smith(未知对方婚否)。若收信人是公司或写信者并不知道其姓名,称呼应写成 Dear Sirs,Gentlemen,Dear Sir/Madam,Export Manager,Import Department,Dear Customers,或者 To Whom This May Concern(致有关人员)。称呼后面通常用逗号或不用标点。

(四)事由(Subject or Caption)

事由的使用可以帮助收信人快速了解来信的意图。在业务较繁忙的公司中,这样可以节省很多时间,登记归档和查阅时也非常便利。事由一般不使用句子,而是一个词组或短

语,甚至只是书信中所涉及的商品名称、合同或订单的编号等。通常情况下,事由在前面加上"Re:"(拉丁文,意思是"关于"),在称呼下面空一行居中或靠左侧书写。

（五）正文(Body)

根据具体格式要求,正文可以从左边齐头(Block Style)或缩行四至五个字母(Indented Style)写起。(注:缩行式封内地址的写法是后行比前行缩进二至三个字母)

1. 开头语(Opening Sentence)

通常是将收到对方来信的日期、编号、主题等加以综合叙述,并表明本封信函需要讨论的问题。例如,We acknowledge, with thanks, receipt of your letter of September 14 under your reference 518, in which you inform us that you intend to place an order with us for 2,500 pieces of combination pliers.（我们已经收到并非常感谢贵方9月14日所发编号为518的来信。在信中,贵公司表示愿意向我们订购2,500套多用老虎钳）。如果是首次通信,可以利用开头语做必要的自我介绍,或说明通过何人或何渠道而得知了该公司或该信息。例如,Your company has been kindly introduced to us by... 经……介绍,我们获知了贵公司。

2. 主体(Main Body)

主体包含着写信人所要传递给收信人的必要信息。信的主体可由一段或多段组成,每一段只谈一个主题。

3. 结尾语(Closing Sentence)

一般用来总结本信所谈的事项,提示对收信人的要求,如希望回复、订货、做必要的说明等。另外,也需要附加一些略带客套的语气。例如,Your prompt attention to this matter would be highly appreciated.（如贵方能立即处理此事,我们将甚为感激）。结尾语的位置是在正文主体结束之后,另起一段。

（六）结束礼词(Complimentary Close)

常用的书信结束礼词有 Truly,Sincerely,Faithfully,Cordially,Respectfully 等,也可组合成 Yours truly,Truly yours,Very truly yours 等。信函结束礼词只需对第一个单词首字母大写。除完全齐头式外,通常居中或从信纸中线处向右写起,并在后面加逗号。

（七）签名(Signature)

结束礼词下方的签名区应该有手写签名、打印签名,以及职位。手写签名通常允许占用3行。对于打印签名,男士姓名前不加性别前缀"先生"(Mr.),女士姓名前可加"小姐"(Miss)或"女士"(Ms.),以便回信时正确称呼。性别前缀一般写在括号内。

（八）附件(Enclosure)

当写信人在信中附有发给收信人的相关文件时,应在信纸的左下角清楚地标注。标注可以使用完整单词 Enclosure,或者它的缩写形式如 Encl. 或 Enc. 如附件不止一件,需要使用复数形式,如 Enclosures 或 Encls. 等,并建议标明附件的数量和具体内容。

（九）经办人代码(Identification Mark)

发信方为明确责任,常使用经办人代码来识别信件的签署人和打印人员。签署或主稿人姓名的首字母用大写形式打出,后面接冒号或斜杠;操作人员(即打印员)姓名的首字母以小写形式打出。典型的经办人代码写法如 JS/ms 或 JS:ms,它表明主稿人为经理 John

Smith(对内容负责),打印人员为其秘书 Marry Stomas(对文字负责)。

(十)抄送(Carbon Copy)

如果信件的副本被抄送给有关单位或人士时,副本接收人应该被完整清楚地注明。这种做法的交际功能是告知你的目标读者,其他的某个(些)人也收到了一封同样的信件。抄送常常被简写为 C. C. ,然后在后边写上抄送单位的名称或个人的名字即可。

(十一)再启(Postscript)

信件写完后,如果想起还有话没说或纯粹是为了强调,可以在信末空两行加 P. S. (Postscripts 的缩写)引出补叙的话,并签署发信人简笔签名(如 Park Davis 只签 P. D.)。

二、于琪的解决方案(信头及封内地址略)

Dear Mr. Smith,

Re: Settlement of Complaint

We regret to learn from your letter dated September 28 that the Children's wear you ordered under the Contract No. 518 were found damaged.

We have checked our records and found that the goods left our factory in good condition and were, as usual, carefully packed as shown by a copy of the clean B/L which we enclose herewith. We then asked our sales representative to take up this matter with stevedoring company at your end and subsequently discovered that the goods had been unloaded by using hooks, although the packages were clearly marked with a warning against using hooks. We therefore do not feel in any way responsible for the damage.

We appreciate, however, that you do not want to accept these damaged clothes as they are. If you return them to us, we will replace them at our expense.

Yours faithfully,
Tianyue Ma
(Signed)
Sales Manager

Enclosure

Review Questions

1. Key Terms

Master brands; Private-label brands; Ingredient branding; Line extensions; Brand extensions; Megabrand strategies

2. Multiple Choices (select one)

(1) A ( ) is a name, term, sign, symbol, or design or a combination of these that identifies the maker or seller of a product or service.

A. brand   B. place   C. corporation   D. firm

(2) All of the following statements are accurate descriptions of the benefits of bran-

ding to buyers, except which one? (　　)

　　A. Brand names help consumers identify products that might benefit them.

　　B. Branding helps the seller to segment markets.

　　C. Buyers who always buy the same brand know that they will get the same features, benefits and quality each time they buy.

　　D. Brand identity is essential to developing brand loyalty.

　　(3) In one study, 72 percent of customers would pay a 20 percent premium for their brand of choice relative to the closest competing brand; 40 percent said they would pay a 50 percent premium. Thus, brands with strong (　　) are very valuable assets.

　　A. popularity　　　　B. low prices　　　C. reputation　　　　D. equity

　　(4) A brand created and owned by a reseller of a product or service is called a (　　).

　　A. manufacturer brand　　　　　　B. private brand
　　C. generic brand　　　　　　　　　D. licensed brand

　　(5) (　　) is the practice of using the established brand names of two different companies on the same product.

　　A. Slotting fees　　B. Premiums　　　C. Co-branding　　　D. Licensing

　　(6) (　　) occur(s) when a company introduces additional items in a given product category under the same brand name, such as flavors, forms, colors, or package sizes.

　　A. Line extensions　　　　　　　　B. Brand extensions
　　C. Multibranding　　　　　　　　　D. Licensing

　　(7) Morton Salt has expanded its line to include regular iodized salt plus Morton Coarse Kosher Salt, Morton Lite Salt, and Morton Popcorn Salt. Thus, Morton Salt has introduced several (　　).

　　A. brand extensions　　　　　　　B. line extensions
　　C. multibranding　　　　　　　　　D. licensing

　　(8) A (　　) involves the use of a successful brand name to launch new or modified products in a new category.

　　A. brand extension　　　　　　　　B. line extension
　　C. license　　　　　　　　　　　　D. slotting fee

　　(9) All of the following are accurate descriptions of risks associated with brand extension strategies, except which one? (　　)

　　A. A brand extension gives a new product instant recognition and faster acceptance.

　　B. A brand extension may confuse the image of the main brand.

　　C. A brand extension may harm consumer attitudes toward the other products carrying the same brand name, if the brand extension fails.

　　D. A brand name may not be appropriate to a particular new product.

　　(10) All of the following are benefits of multibranding, except which one? (　　)

　　A. Each brand might obtain only a small market share, and none may be very profitable.

B. Firms set up flanker and fighter brands to protect their major brands.

C. Multibranding offers a way to establish different features and appeal to different buying motives.

D. It allows a company to lock up more shelf space.

3. Questions for Discussion

(1) What are the main purposes or benefits of branding?

(2) What are the main advantages and disadvantages of brand extension?

(3) How does co-branding affect brand extensions? Suggest a co-branding opportunity in Asia that you believe makes sense from a marketing perspective.

Practical Writing

Scenario: You work as the Managing Director of a clothing company. One day, you got a letter below from one of you clients complaining about the goods received. You are going to write a **Letter** of reply, explaining that you would like to replace any piece of Serges(哔叽布) found not to be satisfactory instead of accepting return of all the unsold balance.

Dear Sirs,

Re: Not Matching Samples

We have recently received a number of complaints from customers about your Serges. The Serges clearly do not match the samples you left with us.

The Serges complained about are part of the batch of 100 pieces of 50 yards supplied to our Order No. AD-190 of May 10. We have ourselves examined some of the Serges complained about and there is little doubt that some of them are shrinkable and others not colourfast.

We are therefore writing to ask you to accept return of the unsold balance of the batch referred to, amounting to 35 pieces in all, and to replace them by Serges of the same quality as the samples.

Yours faithfully,

Unit 12　Getting Support from the Bank

Learning Objectives

◇ 熟悉融资谈判的常用口语表达；
◇ 理解最基本的财务报表——资产负债表的构成和含义；
◇ 理解企业财务管理的基本职能；
◇ 理解企业所面临的财务风险类型和基本的规避技术；
◇ 掌握简历的书写规则和常用套语的正确写法。

Speaking：Borrowing Money from the Bank

【场景1】　与阳光公司建立生产冰激凌合资企业的工作正在紧锣密鼓地进行着。根据合资协议，金色童年公司需要大约300万美元的现金出资。由于目前公司的自有资金不足，这天早晨，公司财务经理 Leila Peterson 女士和中国银行上海分行的业务部经理 Mark Erwin 先生展开了会谈。

【对话1】　A：Leila Peterson 女士　　B：Mark Erwin 先生

A：Mr. Erwin, what credit terms are available for companies that want to invest in Shanghai Pudong District?
欧文先生，想在上海浦东投资的公司能获得哪些信贷条件呢？

B：Generally, there are two possibilities. A medium-term loan can be provided to companies that invest in Shanghai Pudong District at a rate of 11％. The normal rate is 13％, as you know. This loan must be repaid over a minimum period of 2 years or maximum of 7 years. Companies can also apply for a long-term loan at the rate of 10％, but can vary by up to 1％ every year. Of course, with both of these loans, the loan period must be agreed in advance.
通常来说有两种选择，一种是中期贷款，对在上海浦东投资的公司年利率是11％，你要知道一般利率是13％。这种贷款至少在两年内，最多七年内必须还清。还有一种，公司也可以按10％的利率申请长期贷款，但每年可以有1％以内的变动。当然，这两种贷款的期限必须要提前决定。

A：And how much money does the Bank provide for a project, in terms of percentage?
那么贵银行可以为一个项目提供几成的贷款呢？

B：The normal position of the Bank of China is that it will only lend a maximum of half the money for any one project. Also, the Bank will only provide as much as the company invests of its own capital, so for example, if the company borrows 30% elsewhere, the company must invest 35% of its own money, and the Bank will then provide a maximum of 35%. This is normal practice, but it is not a regulation. It depends on the financial position and general profitability of the company, and also on the kind of project it is undertaking.
中国银行一般的规定是最多为一个项目提供五成的贷款。而且，银行提供的贷款最多不超过公司本身投入的资金额。比如说，如果公司从其他渠道获得30%的贷款，那么公司必须要投入35%的资金，银行才会提供最多不超过35%的贷款。这是惯常的做法，但却不是硬性的规定，这要看公司的财务状况和盈利率，以及从事项目的具体性质。

A：You mean it is open to negotiation?
你是说这可以协商是吗？

B：Yes, that's right. Now you must tell me something about the project for which you're applying for a loan.
是的，现在你得告诉我申请贷款的项目到底是什么。

A：We are going to set up a joint venture with a British partner to manufacture best tasting ice-cream with a wide range of flavors. They are popular products and have very good market potential. When the joint venture is fully efficient, say in five years' time, it will produce an annual profit of $1.8 million. The joint venture will hopefully have paid for itself in about ten years, depending on how much interest it has to pay on the loan. The capital contribution on our part is estimated at $3 million. The accountants estimate that it will be two years before the joint venture is operational and four years before it produces any profit. The loan would be needed for a fairly long period, probably about 10 years. We are hoping that the Bank of China will provide 90% of the loan ($2.7 million). We will then make up the other $300,000. We'd like to have the loan interest free for three years. And we are willing to make the first repayment after 5 years. We would then pay back the loan in 5 annual installments.
我们计划和一家英国公司成立一个生产高品质、多口味冰激凌产品的合资企业。它们是流行产品，有非常好的市场前景。如果合资企业全面投产的话，比如说五年内，就能产生180万美元的年利润。公司在十年内很有可能还清贷款，不过这要看获得的贷款利息是多少了。我方对合资企业估计要投入300万美元的资金。据会计师估计，合资企业要经过两年建设才能投产，四年才能盈利。所以贷款可能要较长一段时间，可能是十年。我们公司希望中国银行能提供九成的贷款，也就是270万美元。我们会自筹剩余的 30 万美元。我们希望头三年能免贷款利息，五年后开始返还贷款，在五年内分期还贷。

B: Why don't you try to raise the capital by selling more shares or by applying to an industrial consortium for a loan?

你们为什么不用发行更多股票的方式筹资或向一些工业财团贷款呢？

A: We don't want to sell more shares because the investment market is extremely bad at the moment. Also, we do not want to approach the big consortia for finance, as interest rates are extremely high. We are hoping for a better rate, say 6%, from the Bank of China.

现在投资市场非常不景气，我们不想卖掉更多的股份。而且，我们不想找大财团融资的原因是他们的利率太高了。我们希望从中国银行得到一个较好的贷款利率，比如 6%。

B: Have you taken out any facilities from other commercial banks or are you receiving loans from any other sources?

你们公司还从其他商业银行申请贷款或打算从其他渠道募集资金吗？

A: No, I don't think so. If the Bank of China is willing to support us this time, I don't think we need to approach other bankers.

没有。如果此次中国银行愿意支持我们，我想我们没有必要和其他银行接洽。

B: Well. So can I sum up the details of your requirement? You want the Bank of China to provide $2.7 million out of the $3 million funds needed for the joint venture. You asked for a long-term loan over 10 years at a rate of 6% interest and have the first three years interest free. And you'll start making repayment after five years. Is that right?

嗯。让我来总结一下你的要求好吗？你们需要总额为 300 万美元的资金来筹建合资企业，希望中国银行提供其中的 270 万美元。你们想申请一个十年的长期贷款，利率为 6%，并且头三年免利息，五年后开始还贷。是这样吗？

A: Yes, that's right.

是的，没错。

B: I'm afraid these are not possible. They are against the Bank's policies.

恐怕这些不行。这与中国银行的政策不符。

A: Why not? According to our research, Chinese ice-cream market has great potential. With the products that are especially designed for Chinese market, we are confident that the joint venture will generate high and stable cash flow. In addition, the project will be doing a great public service to the people of Shanghai by providing thousands of jobs. Actually, Shanghai government speaks highly of the significance of setting up joint ventures with foreign partners. For these reasons we are hoping for a loan from the Bank of China on very favorable terms.

为什么不行呢？根据我们的调查，中国冰激凌市场具有巨大的潜力。依靠专门针对中国市场开发的产品，我们相信该合资企业一定会产生高额和稳定的现金流。另外，该项目可以通过提供数以千计的工作来改善上海公共服务的状况。实际上，上海政府高度评价和外国伙伴建立合资企业的意义。因此，我们希望能从中国银行获得优惠的贷款。

B：Well, we may consider offering you a ten-year loan at 8.5% interest. This interest will not vary with the Bank Rate. The Bank will provide 60% ($1.8 million) of the money, provided that you do not go elsewhere for finance, and make up the other 40% ($1.2 million) yourselves. You can have the loan interest free for the first year, and you should make the first repayment in the third year, with the remaining part to be paid in equal installments.

我们可以考虑向贵公司提供十年期的贷款，利率为8.5%，此利率不因央行利率变动而变动。只要你们不在其他地方进行融资，则银行将会提供60%的贷款，即180万美元，其余40%的资金，即120万美元由你们自筹。头一年你们可以得到免息，但你们必须在第三年开始还贷，剩余部分按同样数目分期偿付。

A：I'm afraid your offer is far beyond our expectations.

很抱歉这与我们期望的相差甚远呀。

B：We are making some very generous offers, Ms. Peterson. You should not expect too much from the Bank, as the joint venture is, after all, a commercial organization that makes profits.

我们已经提出非常优惠的条件了，彼特森女士。你们不应当老想从银行获得太多，因为毕竟合资公司才是营利的商业机构。

A：Well, I'm afraid I'll have to report back to my boss.

嗯，我恐怕得向上级汇报此事。

B：All right. If you have made up your mind, please fill in the application form here. It covers most of the basic information about the joint venture, including the capital, the business type, the production and sales forecasts, and also details of all the directors. I will also need Golden Childhood Company's financial statements so that we can conduct a proper assessment on this loan application.

好的。如果你们决定了，请填写这份申请表。表中涵盖了合资企业大部分的基本信息，包括资金、商业类型、生产和销售预测，以及所有董事的情况。我同时还需要金色童年公司的财务报表，以便我们可以对贷款申请进行评估。

【场景2】 从银行信贷部出来，财务经理 Leila Peterson 女士径直回到公司的财务部。财务部里，会计 Sophie Deng 小姐正忙着编制年度的财务报表。

【对话2】 A：Leila Peterson 女士　B：Sophie Deng 小姐

A：How is the financial report coming? Let me take a look at the breakdown.

财务报表编制得怎么样了？让我看看明细。

B：I'm almost done... It's estimated our expenses will be much more than that of last year.

几乎完成了……估计我们的费用支出要比去年多得多。

A：We need to know where the money is going to see if there are any excesses we can easily cut out.（Reads the report）We go over budget by 20% on overhead expenses alone.

我们需要了解钱到哪里去了，以便发现那些容易削减的额外支出。（读财务报表）管理费用一项我们就超过预算 20%。

B：That's true.

没错。

A：Well，from now on，if it's a flight of less than four hours，we're going to ask our managers to fly economy class... And we still have over $100,000 in accounts receivable. We've got to get our customers to pay their bills.

那么，从今天起，凡是不到四个小时的短途飞行，我们要让经理们一律乘坐经济舱……另外，我们还有超过 10 万美元的应收账款。我们得让客户们付钱。

B：The sales people always argue it is better to wait for payment rather than lose a customer，but I think we can tighten up on reminders，statements and so on.

搞销售的人总是说宁肯等待支付货款也不要失去顾客，可是我认为可以把催款信、财务报表等这类工作抓得更紧一些。

A：Well，we must reduce the average delay in payment. It's nearly 45 days now from the date we send out the invoice. We've got to get it down to nearly 30 days.

嗯，我们必须缩短货款拖欠支付的平均期限。现在从我们开出货物发票（到收款）差不多需要 45 天，我们必须把期限缩短在 30 天以内。

Reading：Enhancing Financial Management

财务管理是企业管理的重要组成部分，是有关资金的获得和有效使用的管理工作。财务管理的好坏，直接影响到企业的生存与发展。进入公司后，于琪便很快意识到自己需要好好地补习财务这门功课。

Chapter 12 Financial Management

Section 1 Financial Statement

Financial management consists of all those activities that are concerned with the actual management of a firm's financial operations. The role of financial managers is important because their decisions influence the value of their firms. Within a business organization, the financial manager must not only determine the best way (or ways) to raise money, she or he must also ensure that projected uses are in keeping with the organization's goals. Suppose we take a financial snapshot of a firm called Monterrey Manufacturing Company at a single point in time (Table 12.1). The snapshot should contain a summary of all of the investment and financing decisions made by the firm throughout its relevant history. This type of information is contained in a firm's balance sheet, which shows where and how the company raised its money and how it has spent it.

Table 12.1　　　　　　　　Balance Sheet on 31st December, 2010

Assets	12,000	Liabilities and Equity	12,000
Current Assets	7,200	**Current Liabilities**	2,400
Cash	1,600	Accounts payable	800
Accounts receivable	3,200	Short-term bank loan	1,600
Inventories	2,400	**Long-Term Debt**	**1,600**
Raw materials	900	**Owners' Equity**	**8,000**
Work in process	600	Common stock	1,800
Finished goods	500	Retained earnings	6,200
Supplies	400		
Fixed Assets	4,800		
Plant and equipment (original cost)	6,000		
Less: Accumulated depreciation	1,200		

　　The assets of the firm are on the left-hand side of the balance sheet. Assets represent how a firm has spent its time and money and are usually categorized as either current or fixed. Fixed assets are those that will last a long time, such as a building. Some fixed assets are tangible, such as machinery and equipment. Other fixed assets are intangible, such as patents, trademarks, and the quality of management. The other category of assets, current assets, comprises those that have short lives, such as inventory or accounts receivable. The products that the firm has made but has not yet sold are part of its inventory. Unless the firm has overproduced, the products will eventually be sold. At that time, one asset (inventory) will be converted into another (cash).

　　Before a corporation can invest in an asset, it must obtain funding, which means that it must raise the money to pay for the investment. Many firms obtain funding from a variety of different sources. The right-hand side of the firm's balance sheet summarizes the outstanding different types of financing it has used; hence, we often observe a number of sources rather than just a single provider. A firm will issue (sell) pieces of paper called debt (loan agreements) or equity shares (stock certificates). Debt obligations are owed to creditors, and the stockholders are the debtors. Typically however, shareholders have the right of limited liability, which means they are not personally responsible for repaying the firm's debt obligations. Therefore, lenders base their loan decisions on their assessment of the corporation's ability (and willingness) to repay their credit obligations. Similar to our classification of assets as long-lived or short-lived, so too are liabilities. A short-term loan or debt obligation is called a current liability, which represents loans and other obligations that must be repaid within one year. Long-term debt is debt that does not have to be repaid within one year. Shareholders' equity represents the difference between the value of the assets and the debt of the firm. These are the claims held by the owners of the corporation. In this sense, it is considered a residual claim on the firm's assets. That is, shareholders get paid only after all other financial obligations of the firm have been satisfied.

小 结

财务管理活动涉及对企业财务运作的实际管理。企业在其相对历史时期的所有投资和融资决策信息，通常包含在企业的资产负债平衡表中。企业的资产在资产负债表的左侧，通常划分为流动资产和固定资产。固定资产是持续很长时间的资产，例如建筑。流动资产包含那些寿命期较短的资产，例如库存和应收账款等。企业资产负债表的右侧归纳了企业所使用的不同融资类型。短期负债也叫作流动负债，是企业必须在一年内偿还的贷款和其他责任。长期负债是企业不必在一年内偿还的贷款。股东的所有者权益是公司资产和负债的差额。它是股东在公司资产扣除负债后的剩余索取权。

Section 2 Financial Management Functions

From the balance-sheet model of the firm, it is easy to see why finance can be thought of as the study of the following four questions.

2.1 Fixed Assets Investment Decisions

In what long-lived fixed assets should the firm invest its financial resources? This question concerns the left-hand side of the balance sheet. Of course, the nature of the business the firm has chosen to operate in typically determines the type and proportions of assets the firm needs. We use the terms capital budgeting and capital expenditure to describe the process of committing investment capital and managing expenditures on long-lived assets. An example would be whether Motorola should build a new manufacturing plant to meet the expected increase in demand for its cellular phone products.

A common technique for choosing capital projects is the net present value (NPV) method. NPV is simply the present value of expected future cash inflows minus the initial investment. Future cash inflows are discounted at an appropriate rate which for an average risk project is the firm's cost of capital. The decision rule is simply to accept projects that have positive NPVs. The NPV is theoretically the best capital budgeting method, however, many business professionals prefer the internal rate of return (IRR) method. A project's IRR is simply its expected rate of return. The rationale for the IRR is simply to accept a project that has an IRR greater than the required rate of return.

2.2 Financing Decisions

How should the firm raise the cash necessary to finance its capital expenditures? This question concerns the right-hand side of the balance sheet. These decisions establish the firm's capital structure, which represents the proportions of the firm's financing from current and long-term debt and equity. The four primary types of funding are sales revenue, equity capital, debt capital, and disposal of assets. Future sales generally provide the greatest part of a firm's financing. Equity capital is money received from the sale of shares of ownership in the business. Equity capital is used almost exclusively for long-term financing. Debt capital is money obtained through loans for either short-term or long-term use. The fourth type of funding is the proceeds from the sale of assets. Continuing with our Motorola plant expansion decision, if the management decides to proceed with its planned capital expenditure, should it issue debt or equity to finance the project?

Financial managers must determine and maintain the business's optimal capital structure. Debt financing is beneficial because interest payments are tax deductible whereas dividend payments to stockholders are not tax deductible. Therefore, firms generally prefer debt financing to equity financing. However, debt payments are required and if a firm cannot make principal and interest payments on time it can be forced into bankruptcy. In bankruptcy a firm may have to sell its assets in order to pay creditors. Therefore, some equity financing is desirable. The optimal capital structure balances the advantages and disadvantages of debt and equity financing in order to maximize the value of the firm. A firm's financial manager may decide that the optimal capital structure consists of 40% debt and 60% equity. The optimal capital structure is influenced by many factors such as the stability of the firm's earnings, the liquidity of its assets, and the risk preferences of its stakeholders.

2.3 Operating Cash Flows Decisions

How should short-term operating cash flows be managed? This question concerns the upper portion of the balance sheet. Depending on the business(es) a firm operates, there may be a mismatch between the timing of cash inflows and cash outflows during its operating cycle. Furthermore, both the amount and the timing of operating cash inflows and outflows are not known with certainty. Financial managers must establish policies and procedures to manage the temporary shortfalls (or excess inflows) in cash flow. Short-term management of cash flow is described by a firm's net working capital position. Net working capital is defined as current assets minus current liabilities. Decisions such as how much inventories to carry and how much customer credit should be extended are typical problems addressed here.

2.4 Dividend Policy Decisions

Finally, how much should the firm return the accumulated profits to the shareholders? If there are no good investment opportunities on hand, the financial managers should decide to return the accumulated profits to the shareholders. They should also decide whether to pay dividends or buy back stocks. This is the so-called dividend policy. Most large corporations distribute only a portion of their after-tax earnings to shareholders. The remainder, the portion of a corporation's profits that is not distributed to stockholders, is called retained earnings. Retained earnings are reinvested in the business. Because they are undistributed profits, they are considered a form of equity financing.

小 结

从企业的资产负债表模型，我们很容易理解为什么财务管理活动被看作是对以下四个问题的研究。其一，企业应将其财务资源投入到哪些长期固定资产中？这个问题涉及资产负债表的左侧。我们使用术语资本预算和资本支出来描述计划长期资产投资和管理资金使用的过程。其二，企业应如何获得用于投资的资金？这个问题涉及资产负债表的右侧。这些决策建立了企业的资本结构。其三，企业短期运营现金流应该如何管理？这个问题涉及资产负债表的上部。从财务的角度来说，短期现金流问题源自现金流入与流出的不匹配。最后，如果没有好的投资机会在手，财务经理必须考虑返还股东的累积利润。他们也应考虑是否付红利还是买回股票。这就是所谓的股利政策。

Section 3 Financial Risk Management

Risk is often defined as an exposure to loss and represents uncertainty. While risk cannot be totally eliminated or avoided, it can be retained, transferred, shared, or reduced. Financial managers are responsible for identifying relevant risks confronting the business and efficiently managing those risks.

3.1 Managing Valuable Assets

Businesses generally purchase insurance on valuable assets such as equipment, facilities and finished goods in order to protect against partial or complete destruction. The business signs an indemnity contract with an insurance company agreeing to make regular cash payments called premiums in exchange for a promise by the insurer to reimburse the company if the property is damaged or destroyed by perils such as fire, flood in factory or during transportation. The premiums that are set by actuaries are based on the amount of risk involved and the amount to be paid in case of a loss. Generally, the greater the risk and the amount to be paid, the higher the premium. The contract between an insurer and the person or firm whose risk is assumed is known as the insurance policy. The person or business purchasing the insurance is known as the policyholder. Insurance can thus be considered to be the contractual arrangement where one party agrees to compensate another party for losses proximately caused by the peril insured against.

The purpose of insurance is to provide protection against loss; it is neither speculation nor gambling. This concept is expressed in the principle of indemnity: in the event of a loss, an insured firm or individual cannot collect from the insurer, an amount greater than the actual dollar amount of the loss. Insurance companies will not, however, assume every kind of risk. Those risks that insurance companies will assume are called insurable risks. Risks that insurance firms will not assume are called uninsurable risks. In general, pure risks are insurable, whereas speculative risks are uninsurable. In addition, the policyholder must have an insurable interest. An insurable interest refers to the interest which the policyholder has in the subject matter of the insurance and is recognized by laws. The subject matter of the insurance refers either to the property of the insured and related interests associated therewith, or to the life and body of the insured, which is the object of the insurance. If you would suffer a financial loss because of the death or injury of the person to be insured, or from losses or damage to property, you are considered to have an insurable interest.

3.2 Managing Exchange Rates

Foreign exchange risk can significantly reduce a firm's profit margin on a business transaction. For example, if an American company makes a deal with a firm in Britain to sell it a product for 1 million British pounds, the exchange rate plays a role in exactly how many dollars the American company will receive. If the British company agrees to make the payment in three months, and the dollar strengthens in value relative to the pound, the American company will actually receive fewer dollars than anticipated. For instance, a change in rates from $1.5 per pound to $1.2 per pound will lower the American company's revenue from $1.5 million to $1.2 million.

One of the common ways to reduce exposure to foreign exchange risk is forward contracts. A forward contract is an agreement made today to exchange one currency for another, with the date of the exchange being a specified time in the future, say three months. The rate at which the two currencies will be exchanged is set today. In the case mentioned above, the American company can enter into a forward contract with a bank and fix the exchange rate at $1.5 per pound. The manufacturer will get $1.5 million from the bank when exercising the forward contract, even the exchange rate has fallen to $1.2 per pound. Although forward contracts eliminate uncertainty and foreign exchange risk, they also eliminate any additional profits that can be earned with a favorable movement in exchange rates. Currency option is another way to manage a company's foreign exchange risk. A currency option is a contract that gives the owner the right, but not the obligation, to make either a purchase or sale at an agreed-upon price until the contract expires. Companies reduce exchange rate risk when purchasing currency options because if a rate moves in an unfavorable direction, the company can exercise that option to get their predetermined rate. However, if the rates move in a favorable direction, then the company does not need to exercise that option and can enjoy the additional profits. On the other hand, option contracts cost a fee and may yield less profit if exercised than a forward contract would.

3.3 Managing Interest Rates

Many businesses and organizations are exposed to interest rate risk—the probability that interest rates will unexpectedly change and thus decrease the value of an investment. Interest rate swaps are the oldest and most popular derivatives they use to protect against or hedge interest rate risk. A swap is an agreement between counterparties to exchange cash flows over some period of time. For example, assume a pension fund owns significant debt ($5 million) that pays variable-rate interest while a community bank owns significant debt that pays fixed-rate interest. The pension fund manager may want to lower the fund's exposure to variable-rate interest payments while the community banker may want to increase the bank's exposure to variable-rate interest payments. In this scenario, the pension fund manager may agree to pay a floating interest rate on $5 million to the community bank while the community banker agrees to pay a fixed interest rate on $5 million to the pension fund. In this example, the pension fund manager was able to reduce the fund's exposure to variable interest rates and received a fixed rate on outstanding variable-rate debt. On the other hand, the community banker was able to take advantage of higher interest rates through exposure offered in the swap. Without the swap, the community banker would have had to be content with the fixed interest payments characteristic of the outstanding debt owned by the bank. Essentially, the two entities are swapping their risk positions in a similar market to better meet their institutional goals.

3.4 Managing Commodity Prices

Companies that purchase raw materials are exposed to the risk that the price of these inputs of production will unexpectedly increase. For example, home builders have to deal with the uncertainty of lumber prices. On the other hand, a sugar producer faces the risk of falling sugar prices in the domestic or international market, resulting in a loss of total investment. Companies can hedge these risks by entering into long-term contracts with suppliers and buyers, or investing in derivative contracts.

小 结

企业所面临的财务风险主要体现在四个方面。其一，资产风险。企业通常通过购买保险来对设备、装置的损失风险进行防范。其二，汇率风险。远期合同是减少汇率风险的常见方法。远期合同是当事人之间以一个约定的汇率在未来某个时间进行交易的协议。货币期权是另一种管理公司汇率风险的方式。期权是赋予所有者权利，但不是义务，使其可以以一个议定汇率进行交易，但需支付一定费用。其三，利率风险。利率掉期是最古老和最流行的防止或对冲利率风险的金融衍生工具。掉期是参与者之间的协议,在一段时间内彼此交换现金流。最后,商品价格风险。公司可以通过与交易方签订长期合同或购买金融衍生工具的方式来规避原材料或成品价格变动可能产生的不利影响。

New Words and Key Terms

01. financial management	财务管理
02. balance sheet	资产负债表
03. fixed assets	固定资产
04. current assets	流动资产
05. accounts receivable	应收账款
06. debt obligations	债务责任
07. creditors	债权人
08. debtors	债务人
09. credit obligations	债权责任
10. current liabilities	流动负债
11. long-term debt	长期负债
12. shareholders' equity	股东权益
13. capital budgeting and capital expenditure	资本预算与资本支出
14. net present value	净现值
15. internal rate of return	内部收益率
16. capital structure	资本结构
17. net working capital	净营运资本
18. dividend policy	股利政策
19. retained earnings	留存收益,未分配利润
20. insurance	保险
21. premiums	保险费
22. insurer	保险商,承保人
23. insurance policy	保险单
24. policyholder	投保人
25. principle of indemnity	赔偿原则,补偿原则
26. insurable risks	可保风险
27. uninsurable risks	不可保风险
28. insurable interest	保险利益
29. subject matter	(保险)标的
30. forward contract	远期合同
31. currency option	货币期权
32. interest rate swaps	利率掉期
33. derivatives	金融衍生工具

Writing：Resume or CV

在贷款申请工作进行的同时,金色童年公司也在考虑合资企业未来诸多岗位的合适人选。根据合资协议,合资企业的财务经理将由英方担任,中方派人出任财务助理。公司已刊登了财务助理的招聘广告,应聘者非常多。这天下午,人事部经理 Michael Douglas 先生拿来一些简历,让于琪帮助其筛选重点人员安排面试。

一、简历写作的基本要求和格式

简历(Resume or CV)是对自己资历的总结,提供有关个人背景的重要信息,供深造或求职使用,并构成申请材料的重要组成部分。简历的书写首先应做到简洁,以不超过两页纸为宜。其次应引人入胜,设法突出自己的强项。对于大多数高校毕业生,学历是自己的强项;而有相应工作经历的人,重点则应放在工作经历上。最后一点是要如实填写。简历写作允许锦上添花,但坚决反对无中生有。一份简历通常包括如下内容:

(一)个人信息(Personal Data)

个人信息应当包括如年龄(age)、出生地(birth place)、健康状况(health)、婚姻状况(marital status),以及联系方式等所有申请深造或求职时可能需要的资料。其中联系方式是非常重要的信息,通常要将名字、地址、电话号码、电子邮件地址清楚地列在简历的上部,以及申请材料的封面。不要让读你申请的人到处寻找这些信息。例如,

Date of Birth：July 12，1988　　　　Birth Place：Beijing
Sex：Male　　　　　　　　　　　　Marital Status：Single
Telephone：(010) 88888888　　　　E-mail：career@sohu.com

(二)职业目标(Job Objective)

职业目标是指个人在选定的职业领域内未来时点上所要达到的具体目标。例如,A challenging position in the company's technology field. 在公司技术领域的一个具有挑战性的职位。

(三)教育经历(Education Background)

教育经历应从最后就读的学校写起,并标明学校名称、获取的学位或证书的日期。还要列出所学的相关课程及所获荣誉或奖励。如果学习成绩优异,可列出成绩单。通常情况下,简历中不必填写高中部分的情况,除非申请者认为高中的信息可能会使申请的大学或未来雇主感兴趣。例如,

2010.9～Present　Master of Business Administration　University of Central Florida
　Courses Studied include：Strategy, Marketing, Finance, Accounting, International Trade, E-Commerce, Human Resources Management, etc.
　Honors or Achievement：President of the Student Union.
2006.9～2010.7　Bachelor of Business Administration　East Michigan University

Courses Studied include：Business English，Sales and Marketing，Consumer Behavior，Promotional Strategies，Statistics，etc.

Honors or Achievement：Class monitor，Scholarships for 4 consecutive years.

（四）工作经历（Working Experience）

申请者应着眼于学业或雇主的需求，重点写出满足该学业或雇主需求的资历。必要时更可使用概述的方式，便于主试者深入了解。同样，工作经历要按逆序排列（in reverse chronological order），写清楚雇用时间、雇用单位、具体工作。对于刚毕业的大学生，课下的兼职、假期实践、毕业实习，以及曾参加的一些课外活动都可算是工作经历。例如，

2010.9～Present   BEIJING HUAXIA CONSULTING Co.

Position：Assistant Executive

Duties：Direct regional and national professional training courses，develop and maintain an efficient career counseling and consultancy service，and provide information and advice to user groups.

Achievement：Earned a profit of ＄180,000 for the first half year of 2011 by successfully marketing consultancy and training services.

2006.9～2010.7   JINZHOU TIANLONG ADVERTISING Co.

Position：Marketing Consultant

Duties：Designed promotional campaigns to suit clients' needs，created multimedia advertisements for small and mid-sized companies，collected market information and forecasted market trend，etc.

Achievement：Developed a computer program for analyzing market data，which had been adopted by over twenty firms nationwide by the end of 2009.

Reasons for leaving：Professional and financial advancement afforded by a larger company.

（五）其他信息（Other Background）

包括技能（skill）或资格证书（Certificate），如 Certificate of College English Test Band 6（大学英语六级证书）；社会活动，如 Organizer of the third Culture Festival of Bohai University（渤海大学第三届文化节的组织者）；兴趣爱好（Interests and Hobbies），如 sports and travel（运动和旅游）等。

（六）证明人（Reference）

证明人的目的是给未来的大学或老板提供信息，以便帮助他们做出最后的决定。申请者应选择最合适的人为之推荐，并列出至少两位证明人，一位是学历证明人，另一位是工作经历证明人（有些情况下，需要列出三位证明人）。切记征得证明人的许可方可填写他们的姓名。除姓名外，还应该写上证明人的职务、通信地址，以及电话号码。

二、于琪的解决方案

\multicolumn{3}{c|}{A Resume of Han Wu}		
Home Address	21 Jiefang Road, Jinzhou City, Liaoning Province, P. R. China，121001	Attach a photo taken recently
School Address	Accounting Department，Peking University，Peking，101149	
Job Objective	A position offering challenge and responsibility in the realm of accounting or management.	
\multicolumn{3}{c|}{Personal Data}		
Name	Han Wu	Date of Birth	Oct. 23, 2001
Sex	Female	Marital Status	Single
\multicolumn{3}{c|}{Education Background}		
2019～2023 Peking University	Graduating in December with a BS degree in Accounting. Fields of study include Principles of Accounting, Cost Accounting, Commercial Accounting, Industrial Accounting, Management Accounting, Marketing, and Commercial Law, etc.	
Extracurricular Activities and Rewards	◇ Organizer of the first Cultural Festival of Peking University in 2021 ◇ Class monitor from 2019 to 2023 ◇ Member of the college choir from 2019 to 2023	
\multicolumn{3}{c|}{Working Experience}		
2020～2022 Part-time accountant at the Atlantic Trading Company	◇ Conducted routine bookkeeping in accordance with the requirements of CICPA's Auditing Standards; ◇ Provided financial consultation, financial analysis; ◇ Assisted enterprise to improve its system of internal control.	
Rewards or Achievements	Compiled "China's future market" with colleagues, a 350-page book, published by China Financial and Economic Publishing House, 2021.	
\multicolumn{3}{c|}{Relevant Skills and Abilities}		
\multicolumn{3}{l|}{◇ Being familiar with the PRC Financial and Tax Regulations, having excellent financial analysis skills and financial management ability; ◇ Being capable of handling accounting affairs and prepare financial reports in English; ◇ Being skillful in the use of office software, including Word, Excel and others; ◇ College English Test Band 6; ◇ National Computer Rank Examination Band 4.}		
\multicolumn{3}{c|}{Self-recommendation}		
\multicolumn{3}{l|}{Besides all the qualifications I have acquired in the accounting area, I'm confident, humorous, considerate, goal-driven, reliable, and mature in thought. I believe I would be a great asset to any organization I work for.}		
References	References will be furnished upon request.	

Review Questions

1. Key Terms

Current assets; Net present value; Capital structure; Principle of indemnity; Currency option

2. Multiple Choices (select one)

(1) (   ) is concerned with the acquisition, financing, and management of assets with some overall goal in mind.

 A. Financial management   B. Profit maximization

 C. Agency theory   D. Social responsibility

(2) A major disadvantage of the corporate form of organization is the (   ).

 A. double taxation of dividends

 B. inability of the firm to raise large sums of additional capital

 C. limited liability of shareholders

 D. limited life of the corporate form

(3) Felton Farm Supplies, Inc. has an 8 percent return on total assets of 300000 and a net profit margin of 5 percent. What are its sales? (   )

 A. 3,750,000.   B. 480,000.   C. 300,000.   D. 1,500,000.

(4) A company can improve (lower) its debt-to-total asset ratio by doing which of the following? (   )

 A. Borrow more.   B. Shift short-term to long-term debt.

 C. Shift long-term to short-term debt.   D. Issue common stock.

(5) Which of the following items concerns financing decision? (   )

 A. Sales forecasting.   B. Bond issuing.

 C. Receivables collection.   D. Investment project selection.

(6) Which of the following items is the function of a treasurer? (   )

 A. Cost accounting.   B. Internal control.

 C. Capital budgeting.   D. General ledger.

(7) (   ) is the value at some future time of a present amount of money, or a series of payments, evaluated at a given interest rate.

 A. Future value   B. Present value

 C. Intrinsic value   D. Market value

(8) Which of the following items has the most risk? (   )

 A. Treasury bill.   B. Corporate bond.

 C. Preferred stock.   D. Common stock.

(9) (   ) equals the gross profit divided by net sales of a firm.

 A. Gross profit margin   B. Net profit margin

C. Return on investment　　　　D. Return on equity

(10) A(n) (　　) is a contract that gives the owner the right, but not the obligation, to make either a purchase or sale at an agreed-upon price until the contract expires.

A. forward contract　　　　B. option
C. swap　　　　D. long-term contract

3. Questions for Discussion

(1) What kind of information is contained in a firm's balance sheet? What is the difference between current assets and fixed assets?

(2) Where do a corporation's retained earnings come from? Will financial managers return all the accumulated profits to the shareholders?

(3) How do businesses generally do to protect their valuable assets such as equipment, facilities and finished goods against partial or complete destruction?

Practical Writing

Scenario: Send a **Resume** in reply to the following advertisement. You may invent any name, experience and qualification you consider relevant to the application.

Sales Representatives

Already one of the fast-growing garden products companies in the UK, Jardina will soon be selling its high-quality garden furniture in the USA.

We are looking for experienced sales representatives to help us set up a distributorship in the USA.

If you happen to be aged 25~35 and
√ possess good sales and communication skills,
√ be able to manage people effectively,
√ have an excellent track record,

Why not join Jardina and enjoy the attractive starting salary of $70,000, plus attractive incentive scheme and fringe benefit in keeping the image of a young, dynamic company?

Interested? Please send your C. V. to: Human Resources Department, Jardina furniture plc, Manor Heights, Manor Road, London, 3ED 4AX.

Unit 13　We Need a Hand

Learning Objectives

◇ 熟悉求职面试的常用口语表达；
◇ 理解人员计划、招募与选择的含义和基本方法；
◇ 理解人员报酬的种类和不同类型报酬的作用；
◇ 理解人员培训、开发与表现评估的目的和基本方法；
◇ 掌握劳动合同的书写规则和常用套语的正确写法。

Speaking：Job Interview

【场景1】吴晗小姐是一名即将毕业的大学生。一天，她刚好在报纸上看到"金色童年"即将成立的合资企业招聘财务助理的广告。在提交简历后不久，她接到了公司的面试通知。这天一早，她如约来到了"金色童年"的总部大楼。

【对话1】　A：吴晗小姐　　B：前台接待

A：Good morning.
　　早上好。

B：Good morning, Miss. What can I do for you?
　　早上好，小姐。我能为您做些什么？

A：I'm coming for an interview at nine o'clock in the morning. I received a call the day before yesterday, informing me of my interview.
　　我来这里是为了今天上午9点钟的面试。我前天接到电话，通知我今天参加面试。

B：I see. Can I have your name please?
　　是这样。请问您的名字？

A：Sure. My name is Han Wu.
　　好的。我的名字叫吴晗。

B：(Taking a quick glimpse at the name list) Oh, yes, your number is six. Would you please sit there and wait a moment? I'll call your name when it is your turn.

(快速浏览名单)喔,找到了,您的号码是 6 号。请在那边坐下等一会儿,轮到您的时候我会叫您的名字。

A:OK, thank you.

好的,谢谢。

B:(About twenty minutes later, she gestures to Han Wu.) Miss Wu, it's your turn now, and our interviewers are waiting for you in Room 201. Please come this way.

(大约20分钟后,她向吴晗示意。)吴小姐,现在轮到您了,我们的面试官在 201 房间等您。请这边走。

A:OK. Thank you.

好的,谢谢。

B:Don't mention it. Good luck to you!

不用谢。祝您好运!

【场景 2】 随着前台接待小姐的引领,吴晗小姐来到了 201 房间。面试的主考官是人力资源部经理 Michael Douglas 先生。吴晗知道,真正的考验马上就要开始了。

【对话 2】 A:Michael Douglas 先生　　B:吴晗小姐

A:Please sit down, Miss Wu. Something to drink?

请坐,吴小姐。喝点什么吗?

B:No, thank you, not just now.

不,谢谢,现在不。

A:Well, I think you probably have a fair idea about what sort of job you've applied for.

好的,我想你对申请的工作应该有个基本的了解了。

B:Yes, it was clearly explained in the advertisement.

是的,招聘广告上解释得非常清楚。

A:I have noticed from your Resume that you major in accounting at Peking University. Will you please tell me something about your related courses?

我从你的简历中知道你是北京大学会计专业的。能告诉我你都学了哪些相关课程吗?

B:In the first academic year we learned Principles of Accounting, and in the following years we learned Cost Accounting, Commercial Accounting, Industrial Accounting, and Management Accounting.

第一学年,我们学了会计原理,接下来的几年学了成本会计、商业会计、工业会计和管理会计。

A:From your academic transcript, I can see you did well in every course. But our advertisement says we need an accountant with practical work experience.

从成绩单上可以看出你每门课程都学得很好。可我们广告上说我们需要有实际工作经验的会计。

B：In fact, I took a part-time job as an accountant at the Atlantic Trading Company during my second and third school year. I worked three evenings a week there and I did quite well. Here is the recommendation.

实际上，在我的第二和第三学年，我在大西洋贸易公司做过兼职会计。我每周在那里工作三个晚上，而且做得很出色。这是他们的推荐信。

A：You can speak English fluently but I wonder if you can deal with bookkeeping and accounting in English.

你英语说得很流利，但我不知道你能否用英语记账和清算账目。

B：No problem. The professional English course is just English for Accounting. Moreover, as you know, the Atlantic Trading Company is a Sino-Australian joint venture. When I served part-time there, I became well acquainted with accounting operated in English.

没问题，我的专业英语就是会计英语。而且，你也知道大西洋贸易公司是一家中澳合资企业。我在那里做兼职时，就已经熟练掌握用英语进行会计操作了。

A：What were your responsibilities in that work?

你当时工作的主要职责是什么？

B：My work involved various routine bookkeeping and basic accounting tasks including journal entries, verifying data and reconciling discrepancies, preparing detailed reports from raw data, and checking accounting documents for completeness, mathematical accuracy and consistency.

我的工作包括各种日常记账以及基本的账目清算任务，例如日记账分录、核对数据、理顺差错、以原始数据准备详细的报告，以及检查账目文档的完整性、准确性和一致性。

A：That sounds fine. Why did you choose to apply to our company?

听起来不错，那你为什么选择了我们公司呢？

B：I have a relative working as a manager in your manufacturing department. Her name is Liu Ling. She told me a lot about the projected joint venture program and I became quite interested. I believe I can have a promising career with the development of this joint venture.

我有个亲戚是贵公司生产部的一名经理，她叫刘灵。她告诉我许多有关贵公司计划的合资项目情况，我非常感兴趣。我相信随着合资公司的发展，我的事业也会大有前途的。

【场景3】 求职面试中的技能考核是必不可少的。Michael Douglas 先生，这位哈佛大学 MBA 毕业生，本身就是财务方面的专家。

【对话3】 A：Michael Douglas 先生　B：吴晗小姐

A: Well, I suppose you are familiar with the PRC Financial and Tax Regulations already. Can you tell me the classification of long-term assets?
嗯,我想你应该熟悉中华人民共和国财政和税收条例。你能告诉我长期资产的分类吗?

B: Certainly. There are three major forms, which are constructed assets, natural assets and intangible assets. You know the costs related to the use of long-term assets must be properly calculated and matched against the revenues the assets help to produce.
当然可以。主要有三种,即建造资产、自然资产和无形资产。您知道,与使用长期资产有关的成本必须恰当加以计算,而且要和这些资产所产生的收入相结合。

A: Could you give me some examples about intangible assets?
你能给我举几个无形资产的例子吗?

B: Intangible assets include patents, copyrights, franchises, trademarks, land use rights and so on.
无形资产包括专利、版权、特许经营权、商标、土地使用权等。

A: What shall we do about the costs for periodic maintenance?
对于定期维修的费用,我们应该怎么处理?

B: Usually they are charged to expense. As to the expenditures for extraordinary repairs or betterment, the costs should be capitalized and allocated over the asset's useful life through depreciation. One more thing, betterment improves the quality of an asset and may extend the remaining years of its useful life.
通常是记作费用。至于非正常修理或改良的支出,这些费用应该资本化并以折旧的形式在资产的可使用寿命期内进行分摊。还有一件事,改良提升了资产的品质,可能会延长其剩余使用寿命期。

A: Very good, thanks. Well, can you tell me how you spend your leisure time?
很好,谢谢。那么,能告诉我你业余时间都做些什么吗?

B: I like travel and all kinds of sports, such as basketball, swimming, bike riding and so on. Maybe it is just the reason why I am so energetic and vigorous.
我喜欢旅行和各类体育运动,比如打篮球、游泳、骑车之类的。也许这是我精力如此充沛的原因吧。

A: Very interesting. If hired, when could you start work?
很有意思。如果被雇佣,你何时能开始工作?

B: I'll defend my thesis in late November, so I can set to work in December.
我需要在11月底进行论文答辩,12月份就可以正式上班了。

【场景4】 面试即将结束,按照惯例,考官会在面试最后询问应试者有什么问题,吴晗小姐不想浪费这次机会。

【对话4】 A: Michael Douglas 先生 B: 吴晗小姐

A: Well, we've made a note of that. Now, do you have any questions you'd like to ask?
好了,我们已经做了记录。现在,你有什么问题需要询问吗?

B：Yes, well, I wonder if you could tell me what the salary would be.
是的，嗯，我想知道您是否能告诉我工作的报酬情况。

A：Of course. We'd be offering a starting salary of ＄200 a week, that's for 40 hours.
当然。开始工资是每周 200 美元，一周工作 40 个小时。

B：Do you mean that it might be increased at a later stage?
是否意味着以后还会加薪？

A：Yes, we normally give our staff a month's trial and then, if everything is satisfactory we raise the salary by 20 percent. Any more questions?
是的，我们通常给员工的试用期是一个月，如果工作满意，我们会增加 20％的工资。还有其他问题吗？

B：No. I think that's all.
没有了，就这些。

A：Well, thank you very much for coming in. I have got quite a lot more people to see, of course, but you should be hearing from us in the next few days.
好的，非常感谢你的到来。我还有很多人需要见，当然，你会在随后几天内得到反馈。

Reading：Enhancing Human Resources Management

"人"是组织最重要的资产，也是竞争力的关键因素。于琪清楚，一个不重视人才获得、培养，以及维系的企业，迟早会丧失其竞争力。但是，人力资源管理工作该如何合理、有效地进行呢？

Chapter 13 Human Resources Management

Section 1 Human Resources Planning, Recruiting, and Selection

The human resource is not only unique and valuable; it is an organization's most important resource. The term "human resources" implies that people have capabilities that drive organizational performance (along with other resources such as money, materials, information, and the like). It seems logical that organizations would expend a great deal of effort to acquire and utilize such a resource, and most organizations do. That effort is now known as human resources management (HRM), which consists of all the activities involved in planning, acquiring, maintaining, developing, and appraising an organization's human resources.

1.1 Human Resources Planning

As the definition implies, HRM begins with planning to ensure that personnel needs will be constantly and appropriately met. Human resources planning is the development of strategies for meeting the firm's future human resource needs. The starting point for this planning is the organization's overall strategic plan. From this, human resources planner can forecast the firm's future demand for human resources. Next they must determine whether the needed human resources will be available; that is, they must forecast the supply of human resources within the firm. Finally they have to take steps to match supply with demand.

Forecasts of human resources demand should be based on as much relevant information as planners can gather. The firm's overall strategic plan will provide information about future business ventures, new products, and projected expansions or contractions of particular product lines. Information on past staffing levels, evolving technologies, industrial staffing practices, and projected economic trends can also be very helpful.

The human resources supply forecast must take into account both the present work force and any changes, or movements that may occur within it. Two useful techniques for forecasting human resources supply are the replacement chart and the skills inventory. A replacement chart is a list of key personnel, along with possible replacements within the firm. A skills inventory is a computerized data bank containing information on the skills and experience of all present employees. It is used to search for candidates to fill new or newly available positions.

Once they have forecasts of both the demand for personnel and the firm's supply of personnel, planners can devise a course of action for matching the two. We also need to know the exact nature of a job before we can find the right person to do it. The job analysis for a particular position is significant, which typically consists of two parts: a job description and a job specification. A job description is a list of the elements that make up a particular job. It includes the duties the jobholder must perform, the working condition under which the job must be performed, the jobholder's responsibilities (including number and types of subordinates, if any), and the tools and equipment that must be used on the job. A job specification is a list of the qualifications required to perform a particular job. Included are the skills, abilities, education, and experience that the jobholder must have. The job analysis is the basis for recruiting and selecting new employees—for either existing positions or new ones.

1.2 Human Resources Recruiting

Recruiting is the process of attracting qualified job applicants. Because it is a vital link in a costly process, recruiting needs to be a systematic rather than haphazard process. One goal of recruiters is to attract the "right" number of applicants. The right number is enough to allow a good match between applicants and open positions, but not so many that matching them requires too much time and effort.

The recruitment strategy should be based upon the human resource planning estimates as to the numbers, types, and skill sets of employees needed and upon the organizations' ability to compensate the employees. Based upon the results of the job analyses, job advertisements should be written up identifying the skills and experiences of applicants desired. The advertisement should be designed such that it attracts employees with the types of background experiences and skills desired for the job and in the numbers needed by the organization. An important part of recruitment is the determination of where to advertise the job openings.

Recruiters may seek applicants outside the firm, within the firm, or both. Which source is used generally depends on the nature of the position, the situation within the firm, and (sometimes) the firm's established or traditional recruitment policies. Some firms have a policy of recruiting or promoting from within except in very exceptional circumstances. This policy has three major advantages. First, individuals recruited from within are already familiar with the organization and its members, and this knowledge increases the likelihood they will succeed. Second, a promotion-from-within policy fosters loyalty and inspires greater effort among organization members. Finally, it is usually less expensive to recruit or promote from within than to hire from outside the organization.

However, internal recruitment limits the pool of available talent, reduces the chance that fresh viewpoints will enter the organization, and may encourage complacency among employees who assume seniority ensures promotion. Therefore in most instances the position would be advertised both internally and externally. Internal postings may be done in a variety of ways from newsletters, to e-mail messages, to bulletin boards (both virtual and physical). External postings may also be done electronically, through newspapers, magazines, trade journals, with job placement services, and through word of mouth. Once a pool of applicants has been created it then moves on to the next step—employee selection.

1.3 Human Resources Selection

Selection is the process of gathering information about applicants for a position and then using that information to choose the most appropriate applicant. Note the use of the word appropriate. In selection, the idea is not to hire the person with the "most" qualifications, but rather to choose the applicant with the qualifications that are most appropriate for the job. The actual selection of an applicant often is made by one or more line managers who have responsibility for the position being filled. However, HRM personnel usually facilitate the selection process by developing a pool of applicants and expediting the assessment of these applicants. The most common means of obtaining information about applicants' qualifications are employment applications, tests, interviews, references, and assessment centers.

Employment applications are useful in collecting factual information on a candidate's education, work experience, and personal history. The data obtained from applications are usually used for two purposes: to identify candidates who are worthy of further scrutiny and to familiarize interviewers with applicants' backgrounds. Tests that are given to job candidates usually focus on aptitudes, skills, abilities, or knowledge relevant to the job that is to be performed. The employment interview, which provides an opportunity for the applicant and the firm to learn more about each other, is perhaps the most widely used selection technique. Interviewers can pose problems to test the candidate's abilities. They can probe employment history more deeply and learn something about the candidate's attitudes and motivation. The candidate, meanwhile, has a chance to find out more about the job and the people with whom he or she would be working. A job candidate is generally asked to furnish the names of references—people who can verify background information and provide personal evaluations of the candidate. A newer selection technique is the assessment center, which is used primarily to select current employees for promotion to higher-level management positions.

小 结

人力资源计划是为了满足企业未来人力资源需求所制定的发展战略。它需要根据企业的总体战略计划预测未来的人力需求和供给状况，以便采取措施保证供求平衡。同时，在选择合适的人员之前，人力资源管理者还需要了解某一工作的具体属性。招工是吸引高素质求职者的过程。招工者的目标是吸引适度数额的应聘者，既能够保证求职者与空缺职位间形成良好的匹配，又不能使匹配过程花费大量的时间和精力。选择是指搜集求职者的信息，然后再利用那些信息选择最合适的人选的过程。获取关于求职者素质信息最常用的手段包括：就业申请、测试、面试、推荐书，以及评估中心等。

Section 2 Compensation

After acquisition—getting people to work for the organization, steps must be taken to keep these valuable resources. They are the only business resources that can leave the organization at will. In fact, the use of compensation as motivators has been traced to antiquity.

2.1 Wages and Salaries

Wages and salaries are the monetary form of compensation given to a firm's employees for their contributions. The amount of wage is set according to the number of hours worked (hence the name "time wage") or the number of products made (hence the name "piece rate wage"), or a combination of the two. Salary is money compensation for longer periods of work time (e.g., a month or a year) and mostly paid to middle and upper level managers. A number of factors should be taken into consideration when a firm sets its wage and salary schedules. First, they must be equitable compared with the contributions made by the employees. In addition, they should be competitive in the industry to keep employees from quitting and working for rivals. Within the firm, moreover, employees doing different jobs should be paid different wages or salaries to reflect the skills required for the jobs and/or the importance of the positions. Some firms also pay experienced workers more than they pay newcomers even if the two do the same type of job, because it is felt that the experienced workers usually perform better and therefore should be retained at a higher cost.

2.2 Incentive Programs

With equitable and competitive wages and salaries, the employees should complete their normal tasks. To have employees work harder and become more productive, however, incentive programs of all sorts have been adopted to link above-normal performance with additional income or rewards. A manager who has done exceptionally well would have a big bonus or stock options (the options to buy company stock at a predetermined and favorable price); and a worker who overfulfils the normal production quota by 10% would also get extra pay. The most typical example of incentive programs is probably the ones designed for salespeople. Such people are usually given a low base salary. Any additional income (often called commission) is tied to the sales they make, usually a certain percentage of the sales.

Some other incentive programs are designed for employees as a whole rather than individuals. For example, a company may introduce a gain-sharing plan which stipulates that the gain resulting from the reduction of the firm's overhead costs will be shared as bonus by all employees. In a similar fashion, a firm may announce a profit-sharing plan which will give all employees a bonus if the firm's profits exceed a preset amount.

2.3 Fringe Benefits

Different from wages, salaries and incentive programs which are directly linked with the jobs done, fringe benefits are not directly related with work performance, but given as a result of employment. The most common benefits in the US are life, health and disability insurance, pension plans, and paid vacations. Other benefits may include vision care, dental benefits, discounts on the purchase price of the firm's products, and even free legal services.

As the economy develops and the standard of living rises, the range of fringe benefits has expanded so much that, in some companies, the benefits cost over half of the total money that these companies spend on compensation, so that the term "fringe" is no longer appropriate. To make the benefits programs more tailor-made to suit the needs of individual employees and therefore more cost-effective, many firms have experimented with new arrangements. Cafeteria benefit, one of such experiments, is a flexible arrangement in which each employee is allocated a certain sum to cover benefits of his or her own choice.

小 结

工资和薪酬是对公司员工贡献的货币补偿形式。工资数额可按照工作小时数(计时工资)、产品数量(计件工资),或两者结合计取。薪酬是对较长工作时间(如一个月或一年)的货币补偿形式,主要是支付给中、高层管理人员。工资和薪酬是对员工完成其正常工作的补偿。为让员工更努力地工作和变得更有效率,公司会制定各种激励方案来对员工的超常表现进行奖励。最常见的奖励方案是付给销售人员在底薪基础上的销售提成。员工的福利是间接提供给职工们的报酬。员工福利并非与工作表现有关,而是来自工作本身。它包括各种保险、养老金、带薪休假、折价购买公司产品,甚至免费的法律咨询等。一些公司甚至允许员工采用自选福利的形式。

Section 3 Training, Development and Performance Appraisal

3.1 Training and Development

Once new employees have been hired within an organization, they should be developed to their full capacity to contribute to the firm. Training and development are both aimed at improving employees' skills and abilities. Needless to say, new employees need training to do their jobs well. Experienced employees, in order to be more productive, also need training in more efficient techniques, methods or skills.

Most employee training takes place on the job (while the employee is working). In more complicated work the employee may be trained for the job before being hired and then retrained by the organization after beginning paid employment or they may be trained for the job off-site (while not performing the job, but being paid). For example, modern American bombing crews are trained for their job by the US government before being assigned to a bombing crew and then they are re-trained by the training officers from their squadrons as to what they are supposed to do. They also must then go through refresher courses at predetermined intervals in order to ensure that they remain combat ready and that they do not forget what they were trained to do and how they are supposed to do what they are trained to do. The most common type of training is employee orientation, which is done to acquaint new employees with their organization (organizational culture and policies, etc.) and their working environment (physical surroundings, colleagues, responsibilities, etc.).

While employee training involves making a worker more effective and efficient in his/her current job, employee development involves the preparation of the employee for future positions within the organization. Typically the first type of employee development with which employees become involved is career exploration in which employees decide where they would like to work and what they might like to do in the future. Psychological self evaluations such as the Strong Interest Inventory and the Personal Career Development Profile are two tests which may be very useful for employees trying to decide what they might do in the future as can mission-based goal-setting in which employees develop a mission statement for their life—just as the organization has a mission statement to provide guidance for employees—so too may a personal mission statement provide guidance for employees seeking to decide what type of personal and career development they may desire.

3.2 Performance Appraisal

The final area for human resources management is the evaluation of employees' on-the-job performance. Performance appraisal or job evaluation is the evaluation of employees' current and potential levels of performance to allow managers to make objective human resource decisions. It has three main objectives. First, performance appraisal allows manager to let subordinates know how well they are doing and how they can do better in the future. Second, it provides an effective basis for distributing rewards such as pay raises and promotions. Third, performance appraisal helps the organization monitor its employee selection and training and development activities. If large numbers of employees continually perform below expectations, the firm's selection process may need to be revised, additional training and development may be required.

The various techniques and methods for appraising employee performance are either objective or judgmental in nature. Objective appraisal methods make use of some measurable quantity as the basis for assessing performance. Units of output, dollar volume of sales, number of defective products, and number of insurance claims processed are all objective, measurable quantities. Judgmental appraisal methods are used much more frequently than objective methods. They require that the manager judge or estimate the employee's performance level, relative to some standard.

No matter which appraisal technique is used, the results should be discussed with the employee soon after the evaluation is completed. The manager should explain the basis for present rewards and should let the employee know what he or she can do to be recognized as a better performer in the future. The information provided to an employee in such discussion is called performance feedback.

小　结

培训和开发旨在提高员工们的技艺和能力。员工培训的目的是使员工更有效地做他/她目前的工作,而员工开发涉及员工为其在组织内的未来发展做准备。绩效评估是评价职工目前和潜在的绩效水平。它主要有三个目标。首先,绩效评估使管理者让下属知道他们干得怎么样,怎样才能干得更好。其次,它为诸如涨工资、晋升等奖励分配提供了一个有效的根据。再次,绩效评估有助于组织监测其员工选择、培训和开发等活动是否得当。评价员工表现的方法很多,但不外乎是客观判断和主观判断两大类。不论采用哪种评价方法,其结果都应在评估结束后不久便与员工进行讨论。

New Words and Key Terms

01. human resources management	人力资源管理
02. human resources planning	人力资源计划
03. replacement chart	替换图
04. skills inventory	技艺库
05. job analysis	工作分析,作业分析
06. job description	工作(岗位)说明
07. job specification	工作(岗位)规范
08. recruiting	招工,招募,招聘
09. promotion-from-within	内部提拔
10. selection	选择,挑选;淘汰
11. assessment centers	评估中心
12. compensation	报酬;补偿,赔偿
13. wage	工资
14. time wage	计时工资
15. piece rate wage	计件工资
16. salary	薪酬
17. bonus	红利
18. stock options	股票期权
19. base salary	底薪
20. commission	佣金
21. gain-sharing plan	收益分享计划
22. profit-sharing plan	利润分享计划
23. fringe benefits	福利
24. pension	退休金
25. cafeteria benefit	自助式福利
26. employee training	员工培训
27. employee orientation	员工定位
28. employee development	员工开发
29. Strong Interest Inventory	斯特朗兴趣量表
30. Personal Career Development Profile	个人职业生涯发展规划
31. performance appraisal	绩效评估,业绩鉴定
32. performance feedback	表现反馈

Writing: Contract of Employment

上午面试的吴晗小姐给公司留下了很好的印象。由于人力资源部经理 Michael Douglas 先生还有许多其他职位的面试工作要做,他下午一上班便让于琪先代他起草一份公司和吴晗小姐的劳动合同,以备签署。

一、劳动合同写作的基本要求和格式

劳动合同(Contract of Employment 或 Employment Agreement)是劳动者与用工单位之间确立劳动关系,明确双方权利和义务的协议。劳动合同应当具备以下条款:

(一)约首(Head)

所包括内容与意向书类似。其中,序言写法通常如下:…(the engaging party) has engaged…(the engaged party) as…(position). The two parties in the spirit of friendship and cooperation have entered into an agreement to sign and to comply with the following terms:……(聘方)聘请……(受聘方)为……(职务)。双方本着友好合作的精神,同意签订并遵守本合同。合同条款如下:

(二)正文(Body)

1. 聘任期限(Duration of Employment)

例如,The duration of service is… i.e. from… to… 聘期为……(年限),自……日起,至……日止。

2. 受聘方工作任务细则(Specified Duties of the Engaged Party)

例如,By mutual consultation the work of the Engaged Party is decided as follows:(1) Training teachers of English, research students and students taking refresher courses;(2) Compiling English textbooks and supplementary teaching materials, undertaking tape recording and other work connected with the language;(3) Having 10 to 12 teaching periods in a week. 经双方协商,受聘方的工作任务确定如下:(1)担任英语师资、研究生、进修生的培训工作;(2)编写英语教材和补充读物,以及进行英语录音及其他英语相关的工作;(3)每周授课 10~12 课时。

3. 聘方义务(Obligations of the Engaging Party)

例如,Party A will provide free of charge Party B with suitable accommodation including a color television, washing machine, air conditioner, refrigerator, dishes and cooking utensils (where applicable), and all required bedding. 聘方免费为受聘方提供适宜的住宿和生活条件,包括彩电、洗衣机、空调、冰箱、炊具(视情况)及床上用品。

4. 受聘方义务(Obligations of the Engaged Party)

例如,The Party B shall observe the Party A's work system and regulations concerning foreigners working in China and shall accept the Party A's arrangement, direction, supervision and evaluation in regard to his/her work. 受聘方应遵守聘方的工作制度和国家有关外国人在华就业管理规定,接受聘方的工作安排、业务指导、检查和评估。

5. 薪金支付(Salary and Payment)

例如,Party B's monthly salary will be... Euros, ...% of which can be converted into foreign currency monthly. 受聘方的月薪为……欧元,其中……%可按月兑换外汇。

6. 福利待遇(Welfare)

例如,In addition to being entitled to all Chinese public holidays Party B is also entitled to a 3-week paid holiday. 受聘方除享有所有中国公共节假日外,每年另享有三周带薪假。再如,Party A shall, at his own cost, also pay contribution to the Social Security Scheme of... for Party B to comply with the relevant regulations of... government. 聘方还应该按……政府的规定,为受聘方缴纳……(数额)社会保险。

7. 合同的生效、修改及终止(Validity, Revision and Termination of the Contract)

例如,The present contract shall come into effect on the first day of the term of service herein stipulated and cease immediately to be effective at its expiration. If either party wishes to renew the contract, the other party shall be notified before it expires. Upon agreement by both parties through consultation a new contract can be signed. 合同自受聘方到职之日起生效,聘期届满即自行失效。如一方要求延长聘期,必须在本合同期满之前向对方提出,经双方协商确认后,再另行签订新的聘期合同。

8. 仲裁(Arbitration)

例如,The two parties shall consult with each other and settle any disputes which may arise in the duration of the contract. If all attempts fail, the two parties can appeal to the Municipal Labor Bureau of Zhanjiang. 在合同期内,当事人双方发生任何合同纠纷时,应通过协商或者调解解决。若协商、调解无效,可向湛江市劳动局申请仲裁。

(三)约尾(End)

所包括内容与意向书类似。例如,This contract is signed at Zhanjiang City in duplicate on 1st of October 2007 in the Chinese and English languages, both texts being equally authentic. 本合同于2007年10月1日在湛江签订,一式二份,每份都用中文和英文写成,两种文本效力同等。

二、于琪的解决方案

Contract of Employment

1. The Parties

The parties to this employment agreement are: Golden Childhood Children's Products Co., Ltd., the "Employer" and Han Wu, the "Employee".

2. The Position and the Duties

2.1 Position: The employee is being employed as the Accountant Assistant.

2.2 Duties: The employee shall perform the duties set out in the Job Description attached to this agreement.

3. Obligations of the Relationship

3.1 Obligations of the Employer: The employer shall (i) act as a good employer in all dealings with the employee; (ii) deal with the employee and any representative of the employee in good faith in all aspects of the employment relationship; (iii) take all practicable steps to provide the employee with a safe and healthy work environment.

3.2 Obligations of the Employee: The employee shall (i) comply with all reasonable and lawful instructions provided to him/her by the employer; (ii) perform his/her duties with all reasonable skill and diligence; (iii) deal with the employer in good faith in all aspects of the employment relationship; (iv) comply with all policies and procedures (including any Codes of Conduct) implemented by the employer from time to time.

4. Hours of Work

The employee's normal hours of work shall be 40 hours per week, between the hours of 9 a.m. and 5 p.m. on week days. The employee may also be required to perform such overtime as may be reasonably required by the employer in order for the employee to properly perform his/her duties. $12 should be paid for each overtime hour.

5. Wages and Allowances

5.1 Annual Salary: The employee's salary shall be $12,480 per annum, which shall be paid monthly on the 10th each month, in cash.

5.2 Reimbursement of Expenses: The employee shall be entitled to reimbursement by the employer of all expenses reasonably and properly incurred by the employee in the performance of his/her duties, provided the employee produces appropriate receipt.

6. Holidays and Leave Entitlements

6.1 Annual Leave: The employee shall be entitled to three weeks of paid annual leave after 12 months' continuous employment with the employer.

6.2 Sick Leave: The employee shall, after 6 months' employment with the employer, be entitled to 5 days' sick leave for each subsequent 12 month period of service. Sick leave may be taken when the employee is sick or when the employee's spouse or a person who is dependent on the employee is sick or injured.

7. Termination of Employment

The employer may terminate this agreement without notice for serious misconduct on the part of the employee. Serious misconduct includes, but is not limited to (i) theft; (ii) dishonesty; (iii) harassment of a work colleague or customer; (iv) serious or repeated failure to follow a reasonable instruction; (v) deliberate destruction of any property belonging to the employer; (vi) actions which seriously damage the employer's reputation.

8. Declaration

We, Golden Childhood Co., Ltd. offer this contract of employment to Han Wu.

Signed: Date:

I, Han Wu, declare that I have read and understand the conditions of employment detailed above and accept them fully.

Signed: Date:

Review Questions

1. Key Terms

Replacement chart; Job description; Fringe benefits; Employee orientation; Performance feedback

2. Multiple Choices (select one)

(1) Questions contained in structured job interviews should be based on (   ).

A. job analysis   B. job design

C. job specialization   D. job utilization

(2) Reasons for not hiring from within include all of the following except(   ).

A. motivational concerns   B. lack of qualified internal candidates

C. a need for new ideas   D. the risk of "employee cloning"

(3) Recruiting from within means that an organization prefers to recruit people from (   ).

A. regional labor market   B. national labor market

C. internal labor market   D. international labor market

(4) Human resource and succession planning provides information on (   ).

A. the direction in which the organization is going

B. future skill requirements and management training needs

C. deficiencies in training arrangements

D. any gaps between expectations and results or negative trends

(5) The most common means of obtaining information about applicants' qualifications are (   ).

A. employment applications   B. interviews

C. test   D. all of above

(6) Compensation programs that compensate employees for the knowledge they possess are known as (   ).

A. skill-based pay plans   B. performance-based pay plans

C. merit-based pay plans   D. seniority-based pay plans

(7) Which of the following isn't a form of performance-based compensation? (   )

A. Piece-rate   B. Profit-sharing

C. Minimum wage   D. Lump-sum bonuses

(8) Coaching is a (　　) technique that can be used to develop individual skills, knowledge and attitudes.

　　A. on-the-job　　　　　　　　B. off-the-job

　　C. web-based training　　　　D. classroom training

(9) Performance appraisal has the following main objectives except (　　).

　　A. lets employees know how well they are doing and how they can do better

　　B. provides an effective basis for distributing rewards

　　C. helps the organization monitor its other HRM activities

　　D. helps the organization develop new products that satisfy customers' needs

(10) The following quantities are commonly used for objective appraisal methods except (　　).

　　A. units of output or dollar volume of sales

　　B. working hours

　　C. number of defective products

　　D. number of insurance claims processed

3. Questions for Discussion

(1) What are the advantages and disadvantages of external recruiting? Of internal recruiting?

(2) In your opinion, what techniques are needed for gathering information about job candidates? Explain them.

(3) What are the most common methods of training and development?

(4) Describe the techniques and methods for appraising employee performance.

Practical Writing

Scenario: You work in the School of Foreign Studies of South China University. Your school (the engaging party) has agreed to hire Mr. Smith (the engaged party) as a teacher of English. You are asked by the dean to draft a **Contract of Employment**. This contract should include the period of time of employment, both sides' obligation, the salaries provided by the employer and the clause for breaching of the contract as well as the termination of the contract, etc.

Unit 14 Storage and Transportation Problems

Learning Objectives

◇ 熟悉主持会议的常用口语表达；
◇ 理解物流的性质和重要性；
◇ 理解企业物流活动的主要功能；
◇ 理解第三方物流的含义和意义；
◇ 掌握会议记录的书写规则和常用套语的正确写法。

Speaking：Chairing a Meeting

【场景】　随着公司日益扩大，现有厂房生产空间不足，熟练工人短缺等问题逐渐显现。公司已决定将原厂房扩建，等待获得相关部门的批准。但厂房扩建后最大的问题是现有的染料油漆间将紧挨厂房扩建部分，存在潜在的火灾隐患。与此同时，加拿大客户 Alex Johnson 刚刚发来传真，希望在广州展销会上与公司签订的玩具销售合同能够提前交货。总经理 Robert Liu 召集办公会议，讨论一系列相关问题。会议刚刚开始……

【对话】　A：总经理 Robert Liu　B：销售经理马天跃　C：生产部经理 Peter Phillips　D：人力资源部经理 Michael Douglas　E：建筑设计师 Edward White　F：于琪

A: Mr. Ma, Mr. Phillips, Mr. Douglas, Mr. White... Well, gentlemen, I think everyone's here, except the Financial Manager, Ms. Peterson. I'm afraid she can't join us this morning because she has to meet Mr. Erwin again for the loan business. To start with, I don't think we need to read the minutes of the last meeting, as copies of them have already been circulated to you. (Murmurs of agreement) During our last meeting, it was agreed that the complaint from Mr. Smith should be investigated and the Marketing Department should send him a letter. Tianyue, have you completed the investigation?

马先生、菲利普斯先生、道格拉斯先生、怀特先生……诸位，除了财务经理彼得森女士外，其他人都到齐了。彼得森女士恐怕不能参加今早的会议了，因为她要继续与欧文先生会面探讨贷款事宜。首先，上次会议的纪要大家都传阅了，我想就不必再在会上宣读啦。（大家一片同意声）在上次会议中，我们决定对史密斯先生的投诉进行调查，并安排营销部写回信。天跃，你已经完成调查了吗？

B：Yes. According to the investigation, the goods left our factory in good condition and were, as usual, carefully packed. However, they were handled badly by the men in the stevedoring company who unloaded the goods from the containers. Even though the clothes were wrapped in strong cardboard, it was not strong enough to protect them, as hooks were used for unloading. Although we are not in the wrong, we have sent Mr. Smith a letter telling him to have the damaged clothes replaced. We consider that the time and money involved is small in comparison with the importance of keeping a customer satisfied.

是的。根据调查，货物离开我们工厂的时候状况良好并且与往常一样经过仔细地包装。然而，它们被装卸公司的员工从集装箱内卸货时处置不当。尽管衣服被放置在结实的硬纸箱里，但因装卸工人使用了吊钩，货物还是受到了损坏。虽然我们在这个事情上并无差错，但仍写信给史密斯先生同意更换损坏的衣物。我们认为同保证客户满意的大局相比，这样做所需的时间和费用实在是微不足道的。

A：Thanks, Tianyue. So, if there is nothing else we need to discuss, let's move on to today's agenda. Mr. Phillips, will you report, please, on the result of our application to build an extension to the present factory?

谢谢，天跃。如果没有什么其他的需要讨论，让我们转入今天的议程吧。菲利普斯先生，请你就我们扩建现有厂房的申请结果进行一下汇报，好吗？

C：Our I. D. C. was granted provided the Dye and Paint Store was placed in a different position to avoid the danger of fire. Mr. White has now proposed that we rebuild the present Managers' garage as a Dye and Paint Store. It's on the other side of the delivery bay, and would halve the time taken to unload and store the stuff.

工业发展证书（即扩建许可）同意发放，条件是我们的染料油漆间应设在不同场所，以防止发生火灾。怀特先生建议把现在经理们的车库改建为染料油漆间。它就在卸货平台的另一头，可使卸货和存仓的时间减少一半。

D：Where shall we put our cars?

那我们在哪里停放车辆呢？

C：Well, they can stand in the car park like everyone else's.

像其他人一样在停车场停放嘛。

A：Just a minute, gentlemen. I don't think our present Managers' garage is big enough to store all the dyes and paints we need.

等一下，诸位。我认为用现在经理们的车库来存放我们所需的染料和油漆不够大。

B：We'd better think about the ways to improve our storage capacity.

我们需要考虑提高存储能力的方式。

A：I'm afraid that's outside the scope of the meeting, Tianyue. Edward, we have not

heard from you, what do you think of it?
恐怕这超出了本次会议的讨论范畴,天跃。爱德华,我们还没听到你的高见呢,你怎样看这个问题?

E: I propose to extend the present garage to meet the west wall of the delivery bay and knock in a door here. The present Dye and Paint Store can then be used for other storage.
我建议把目前的车库扩建到卸货平台的西墙,就在这里开个门。这样,现在的染料油漆间还可用来存放其他物资。

A: Very well—yes, this does seem a sensible solution. If we are all agreed...? (Murmurs of "yes") Right. Now we come to item number two on the agenda. Tianyue?
很好,是的,看来这是一个合理的解决办法。要是大伙同意的话?（众人同意）好的。现在让我们进入议程的第二项内容。天跃?

B: Yes. Mr. Alex Johnson, one of our clients from Canada, faxed us yesterday, asking to advance the shipment of the order for 1,000 pieces of children's toys contracted during the Guangzhou Exhibition Fair to November 20. We have contacted the shipping company. We are advised that because direct vessels, either liner or tramp, sailing for their port are few and far between, the shipping space has been fully booked up to the end of November.
好的。加拿大客户阿莱克斯·约翰逊先生昨天发来传真,希望将广州展销会上所订的1,000件儿童玩具交货期提前到11月20日。我们已经联系了运输公司。得到的回复是由于直达他们港的轮船,无论是班轮还是不定期货轮,都非常少,舱位已经预订到了11月末。

A: How about multimodal combined transport by rail and sea? We can first ship the goods from Shanghai to Hong Kong by train and then load them on the ship to Canada.
那采用海陆联运呢?我们可以先用火车将货物从上海运到香港,再装上轮船,运到加拿大。

B: From personal point of view, I am not inclined to the way of combined transport. Because firstly it has complicated formalities and secondly it's easy to cause a delay in shipment or even lose the goods completely if we arrange such combined transport.
就个人而言,我并不倾向于联运方式。因为首先这有很复杂的手续要办。其次,如果安排联运的话,容易误期,甚至是丢货。

A: But this is the fastest and cheapest way we can find.
但这是我们能找到的最快、最省钱的方法了。

B: However, if they would allow part shipment and transshipment at Hong Kong, we could do our best to make further consideration with the shipping company. In this case, they must bear the additional charges.
可是,如果他们能够允许分运和在香港转船的话,我们还可以继续努力与运输公司进行协商。在这种情况下,他们必须支付额外的费用。

A: That's for sure. Peter, when is the earliest we can produce enough products?

Unit 14
Storage and Transportation Problems

这个自然。彼得，我们最早何时能生产出足够的产品？

C：As per the order No. 588, the shipment is to be made in early December. Our factories are fully committed for the fourth quarter. If they desire an earlier delivery, we can only deliver 600 pieces in November and the remainder in December.

编号 588 的订单，装运期是 12 月初。我们工厂第四季度的生产任务已经全部排满。如果他们希望提前交货的话，我们只能在 11 月交货 600 件，余下的 12 月交货。

A：Well, fax Mr. Johnson after the meeting to make sure that our arrangement is satisfactory with them. All right, we are running short of time. The next item on the agenda is the report from the HR Manager about the additional labor that's going to be required. So far, Michael, we've had no difficulty in obtaining skilled workers, but is this situation likely to continue or not?

嗯，会后给约翰逊先生发份传真，确保他对我们的安排满意。好吧，现在时间不多了。议程中的下一个议题是，人事部经理就将来需要再增加的劳动力做汇报。迈克尔，到现在为止，招收熟练工人没有什么困难，不过目前这种情况在今后能否继续下去呢？

D：Well, the position is this: skilled labor is getting harder to find. There's plenty of unskilled labor, and I think we should start a training program now. Then by the time the new extension is ready we should have the right number of trained men.

嗯，情况是这样的，熟练工越来越难找了。非熟练工人有很多。我想我们现在就应当开始实施一项培训计划。这样，到扩建竣工之时我们就能有足够数量的受过培训的工人了。

A：Let's see. Mr. White, how long will the factory extension take to build once we've got our permission?

让我们看看，怀特先生，获得批准后扩建厂房需要多长时间？

E：If the contractors are very efficient, I'd say three months, possibly less.

要是承包单位效率高的话，我看要 3 个月吧，也许还用不了 3 个月。

A：Well, Michael, can you produce enough skilled workers in, say, three months from now?

嗯，迈克尔，你能在从现在算起的 3 个月内培训出足够数量的技术工人吗？

D：Yes, I think so.

是的，我想可以。

A：Very well, I think we all agree that a training program should be started immediately. (Murmurs of assent) Good. You will minute that, Qi Yu, won't you? Also that Mr. Douglas will make an estimate of the cost. Any other business?

好极了，我看大家一致同意应当立即开始培训工人的计划。（大家表示同意）好！于琪，请记录在案，好吗？还有，道格拉斯先生要对培训费用做个估算。还有其他事情吗？

D：Yes. Sheila Anderson's husband is ill and in hospital. We should send a gift to Sheila's husband, expressing the company's sympathy and support.

是的。希拉·安德森的丈夫生病住院了。我们应该给希拉的丈夫送去一份礼物，来表达公司的慰问和支持。

A：Absolutely. If we are all agreed...? (Murmurs of "yes") Right. I presume there is no other business? (Chorus of "no", "don't think so") So, the next meeting will be on Wednesday, the 5th of December at the Conference Room. Michael, do you think you could make a draft of the training program by the time of our next meeting?
非常必要。要是大伙同意的话？（众人同意）好的。我想现在没有其他要讨论的问题了吧。（众人都说"没有了"）那么，我们下次会议于星期三，12月5日在会议室召开。迈克尔，你觉得你可以在下次会议开始前起草一份培训计划的草案吗？

D：Sure.
没问题。

A：Right. I'd like to thank all for attending the meeting. Now, I declare the meeting closed.
好的。谢谢大家出席会议。现在，我宣布闭会。

Reading: Enhancing Logistics Management

在进入企业以前，于琪便听说物流被称为企业"降低成本的最后边界"，是排在降低原材料消耗、提高劳动生产率之后的"第三利润源泉"。为什么会对物流活动有如此高的评价？现代企业的物流活动到底包括哪些内容？

Chapter 14 Logistics Management

Section 1 The Nature and Importance of Marketing Logistics

In today's global marketplace, selling a product is sometimes easier than delivering it to customers. Companies must decide on the best way to store, handle, and move their products and services so that they are available to customers in the right assortments, at the right time, and in the right place. Physical distribution and logistics effectiveness has a major impact on both customer satisfaction and company costs.

To some managers, marketing logistics means only trucks and warehouses. But modern logistics is much more than this. Marketing logistics—also called physical distribution—involves planning, implementing, and controlling the physical flow of goods, services, and related information from points of origin to points of consumption to meet customer requirements at a profit. In short, it involves getting the right product to the right customer in the right place at the right time.

In the past, physical distribution typically started with products at the plant and then tried to find low-cost solutions to get them to customers. However, today's marketers prefer customer-centered logistics thinking, which starts with the marketplace and works backward to the factory, or even to sources of supply. Marketing logistics addresses not only outbound distribution (moving products from the factory to resellers and ultimately to customers) but also inbound distribution (moving products and materials from suppliers to the factory) and reverse distribution (moving broken, unwanted, or excess products returned by consumers or resellers). That is, it involves entire supply chain management—managing upstream and downstream value-added flows of materials, final goods, and related information among suppliers, the company, resellers, and final consumers, as shown in Figure 14.1.

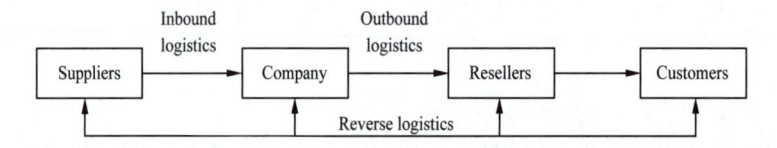

Figure 14.1 Supply Chain Management

Thus, the logistics manager's task is to coordinate activities of suppliers, purchasing agents, marketers, channel members, and customers. These activities include forecasting, information systems, purchasing, production planning, order processing, inventory, warehousing, and transportation planning.

Companies today are placing greater emphasis on logistics for several reasons. First, companies can gain a powerful competitive advantage by using improved logistics to give customers better service or lower prices. Second, improved logistics can yield tremendous cost savings to both the company and its customers. Third, the explosion in product variety has created a need for improved logistics management. Finally, improvements in information technology have created opportunities for major gains in distribution efficiency.

小 结

今天的营销物流不仅仅强调外向物流(指产品从工厂到中间商再到最终客户),还包括内向物流(指产品和原材料从供应商到生产工厂)和反向物流(指将损毁的、不想要的或者多余的产品退回来)。也就是说,物流活动包括整个供应链管理,即在上游和下游的企业之间管理原材料、最终产品和相关信息的流动。今天的公司出于如下原因更加重视营销物流。第一,通过改善营销物流,公司可以提供给客户更好的服务和更低的价格,从而获得强有力的竞争优势。第二,先进的物流可以为公司和客户节省巨额的成本。第三,产品品种的激增使公司有改善物流管理的需求。最后,信息技术的发展为提高分销效率创造了机会。

Section 2 Major Logistics Functions

2.1 Order Processing

The role of proper order processing in providing good service cannot be overemphasized. As an order enters the order processing system, management must monitor two flows: the flow of goods and the flow of information. Often the best-laid plans of marketers can get entangled in the order processing system. Obviously, good communication among sales representatives, office personnel, and warehouse and shipping personnel is essential to correct order processing. Shipping incorrect merchandise or partially filled orders can create just as much dissatisfaction as stockouts or slow deliveries. The flow of goods and information must be continually monitored so mistakes can be corrected before an invoice is prepared and the merchandise is shipped.

Order processing is becoming more automated through the use of computer technology known as electronic data interchange (EDI). The basic idea behind EDI is to replace the paper documents that usually accompany business transactions, such as purchase orders and invoices, with electronic transmission of the needed information. Companies that use EDI can reduce inventory levels, improve cash flow, streamline operations, and increase the speed and accuracy of information transmission. EDI is also believed to create a closer relationship between buyers and sellers.

It should not be surprising that retailers have become major users of EDI. For Wal-Mart, Target, Kmart, and the like, logistics speed and accuracy are crucial competitive tools in an overcrowded retail environment. Many big retailers are helping their suppliers acquire EDI technology so that they can be linked into the system. EDI works hand in hand with retailers' efficient consumer response (ECR) programs, which are designed to have the right products on the shelf, in the right styles and colors, through improved inventory, ordering, and distribution techniques. In a full implementation of ECR, products are scanned at the retail store when purchased, which updates the store's inventory lists. Headquarters then polls the stores to retrieve the data needed to produce an order. The vendor confirms the order, shipping date, and delivery time, then ships the order and transmits the invoice electronically. The item is received at the warehouse, scanned into inventory, and then sent to the store. The invoice and receiving data are reconciled, and payment via an electronic transfer of funds completes the process. Some retailers even go so far as to shift inventory and delivery costs to the supplier by asking suppliers to track retailers' inventory levels, generate orders as needed and arrange deliveries for them.

2.2 Warehousing

Warehousing includes a number of activities, such as receiving goods, identifying goods, sorting goods, dispatching goods to warehouse, storage, recalling, selecting or picking goods, marshaling shipments and dispatching shipments. Warehousing supports production by consolidating inbound materials and distributing them to the production facility at the appropriate time. Warehousing also helps marketing to serve current customers and expand into new markets.

One of the most important aspects of warehousing concerns questions related to inventory. The amount of inventory that should be held and its location within a company's logistic structure are crucial in order to meet customer service requirements and expectations. But, there is potentially a large cost associated with holding inventory. It is vital to get right this balance of service versus cost. ABC analysis is a method for dividing on-hand inventory into three classifications A, B, C based on annual consumption unit. A-items (money value is highest 70%, represent only 10% of items) should have tight inventory control under more experienced management. Re-orders should be more frequent. B-items (money value is medium 20%, represent about 20% of items) require medium attention for control. C-items (money value is lowest 10%, represent about 70% of items) require minimum attention and may be kept under simple observation. Re-ordering is less frequent. ABC analysis for prioritization allows the management to decide which items require most effort in controlling.

After the inventory has been classified, the two fundamental questions posed to any inventory system are how much and when to order? The periodic review system works on the premise that the stock level of the product is examined at regular intervals and, depending on the quantity in stock, a replenishment order is placed. The size of the order is selected to bring the stock to a predetermined level. Thus, the order size will vary each time a new order is placed. For the fixed point reorder system, a specific stock level is determined, at which point a replenishment order will be placed. The same quantity of the product is reordered when that stock level is reached. Thus, for this system it is the time when the order is placed that varies. To ensure that inventories of both raw materials and finished goods are sufficient to meet customer demand without undue delay, some firms utilize sophisticated just-in-time (JIT) inventory control systems. New stock arrives exactly when needed, rather than being store in inventory until being used. Just-in-time systems require accurate forecasting along with fast, frequent, and flexible delivery so that new supplies will be available when needed.

Storage, another important consideration in warehousing operation, is that warehouse utilization should position products based upon individual characteristics. The most important product variables to consider in a storage plan are product volume, weight, and storage requirements. Product volume or velocity is the major factor driving warehouse layout. High-volume product should be positioned in the warehouse to minimize movement distance. For example, high-velocity products should be positioned near doors, primary aisles, and at lower levels in storage racks. Such positioning minimizes warehouse handling and reduces the need for frequent lifting. Conversely, products with low volume should be assigned locations more distant from primary aisles or higher up in storage racks. Similarly, the storage plan should take into consideration product weight and special storage requirements. Relatively heavy items should be assigned storage locations low to the ground to minimize lifting. Bulky or low-density product requires cubic space. Floor space along outside walls is ideal for such items. On the other hand, smaller items may require storage shelves, bins, or drawers. The integrated storage plan must consider individual product characteristics.

Materials handling is short distance movement of goods or materials, in warehousing as well as during transportation. Since materials handling tends to add costs rather than value to logistics system, managers tend to minimize the number of handling whenever possible. Proper materials-handling procedures and techniques can increase the usable capacity of a warehouse or that of any means of transportation, and reduce breakage and spoilage. The unit loading and unloading concept puts product in or on to appropriate standard modules, such as containers, pallets, etc. for handling and storage, movement, loading and unloading. It enables the use of standard equipments irrespective of the products being handled, at the same time as achieving product protection and security, and economy in the use of space, and the amount of handling required for a given quantity of materials.

2.3 Transportation

As a part of physical distribution, transportation is simply the shipment of products to customers. The greater the distance between seller and purchaser, the more important is the choice of the means of transportation and the particular carrier. Firms that offer transportation services are called carriers. A common carrier is a transportation firm whose services are available to all shippers. Railroads, airlines, and most long-distance trucking firms are common carriers. A contract carrier is a transportation firm that is available for hire by one or several shippers. Contract carriers do not serve the general public. An efficient and inexpensive transportation system contributes to greater competition in the marketplace, greater economies of scale in production, and reduced prices for goods.

Railroads are the most reliable and one of the most cost-effective modes for shipping large amounts of bulk products—coal, sand, minerals, farm and forest products—over long distances. In contrast with rail, trucking is a transportation service of semi-finished and finished products. Trucking firms have added many services in recent years. For example, most advanced carriers may offer satellite tracking of shipments, and in-truck computer systems allow drivers and dispatchers to make last-minute changes in scheduling and delivery. The inherent advantages of trucking are its door-to-door service such that no loading or unloading is required between origin and destination (as is often true of rail and air modes), its frequency and availability of service, and its door-to-door speed and convenience.

Air transportation is being considered by increasing numbers of shippers for regular service, even though air freight rates exceed those of trucking by more than 2 times and those of rail by more than 16 times. The appeal of air transportation is its unmatched origin-destination speed, especially over long distances. Water transportation service is limited in scope for several reasons. Firstly, domestic water service is confined to the inland waterway system, which requires shippers to be located on the waterway or to use another transportation mode in combination with water. Secondly, water service on the average is slower than rail. In addition, availability and dependability of water service are greatly influenced by the weather. Finally, Movement on the waterway in the northern part of the country during the winter is impossible, and service is interrupted by floods and droughts.

To date, pipeline transportation offers a very limited range of services and capabilities. The most economically feasible products to move by pipeline are crude oil and refined petroleum products. However, there is some experimentation with moving solid products suspended in liquid, called "slurry" or containing the solid products in cylinders that in turn move in a liquid. If these innovations prove to be economical, pipeline service could be greatly expanded. Product movement by pipeline is very slow, only about 3 to 4 miles per hour. In regard to transit time, however, pipeline service is the most dependable of all modes, because there are few interruptions to cause transit time variability.

Nowadays, shippers increasingly are using intermodal transportation—combining two or more modes of transportation. Piggyback describes the use of rail and trucks; fishyback, water and trucks. Each combination offers advantages to the shipper. For example, not only is piggyback cheaper than trucking alone but it also provides flexibility and convenience. In choosing a transportation mode for a product, shippers must balance many considerations: speed, dependability, availability, cost and others.

小 结

物流管理可以从订货、存储和运输三大环节进行研究。物流的第一个功能是订单处理。随着计算机技术(如EDI)的飞速发展，订单处理越来越自动化。物流的第二个功能是仓储功能，是指接收商品、商品鉴别、商品分类、商品发送到库房、商品存储、撤销进货、商品挑选或拣选，以及运输调度等一整套业务活动。其中，ABC分类法和库存补充系统被设计出来以减少库存数量高低波动的负面影响。根据产品规模、重量，以及存储要求等因素制定的存储计划最大限度优化了库房的利用。而恰当的物资搬运过程和技术，可以增加库房和运输工具的利用能力，并且减低破损和损耗。最后，物流的运输功能是指将产品发运给客户。铁路是长距离运输原材料和低价值产品的基本承运工具。卡车提供半成品和产成品的运输服务。空运尽管费用高但因其无可比拟的速度优势正在被越来越多的货主考虑。而水路运输和管道运输目前仅提供非常有限的服务和运输能力。

Section 3 Outsourcing Logistics Functions

External partners are becoming increasingly important in the efficient deployment of supply chain management. Third-party logistics (TPL), or contract logistics, is a rapidly growing segment of the distribution industry in which a manufacturer or supplier turns over the entire function of buying and managing transportation or another function of the supply chain, such as warehousing, to an independent third party. Many manufacturers are turning to outside partners for their logistics expertise in an effort to focus on the core competencies that they do best. Partners create and manage entire solutions for getting products where they need to be, when they need to be there. Logistics partners offer staff, an infrastructure, and services that reach consumers virtually anywhere in the world. Because a logistics provider is focused, clients receive service in a timely efficient manner, thereby increasing customers' level of satisfaction and boosting their perception of added value to a company's offerings. A recent study found that nearly 75 percent of U.S. manufacturers and suppliers are either using or considering using a third-party logistics service.

Third-party contract logistics allows companies to cut inventories, locate stock at fewer plants and distribution centers, and still provide the same service level or even better. The companies then can refocus investment on their core business. Ford Motor Company decided to use third-party logistics provider UPS Worldwide Logistics Group to manage the delivery of Ford, Lincoln, and Mercury cars and trucks in the United States, Canada, and Mexico. The companies say they expect the alliance will reduce the time it takes to move vehicles from Ford's plants to dealers and customers by up to 40 percent. The alliance will also provide web-based information systems that allow Ford and its dealers to track individual vehicle status from production through final delivery.

Many firms are taking outsourcing one step further by allowing business partners to take over the final assembly of their product or its packaging in an effort to reduce inventory costs, speed up delivery, or meet customer requirements better. Ryder assembles and packages twenty-two different combinations of shrink-wrapped boxes that contain the ice trays, drawers, shelves, doors, and other accessories for the various refrigerator models Whirlpool sells. Before, Whirlpool would install the accessories in the refrigerators at the plant—a source of considerable factory-floor confusion. IBM, for example, allows some of its distributors to do more of the final product assembly. Today, about 31 percent of its U.S. desktop personal computers are assembled by eleven business partners, many of whom may install non-IBM components. One reseller actually assembles some of its IBM orders in a warehouse right next to IBM's factory in North Carolina, saving on distribution costs. For Nike's new athletic-equipment division, contract logistics provider Menlo Logistics inflates basketballs, soccer balls, and footballs, which come in half-inflated because they take up less room. The logistics company also puts the balls in colorful packages and sticks on price tags for some sports retailers.

小 结

分销和物流领域的一个最重要的发展是第三方物流提供商的涌现,或者叫作物流作业外包。物流管理愈来愈被看作是专业化的活动,许多公司开始把物流作业的全部或部分外包给独立的专业机构,从而使得企业管理者可以把精力集中在公司的核心活动中。许多公司将外包工作更进一步,他们允许这些商业伙伴接管他们的产品最终装配或产品包装工作,以降低库存成本、加快交货,或更好地满足顾客的要求。

New Words and Key Terms

01.	marketing logistics	营销物流
02.	physical distribution	实物流通,实体分销(物流的最初表述)
03.	outbound distribution	运出分销,外向物流
04.	inbound distribution	运入分销,内向物流
05.	reverse distribution	反向分销,逆向物流
06.	order processing	订货单处理,订货单加工
07.	order processing system	订单处理系统
08.	electronic data interchange(EDI)	电子数据交换
09.	efficient consumer response(ECR)	有效客户反应
10.	warehousing	仓储管理
11.	ABC analysis	ABC 分类法
12.	periodic review system	周期性评价系统,定期订货方式
13.	fixed point reorder system	固定量订货系统,定点订货方式
14.	just-in-time(JIT) inventory control systems	精准库存控制系统
15.	storage	存储,贮存
16.	warehouse layout	仓库布局
17.	rack	货架
18.	materials handling	物料搬运
19.	unit loading and unloading	单元装卸
20.	transportation	运输;运输费
21.	carrier	承运人,运输公司
22.	common carrier	公共承运人
23.	shippers	托运人,货主
24.	contract carrier	契约承运人
25.	intermodal transportation	联合运输,多式联运
26.	third-party logistics(TPL)	第三方物流
27.	contract logistics	合同物流(第三方物流的另外表述)
28.	distribution centers	配送中心

Writing: Minutes

下午一上班,总经理 Robert Liu 便打来电话,让于琪将上午的会议记录给他送过去。

于琪已经完成了会议记录的初稿,他需要再整理一下,然后交给总经理签收。

一、会议记录写作的基本要求和格式

会议记录(Minutes)正式记录一次会议的进展情况,记载和传达会议议定事项和主要精神,要求与会单位或个人共同遵守和执行,具有纪实性和指导性。会议记录重要的是要客观记载会议情况,而不可添加记录人自己的看法或主观评述。由于会议记录是对过去发生的会议的真实记录,因此行文要用过去时态。一次会议中所讨论的议题通常比较复杂。因此,一个清晰的结构将有助于与会者回顾要点,尤其是在会议结束很长时间再阅读会议记录的时候。会议记录的格式如下:

(一)标题(Title)

会议记录的标题包括公司名称、文体名称和会议类型,诸如例会(regular meeting,又称办公会议)、特别会议(special meeting)、部门会议(department meeting)、董事会会议(board meeting)和年会(annual general meeting)等。

(二)会议的组织(Organization)

会议记录开篇部分详细记述开会时间(会议时间要写明年、月、日,上午、下午或晚上)和地点(如 Conference Room,Main Hall,Chairman's Office 等;有时,会议的时间和地点亦可直接置于标题下)、会议主持人(包括主持人的职务、姓名,如 Chairman ×××,CEO ××× 等)、出席人(根据会议的性质、规模和重要程度的不同,出席人一项的详略也会有所不同。有时可以只显示身份和人数,如 Board of Directors 8P,Department Heads 12P 等)和缺席人(如有重要人物缺席,应做出记录)。例如,The meeting was held on... (date), at... (time), in/at... (place). A quorum was present. Apologies were received from... (sb.), who was attending a business conference. 会议于……(日期)……(时间)在……(地点)举行。与会者达到了法定人数。会议收到……(某人)的请假,他/她正在参加一个商务会议。

(三)会议的具体内容(Content)

会议记录接下来的部分记述本次会议的各项议题和采取的行动。高效地书写会议记录并不意味着逐字记录会议中说过的每一句话,因为这样很容易导致失去重点。会议若无特殊目的,按下列通常的惯例记述:

1. 上次会议记录(Minutes of Last Meeting)

例如,As the first item on the agenda, the chairman asked for approval of the minutes of the meeting held on 14 December 1999, which were agreed and signed, subject to the following amendments: In Manager's report, Line 3 "$30,000" should be amended to read "$3,000". 根据议程第一项,主席要求通过1999年12月14日召开的会议的会议记录。该会议记录做以下修改后同意签发:"经理报告"中第三行的"30,000美元"改为"3,000美元"。

2. 上次会议记录跟进事项(Matters Arising from the Minutes)

例如,Mr. John Smith, the Production Manager, reported back on his investigation into the production problems the company had been experiencing at the time of the last meeting. He reported that those had now been completely overcome, and stated that the production was now back at its expected level. He would be producing a report shortly. 生产经理约翰·史密斯先生对上次会议时公司所经历的生产问题的调查结果进行了汇报。他说那些问题现在已经完全克服,生产回到预计水平。他将在不久提交一份报告。

3. 本次会议的议题(Special or New Business),包括报告、讨论,以及通过的决议等

例如,The Personnel Manager reported on labor available for the new extension, and suggested a program should be put in hand to train workers. 人事部经理就新扩建工厂招募劳动力问题进行了汇报,并建议迅速制订出培训工人的计划。再如,The draft for... was discussed and the following amendments were made:... should be deleted;... should read...;... should be amended to read... 会上讨论了关于……的草案,并做出如下修改:删去……;……应改为……;……修正为……

4. 其他事项或例外事件(Any Other Business [AOB] or Unusual Occurrences),包括发言人、仪式等

例如,Mr. Gordon Brown mentioned that staff member, Sheila Anderson's husband was ill and in hospital. He motioned to send a gift to Sheila's husband, expressing the organization's sympathy and support; seconded and passed. 戈登·布朗先生提到,员工希拉·安德森的丈夫因病住院。他提议送份礼物给希拉的丈夫表达组织的慰问与支持。附议并通过。

5. 下次会议时间(Date of Next Meeting)

例如,The next meeting scheduled for 11 February will be postponed because of the coming Spring Festival. The participants would be notified in due course of the new date. 原定于 2 月 11 日的下次会议因春节放假而延期。具体开会时间待确定后另行通知。

6. 休会时间(Adjournment Time)

例如,The meeting adjourned at 6:00 p.m. 会议在下午六点结束。

(四)结束(Ending)

通常会议记录的结尾部分为结尾礼词 Respectfully submitted,以及记录人的手写和打印签名。

二、于琪的解决方案

GOLDEN CHILDHOOD COMPANY
MINUTES OF REGULAR MEETING
HELD ON MONDAY, 5 NOVEMBER, 2023

PRESIDING: Mr. Robert Liu (CEO)

PRESENT: Mr. Tianyue Ma (Sales Manager), Mr. Peter Phillips (Production Manager), Mr. Michael Douglas (Human Resources Manager), Mr. Edward White (Architect), Mr. Qi Yu

APOLOGIES FOR ABSENCE WERE RECEIVED FROM: Leila Peterson

PROCEEDINGS:

The meeting was called to order on Monday, 5 November, 2023, at 8:00 a.m. by Mr. Robert Liu, the Chief Executive Officer, in the conference room.

1. Minutes of Last Meeting

At the beginning of the meeting, the Chairman asked for approval of the minutes of the meeting held on 5 October, 2023, which were agreed and signed.

2. Matters Arising from the Minutes

Mr. Tianyue Ma, the Sales Manager, reported back on his investigation about the complaint from Mr. Smith. He reported that the goods were handled badly by the men in the stevedoring company, as hooks were used for unloading. Although we were not in the wrong, the damaged clothes would be replaced to keep the customer satisfied.

3. Production Manager's Report on Factory Extension

(a) The Production Manager reported that the I. D. C. was granted, provided that the Dye and Paint Store was placed in a different position to avoid the danger of fire.

(b) The Architect's proposal to rebuild the present Managers' garage as a Dye and Paint Store was agreed.

4. Sales Manager's Report on Advancing Shipment

(a) Mr. Alex Johnson, one of our clients from Canada, asked us to advance the shipment of the order No. 588. The Sales Manager proposed to make part shipment and transshipment at Hong Kong. Meanwhile, the Production Manager mentioned we could only deliver 600 pieces in November and the remainder in December.

(b) The Chairman asked to fax Mr. Johnson after the meeting to make sure that he was satisfied with our arrangement.

5. HR Manager's Report on Labor Availability

(a) The HR Manager reported on labor available for the new extension, and suggested a program should be put in hand to train workers.

(b) It was agreed that a training program should be started immediately, and that an estimate of the cost should be provided by the HR Manager.

6. Other Business

The HR Manager mentioned that staff member, Sheila Anderson's husband was ill and in hospital. He motioned to send a gift to Sheila's husband; seconded and passed.

7. Date of Next Meeting

The next meeting will be on Wednesday, the 5th of December at the Conference Room.

8. Adjournment

The meeting adjourned at 11:30 a.m.

(Prepared by: Qi Yu)

Review Questions

1. Key Terms

Marketing logistics; Periodic review system; Materials handling; Common carrier;

Contract logistics

2. Multiple Choices (select one)

(1) What is the same meaning of reverse distribution? (　　)

　A. Sales.　　　　　　　　　B. Sales and logistics.

　C. Returned logistics.　　　　D. Back and forth.

(2) (　　) is software about the relation between the customer and the supplier in marketing.

　A. Customer Relationship Management (CRM)

　B. Customer service

　C. Sales planning

　D. Distribution channel

(3) (　　) is the method to keep the best inventory level and position with the minimum cost to satisfy the demand.

　A. Warehouse management　　　B. Inventory control

　C. Stock management　　　　　D. Storage management

(4) The transportation method that is restricted to a small number of products is (　　).

　A. pipelines　　B. planes　　C. ships　　D. trucks

(5) The transportation method that can carry large volumes and great weights at a relatively slow pace is (　　).

　A. pipelines　　B. planes　　C. ships　　D. trucks

(6) The disadvantage of rail transport compared with motor carrier is (　　).

　A. cost　　　　　　　　　　　B. speed

　C. lost and damage ratios　　　D. transit time and frequency of service

(7) Container is most benefit for (　　).

　A. transport carrying, loading and unloading　　B. storage

　C. transporting　　　　　　　　　　　　　　　D. distribution

(8) What are the major goods moved in pipeline transport? (　　)

　A. Natural gas.　B. Crude oil.　C. Water.　D. A, B and C.

(9) The advantage of Third-party logistics are (　　).

　A. better service　B. lower cost　C. cheaper　D. A and B

(10) A manufacturer turns over the function of transportation or warehousing to an independent third party. This practice is called (　　).

　A. outsourcing　　　　　　　B. third-party logistics

　C. contract logistics　　　　　D. All of above

3. Questions for Discussion

(1) Explain the three main inventory replenishment systems.

(2) Describe the primary modes of transportation and please compare the cost of rail with water.

(3) Why is information viewed as one of the keys to logistics competitive advantage for the future? Give some examples about logistics information technology.

(4) What is third-party logistics, and why does it exist?

Practical Writing

Scenario: The following dialogue is taken from a meeting of the Welfare Committee of Hudson Enterprises Inc., which was held at 4 p.m. on Tuesday 21 October 1999 in the Chairman's Office. Prepare the **Minutes** in narrative style.

Mrs. Pryse: (Chairman): Well, it's 4 o'clock and we all appear to be here so shall we get started? Anthony Long won't be joining us as he's attending a business conference this week. Do you all have the last meeting's minutes? (agreement) Are there any amendments, or can I sign them as a correct record? (Chairman signs) Good, matters arising? Anything to report?

Mr. Crook: Yes, Miss Bolan and I visited Maria Roberts in hospital on the 16th to deliver our Committee's basket of flowers and our good wishes for a speedy recovery. She hopes to be back at work in a week on Monday, so she'll be with us again when we next meet.

Chairman: That's marvelous news. Right, let's move on to Item 4. Gordon, you were going to talk about the restaurant, I believe. Did you bring along the accounts for the half year ending 31 July?

Mr. Caign: Yes, I have copies for everyone. (distributes copies) As you'll see, the accounts show we made a profit of $1,300,000 over the first 6 months of the year. I'd like to suggest that we utilize some of this by purchasing a new coffee machine, as the present one is rather old and frequently breaks down.

Chairman: Right, we'll move on to Washroom Facilities now. I've received several complaints about the female toilets on the second floor. I've been there to see what all the fuss is about and I agree they do need upgrading.

Miss Paterson: Yes, these are near my office, and apart from several locks being faulty, there are chipped tiles, and the state of decoration is very poor.

Chairman: I'd like a volunteer to arrange for some local workmen to look at the washroom and give us an estimate on the cost of the repairs.

Miss Paterson: I'll gladly do that. Something needs to be done quickly.

Chairman: Right, that's something else to continue with next time. Leonard, you're next, I believe...

Mr. Leighton: Thank you. Well, as you know, as Training Officer, I have a lot of contact with our young trainees. Many of them are attending Cliff College on evening courses which the Company sponsors. Examinations are coming up in December and these people don't have much time to study. I'd like to suggest that they be given two weeks' study leave prior to their exams.

Mrs. Shirley: That's a valid point, Natasha Len, in my department, bless her, she works very hard for us, and I know she goes to College three evenings a week. It would kill me!

Chairman: I can sympathize, but I really don't think it's within our power as a Committee to make such a decision. Leonard, can I suggest you write a formal memo to the Board? They have a Board meeting early November I believe, so you should ask them to include this item on the agenda. By the time we meet again, we should have an answer from them.

Mr. Leighton: Yes, I think that will be best. I'll get a memo out tomorrow.

Chairman: Now, the final item, Christmas Dinner and Dance, Miss Bolan, did you get some specimen menu from hotels?

Miss Bolan: Yes, I have some samples for us to look at. (distributes copies)

Mr. Knight: This one looks brilliant—the Marina Hotel—quite reasonable too.

Mr. Crook: I agree, it seems far superior to the others.

Miss Bolan: That's what I thought too. I suggest we should confirm with the Marina, if everyone agrees? (agreement)

Chairman: Good, now shall we fix a date? What about the last Saturday before Christmas? That's the 21st. (agreement)

Chairman: Right then Miss Bolan, can we leave it to you to make all the necessary arrangements?

Miss Bolan: Oh sure. I'll get in touch with the Marina to confirm with them, and I'll also put up a notice on the staff bulletin board. I hope it'll be as successful as last year's.

Chairman: When everything is left to you, Miss Bolan, I'm sure it can't fail to be successful. Right, moving on, is there anything else anyone wants to discuss? No? Right, then let's decide on a date for the next meeting... 6 weeks as usual? Can I suggest 24th November, same time? (agreement) OK then, thank you all for attending.

Part 5

Expanding Marketing Concept
拓展营销理念

经典营销名言:

Innovation has no limits. The only limit is your imagination. It's time for you to begin thinking out of the box... Innovation distinguishes between a leader and a follower.

—Steve Jobs

创新无极限。只要敢想,没有什么不可能。立即跳出思维的框框吧……领袖和跟风者的区别就在于创新。

——史蒂夫·乔布斯

本部分内容导读:

21世纪,服务行业飞速发展。与此同时,先进的通信、交通以及技术的进步令世界变得越来越小。一些注重可持续发展的公司更是努力将企业、顾客和社会的利益结合在一起。营销学本身正随着企业日益拓展的实践活动不断地获得丰富和完善。

内容	口语	阅读	写作
单元 15	保险	从产品营销到服务营销	通知/邀请函(请柬)
单元 16	演讲词	21世纪的营销创新	代理协议

Unit 15　It's an Insurance Salesperson

Learning Objectives

◇ 熟悉保险销售的常用口语表达；
◇ 理解服务的性质与特点；
◇ 理解衡量服务质量的基本方法和技术；
◇ 理解服务营销组合与产品营销组合的差异；
◇ 掌握通知与邀请函(请柬)的书写规则和常用套语的正确写法。

Speaking：Insurance

【场景1】　早上7点刚过，于琪家中的门铃忽然响起。他打开房门，一位年轻的女孩正站在门口。还未等于琪说话，对方便主动递上名片并介绍自己是太平洋保险公司的琳达小姐。

【对话1】　A：保险公司业务员 Linda Zhang　　B：于琪

A：Good morning. My name is Linda Zhang and I'm with Pacific Insurance Company. May I come in and show the new life insurance package Pacific is offering this year?
早上好。我叫张琳达，来自太平洋保险公司。我可以进来向您展示一下太平洋保险公司今年推出的最新保险计划吗？

B：How long will it take?
需要多长时间？

A：I can give you a general overview in less than ten minutes.
我可以在10分钟之内向您做一个大致的介绍。

B：Well，okay then. Come in，please.（Sitting down to talk）
那么，好吧。请进。（坐下来交谈）

A：May I have your name?
可以问一下您的姓名吗？

B：It's Qi Yu.

我叫于琪。

A: Mr. Yu, do you have life insurance right now?
于先生，您现在有人寿保险吗？

B: No, I don't. I don't have a family of my own, so I don't think I really need it right now.
还没有。我自己还没有组建家庭，因此我认为我现在还不需要。

A: Well, let me tell you a real story, Mr. Yu. Once I had a very good friend who had already received an insurance plan by a certain agent. But he left it unsigned because he went on a business trip the next day. Then something really terrible happened. He died in an accident in another city, leaving his family unsupported. I could do nothing but feel sorry for him. Actually that's why I have joined this line. Mr. Yu, I suppose your parents love you very much?
嗯，让我给您讲一个真实的故事，于先生。我曾经有一个非常要好的朋友，他已经收到某代理给他办理的保险计划。可是由于第二天要出差，他没有签署该保险文件。接下来，可怕的事情发生了，他在另外一个城市死于一场意外，造成他的家庭无人供养。除了感到惋惜，我什么都做不了。实际上，这就是我为什么要加入这个行业的原因。于先生，我想您的父母是非常爱您的吧？

B: Yes, of course.
是的，当然。

A: And you love them, too?
您也爱他们，是吧？

B: Sure.
当然。

A: Surely you wish they could live a happy and long life without any financial worry. Am I right?
您一定希望他们能够快乐长寿，不必有任何经济上的担心，对吧？

B: Yes.
是的。

A: Then it is advisable for you to buy life insurance and leave the money to your parents in case anything should happen to you. It is actually a way of expressing your love for them.
那么我向您建议购买人寿保险，如果任何事情发生在您的身上，您可以留下一笔钱给您的父母。这实际上是向他们表达您的爱的一种方式。

B: It sounds reasonable.
听起来有些道理。

A: At Pacific, we have a plan that increases the amount of the benefits over time. The longer you pay into it, the more the beneficiary will get out of it in the end. If you are interested in it, how much will you pay for this plan each year?
在太平洋保险公司，我们有一个随着时间的推移而不断增加保险金数额的保险计划。

您付款的时间越长,受益人最终获得的赔偿就越多。如果您对这个计划感兴趣,每年您愿意支付多少?

B：About 1,000 yuan.

大约一千元。

A：And your date of birth, please?

请问您的出生日期是?

B：July 27, 2000.

2000年7月27日。

A：Then I will design a plan most suitable for you according to the information, Mr. Yu. It may take one or two days. When will you be available the day after tomorrow, just this time or at four in the afternoon?

那么,于先生,我将根据您的信息为您设计一个最合适的计划。这可能需要一到两天的时间。后天您什么时间有空,这个时间还是下午4点?

B：At four in the afternoon.

下午4点吧。

A：OK. I'll be here on time. Next time, it may take us about 25 minutes. Please take a note about it and if there is any change, inform me in advance. Thank you very much, Mr. Yu. See you later.

好的。我会准时到这儿。下次,我大约要占用您25分钟左右的时间。请对此做个记录。如果有任何改变的话,事先通知我一下。非常感谢,于先生。再见。

B：See you.

再见。

【场景2】 早上上班时在公司大门口,于琪正好碰上销售经理马天跃。马经理告诉于琪,公司刚刚从新西兰进口了一批布料,用于生产高档童装。该笔交易执行FOB价格条款,由买方金色童年公司办理保险。销售经理交代于琪负责保险事宜,于琪马上想到了太平洋保险公司的张琳达。电话预约后,双方又见面了。

【对话2】 A:保险公司业务员Linda Zhang B:于琪

A：Good morning, Mr. Yu. So glad to see you again.

早上好,于先生。很高兴又见到你。

B：Good morning, Miss Zhang.

早上好,张小姐。

A：Take a seat, please. What can I do for you?

请坐。我能为您做些什么?

B：Thank you. I'm here to ask you what kind of insurance you are able to provide for my consignment, Miss Zhang?

谢谢。我来这儿是想向你了解贵公司能为我的货物提供哪些保险呢,张小姐?

A：We've been able to cover all kinds of risks for transportation by sea, land and air.

我们可以办理海运、陆运和空运的所有险种。

B: I have a batch of cloth to be shipped to Shanghai. What risks should be covered?
我有一批布料要海运到上海,我应该保哪些险呢?

A: We can serve you with a broad range of coverage against all kinds of risks for sea transport, such as free from particular average, with particular average, all risks and extraneous risks. It's better for you to scan this leaflet first, and then make a decision.
我公司可以承保海洋运输的所有险种,如平安险、水渍险、一切险和附加险。您最好先看看说明书,再决定保什么险。

B: (After reading the leaflet) FPA... that means free from particular average. It's good enough, what do you think?
(看了材料后)FPA……它的意思是平安险。这个险种足够了,你觉得呢?

A: Surely, you can do as you pleased. But don't you wish to arrange for WPA and additional coverage against risk of contamination? This suits your consignment.
当然,您满意就好。但是不考虑投保水渍险附带污渍险吗?这适合您的货物。

B: Perhaps you're right. I'll have the goods covered as you said.
也许你是对的。就投你所说的险种。

A: Very good, please fill in the application form. You need to write every word clearly.
很好,请填写这份表格。您需要清楚地书写每一个字。

B: Surely, I'll. (After a while) Miss Zhang, I finished. Please help me to have a check to see if everything is correct.
当然,我会的。(过了一会儿)张小姐,我填好了。请帮我核对一下是否填写正确。

A: OK, let me read it. (Reading in a low voice) Insured: Qi Yu; Description of the goods: Top-grade Cloth; Mode of transport and the name of vessel: S. S. "HUA-YUAN"; Coverage: WPA plus risk of contamination. Oh, Mr. Yu, why both the loading port and unloading port are missing?
好的,让我看一下。(低声地读)投保人:于琪;货物描述:高档布料;运输方式和运输工具名称:"华远"号轮船;险种:水渍险附带污渍险。噢,于先生,为什么装运港和目的港都没有填?

B: Oh, terribly sorry. I forgot that. The loading port is Wellington and the unloading port is Shanghai. Here you are. Now, what is the insurance premium?
哎,太对不起了。我忘填了。装运港是惠灵顿,目的港是上海。给你。那么,需要交纳的保险费是多少?

A: The premium is to be calculated in this way. First find out the premium rate for cloth, that is 0.3 percent. And secondly consider what risks are covered. What you have covered is WPA plus risk of contamination. So the total premium rate is 0.8%. According to international practice, insurance coverage is for 110% of the invoice value.
保险费是这样计算的。首先找到布料的保险费率,0.3%。然后看投保了哪些险。您投保的是水渍险附带污渍险。因此,总的保险费率是0.8%。按照国际惯例,保险额为发票金额的110%。

B：Good, Miss Zhang, thank you for your assistance.
好的，张小姐，谢谢你的帮助。
A：Don't mention it. See you again.
不用客气。再见。
B：See you again.
再见。

Reading：From Product Marketing to Service Marketing

于琪与琳达小姐都是销售人员，于琪销售的是产品，琳达小姐销售的是服务。那么，产品营销和服务营销有什么样的区别呢？

Chapter 15 Services Marketing

Section 1 Nature and Characteristics of a Service

There is general agreement that inherent differences between goods and services exist and that they result in unique, or at least different, management challenges for service businesses and for manufacturers that offer service as a core offering.

1.1 Intangibility

Intangibility means that services can't be held, touched, or seen before the purchase decision. In contrast, before purchasing a traditional product, a consumer can touch a box of laundry detergent, kick the tire of an automobile, or sample a new breakfast cereal. Because services are performances or actions rather than objects, they cannot be seen, felt, tasted, or touched in the same manner that we can sense tangible goods. For example, health-care services are actions (e.g., surgery, diagnosis, examination, treatment) performed by providers and directed toward patients and their families. These services cannot actually be seen or touched by the patient, although the patient may be able to see and touch certain tangible components of the service (e.g., equipment, hospital room).

Intangibility presents several marketing challenges. For example, services cannot be patented legally, and new service concepts can therefore easily be copied by competitors. Services cannot be readily displayed or easily communicated to customers, so quality may be difficult for consumers to assess. Decisions about what to include in advertising and other promotion materials are challenging, so is pricing. The actual costs of a "unit of service" are hard to determine and the price/quality relationship is complex. To reduce uncertainty, buyers will look for signs of evidence of the service quality. They will draw inferences about quality from the place, people, equipment, communication material, symbols, and piece that they see. Therefore, the service provider's task is to "manage the evidence", to "tangibilize the intangible."

1.2 Inseparability

Inseparability refers to the fact that production and consumption of the service are inextricably intertwined. Whereas most goods are produced first, then sold and consumed, most services are sold first and then produced and consumed simultaneously. For example, an automobile can be manufactured in Detroit, shipped to San Francisco, sold two months later, and consumed over a period of years. But restaurant services cannot be provided until they have been sold, and the dinning experience is essentially produced and consumed at the same time.

The implications of this are that the consumer is involved in production. Further, in many cases other consumers are also involved at the same time, as in most retailing situations. This may be a positive aspect of the benefits delivered (in a theatre or club), or it may be a potential negative aspect (waiting in queues at the post office). Whether the buyer is physically present or not, the product comes into existence only when it is bought; it cannot be mass produced in advance (although the physical components may be, to some extent).

1.3 Variability

Variability (or heterogeneity) is a result of the fact that services are usually delivered by human beings, whose performance is necessarily variable. Tangible products can be of good or bad quality but with modern production lines the quality will at least be consistent. Heterogeneity also results because no two customers are precisely alike; each will have unique demands or experience the service in a unique way. Thus, the heterogeneity connected with services is largely the result of human interaction (between and among employees and customers) and all of the vagaries that accompany it. For example, a tax accountant may provide a different service experience for two different customers on the same day depending on their individual needs and personalities and on whether the accountant is interviewing them when he or she is fresh in the morning or tired at the end of a long day of meeting.

Because services are heterogeneous across time, organizations, and people, ensuring consistent service quality is challenging. Service firms can take three steps toward quality control. The first step is investing in good hiring and training procedures. Recruiting the right service employees and providing them with excellent training are crucial regardless of whether employees are highly skilled professionals or low-skilled workers. The second step is standardizing the service-performance process throughout the organization. This is helped by preparing a service blueprint that depicts events and processes in a flowchart, with the objective of recognizing potential fail points. The third step is monitoring customer satisfaction through suggestion and complaint systems, customer surveys, and comparison-shopping.

1.4 Perishability

Perishability means that the service cannot be stockpiled. If a seat is unfilled when the plane leaves or the play starts, it cannot be kept and sold the next day or next week; that revenue is lost for ever. In some cases, such as insurance or banking, it could be argued that potential stocks remain, in the sense that the service is there to be sold every day as long as underwriting or loan capacity exists. Retailers can keep stocks of products for the duration of their shelf-life—a day for fresh product, several months for clothes, longer still for furniture. Most services, however, are clearly time-dependent in a way that physical products are not.

A primary issue that marketers face in relation to service perishablity is the inability to inventory. The perishability of services is not a problem when demand is steady. When demand fluctuates, service firms have problems. Demand forecasting and creative planning for capacity utilization are therefore important and challenging decision areas. The fact that services cannot typically be returned or resold also implies a need for strong recovery strategies when things do go wrong. For example, while a bad haircut cannot be returned, the hairdresser can and should have strategies for recovering the customer's goodwill if and when such a problem occurs.

小 结

服务和产品的不同主要体现在四个方面。第一,服务是无形的,也就是说在购买前他们不能被持有、触摸或看见。这对营销人员提出新的要求,尽量将无形的服务有形化。第二,服务具有不可分性,即服务的生产和消费不能确切地分离。这意味着消费者也参与到服务提供的过程中,而且其他消费者的参与也可能对服务消费过程产生积极或消极的影响。第三,服务具有易变性,即服务的质量受提供人,以及其他许多因素的影响。这对如何保证服务的质量提出新的挑战。第四,服务具有易逝性,即不能被储存。当需求波动时,服务企业将面临问题。

Section 2 Service Quality Measurement

Because the customer's experience of a service determines if she or he will return to the provider in the future, service marketers feel that measuring positive and negative service experiences is the "Holy Grail" for the services industry.

2.1 SERVQUAL

The SERVQUAL scale is one popular instrument to measure consumers' perceptions of service quality. SERVQUAL identifies five dimensions, or components, of service quality: Tangibles mean the physical facilities and equipment and the professional appearance of personnel; Reliability means the ability to provide dependably and accurately what was promised; Responsiveness means the willingness to help customers and provide prompt service; Assurance means the knowledge and courtesy of employees, and the ability to convey trust and confidence; Finally, empathy means the degree of caring and individual attention customers receive.

Thousands of service businesses apply the SERVQUAL scale. They usually administer it in a survey format through a written, on-line, or phone questionnaire. Firms often track SERVQUAL scores over time to understand how their service quality is (hopefully) improving. They also can use this measure to apply the gap analysis approach we'll describe next.

2.2 Gap Analysis

Gap analysis is a measurement approach that gauges the difference between a customer's expectation of service quality and what actually occurs. By identifying specific places in the service system where there is a wide gap between what customers expect and what they receive, services marketers can get a handle on what needs improvement. Some major gaps include the following:

◇ Gap between consumers' expectations and management's perceptions: A major quality gap occurs when the firm's managers don't understand what its customers' expectations are in the first place.

◇ Gap between management's perception and quality standards the firm sets: Quality suffers when a firm fails to establish a quality-control program. American Express found that customers complained most about its responsiveness, accuracy, and timeliness. The company established 180 specific goals to correct these problems, and it now monitors how fast employees answer phones in an effort to be more responsive.

◇ Gap between established quality standards and service delivery: One of the biggest threats to service quality is poor employee performance. When employees do not deliver the service at the level the company specifies, quality suffers.

◇ Gap between service quality standards and consumers' expectations: Sometimes a firm makes exaggerated promises or does not accurately describe its service to customers. A services firm is better off when it communicates exactly what the customer can expect and how the company will make it right if it doesn't deliver on its promises.

◇ Gap between expected service and actual service: Sometimes consumers misperceive the quality of the service. Thus, even when communications accurately describe what service quality the firm provides and what customers can expect, buyers are less than satisfied. Some diners at fine restaurants are so demanding that even their own mothers couldn't anticipate their every desire (that's probably why they're eating out in the first place).

2.3 The Critical Incident Technique

The critical incident technique is another way to measure service quality. Using this approach, the company collects and closely analyzes very specific customer complaints. It can then identify critical incidents—specific contacts between consumers and service providers that are most likely to result in dissatisfaction.

Some critical incidents happen when the service organization simply can't meet a customer's expectations. For example, it is impossible to satisfy a passenger who says to a flight attendant, "Come sit with me. I don't like to fly alone." In other cases though, the firm is capable of meeting these expectations but fails to do so. For example, the customer might complain to a flight attendant, "My seat won't recline." A service provider can turn a potentially dissatisfied customer into a happy one if it addresses the problem or perhaps even tells the customer why the problem can't be solved at this time. Customers tend to be fairly forgiving if the organization gives them a reasonable explanation for the problem.

Of course, no one (not even a marketing professor) is perfect, and mistakes happen. Some failures, such as when your dry cleaner places glaring red spots on your new white sweater, are easy to see at the time the firm performs the service. Others, such as when the dry cleaner shrinks your sweater, are less obvious and you recognize them only at a later time when you're running late and get a "surprise". But no matter when or how you discover the failure, the important thing is that the firm takes fast action to resolve the problem. A timely and appropriate response means that the problem won't occur again (hopefully) and that the customer's complaint will be satisfactorily resolved. The key is speed. Research shows that customers whose complaints are resolved quickly are far more likely to buy from the same company again than from those that take longer to resolve complaints.

To make sure that they keep service failures to a minimum and that when they do blow it they can recover quickly, managers should first understand the service and the potential points at which failures are most likely to occur so they can plan how to recover ahead of time. That is why it's so important to identify critical incidents. In addition, employees should be trained to listen for complaints and be empowered to take appropriate actions immediately. For example, Marriott allows employees to spend up to $2,500 to compensate guests for certain inconveniences.

小 结

SERVQUAL量表是比较流行的从五个方面衡量顾客服务满意度的方法。这五个方面包括可感知性、可靠性、反应/响应性、保证性，以及情感性/移情性。差距分析是通过分析顾客所接受的服务和期望之间的差距来寻求改进的方法。差距可能来自顾客期望和管理层的认知、管理层的认知和企业质量标准、企业质量标准和实际服务质量、企业质量标准和顾客期望，以及顾客期望服务和实际提供服务五个方面。最后，关键事件技术是通过识别工作环境中影响服务质量的关键点来合理计划和预防的一种技术手段。当然，在提供服务的过程中出现失误是不可避免的，重要的是能够迅速地进行弥补。

Section 3 Marketing Mix for Services

3.1 Traditional Marketing Mix

One of the most basic concepts in marketing is the marketing mix, defined as the elements an organization controls and use to satisfy or communicate with customers. The traditional marketing mix is composed of the four P's: product, price, place (distribution), and promotion. These elements appear as core decision variables in any marketing text or marketing plan. The notion of a mix implies that all of the variables are interrelated and depend on each other to some extent. Further, the marketing mix philosophy implies that there is an optimal mix of the four factors for a given market segment at a given point in time.

Careful management of product, place, promotion, and price will clearly also be essential to the successful marketing of services. However, the strategies for the four P's require some modifications when applied to services. For example, traditional promotion is thought of as involving decisions related to personal selling, advertising, sales promotions, and publicity. In services, these factors are also important, but because services are produced and consumed simultaneously, service delivery people (such as clerks, ticket-takers, nurses, phone personnel) are involved in "real time" promotion of the service even if their jobs are typically defined in terms of the operational function they perform. Pricing also becomes very complex in services. First, in order to price a service, it is important to define the unit of service consumption. For example, should pricing be based on completing a specific service task (cutting a customer's hair), or should it be time based (how long it takes to cut a customer's hair). Second, for services that are composed of multiple elements, the issue is whether pricing should be based on a "bundle" of elements or whether each element should be priced separately. A bundled price may be preferable when consumers dislike having to pay "extra" for every part of the service (for example, paying extra for baggage or food on an airplane).

3.2 Expanded Mix for Services

In addition to the traditional four P's, three new marketing-mix elements (people, physical evidence, and process) are included in the marketing mix for service because they are within the control of the firm and any or all of them may influence the customer's initial decision to purchase a service, as well as the customer's level of satisfaction and repurchase decisions.

All of the human actors participating in the delivery of a service, namely, the firm's personnel, the customer and other customers in the service environment provide cues to the customer regarding the nature of the service itself. How these people are dressed, their personal appearance, and their attitudes and behaviors all influence the customer's perceptions of the service. The service provider or contact person can be very important. In fact, for some services, such as consulting, counseling, teaching, and other professional relationship-based services, the provider is the service. In other cases the contact person, may play what appears to be a relatively small part in service delivery, for instance, a telephone installer, an airline baggage handler or an equipment delivery dispatcher. Yet research suggests that even these providers may be the focal point of service encounters that can prove critical for the organization.

The physical evidence of service includes all of the tangible representations of the service such as brochures, letterhead, business cards, report formats, signage, and equipment. In some cases it includes the physical facility where the service is offered, for example, the retail bank branch facility. In other cases, such as telecommunication services, the physical facility may be irrelevant. In this case other tangibles such as billing statements and appearance of the repair truck may be important indicators of quality. Especially when consumers have little on which to judge the actual quality of service they will rely on these cues, just as they rely on the cues provided by the people and the service process. Physical evidence cues provide excellent opportunities for the firm to send consistent and strong messages regarding the organization's purpose, the intended market segments, and the nature of the service.

The actual delivery steps the customer experience, or the operational flow of the service, will also provide customer with evidence on which to judge the service. Some services are very complex, requiring the customer to follow a complicated and extensive series of actions to complete the process. Highly bureaucratized services frequently follow this pattern, and the logic of the steps involved often escapes customer. Another distinguishing characteristic of the process that can provide evidence for the customer is whether the service follows a production-line/standardized approach or whether the process is an empowered/customerized one. None of these characteristics of the service is inherently better or worse than another. Rather, the point is that these process characteristics are another form of evidence used by the consumer to judge service. For example, two successful airline companies, Southwest in the U.S. and Singapore Airlines, follow extremely different process models. Southwest is a no-frills, no food, no assigned seats, no exceptions, low-priced airline that offers frequent, relatively short length domestic flights. All of the evidence it provides is consistent with its vision and market position. Singapore Airlines, on the other hand, focuses on the business traveler and is concerned with meeting individual traveler's needs. Thus, its process is highly customized to the individual, and employees are empowered to provide nonstandard service when needed. Both airlines have been very successful.

小 结

服务营销组合将传统的4P扩展到了7P。增加的第一个P是人员,这是7P营销组合很重要的一个观点。所有的人都直接或间接地被卷入某种服务的提供过程中,他们的穿着、外貌、态度和行为都会对服务质量产生影响。增加的第二个P是物证,包括小册子、信笺、名片、报告格式、标识、设备,以及服务环境等。当顾客对服务质量无从判别时,他们会更多地依靠这些物证。增加的最后一个P是过程。服务是通过一定的程序、机制以及活动得以实现的,服务提供过程也会成为判断服务质量的一个关键要素。

New Words and Key Terms

01. intangibility	无形性
02. inseparability	不可分性
03. variability	易变性
04. perishability	易逝性
05. SERVQUAL scale	SERVQUAL 量表
06. tangibles	可感知性
07. reliability	可靠性
08. responsiveness	反应性,响应性
09. assurance	保证性
10. empathy	情感性,移情性
11. gap analysis	差距分析
12. critical incident technique	关键事件技术
13. physical evidence	物证

Writing: Notice / Invitation Letter or Card

新年就要到了,这也是"金色童年"的第四十个年头。公司决定举办一场盛大的新年联欢晚宴。总经理 Robert 让于琪在公司内部发布一个通知,并向重要的嘉宾发送邀请函或请帖。Robert 特别提到,一定要邀请到英国阳光公司的代表来参加年末的这次盛宴。

一、通知与邀请函(请柬)写作的基本要求和格式

(一)通知(Notice)

通知通常是上级对下级、组织对成员(或公众)或平行单位之间部署工作、传达事情或告知情况时所使用的应用文。书面通知通常有两种类型:一种是以书信的形式,把某一具体事项发送给相关人员;另一种是以布告形式发布在布告栏(这类通知又称为告示、启事)。一份通知应包括以下内容:时间和日期、地点、人员、活动或事件,以及其他需要说明的信息或细节,如发布人(或单位)、相关要求等。书信类通知的写作参考商务信函,而对于告示或启事类通知,其写法可以采用以下四种形式。

1. 简洁式

通知的这种写法充分体现简洁明了的特点,表述直截了当,不用完整的句子,而只使用名词或名词短语。

LECTURE

Topic: Across Cultures—Digital Media and Literate Activity

Lecturer: Professor Robert Johnson from University of Pennsylvania

Date: Monday, December 10th, 2023

Time: from 9.30 a.m. to 11.30 a.m.

Place: the Meeting Room of English Department

All Welcome

2. 灵活式

通知的这种写法在注重简洁明了的同时,又充分展现了灵活性,通常被具有一定语言文字功底的中高级写作者所采用。

LECTURE

By

Professor Robert Johnson

From

University of Pennsylvania

On

Across Cultures—Digital Media and Literate Activity

Meeting Room,English Department

9.30 a.m.,Monday,December 10th,2012

3. 混合式

通知的这种写法通常是由于要包含一些只能用文字叙述的细节,因此采用句子和短语混合使用的书写方式。

LECTURE

Topic:Across Cultures—Digital Media and Literate Activity

Lecturer:Professor Robert Johnson from University of Pennsylvania

Date:Monday,December 10th,2012

Time:from 9.30 a.m. to 11.30 a.m.

Place:the Meeting Room of English Department

Professor Johnson is well known for his unique probing of the many connections between literate activity and new information technologies.

4. 段落式

尽管完全使用句子来发布通知越来越不被推崇(除非没有其他选择),有些人仍习惯于这种写法。采用段落式书写通知,文字应干净利落,不要拖泥带水。

NOTICE

There is going to be a lecture titled "Across Cultures—Digital Media and Literate Activity" by Professor Robert Johnson from the Department of English Literature of University of Pennsylvania in the Meeting Room of English Department from 9.30 a.m. to 11.30 a.m. on Monday December 10th. All the teachers and students are welcome to attend this lecture.

English Department

(二)邀请函(请柬)(Invitation Letter or Card)

邀请函(Invitation Letter)是一种重要的社交书信,它包括正式和非正式两种。非正式邀请函实际上就是一封普通的私人信件,使用相对随意的口头语言,语气与便条语气相似。例如,下面是一封私人家宴邀请函的正文。My husband and I should be very much pleased if you and your daughter would dine with us next Sunday, the eleventh, at 6:30. I am asking a few other people and I hope we may have some Karaoke after dinner. If Anne would only consent to bring her violin with her, I feel sure we would have a wonderful evening.（我和我的丈夫高兴地邀请您和您的女儿下个星期天11号6点半和我们共进晚餐。我同时也邀请了一些其他朋友，并计划在晚餐后唱唱卡拉OK。如果安妮愿意带上她的小提琴，我相信我们一定会度过一个愉快的夜晚）。而对于正式的邀请函，通常由机构或公司发出，篇幅较长并往往带有公务的性质，使用正式的书面语言，语气偏向中性。

请柬（Invitation Card）属于非信函形式的正式邀请。需排成两边整齐对称的锯齿形，一般使用第三人称，"先生"通常写在其"夫人"前，行末不用标点符号。具体书写时先写邀请人的姓名，前面需带称谓或头衔。然后是套语，如"request the pleasure（honour）of the presence of"，或"request the pleasure（honour）of the company of"。套语后是被邀请人的姓名，也需带称谓或头衔。接下来，书写邀请的具体内容和时间。时间安排的顺序是星期几，几月几日，年和点钟，数字最好使用英语而非阿拉伯数字。最后是地点。写请柬的日期一般不出现在请柬上。对于需安排座位的宴请活动，应要求被邀者答复能否出席。最经常的表述是使用"R.S.V.P."（法语缩略词，意思是"请赐复！"）或"Regrets only"（如不能出席，请告知）并最好注明联系电话，也可用电话询问能否出席。若邀请人对被邀者出席服装有要求，可在请柬的左下角或右下角加以注明。

二、于琪的解决方案

（一）通知（公司员工）

GOLDEN CHILDHOOD COMPANY

NEW YEAR DINNER PARTY

All Are Cordially Welcome

Thursday, 28th December 2023

Multi-functional Hall in Oriental Riverside Bund View Hotel

4:30 p.m. —6:30 p.m.

You may bring up to two friends. Please bring a small gift (suggested price US $ 20) to be swapped between others.

（二）邀请函（阳光公司代表）

Dear Mr. Jimmy Wales,

It's our great honor to invite you and other representatives from Sunshine Food Company to come to our New Year Dinner Party which will be held on 28th December, 2023.

As a leading producer of high-quality children's wear and toys, Golden Childhood has experienced four decades of hard struggle. This is a brilliant four-decade, a fruitful four-decade. We would like to take this opportunity to express our sincere thanks to all the friends who have been supporting us all the time. Meanwhile, we hope this party will provide an excellent opportunity to increase our friendship and communicate our future business cooperation in detail.

We should be very pleased if you let us know as soon as possible whether you can attend the Party. All arrangements for your stay will, of course, be made by us at our expense.

We are all looking forward to seeing you soon.

Yours truly,

(三)请柬(嘉宾)

INVITATION CARD

The Golden Childhood Company
requests the honour of the presence of
Mr. & Mrs. Hillman
at the New Year Dinner Party on Friday
the twenty-eighth of December twenty twenty-three
at Four Thirty P. M.
Multi-functional Hall, Oriental Riverside Bund View Hotel
2727 Binjiang Avenue, Pudong District

R. S. V. P.

Review Questions

1. Key Terms

Inseparability; Variability; Responsiveness; Empathy; Critical incident; Physical evidence

2. Multiple Choices (select one or more)

(1) The provision of auditing and taxation advice by a firm of accountants is an example of ( ).

A. brand　　　　B. goods　　　　C. product　　　　D. service

(2) What are NOT belonging to "service"? ( )

A. Time of the lawyer.　　　　B. Good package of the candy.

C. Skill of the doctor.　　　　D. Smile of a waiter.

(3) How can we tangiblize our service to customers? ( )

A. Describe the function of our service by the salesperson.

B. Fine equipment.

C. High quality.

D. Employees' appearance.

(4) Service has been described as something that may be bought and sold, but which cannot be dropped on your foot. What does the sentence infer? ( )

A. Service is intangible.　　　　B. Service is a process.

C. Service cannot be stored.   D. Service has value.

(5) In the following statements, which can explain that service is heterogeneous? (   )

A. Service delivery and customer satisfaction depend on each other.

B. Customers affect each other.

C. Service quality depends on the service provider.

D. Customers participate in and affect the transaction.

(6) Which CANNOT be controlled by service supplier? (   )

A. The ability of the consumer to articulate his or her needs.

B. The ability and willingness of personnel to satisfy those customers.

C. The level of demand for the service.

D. The ability of his allocation of resources.

(7) What is the result of the service being produced and consumed at the same time? (   )

A. Mass production is difficult.

B. One's experience of service production may affect others' experience.

C. People can produce in one place but consume in another place.

D. Standardization could be possible.

(8) Which can help the service firm reduce the inventory cost? (   )

A. Commission.   B. Part-time employee.

C. Upgrading the guest in hotels.   D. Reduce the price of service.

(9) In the SERVQUAL scale approach, (   ) means the willingness to help customers and provide prompt service.

A. reliability   B. responsiveness

C. assurance   D. empathy

(10) What is NOT the physical evidence of a service? (   )

A. Brochure.   B. Letterhead.

C. Report format.   D. Commitment.

3. Questions for Discussion

(1) What is a service? What are the important characteristics of services that make them different from goods?

(2) How do marketers measure service quality? How should marketers respond to failures in service quality?

(3) Identify the additional marketing considerations that services require.

Practical Writing

Scenario: You (Mike Simmons) work for Pleasure Cruise Tourist Agency of 14 Sherry Street, Canterbury, Kent, CJ199AB. Jenny Jones is the manager. One day, you arrive at work in the morning and find the following note from Jenny Jones on your desk. Please write a **Notice** as required. Also, your daughter Mary and Mr. John Smith are going to get married. So you need to write an informal **Letter of Invitation** to one of your best friends and an **Invitation Card** to your boss.

Mike,

  Before you do anything else, please write a notice for me. When I arrived this morning I found the office floor covered with water. I have phoned for a plumber to come and check the problem. I also rang Peter Armstrong, who owns the Golden Pond Restaurant at 11 Pond Road. He's put a small room at our disposal until this mess is cleared up. We'll be open for business during the usual hours. Apologize to customers for any inconvenience this may cause them and put the notice in the window. I'll be back tomorrow at the latest.

Jenny

Unit 16 Hearing Some New Words

Learning Objectives

◇ 熟悉演讲和就餐的常用口语表达；
◇ 理解企业进入国际市场面临的障碍、主要方式，以及开展全球营销的基本策略；
◇ 理解绿色营销的含义、产生原因，以及基本的营销组合策略；
◇ 理解电子商务的含义、基本商务类型，以及网络营销目前面临的挑战；
◇ 掌握代理协议的书写规则和常用套语的正确写法。

Speaking：Speech

【场景1】　在公司新年晚宴上，总经理 Robert Liu 首先向到场的各位领导和来宾表示热烈欢迎，随后谈到公司的发展前景，并特别提及即将建立的冰激凌合资企业。对于来自合资方——英国阳光公司的代表们，Robert 希望他们能够尽情享受美好时光。

【演讲1】　演讲人：总经理 Robert Liu

Excellencies, Distinguished Mayor, Ladies and Gentlemen,
尊敬的各位，市长阁下，女士们和先生们：

　　It is with great pleasure that I extend my warm welcome to our distinguished Mayor, colleagues, and friends. I'm very happy that you are here to attend our New Year's Dinner Party. I would like to take this opportunity to express our warm greetings to all!
　　我荣幸地向尊敬的市长阁下，所有同仁、朋友们表示热烈的欢迎！很高兴大家光临我们的新年宴会，我想借此机会向大家表达我们衷心的祝福！
　　During the past four decades, with the help and supports of our local government, and through the hard work and efforts of the staff and workers in our company, we have made great progress. Our sales are up and our market share is expanding. On this big occasion, the old year is leaving, and the new year is coming. I hope we will be able to share the brightest common future and happiness, and work together for a new success.
　　在过去的四十年里，由于地方政府的帮助与支持和本公司全体职工的辛勤工作与竭诚努力，我们公司取得了很大进展。销售额上涨，市场份额正在扩大。借此辞旧迎新之际，我希望与各位分享美好的未来和幸福，携手共创佳绩。

Also, I'm happy to tell you a little bit more about the cooperation between Golden Childhood and Sunshine. There is to be an all-share joint venture of the two companies under the name of Golden-Sunshine. The establishment of the joint venture is a natural step for both partners as we all share the same science-based culture and a common vision concerning the future of Chinese ice-cream market. I believe that the new joint venture will combine strength of the two companies and allow us to develop innovation-led growth.

同时，我很高兴向大家通报一点儿有关金色童年与阳光公司的合作事宜。两家公司将采取纯股份式合资，新公司叫作金色阳光。鉴于两家公司均持有以科学为基础的理念以及对未来中国冰激凌市场的共同展望，合资企业的成立对双方来讲是自然的一步。我相信新的合资企业将结合两家公司的实力，并将取得创新性的发展。

Tonight we are very fortunate to have Mr. Jimmy Wales and other friends from Sunshine Company with us here to celebrate the coming New Year together. Sunshine is one of the world's leading nutrition, health and wellness companies, providing customers with the highest quality and best tasting ice-cream of more than 50 different flavors. Now, led by the CEO Mr. Wales, the company has been growing steadily with factories or operations in many countries in the world. We all hope our friends from Sunshine will be able to have a good time today, tasting the Chinese cuisine, drinking the Chinese wine, and above all, enjoying the "authentic" Chinese entertainment our young talented employees are going to perform.

今天，我们非常荣幸地邀请到吉米·威尔士先生和其他来自阳光公司的朋友们同我们一起庆祝即将到来的新年。阳光公司是世界领先的营养、健康、保健食品公司之一，向消费者提供超过50种不同口味的高质量、好口感的冰激凌产品。现在，公司在执行官威尔士先生的领导下，快速稳步增长，在世界许多国家拥有自己的工厂或项目。我们希望来自阳光公司的朋友们今天能度过一段美好时光，品尝中国美食，享用中国美酒，尤其是能够欣赏到由我们年轻员工表演的"正宗"的中国娱乐节目。

Now, let me propose a toast to the coming New Year, to friendship and cooperation, to a happy life and good health. Cheers!

现在，我建议为即将到来的新年，为了我们的友谊和合作，为了我们的幸福生活和健康，干杯！

【场景2】宴会正式开始了。随着宴会的进行，宾主双方频频举杯，气氛非常热烈。

【对话2】A：总经理 Robert Liu　B：Jimmy Wales 先生　C：销售经理马天跃

A：I'm so glad you were able to come, Mr. Wales. What would you like to drink?
真高兴您能来，威尔士先生。您想喝点什么？
B：Juice or some wine, I'm off alcohol.

果汁或葡萄酒，我不喝烈酒。

A：Apple juice, then? Would you also like to have a very light beer?
那就苹果汁如何？给您来点低度的啤酒，好吗？

B：OK. Apple juice and a glass of beer.
好吧，苹果汁和一杯啤酒。

A：I propose a toast to your pleasant tour in China!
我提议为您在中国愉快的旅行干一杯！

B：Thank you very much.
非常感谢。

C：This dish is a specialty of this restaurant. Please help yourself.
这是这家餐馆的一道特色菜。请随便尝尝。

B：Thank you. It's very nice. The cuisine takes care of color, flavor and taste. Can you tell me what this is?
谢谢你。味道真不错。整道菜色、香、味俱佳。您能告诉我这是什么菜吗？

C：It's ox tendon with prawn eggs. Have some more, please.
这是虾籽牛筋。多吃点。

A：Mr. Wales, you seem to be quite expert at chopsticks.
威尔士先生，看起来您的筷子用得很好啊。

B：I had practiced in them for a week in the UK before I came here.
来之前我在英国练习了一个星期。

A：No wonder. Well, this calls for a drink. To your progress in chopsticks, cheers!
怪不得。好，为这我们得干一杯。为您学会使用筷子，干杯！

C：Here comes mapodoufu, one of my favorite dishes.
我最喜欢的菜麻婆豆腐来了。

B：Sorry. Ma...
对不起。麻……

C：I don't know the English for it, but it's a kind of bean curd cooked with spicy sauce.
我不知道它用英文怎么说，不过它是一种豆腐，烹制时加了辣酱。

B：It's really a treat. By the way, I want to know the diet habit in your country.
真是美味。顺便问一下，我想知道一些你们国家的饮食习惯。

C：It's quite characteristic, you know, a lot depends on your way of life. Usually we have three meals a day.
我们的饮食习惯是很有特色的，您知道，饮食习惯大多取决于人们的生活方式。我们通常是一日三餐。

B：How many types does Chinese food include?
中国菜都包括哪些种类呢？

C: It's very abundant. There are four types of most famous Chinese food in our country. They are Sichuan Food, Cantonese Food, Jiangsu Food and Shandong Food. Here is a Guangdong Food restaurant, which is famous for its lightness, freshness and delicacy.

非常丰富。我们国家有四大菜系,川菜、粤菜、苏菜和鲁菜。这是一家广东菜馆,粤菜以清淡、新鲜、美味而著名。

B: Very interesting! I like Chinese food very much and I think Chinese cooking is the best in the world.

真有意思!我非常喜欢中国美食,并且我认为中国的烹饪术是世界上最好的。

A: I think your food is very tasty, too. Mr. Wales, try some of this...

我认为你们的饭菜也是非常可口的。威尔士先生,尝尝这个……

> 【场景3】 宴会已经进行将近一个小时了。大家都吃得很高兴,聊得很痛快。这时,吉米·威尔士先生举着一杯葡萄酒站了起来。
>
> 【演讲3】 演讲人:吉米·威尔士先生

Dear Mr. Mayor, Friends, Ladies and gentlemen,

亲爱的市长先生,朋友们,女士们,先生们:

Thank you very much, Mr. Liu, for all the good things you said about me and Sunshine Company. I believe doing business with Golden Childhood will be one of the most enjoyable experiences in my life.

非常感谢您,刘先生,感谢您对我和阳光公司做出的所有好评。我相信,同金色童年公司做生意将是我一生中最愉快的经历之一。

About five years ago, I was told that the most trustworthy people in the world are Chinese. Now, I find you are not only trustworthy, but also full of new ideas. You are willing to explore every possibility for new business. So, I already regret that during this visit we have only one project to work on. Why not ten, a hundred? (All laugh.) I'm serious. (All laugh more loudly.) Well, joking aside, I'm really excited at the new opportunities your economic reform has offered us and many preferential treatments adopted by Chinese government to create a more favorable investment environment for foreign investors. It's a great time to get going and get on with making some significant investments here. Like you, we'll explore every new possibility to expand our cooperation and contribute more to your modernization.

大约在五年前,我被告知世界上最可信赖的人是中国人。现在,我发现你们不仅可以信赖,而且富有创新精神。你们愿意探索各种可能性,以开拓新的业务。所以,我已经开始后悔了,因为这次访问期间我们只有一个项目要谈。为什么不是十个,一百个?(众笑。)我可是认真的。(众人笑得更厉害了。)好了,玩笑归玩笑,你们的经济改革所带来的新机会,以及中国政府为建立良好投资环境所采用的各项鼓励外商投资的优惠待遇,使我感到非常振奋。目前是行动起来,在贵国进行大规模投资的最佳时机。同你们一样,我们也将探索各种可能性,以扩展我们的合作,为你们的现代化做出更多贡献。

Finally, on behalf of all the members of our mission, I would like to express our sincere thanks for inviting us to such a marvelous New Year Party. We really enjoy the delicious food and wine. We really enjoy meeting and talking to you, and sharing the time together.

最后,我想代表我们团的所有成员,对邀请我们参加这场盛大的新年宴会表示感谢。我们非常喜欢这里的美食和美酒。我们也非常愿意和你们见面,进行交流,一起共度这段美好时光。

Now, may I propose a toast? Here is to the success of our cooperation, to the continuation of our partnership, and to the success of your great reform. Cheers!

现在,请允许我让大家举杯。为我们的合作成功,为我们的伙伴关系长存,也为你们伟大的改革成功,干杯!

Reading: Marketing Innovation in the Twenty-First Century

最近,于琪经常会听到一些诸如"全球营销""绿色营销""网络营销"等新名词。这些名词让于琪感到非常新奇,可又似懂非懂。

Chapter 16 Innovative Marketing

Section 1 Global Marketing

1.1 Understanding the International Trade System

When selling to another country the firm faces various trade restrictions. An import duty is a tax that is levied on a particular foreign product entering a county. This tax, which is also called a tariff, has the effect of raising the price of the product in the importing nation. Because fewer units of product will be sold at the increased price, fewer units will be imported. An import quota is a limit on the amount of particular goods that may be imported into a country during a given period of time. The limit may be set in terms of either quantity (so many pounds of beef) or value (so many dollars worth of shoes). Quotas may also be set on individual products imported from specific countries. Government subsidies are payments from public funds to domestic producers. In general, subsidies benefit domestic producers by enabling them to compete with low-cost imports in the home market, and by helping them to compete in export markets. An embargo is a complete halt to trading with a particular nation or in a particular product. Most often the embargo is used as a political weapon. A foreign exchange control is a restriction on the amount of a particular currency that can be purchased or sold. By limiting the amount of foreign currency that importers can obtain, a government limits the amount of goods that importers can purchase with that currency. Currency devaluation is the reduction of the value of a nation's currency relative to the currencies of other countries. Devaluing a country's currency will have the immediate effect of making exports cheaper and imports more expensive. The company also may face nontariff trade barriers, such as biases against foreign company bids or restrictive product standards or other rules that go against foreign product features.

At the same time, certain forces help trade between nations. The General Agreement on Tariffs and Trade (GATT), which was replaced by WTO in 1995, is the only global international organization dealing with the rules of trade between nations. The primary objective of GATT/WTO is to remove barriers to trade on a worldwide basis. On a smaller scale, certain countries have formed free trade zones or economic communities—groups of nations organized to work toward common goals in the regulation of international trade. One such community is the European Union (EU). Formed in 1957, the European Union—then called the Common Market—set out to create a single European market by reducing barriers to the free flow of products, services, finances, and labor among member countries and developing policies on trade with nonmember nations.

1.2 Determining the Best Mode of Entry

At a fairly basic level of international business is licensing. Licensing is a contractual agreement in which one firm permits another to produce and market its product and use its brand name in return for a royalty or other compensation. The advantage of licensing is that it provides a simple method of expanding into a foreign market with virtually no investment. On the other hand, if the licensee does not maintain the licensor's product standards, the product's image may be damaged. Another disadvantage is that a licensing arrangement does not usually provide the original producer with any foreign marketing experience. A firm may also manufacture its products in its home country and export them for sale in foreign markets. Like licensing, exporting can be a relatively low-risk method of entering foreign markets. It does, however, open up several levels of involvement to the exporting firm. A joint venture is a partnership that is formed to achieve a specific goal or operate for a specific period of time. A joint venture with an established firm in a foreign country provides immediate market knowledge and access, reduced risk, and control over product attributes. However, joint-venture agreement established across national borders can become extremely complex. At a still deeper level of involvement in international business, a firm may develop its own production and marketing facilities in one or more foreign nations. This direct investment provides complete control over operation, but it carries a greater risk than the joint venture. The firm is really establishing a subsidiary in a foreign country. Most firms do so only after they have acquired some knowledge of the country's market.

1.3 Deciding on the Global Marketing Program

Within each foreign nation, the firm is likely to find a combination of marketing environment and target markets that is different from those of its home country and other foreign countries. In terms of cultural and social environment, even so simple a thing as the color of a product or its package can present a problem. As far as economic environment is concerned, international marketers tend to concentrate on higher-income countries for obvious reasons. However, some producers have found that their products sell best in countries with a low income per capita. As in domestic marketing, the determining factor is how well the product satisfies its target market. The legal and political atmosphere also varies across national borders. Gifts to authorities—sometimes quite large ones—are standard business procedure in some countries. In others, including the United States, they are called bribes or payoffs and are strictly illegal.

Accordingly, marketing mix must be adapted to local conditions. An international marketer can adopt any of several strategies regarding its product and promotion. The possibilities include: (1) Marketing one product via a single promotional message worldwide; (2) Marketing one product but varying the promotion; (3) Adapting the product but using the same promotional mix; and (4) Adapting both the product and its promotion. Distribution strategies depend on the firm's international organization—whether it is licensing, exporting, or manufacturing in the host country, etc. For the most part, however, the international marketer uses existing distribution channels. Cost-based pricing is more common in international marketing than in domestic marketing. The added costs of shipping, paying import duties, and complying with various regulations tend to make this the most logical pricing method. Prices are also affected by exchange rates, especially changes in these rates.

小 结

面向国际的公司必须了解国际贸易体系。进口税是指对进入一个国家的特定外国产品所征收的税金。进口配额是指在一定时期内，对某个国家可能进口的特定商品在数量或金额上的限制。政府补贴是政府从公共基金中给国内生产者提供的补助。禁运是指与一个特定国家完全停止贸易往来，或停止某一特定产品的贸易。外汇管制是对某种货币买卖量的限制性措施。货币贬值是指一个国家的货币相对于其他国家货币的价值减少，从而刺激出口。关税及贸易总协定作为唯一一个处理国家之间贸易规则的国际组织，主要目标是消除世界范围内的贸易障碍。打算进入国际市场的企业可以通过许可证交易、出口、合资经营和独资企业等方式来进行，但营销计划必须与国外市场相适应。

Section 2 Green Marketing

2.1 What Is Green Marketing?

A majority of people believe that green marketing refers solely to the promotion or advertising of products with environmental characteristics. Terms like Phosphate Free, Recyclable, Refillable, Ozone Friendly, and Environmentally Friendly are some of the things consumers most often associate with green marketing. While these terms are green marketing claims, in general green marketing is a much broader concept, one that can be applied to consumer goods, industrial goods and even services. For example, around the world there are resorts that are beginning to promote themselves as "ecotourism" facilities, i. e., facilities that "specialize" in experiencing nature or operating in a fashion that minimizes their environmental impact.

Yet defining green marketing is not a simple task where several meanings intersect and contradict each other; an example of this will be the existence of varying social, environmental and retail definitions attached to this term. Indeed the terminology used in this area has varied, and it includes: Green Marketing, Environmental Marketing and Ecological Marketing. So far the following definition has gained wide acceptance: green marketing consists of all activities designed to generate and facilitate any exchanges intended to satisfy human needs or wants, such that the satisfaction of these needs and wants occurs, with minimal detrimental impact on the natural environment.

2.2 Reasons for Green Marketing

First, it appears that all types of consumers, both individual and industrial are becoming more concerned and aware about the natural environment. A 1994 study in Australia found that 84.6% of the sample believed all individuals had a responsibility to care for the environment. A further 80% of this sample indicated that they had modified their behavior, including their purchasing behavior, due to environmental reasons. As demands change, many firms see these changes as an opportunity to be exploited.

Second, many firms are beginning to realize that they are members of the wider community and therefore must behave in an environmentally responsible fashion. This translates into firms that believe they must achieve environmental objectives as well as profit related objectives. Organizations like the Body Shop heavily promote the fact that they offer consumers environmentally responsible alternatives to conventional cosmetic products. This philosophy is directly tied to the overall corporate culture, rather than simply being a competitive tool.

In addition, as with all marketing related activities, governments want to "protect" consumers and society; this protection has significant green marketing implications. Governmental regulations relating to environmental marketing are designed to protect consumers in several ways: (1) Reduce production of harmful goods or by-products; (2) Modify consumer and industry's use and/or consumption of harmful goods; or (3) Ensure that all types of consumers have the ability to evaluate the environmental composition of goods.

Furthermore, competitive pressure has forced a firm or an entire industry to modify and thus reduce its detrimental behavior to environment. For example, it could be argued that Xerox's "Revive 100% Recycled Paper" was introduced a few years ago in an attempt to address the introduction of recycled photocopier paper by other manufacturers. In another example when one tuna manufacturer stopped using driftnets the others followed suit.

Finally, firms may also use green marketing in an attempt to address cost or profit related issues. Disposing of environmentally harmful by-products is becoming increasingly costly and in some cases difficult. Therefore firms that can reduce harmful wastes may incur substantial cost savings. In these cases they often develop more effective production processes that not only reduce waste, but reduce the need for some raw materials. This serves as a double cost savings, since both waste and raw materials are reduced.

2.3 Deciding on the Green Marketing Program

A model of a green marketing mix should, of course, contain all 4P's. A producer should offer ecological products which not only must not contaminate the environment but should protect it and even liquidate existing environmental damages. Prices for such products may be a little higher than conventional alternatives. But target groups like for example LOHAS are willing to pay extra for green products. A distribution logistics is of crucial importance; main focus is on ecological packaging. Marketing local and seasonal products such as vegetables from regional farms is much easier to be marketed "green" than products imported. As far as promotion is concerned, a communication with the market should put stress on environmental aspects, for example that the company possesses a CP certificate or is ISO 14000 certified. This may be publicized to improve a firm's image. Furthermore, the fact that a company spends expenditures on environmental protection should be advertised. In addition, sponsoring the natural environment is also very important. Firms may contribute funds directly to an environmental organization to further the organization's objectives. And last but not least, ecological products will probably require special sales promotions.

In fact, Green marketing covers more than a firm's marketing claims. While firms must bear much of the responsibility for environmental degradation, ultimately it is consumers who demand goods, and thus create environmental problems. Green marketing requires that consumers want a cleaner environment and are willing to "pay" for it, possibly through higher priced goods, modified individual lifestyles, or even governmental intervention. Until this occurs it will be difficult for firms alone to lead the green marketing revolution.

小结

绿色营销强调企业在满足顾客需要的同时,尽量降低对环境的损害。绿色营销的产生源于多种因素,包括消费者对环保的关注、企业社会责任意识的提高、政府对企业活动的干预、企业面临的竞争压力,以及企业自身出于成本和利润的考虑等。企业的绿色营销策略当然应该紧密围绕4P进行开展,但绿色营销不是企业的单方责任。绿色营销需要消费者认识到清洁环境的重要性,并通过支付更高价格,调整个人生活方式,甚至是政府干预下愿意为此做出必要的"牺牲"。没有他们的支持,公司独自引领绿色营销革命是很困难的。

Section 3 E-Commerce and Internet Marketing

3.1 What Is E-Commerce?

Like so many popular words in use today, Electronic Commerce may mean different things to different people. The term commerce is viewed by someone as transactions conducted between business partners. Therefore, EC seems to be quite narrow. However, many use the term E-Business. It refers to a broader definition of EC, not just buying and selling but also servicing customers, cooperating with business partners over networks, and conducting electronic transactions within an organization (Figure 16.1). Essentially, E-Business technologies empower customers, employees, suppliers, distributors, vendors and partners by giving them powerful tools for information management and communications.

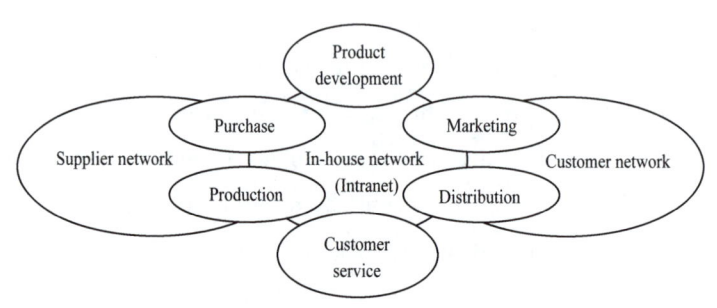

Figure 16.1 E-Business Overview

Firms can gain a number of benefits from E-Commerce. An Intranet can minimize the number of physical meetings, facilitate information sharing, increase speed and consistency of information, and be used to coordinate internal company operations such as product design, production, inventory control, and shipping, etc. Businesses also can gather information on products, buyers and competitors through the Internet so as to increase their own competitiveness. Most significantly, the Internet truly flattens the world. SMEs (small and medium-sized enterprises) that cannot afford to establish overseas offices and strongholds can now increase their exposure to every corner of the world.

3.2 Classifying Major Internet Business

◇ Business-to-Business (B2B) EC is now and will remain by far the largest in revenue—around 70 percent of the total. By extending the benefits of computers to the exchange of information between suppliers, manufacturers and retailers, B2B applications give companies the added advantage that they need to achieve productivity gains.

◇ Business-to-Consumer (B2C) EC is retailing transaction with individual shoppers. B2C Businesses provide consumers with online shopping through the Internet, allowing consumers to shop and pay their bills online. This type of offering saves time for both retailers and consumers.

◇ Consumer-to-Consumer (C2C) EC means consumer sells directly to consumers. Consumers can post their own products online through some agent websites for other consumers to bid. One of the most successful launches has been eBay, which sets up a huge auction site on which individuals can buy and sell.

◇ Consumer-to-Business (C2B) EC takes two forms, reverse auctions and buying groups. In a reverse auction, an individual posts the price he or she is willing to pay for something, say a flight from London to New York, and airlines bid for the custom. Buying groups are another idea, which use the Internet to assemble a group, and then negotiate with the supplier. Companies such as LetsBuyIt.com offer this service.

3.3 Understanding Challenges for Internet Marketing

Internet marketing, also known as web marketing, online marketing, or e-marketing, is referred to as the marketing of products or services over the Internet. Marketing strategies include search engine optimization and search engine submission, copywriting that encourages site visitors to take action, web site design, online promotions, reciprocal linking, and email marketing, etc. Although Internet offers new opportunities for companies, some barriers to Internet-related marketing activities have come up. For example, some stringent privacy regulations make it illegal to solicit via email without the express permission of the consumer. Legal proceedings may increase the expenses of doing business online and any of such actions could have a material adverse effect on the business operations.

Furthermore, security breaches on the network-based systems could significantly harm the future growth of online business. Some new technologies so far have been developed to ensure the privacy and security in online transactions. A firewall, for example, is a specialized computer running firewall software that prevents unauthorized communications from flowing between the Internet and an Intranet. Some companies also use data-hiding techniques and digital signature technologies to enhance online security.

小 结

广义电子商务不仅包含商品买卖,还涉及服务客户,商务伙伴间网络协作,以及组织内部的电子交换。目前,网络商务活动的主要形式有:供应商、制造商和零售商之间的 B2B 商务活动;企业同个体买主进行零售交易的 B2C 商务活动;消费者直接销售产品给其他消费者的 C2C 商务活动;包括逆向竞价和群体购买的 C2B 商务活动。虽然互联网为企业发展提供了新机会,但是网络营销人员要遵守法规,并充分认识网络安全问题。

New Words and Key Terms

01. global marketing	全球营销
02. import duty (or tariff)	进口税,关税
03. import quota	进口配额
04. government subsidies	政府补贴
05. embargo	禁运
06. foreign exchange control	外汇管制
07. currency devaluation	货币贬值
08. General Agreement on Tariffs and Trade	关税及贸易总协定
09. WTO	世界贸易组织
10. economic community	经济共同体
11. licensing	许可证;许可经营
12. joint venture	合资企业,合资经营
13. green marketing	绿色营销
14. Electronic Commerce	电子商务
15. Intranet	公司内联网
16. Business-to-Business（B2B）EC	企业对企业电子商务
17. Business-to-Consumer（B2C）EC	企业对消费者电子商务
18. Consumer-to-Consumer（C2C）EC	消费者对消费者电子商务
19. Consumer-to-Business（C2B）EC	消费者对企业电子商务
20. Internet marketing	互联网营销
21. firewall	防火墙
22. data-hiding techniques	数据加密技术
23. digital signature technologies	数字签名技术

Writing：Agency Agreement

这一年对于金色童年公司来说是收获的一年,不仅合资企业成立在即,多家公司都提出申请希望成为金色童年在当地的销售代理。经过董事会的商讨,公司最终决定接受 John

Brown 先生成为北美地区独家代理的请求,并安排于琪起草一份代理协议。

一、代理协议写作的基本要求和格式

协议书(Agreement)是当事人双方或多方为解决或预防纠纷,或确立某种法律关系,实现一定的共同利益、愿望,经过协商一致后所签署的具有法律效力的书面材料。协议的作用和效力与合同基本相同,常不做区分。销售代理协议书一般包括如下内容:

(一)约首(Head)

所包括内容与意向书类似。序言写法通常如下:This agreement is made and entered into by and between...（Supplier, hereafter called "Party A"）and...（Agent, hereafter called "Party B"）, on the basis of equal and friendly business relationship. Both parties agree to develop business of agency on the terms and conditions stipulated as follows:本协议由……(供货方,以下称甲方)与……(代理方,以下称乙方)在平等友好的业务关系基础上达成。双方同意按下列条件开展代理业务:

(二)正文(Body)

1. 代理产品(Commodity)

例如,Party A hereby appoints Party B to act as his selling agent to sell the commodity mentioned below:甲方委托乙方为销售代理,销售下列商品:

2. 代理区域(Territory)

例如,The territory covered under this agreement shall be expressly confined to...（hereinafter called Territory）.本协议所指的代理区域是……(以下简称区域)。

3. 最低业务量(Minimum Turnover)

例如,Party B shall undertake to solicit orders for the above commodity from customers in the above territory during the effective period of this agreement for not less than USD 1,000,000. 乙方应保证,在此协议的有效期内,从上述区域内的顾客处招揽的上述商品的订单价值不少于一百万美元。

4. 价格与支付(Price and Payment)

例如,The price for each individual transaction shall be fixed through negotiations between Party B and the buyer, and subject to Party A's final confirmation. Payment shall be made by confirmed, irrevocable L/C opened by the buyer in favor of Party A, which shall reach Party A 15 days before the date of shipment. 每笔交易的货物价格应由乙方与买主通过谈判确定,并须经甲方最后确认。付款使用保兑的、不可撤销的信用证,由买方开出,以甲方为受益人。信用证须在装运日期前 15 天送达甲方。

5. 供货方责任与义务(Obligations of Supplier)

例如,Party A shall not supply the contracted commodity to any other buyer(s) in the above mentioned territory. 甲方不得向经销地区其他买主供应本协议所规定的商品。再如,The Supplier shall from time to time furnish the Agent with a statement of the minimum prices and the terms and conditions of sales at which the goods are respectively to be sold. 供货方应经常向代理商提供最低的价格表以及每个商品可以成交的条款、条件。

6. 代理方责任与义务(Obligations of Agent)

例如,In order to keep Party A well informed of the prevailing market conditions, Party B should undertake to supply Party A, at least once a quarter or at any time when necessary, with market reports concerning changes of the local regulations in connection with the import and sales of the commodity covered by this agreement, local market tendency and the buyer's comments on quality, packing, price, etc. of the goods supplied by Party A under this agreement. Party B shall also supply party A with quotations and advertising materials on similar products of other suppliers. 为使甲方充分了解市场情况,乙方应至少每季度一次或在必要时随时向甲方提供市场报告,报告内容包括与本协议代理商品的进口与销售有关的地方规章的变动、当地市场发展趋势以及买方对甲方按协议供应的货物的质量、包装、价格等方面的意见。乙方还承担向甲方提供其他供应商类似商品的报价和广告资料。再如,Party B shall bear all expenses for advertising and publicity in connection with the commodity in question in Singapore within the validity of this agreement, and shall submit to Party A all audio and video materials intended for advertising for prior approval. 乙方负担本协议有效期内在新加坡销售代理商品做广告宣传的一切费用,并向甲方提交所用于广告的声像资料,供甲方事先核准。

7. 佣金及支付(Commission and Payment)

例如,Party A shall pay Party B a commission of 5％ on the net invoiced selling price on all orders directly obtained by Party B and accepted by Party A. No commission shall be paid until Party A receives the full payment for each order. 对乙方直接获取并经甲方确认接受的订单,甲方按净发票售价向乙方支付5％的佣金。佣金在甲方收到每笔订单的全部货款后才会支付。

8. 代理期限、修改及终止(Validity, Revision and Termination of the Agreement)

例如,This agreement, after its being signed by the parties concerned, shall remain in force for... days from... to... If either party wishes to extend this agreement, he shall notice, in writing, the other party one month prior to its expiration. The matter shall be decided by the agreement and by consent of the parties hereto. Should either party fail to implement the terms and conditions herein, the other party is entitled to terminate this agreement. 本协议经双方签字后生效,有效期为……天,从……至……。若一方希望延长本协议,则须在本协议期满前1个月书面通知另一方,经双方协商决定。若协议一方未履行协议条款,另一方有权终止协议。

9. 争议的解决(Dispute Settlement)

例如,All disputes arising from the execution of this agreement shall be settled through friendly consultations. In case no settlement can be reached, the case in dispute shall then be submitted to the Foreign Trade Arbitration Commission of the China Council for the Promotion of International Trade for arbitration in accordance with its provisional rules of procedure. The decision made by this Commission shall be regarded as final and binding upon both parties. Arbitration fees shall be borne by the losing party, unless otherwise awarded. 在履行协议过程中,如产生争议,双方应友好协商解决。若通过友好协商达不成协议,则提交中国国际贸易促进委员会对外贸易仲裁委员会,根据该会仲裁程序暂行规定进行仲裁。该委员会的决定是最终的,对双方均具有约束力。仲裁费用,除另有规定外,由败诉一方负担。

(三)约尾(End)

所包括内容与意向书类似。例如,This agreement is in two originals effective since being signed/sealed by both parties, each party holds one. 本协议有正本两份,自双方签字(盖章)之日生效,每方各执一份。

二、于琪的解决方案

AGENCY AGREEMENT

GOLDEN CHILDHOOD CHILDREN'S PRODUCTS CO., LTD., Shanghai (hereinafter called "Manufacturer") and SMART CHILDREN'S TOYS CO., LTD., New York (hereinafter referred to as "Agent") have on this 30th day of December, 2023 entered into a sales agency agreement under the terms and conditions stated below:

1. Agent shall act as the sole and exclusive agent in the U.S.A., Canada and Mexico for Manufacturer for the sale of the products herein specified.

2. The products covered by this agreement are: Golden Childhood Brand Toys.

3. Manufacturer shall furnish Agent with the price lists of his products stated above, all in terms of CIF New York. Agent is under obligation to push sales energetically at price quoted by Manufacturer. Each transaction is subject to Manufacturer's final confirmation.

4. Agent shall place orders with Manufacturer for not less than US$ 4 million annually.

5. Payment is to be made by confirmed, irrevocable Letter of Credit available by sight draft upon presentation of shipping documents, reaching Manufacturer 30 days before the date of shipment. Should Agent fail to establish the Letter of Credit in time, any loss or losses which Manufacturer may sustain shall be borne by Agent.

6. Manufacturer agrees to pay Agent a commission of 4 percent on CIF value of orders. If the annual turnover exceeds US$ 6 million, Agent can get 6% commission. The commission is to be paid after full payment for each order is received by Manufacturer.

7. Agent shall have the obligation to forward once every three months to Manufactur-

er detailed reports on current market conditions and on consumers' comments.

8. This agreement shall remain in force until terminated by either party by giving a written notice at least 90 days in advance to the other party by registered airmail.

This agreement is made out in quadruplicate, each party holding two copies.

GOLDEN CHILDHOOD CO., LTD.　　SMART CHILDREN'S TOYS CO., LTD.

（Signature）　　　　　　　　　　　（Signature）

Review Questions

1. Key Terms

Import quota; Economic community; Licensing; Green marketing; C2B EC; Firewall

2. Multiple Choices（select one）

（1）Which one is NOT the level of involvement in global marketing?（　）

A. Licensing.　　　　　　　　B. Exporting.

C. National marketing.　　　　D. Joint venture.

（2）Marketing mix standardization（　）.

A. reduces costs related to marketing

B. increases costs related to marketing

C. complicates the multinational marketer's job

D. can easily be controlled by the multinational company

（3）Taxes, import duties, inflation, unstable governments, and regulations are all factors that affect（　）.

A. corporate citizenship　　　B. export pricing

C. favorable pricing　　　　　D. transfer pricing

（4）An example of a multinational marketing publicity campaign would be（　）.

A. Kellogg inserting a coupon into every box of cereal it sells in Canada

B. Ford offering rebates on all trucks sold in Mexico

C. IBM donating computers to universities in Guatemala

D. Motorola advertising its new line of phones in Spain

（5）Which one is NOT the reason for green marketing?（　）

A. Governmental pressure.　　B. Price pressure.

C. Competitive pressure.　　　D. Consumers' awareness.

（6）In addition to the original "4P's", green marketing adds a few more "P's". What are they? (　　)

A. Price, promotion, position, and process.

B. Process, place, policy, and purse strings.

C. Publics, partnership, policy, and purse strings.

D. Publics, process, policy, and purse strings.

(7) (　　) marketing consists of all activities designed to generate and facilitate any exchanges intended to satisfy human needs or wants, so that the satisfaction of these needs and wants occurs, with minimal detrimental impact on the natural environment.

A. Online　　B. Natural　　C. Green　　D. Relationship

(8) These "bricks-and-clicks" companies have turned out to be the real winners, combining their infrastructures with the new (　　) and capabilities that the internet offers.

A. minds　　B. ideas　　C. tools　　D. techs

(9) Which one of the following sentences is right? (　　)

A. The internet has destroyed all the traditionally successful companies.

B. An internet experience is to feel "cold" and mechanical.

C. Computers are logical, but not intelligent.

D. The internet will eliminate none of your employees from the processes that you have moved online.

(10) If you want to call yourself a (an) (　　) marketer, you need to effectively maintain and utilize e-mail marketing databases to create long-term relationships with past clients and website visitors.

A. social　　B. internet　　C. relationship　　D. green

3. Questions for Discussion

(1) What is protectionism? Explain import quotas, embargoes, and tariffs. What is the role of the WTO and economic communities in encouraging free trade?

(2) How to understand "Green marketing covers more than a firm's marketing claims"?

(3) Overview the promise and challenges that Internet marketing presents for the future.

Practical Writing

Scenario: You received a letter below from a trading company asking for sole agency in Spain. After careful consideration and following discussions with representatives from the company, you have decided to offer them an appointment for a trial period of twelve months in the first instance. Please make up necessary information and draft an **Agency Agreement** between you and your agent.

Dear Sirs,

　　We write to offer our services as your agent in Spain. If, however, you are already satisfactorily represented here, please ignore this letter.

　　There is a growing demand here for Chinese textiles, especially printed cotton fabrics, and the prospects are really excellent for good quality fabrics at competitive prices. As soon as we are in possession of details of your ranges with samples and prices, we shall be in a position to advise you on their suitability for this particular market and to choose goods that are likely to sell well.

　　With regard to references, you may write to our bank, Banco Espanol de Credito in Madrid, or any of our major customers.

　　We look forward to hearing from you and to the possibility of representing you in Spain.

　　　　　　　　　　　　Yours faithfully,

参考文献

[1] 邓镝.商务英语综合教程[M].北京:人民大学出版社,2008.

[2] 邓镝.实用英语写作——商务篇[M].北京:清华大学出版社 & 北京交通大学出版社,2012.

[3] 任书梅,王路.商务英语入门[M].北京:外语教学与研究出版社,2005.

[4] 应斌.市场营销学[M].武汉:武汉理工大学出版社,2005.

[5] 雷涯邻,John A. Parnell.工商管理英语[M].北京:高等教育出版社,2003.

[6] 金阳,陆红菊.营销英语[M].北京:高等教育出版社,2003.

[7] 吴颖.外企白领速成英语之商务谈判高手[M].北京:石油工业出版社,2008.

[8] 张晓燕,张萍.商务英语口语[M].北京:经济管理出版社,2009.

[9] 李雪,李铁红,范宏博.商务英语口语大全[M].北京:机械工业出版社,2010.

[10] 刘文宇,王慧莉,张旭.商务英语口语大全[M].大连:大连理工大学出版社,2007.

[11] 盛小利.商务英语开口就会说[M].北京:科学出版社,2009.

[12] 王正元.大学能力英语——走进国际商务[M].北京:机械工业出版社,2005.

[13] 范红.英文商务写作教程[M].北京:清华大学出版社,2000.

[14] 刘静华.国际货物贸易实务[M].北京:对外经济贸易大学出版社,2005.

[15] 熊锟,陈咏.商务英语写作[M].北京:中国人民大学出版社,2003.

[16] 付美榕.现代商务英语写作[M].北京:北京理工大学出版社,2002.

[17] 高恩光,戴建东.英语写作新论[M].上海:上海外语教育出版社,2004.

[18] 李东云.用英语写商务文书[M].广州:世界图书出版公司,2007.

[19] 石定乐,蔡蔚.实用商务英语写作[M].北京:北京理工大学出版社,2003.

[20] 边毅.商务英语写作[M].北京:清华大学出版社 & 北京交通大学出版社,2003.

[21] 姚嘉五.最新英文公文写作大全[M].广州:广东旅游出版公司,2005.

[22] Kotler, Philip, et al. Principles of Marketing—An Asian Perspective [M]. 北京:机械工业出版社,2008.

[23] Solomon, Michael R., Greg W. Marshall, and Elnora W. Stuart. Marketing—Real People, Real Choices [M]. 6th ed. 北京:清华大学出版社,2010.

[24] Boone, Louis E., David L. Kurtz. Contemporary Marketing [M]. 11th ed. 北京:北京大学出版社,2004.

[25] Lamb, Charles W., Joseph F. Hair, and Carl McDaniel. Marketing [M]. 6th ed. 北京:北京大学出版社,2003.

[26] Best, Roger J. Market-Based Management—Strategies for Growing Customer Value and Profitability [M]. 5th ed. 北京:清华大学出版社,2010.

[27] Randall, Geoffrey. Principles of Marketing [M]. 2nd ed. 北京:经济科学出版社,2004.

[28] Mack, Angela. The Language of Business [M]. 沈瑞年,译. 北京:世界图书出版公司,1996.